Aggression and Evolution

Aggression and Evolution

Charlotte M. Otten

Northern Illinois University

Xerox College Publishing

Lexington, Massachusetts / Toronto

Acknowledgments

I wish to thank all of the authors and publishers whose cooperation made this book possible. My particular gratitude goes to Louise E. Sweet and Morton Fried, who wrote original articles, and to David E. Davis, Derek Freeman, and Saleem A. Shah, who edited and adapted their articles for this volume. I am also grateful to William Berman for his assistance, and to Mrs. Susan L. Gleason of Xerox College Publishing for her patience and helpfulness in editing.

ISB Number: 0-536-00407-2

Library of Congress Catalog Card Number: 79-179422

Printed in the United States of America.

Contents

PART FIVE Further views from psychologists and psychiatrists

PART SIX Viewpoints of cultural anthropologists

Introduction

A little over twenty years ago, one could write in a prologue, "Outside my study window . . . rises a forest of stately and ancient Ponderosa pines. There is a stream bordered by alders, willows, and cottonwoods. . . . By night a bear wanders by and mule deer track the mountain." (Simpson, 1949)

In contrast, in 1970, out of my study window I see a tired university campus patrolled by squad cars. A half-dozen irate merchants are sweeping up the many fragments of plate glass that glint on the sidewalk in the morning sun. The charred wreckage of a university car, burned in the night by protesting students, is being towed away.

My morning paper tells of savage bombings, plans to build new and ever more frightening weaponry. Middle East forays are routine, as are riots in overheated ghettos, the response of black citizens to the hardening of prejudiced and self-righteous whites against threatening forces that they cannot comprehend, or will not understand. Alaskans object to the storing of deadly nerve gas in their state; Floridians and Bahamians to its uneasy burial in nearby seas. Having grasped the serpent, we cannot put it down. Reports of massacres of civilian peasants in Asia by American soldiers shock some, while others appear to accept genocide as a fact of life. The seething unrest permeates our very bones. Everyone offers different explanations: historical, economic, political, psychological, cultural, genetic. Little wonder that the suggestions of Konrad Lorenz (1966) and Robert Ardrey (1966), which hold that the source of human violence lies irrevocably in our genes and not our wills or our cultural traditions, were embraced with something of relief. We experienced a sense of release from guilt or the necessity of changing something, whether TV programs, or political parties, or a philosophy, or an economic system.

But it is not all that simple. I believe that some of the less easily available evidence bearing upon the problem of aggression, tends to modify or call into question these attractive conclusions and should be given wider distribution. Three years ago M. F. Ashley Montagu issued an anthology titled *Man and Aggression,* a valuable collection with a similar purpose. Much information dealing with a number of viewpoints has accumulated in the ensuing years, and this volume represents a supplement to his, rather than a replacement.

No one can doubt that man carries a great potential for extreme forms of aggression, as for many other kinds of behavior. As the writers in Part II note, it is easy to teach man to kill, but testimony also exists in support of the opinion that this behavior is not spontaneous and inevitable. Even the evidence from our non-human primate cousins (which may well be no evidence at all) is not so damning as once believed. Aggressive behavior, according to the observations which are presented here, relates to education and ideals, to ecology, to population density (both isolation and crowding), to food supply, to frustration on many levels, to drugs, to the hypothalamus and its intricate relationship with pituitary, adrenal, and sex hormones, to breakdown in social organization, to strange or unnatural habitat or confinement, to fear and pain, and a score of other variables, rather than to species-specific genetic programming alone.

In December 1967, when sociologist Donald Granberg questioned 297 randomly chosen undergraduates at Northern Illinois University as to whether, in their opinion, "the roots of war lie in man's basic nature," 72 percent answered affirmatively. They were also asked several questions concerning the present Vietnam conflict. Granberg concluded that students comprising that 72 percent were more likely to view military involvement as rational and justified than the remaining 28 percent (1969:547-548).

These findings serve to emphasize both the tenacity of the conviction that human aggression is innate, and the importance of understanding the nature and complexity of the problem in formulating one's political views, since some sort of interdependence is clearly present. One can further observe that the children of pacifists are also usually pacifists (although not in Mendelian ratios). Policy and practice seem here of greater importance than predisposition in determining viewpoint.

Aggression as a term has been variously defined and applied. Most ethologists have used it with reference to intraspecific aggression, excluding interspecific encounters such as prey-predator relationships, "maternal" protective behavior against intruders, and competition for food within the same ecological niche. Intraspecific aggressive behavior has most often meant to scientists the predictable conflict attending the establishment of status hierarchies and the defense of territories. Territoriality may involve individuals only (as among fish), or pairs (in birds), or entire breeding populations or demes among many social mammals, including primates. Transitory squabbles between individuals over food or mates have been of less interest except insofar as they demonstrate dominance relationships.

Ethologists have long recognized the adaptive function of status hierarchies in minimizing individual conflicts, distributing food supplies, regulating sexual access and population increase, and controlling predators. Territoriality likewise functions to decrease opportunities for conflict, to distribute resources, and to allocate living space. Irven DeVore (1963), John H. Crook and J. S. Gartlan (1966), and others have analyzed territorial and status-hierarchy behaviors with regard to ecological factors; the import of such studies appears in several contexts in this volume. One cannot overemphasize, I think, the significance of the high correlation of degree and kind of organizational and territorial "aggression" with the nature, size, and resources of the habitat or niche. Such findings should cause one to approach very cautiously the presumption of innate aggressive predilections carried by primates as a genetic heritage.

With regard to man himself, the term *aggression* has been applied to everything from competition in dress, athletics, business, and politics, to warfare and murder. The many individual interpretations of this aspect of human interaction are interesting and significant in themselves. As two ethnologists may find the same tribe friendly and attractive or, conversely, forbidding and repugnant, so there is an existential or non-rational quality about man's inconsistent assessments of his own "nature." The interpretation may reveal as much about the scientist as about his subject.*

The degree and kind of aggression "natural" or "normal" to a species, and the neuroendocrine bases of its arousal and suppression are now undergoing vigorous investigation. "Aggressive" states in non-human animals are being observed in the field, in zoos, and in laboratories, under situations of every imaginable sort, including brain stimulation of pain centers, electric shocks, starvation, and long-term isolation. It seems questionable whether, in the repeated construction of such research designs, more is learned about aggression in animals or in research psychologists, and I seriously question the ethics involved in many of these prolonged explorations, in view of their limited applicability to the human condition.

Be that as it may, the research field has been largely laid out by ethologists and psychologists. Ethologists have mostly attended to what they believe to be "innate" behaviors. Most differences between the behavioral responses of their observed subjects and those that the learning-theory psychologists report, they attribute to genetics. Too often, as has been pointed out by several workers, such distinctions may be in the nature of unrecognized learning superimposed upon species-specific behavior. Further, psychologists have given too little cognizance not only to species differences, but to the sensitivities and responsiveness of the mammalian families with which they work. The reaction patterns of research animals, therefore, are interpreted as constants in spite of the individual learning that must occur in coping with their highly uncongenial environments and the too-frequent insensitivities of the experimenters. Certainly a growing number of workers are becoming aware that

*I refer here to individual philosophy, not personality.

it is a logical impossibility to study that which is innate without considering learning, since the two are, in fact, inextricable.

Further, I find it difficult to believe, as do some other students of the field, that "aggression" exercised in the regulation of social life of a non-human species is of the same order as that evidenced in predation or, again, in sexual encounter or displacement of frustration, or in response to pain or brain stimulation. Most importantly, I doubt whether such reactions are comparable to the multitudinous activities involving conflict that arise from the symbolic construction and fantasies of men. Our daily motivations are not ordinarily conditioned to involve bells, food bars, or foot shocks, but are rather influenced by such highly charged ambiguities as God, communism, freedom, loyalty, status, race, power, love, cleanliness, and motherhood. Because of learned reactions attached to these cultural (and sub-cultural) concepts, they function not only as inevitable sources of human conflict and frustration, but are in turn manipulated as outlets. Ideas that are cultural constructions are thus interpreted as empirical absolutes, and insignia of membership in a particular class, caste, or polity may become a popular cause as well as its identification. In spite of these differences in the "aggressive behaviors" of man and other vertebrates, many research psychologists approach them as a unity resting upon different substrates, a property common to the behavior of almost the entire animal kingdom.

The widespread acceptance of the Lorenz-Ardrey hypothesis of human aggression as an evolutionary inevitability reflects also the current trend toward biological explanation in the social sciences, a trend that has been greeted with apprehension in some quarters (Fried, 1968:130; Hirsch, 1968:41; Holloway, 1969:398) and with more approval in others (Freeman, 1966; Ginsberg, 1968; Tiger and Fox, 1966; Fox, 1970). We have seen, in fact, a rash of ambitious constructions built upon the interaction of ethology, physiology, psychology, and genetics, involving not only non-human primate responses (extrapolated to man) but even concerned with presumed innate psychological and behavioral differences between human races (Jensen, 1968, 1970a, 1970b) as well as between the sexes (Tiger, 1969).

This reductionism, which denies or ignores a symbol-based concept of culture, fails in most ways to explain the capacity of human cultural concepts to produce conflicts (with attendant "aggression") *sui generis,* without necessary reference to direct physical stimuli derived from the immediate sensory present or from inner physiological states. It is this feedback phenomenon, by which man symbolically transforms his environment and is then, in turn, influenced by the transformation, that Holloway details in his important article "Culture; a human domain" (1969). Having invented the ideas of holy water, chastity, totem animals, napalm, and water spirits, man is influenced quite differently by the symbolic import of these realities than by their actual physical referents. This is why research data involving non-human animals is of dubious usefulness in its application to man. Rather, I believe (to quote Holloway) that: ". . . it is power, organizations, socio-economic conditions, and symbol systems that need study" rather than mice, monkeys, and the brains of cats.

Several of the contributing authors have told me that they are preparing further papers, some of which are already in press. Obviously, interest in aggression and its human manifestations is developing rapidly, and hopefully a wider range of evidence is becoming known to policy-makers and instructors who will influence the next generation. Only the problems of ecological salvage and population control are of equal importance. If this collection helps to dispel a few dangerous popular myths, it will have fulfilled its purpose.

Charlotte M. Otten
DeKalb, Illinois

References

Ardrey, Robert. 1966. *The Territorial Imperative.* New York: Atheneum.

Crook, John H. and J. S. Gartlan. 1966. Evolution of primate societies. *Nature* 210:1200-1203.

DeVore, Irven. 1963. A comparison of the ecology and behavior of monkeys and apes. *Classification and Human Evolution,* ed. S L. Washburn. Chicago: Aldine, pp. 301-319.

Fox, Robin. 1970. The cultural animal. *Encounter* 35:31-42 (July).

Freeman, Derek. 1966. Social anthropology and the scientific study of human behavior. *Man* (n.s.) 1:330-342.

Fried, Morton. 1968. The need to end the pseudo-scientific investigation of race. *Science and the Concept of Race,* ed. M. Mead, T. Dolzhansky, E. Tobach, and R. E. Light. New York: Columbia Univ. Press, pp. 122-131.

Ginsberg, B. E. 1968. Genetic parameters in behavioral research. Hirsch (1968b), pp. 135-153.

Granberg, Donald. 1969. War expectancy and the evaluation of a specific war. *Journal of Conflict Resolution* 13:546-549.

Hirsch, Jerry. 1968a. Behavior-genetic analysis and the study of man. *Science and the Concept of Race,* ed. M. Mead *et al.,* pp. 37-48.

_____. 1968b. *Behavior-Genetic Analysis.* New York: McGraw-Hill.

Holloway, Ralph. 1969. Culture: a human domain. *Current Anthropology* 10:395-412.

Jensen, Arthur R. 1968. How much can we boost I.Q. and scholastic achievement? *Harvard Educational Review*: 1-123 (Winter).

_____. 1970a. Race and the genetics of intelligence: a reply to Lewontin. *Bulletin of Atomic Scientists* 26 (5):17-23.

_____. 1970b. The heritability of intelligence. *Engineering and Science* 33 (6):40-44.

Lorenz, Konrad. 1966. *On Aggression.* New York: Harcourt, Brace and World.

Montagu, M. F. Ashley. 1968. *Man and Aggression.* New York: Oxford Univ. Press.

Simpson, G. G. 1949. *The Meaning of Evolution.* New Haven: Yale Univ. Press.

Tiger, Lionel. 1969. *Men in Groups.* London: Thomas Nelson & Sons, Ltd.

Tiger, Lionel and Robin Fox. 1966. The zoological perspective in social sciences. *Man* (n.s.) 1:73-81.

PART ONE
The biology of aggression

The following four articles, representative of an immense and growing literature, are intended to provide certain basic information on the neurophysiological background of (or accompaniment to) states of conflict, rage, attack, and severe stress.

Davis sketches the interrelations of the hypothalamus and the endocrine organs in aggression, correlating an increase in adrenal size with rank order in mice.

Michael's article deals with changes in intragroup aggression associated with the secretion of gonadal hormones in monkeys. Androgens administered prenatally to primates (as well as other vertebrate species) have been shown to have a masculinizing effect upon females, even to the extent of creating true morphological hermaphroditism. Such intersex "female" monkeys demonstrate more aggressive and boisterous play patterns than untreated females, as well as a switch in sex roles in mating behavior and partner choice. Attempts to reestablish female patterns by the administration of estrogens have been notably unsuccessful. The presence of androgens in the blood stream, as both Michael and Moyer point out, are critical to the development of inter-male aggression in status establishment and competition in mate selection.

Moyer reviews the literature on substrate mechanisms, including the results of brain stimulation, brain lesions, brain surgery, and drugs in the production of states that are called "aggressive" in research animals. It is well to bear in mind that we have no clear idea of what, exactly, is happening to the research animal undergoing brain stimulation: what it really "feels," or what specific response is being stimulated when it rages, claws, or kills. Further, although such extreme excitations resembling aggression can be elicited by stimulation oı certain brain centers in the hen, rat, cat, or monkey, we cannot thereby conclude that culturally patterned anger is in any way analogous, or that it can be analyzed and described in biochemical and biophysical terms.

Because of the widespread misunderstandings fostered by the popular press concerning the supposed relationship between the XYY chromosome component and a tendency toward criminality, Saleem Shah's excellent account of the current status of the problem is included.

1

The physiological analysis of aggressive behavior

David E. Davis

Aggressive actions are among the most prominent social activities of animals, including man. Such actions often appear antisocial, but the fighting, bluffing, and threatening may serve to promote, with some individual suffering, survival of the species. In this chapter aggressive behavior will be operationally defined as action involving two or more animals that threaten, bluff, or attack each other. The action may result in physical combat, but, more frequently, one individual flees before combat starts or at least before injury occurs. Learning plays a prominent role, since an individual may learn through experience that a particular individual or a type of individual can inflict damage. When such learning has occurred, one individual will retreat or flee at the sight or odor of another. For example, young woodchucks retreat or watch carefully even when an adult is as far as from 75-100 feet away. Although no contact occurs, social behavior is emphatically present.

Aggressive behavior is widespread throughout the animal kingdom. Among the vertebrates, aggressive behavior is found in species from fish to man. Relatively few species of fish have been studied, and these represent the most advanced forms (teleosts). As might be expected, birds and mammals have been frequently studied from both the behavioral and physiologic viewpoints.

SOURCE: Revised from *Social Behavior and Organization among Vertebrates*, William Etkin, ed., University of Chicago Press.

The reciprocal effect of behavior on physiologic processes has recently attracted attention and research. This chapter considers only those features of aggressive behavior now known to affect physiologic processes, the study of which promises to produce great advances in our knowledge of physiology. Thus, many psychologic and psychiatric aspects (McNeil, 1959) are here completely excluded. Also, many homeostatic processes are ignored.

The term "aggressive behavior" usually excludes predaceous behavior or defensive actions against a predator. The flight of a rabbit from a dog or the alarm cries of nesting birds at a cat are considered defensive, rather than aggressive, social behavior. It is true that these actions include attack, threat, and defense and that many muscular actions in a fight are the same as those occurring in social behavior. The distinction between predaceous and aggressive behavior rests, however, on two main features. First, predatory attacks (with some rare exceptions) are not upon the same species, i.e., they are interspecific. Second, the actual behavior leading up to the predatory attack is different from that shown in intraspecific aggression. When a dog is ready to attack another dog to settle problems of social behavior, he uses motions of the tail, head, etc., different from those he uses preparing to attack a cat. A complicating feature of this distinction is that the physiologic repercussions (to be described in detail later) appear to be very similar, if not identical, in the two types of behavior.

The actual patterns of aggressive behavior differ from species to species. Detailed descriptions are readily available in current literature and may be summarized briefly. Fish generally attack by butting and nipping. Lizards threaten by flashing the dewlap (skin under the throat). Birds attack with bill, wings, or feet, or threaten and bluff by song and by displays involving exposure of bright or striking colors or patterns. Mammals use a variety of patterns to intimidate another member of the same species. For example, cows and sheep butt heads, mice vibrate their tails and hunch their backs, and primates threaten vocally. One more point requires emphasis. The aggressive action may be very subtle and its detection may depend on remarkable powers of observation and of induction.

The aggression involved in social behavior evolves out of two fundamental patterns. Some species divide an area into territories and others arrange themselves into a social rank. These patterns may be at the poles of one continuous phenomenon (Davis, 1958), but for the present we can consider them distinct.

The major function of aggressive behavior is to determine and maintain rank or territory. In every species, regardless of its type of social organization, the aggressive individuals assert their position and maintain it by certain behaviors, some of which were mentioned above. In this action, many physiologic processes participate, some stimulating aggressive behavior and others responding to it. The next two sections of this chapter will consider these processes in some detail.

An unsolved problem or set of problems is the extent to which aggressive behavior is learned. Presumably, many details are learned, or at least perfected, through experience. Other aspects, especially the disposition to aggressiveness, are apparently innate. Experimental evidence is meager, but some items are relevant. Most of the work has been done with domesticated mice, but the little work done with other species confirms the results. It is commonly known that male mice isolated at weaning will fight when put together at three or four months of age. Since it appears unlikely that the fighting is learned during suckling, it is inferred that the disposition to fight is innate. Early social experience nevertheless greatly affects subsequent aggressive behavior (King, 1957). As Scott (1958) has pointed out, the learning of fighting procedures follows psychologic principles. When male mice raised in isolation are placed together, most individuals will start to fight. Within a few hours or days a social rank is organized, and the mice have learned their places. Fighting then becomes rare, since the subordinate mice no longer fight. If a dominant mouse is put with other mice, he will again fight and usually win. In contrast, subordinate individuals will rarely assert themselves. However, by special techniques consisting of artificially producing a "win" by the subordinate mouse, it is possible to teach the formerly submissive mouse to fight and to win. With another type of experiment, it is possible to train some mice, while still relatively young, to win and others to lose. These individuals then will maintain their status unless another teaching program reverses it. It is clear from this type of research that learning plays an important role in modifying the physiologic basis of aggressive behavior.

Some work suggests that the object of aggression is learned but the actual motions are innate. Goats and sheep were raised under three situations: a goat with a goat, a sheep with a sheep, and a goat with a sheep. In each combination the animals, when tested with a strange individual of either species, attacked the kind with which it had been raised. For example, when a sheep which had been raised with a goat was put with a sheep, no fight occurred since the sheep did not attack the other sheep. In contrast, when the sheep was put with a goat, it attacked. However, it fought by butting in the manner of a sheep rather than by jumping in the manner of a goat. No effective fight occurred because the sheep tried to butt the goat and the goat tried to jump on the sheep. No contact was maintained and the attacking soon ceased.

Physiologic factors in aggressive behavior

A major purpose of this chapter is to place in perspective the physiologic factors in social behavior. To understand the causation of behavior, it is necessary to consider the hormones as "agents" that carry a message concerning a state or condition. Hormones are a means of communication supplementing the nervous system but sometimes acting in different ways. Hormone action is slow because the chemical must travel in adequate quantities from the gland to the site of action. When the hormone is present at the proper structure, however, action may be almost instantaneous. The well-known rapid action of adrenalin is an example.

The "agent" cannot deliver its message unless suitable conditions are present.

Thus, testosterone, when injected into a capon, can cause no behavioral expression unless another bird is present and reacts in certain stereotypic ways. Furthermore, the environment must be suitable (familiar; contain certain items). For example, some birds will not demonstrate aggressiveness unless a particular type of perch is available.

The role of hormones in aggressive behavior has been recognized for a century. Many species have been experimentally tested, either by injection of an androgen such as testosterone or by castration. In many cases female or sexually immature individuals respond to androgens as characteristically as do males (Edwards, 1969). In addition to the aggressive behavior, several other masculine features appear. This almost universal reaction of animals to androgens unfortunately has permitted the assumption that aggressive behavior always depends upon androgens. An exception will be mentioned below.

Females fight much less vigorously than do males but nevertheless show aggressive behavior that can often be accentuated by injection of testosterone. Presumably the endocrine glands in females produce enough androgens to stimulate aggressive actions. In mammals some special androgens apparently arise in the adrenal glands, and in birds androgens come from the ovary as well.

The hormones (estrogens) normally associated with female characters apparently stimulate aggressive behavior under some circumstances. For example, Birch and Clark (1946) and Kislak and Beach (1955) found evidence that estrogens accentuated aggressiveness in chimpanzees and hamsters.

Since the production of male and female hormones depends upon the activities of several organs, it is now necessary to consider these individually in order to explain the source of aggressive behavior. An area in the brain called the hypothalamus influences aggressive behavior through many channels. By its control of the pituitary it acts upon the gonads and the adrenal cortex. The gonads, in turn, produce testosterone, which promotes aggression. The adrenal cortex produces corticoids which act upon the organs involved in such behavior. Acting through the sympathetic nerves to the adrenal medulla, the hypothalamus also controls the release of adrenalin, which is concerned in physiologic processes active during aggressive behavior.

Until recently the hormones of the pituitary were not known to affect aggressive behavior directly. However, numerous observations of social behavior in nature suggested that testosterone could not be responsible for the level of aggressiveness in some species. For example, Davis (1957) showed that testosterone did not affect the rank of starlings in the group hierarchy. Subsequently, Mathewson (1961) found that luteinizing hormones (LH) increased aggressiveness and caused birds to reverse rank. Several hitherto unexplained behaviors may be now clarified by experimental or field study. For example, many birds (e.g., blackbirds) defend a territory in the fall and winter when the gonads are very small (Snow, 1961). The usual explanations have been that minimal amounts of androgens are derived either from the tiny gonads or from the adrenals. It may be that the LH produced by the pituitary is responsible. It has long been known (Greeley and Meyer, 1953) that gonadotropins (LH and FSH) are produced in large amounts in the fall. Another example of unexplained behavior is the aggressive behavior of female mammals immediately after copulation. It is well known (Sawyer, 1959) that LH appears in large amounts at ovulation in mammals and that it stimulates ovulation in birds. Aggressive behavior occurring at this time might result from LH.

The hormones mentioned thus far are produced in the gonads or pituitaries and are concerned with reproductive activities. Several additional hormones (progesterone, relaxin, etc.) are associated directly with reproduction, but investigations have thus far not demonstrated any influence on aggressive behavior except associated with changes in sexual receptivity (see Chapter 2, p. 15). Because there are no suggestions that such hormones influence aggression, only a few studies have been made. Other organs, such as the adrenal, thyroid, and pancreas, produce various hormones. But only certain hormones from the adrenal are important in the study of aggressiveness.

The adrenal gland is a complicated structure composed of two very different parts, the cortex and the medulla. The cortex encompasses the medulla and consists of several zones. Some areas produce various hormones called glucocorticoids, which affect carbohydrate metabolism, certain reproductive processes, and inflammation. Other areas produce mineralocorticoids and affect the mineral balance. Also, some androgens appear. The direct measurement of corticoids and androgens is very difficult. Usually the best procedure is to determine the amounts of breakdown products in the urine. Since this measure requires careful interpretation, the results are often dubious.

The medulla may be considered part of the autonomic nervous system, since it develops from the same embryonic source and is homologous with a sympathetic ganglion. In keeping with this origin the medulla produces hormones – adrenalin (epinephrine) and noradrenalin (norepinephrine) – that are collectively called catechol amines. Since a number of detailed reviews (Elmadjian *et al.*, 1958; Christian, 1963) are available, only a summary of pertinent functions will be given here. In general the effects of these two medullary hormones mimic those of the sympathetic nervous system. Both hormones act on the circulatory system to constrict the visceral vessels, but noradrenalin constricts the vessels in muscles while adrenalin dilates skeletal muscles. Adrenalin causes a greater rise in blood sugar than does noradrenalin. Both hormones have various effects on smooth muscle, the spleen, and the bladder, but an effect considered important for current purposes is the mobilization of sugar from the liver. Adrenalin is more effective than is noradrenalin, but the end result is to move carbohydrate from the liver to the muscles.

The sympathetic nervous system responds promptly in a difficult situation, whether it be environmental (cold, poison, etc.) or behavioral (sexual, aggressive). The various effects of the hormones prepare the animal for action in the classic "fight or flight" picture. Recent studies (Elmadjian *et al.*, 1958) suggest that aggressive or active situations tend to stimulate production of noradrenalin whereas tension produces more adrenalin. Thus, professional hockey players had a sevenfold rise in noradrenalin and a threefold rise in adrenalin during a game. Two men who sat on the bench had a trivial change in noradrenalin and a doubling of adrenalin. Several other studies with prize fighters confirmed these results, as did studies on psychotic patients, although the data here are meager at this time.

The pathways in the brain that conduct stimuli causing secretion of adrenalin are not known. Experimental work shows that the hypothalamus is involved, but the mechanism remains to be convincingly demonstrated. Certainly hormones (vasopressin) from the posterior pituitary can release adrenalin, but many details need clarification. Innumerable studies show that an increase in catechol amines follows psychologic stresses, presumably acting through the limbic region (MacLean *et al.*, 1960).

While the action of the hormones from the medulla produces this vast array of physiologic responses, it is clear that these are merely symptoms of a situation associated with aggressive behavior rather than causes of it. Medullary hormones permit an animal to carry out aggression rather than cause it to be aggressive. For example, persons receiving adrenalin demonstrate the physiologic reactions but do not feel mad or become aggressive. The physiologic responses of the adrenal medulla are merely concomitants of the phenomenon called emotion.

Physiologic consequences of aggressive behavior

The knowledge of the physiologic repercussions of aggressive behavior has a long and complex history. In brief it was as follows: In studies of animal populations, various persons noted that the reproductive rate declined at high densities. Introduction of strange individuals into a population also resulted in a decline, presumably because of social turmoil (Davis, 1949). A little later Christian (1950) proposed that the crash of populations in the rodents of Arctic regions resulted from exhaustion of the adrenals due to the added stress of reproduction and other factors.

Subsequent research showed that social behavior caused changes in the adrenal cortex. The evidence (given in detail by Christian, 1963) is as follows: When certain mammals are brought together in groups, fighting begins and the adrenal cortex enlarges, reaching a maximum in about ten days. The relationship between population density and size of adrenal cortex has been demonstrated in mice, rats, woodchucks, voles, monkeys, and chickens and presumably occurs in other species that form social ranks. When mice were put together in cages containing 1, 4, 6, 8, 16, or 32 males (same age and weight), the weight of the adrenals increased from 4.92 mg. to 5.33 mg. at 16 animals per cage but dropped to 4.95 mg. at 32 animals per cage. Numerous other experiments confirm that grouping results in an increase of adrenal size, until, at high density, exhaustion occurs (Fig. 1). Another type of experiment consists of permitting a few pairs of animals (usually mice) to reproduce in a large cage. In about six months the population reaches a high level. Under these circumstances the size of the adrenals increases about 25 percent over the adrenal size of controls (mice in isolation). At the halfway point of population increase, the adrenals weigh about 15 percent more than those of controls.

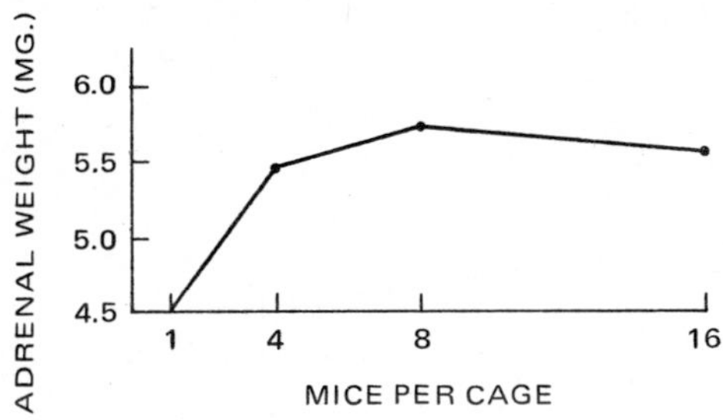

Figure 1. Increase of adrenal weight with increase in number of mice in a cage.

The above results were obtained with caged animals and might be only artifacts of domestication. In natural populations of rats, however, the adrenals in dense populations were about 20 percent larger than the adrenals of rats in sparse populations. Furthermore, the experimental reduction of natural populations of rats had the predicted result, namely, a reduction (26 percent) in adrenal weight.

The above measurements ignore the social organization of the group. Experiments designed to compare adrenal weight with rank showed that the adrenals of the dominant mice were the same size as those of controls, but the adrenals of subordinate mice were enlarged (Fig. 2). Thus, an important consequence of aggressive behavior is the physiologic advantage gained from winning, since the adrenals of winners are normal in size rather than hypertrophied and thus have normal function – we assume.

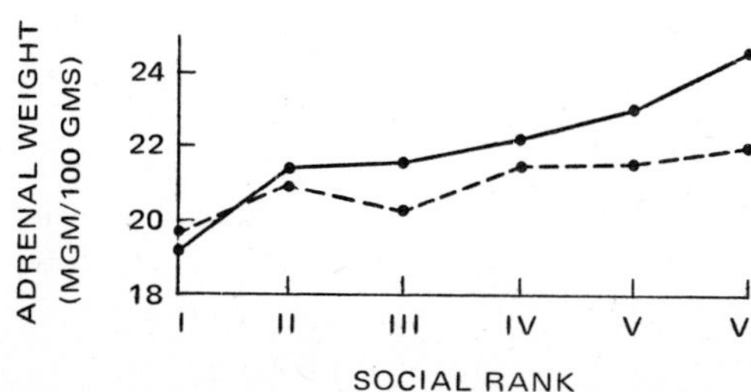

Figure 2. Relation of adrenal size and rank in mice. Dotted line refers to weight at start and solid line refers to weight at end of ten days.

A number of indirect measures show that an enlarged adrenal secretes increased amounts of hormones. One specific measure is the degree of involution of the thymus gland, which is a lymph organ in the throat region. Injection of corticoids involutes the thymus, as does grouping animals under conditions conducive to aggression (Fig. 3). Another indirect measure of adrenal activity is the condition of the gonads. The testes of male animals in groups are smaller than those of male animals in isolation. For example, when mice in a growing population were compared with their controls in isolation, it was found that the testes in adults weighed 20 percent less. Furthermore, an index of sperm production showed a measurable decrease in the grouped mice.

All of these effects (and many others) can be experimentally obtained by injection of appropriate corticoids or ACTH. The evidence from the size of the adrenal, degree of involution of the thymus, inhibition of growth, and retardation of sexual development lead to the following conclusion: that aggressive behavior manifested in crowded populations stimulates the adrenal, through the pituitary, to secrete various corticoids. Recently, direct measurements of hormones from the adrenal vein support this conclusion.

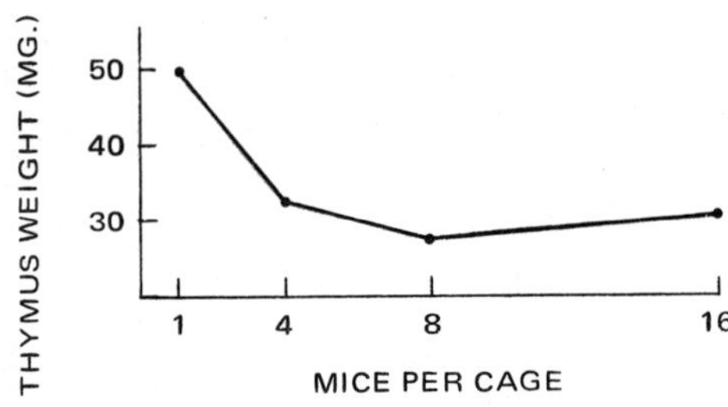

Figure 3. Decline of thymus weight with increase in number of mice in a cage.

The important point to be derived from the physiologic relationships is that corticoids are increased under conditions where aggression occurs. Aggressive behavior is thus recognized as one of many environmental variables (Arvay *et al.*, 1959) stimulating the hypothalamic-pituitary-adrenal axis. The sequence of responses are now documented for many situations. Any potentially harmful stimulus in the environment brings into action the general adaptation syndrome (Selye, 1957). For example, cold, poisons, noise, and behavioral situations will initiate the responses. Such a factor is called a "stressor" and is said to produce stress. The typical (and highly simplified) sequence of physiologic responses is as follows: first, the alarm reaction, then a stage of resistance or adaptation, and, finally – if the stressor persists – exhaustion and death. Occasionally, the stress may be so great as to produce death during the alarm reaction. The physiologic responses differ in the various phases. At first the available adrenal corticoids are exhausted and the catechol amines are secreted from the medulla; then the cortex slowly enlarges, producing more corticoids and the catechol amines return nearly to normal; lastly, after prolonged stress, exhaustion may occur.

The consequences of aggressive behavior, acting through the pituitary-adrenal mechanism, are very important for the individual and for the population. Three major, interlocking effects result: (1) decline in reproduction, (2) increase in mortality, and (3) retardation of growth in various features.

The decline in reproduction occurs in several ways. As mentioned above, the testes are smaller in crowded mice. Also, young mice have testes weighing 84 mg. while the isolated controls had testes weighing 143 mg. The ovaries also reduced in animals under crowded conditions. Crowded female mice produced 5.4 viable embryos per pregnancy, but the controls had 6.2 viable embryos. The difference was not caused by a decrease in the number of ovulations but by loss of embryos after implantation. These effects on the gonads may result from an increase in corticoids or pituitary hormones or both. Another effect of population crowding is interference with lactation. When baby mice born to females living in crowded conditions before conception are reared by their mothers, their growth is reduced in comparison to that of litter mates reared by foster mothers in noncrowded conditions. Whether quantity or quality of milk is affected is not known, but the reduction of growth lasts for at least two generations.

Another action following aggression is the change in resistance to infection by pathogenic organisms. Corticoids inhibit inflammation (which protects against infection) and production of antibodies in many cases. Studies on mice show grouped animals to be less resistant to parasites (*Trichinella*) and to tetanus toxin. In the first case, inflammation is inhibited; and in the second, the level of antibodies is reduced. These effects also may be produced by corticoids and serve to increase mortality in high populations. An important point (though not a central theme of this chapter) is that aggressive behavior, acting through the adrenals, regulates the population by a feedback mechanism. As numbers increase, reproduction declines and mortality increases, thereby retarding the increase in population (Thiessen and Rodgers, 1961).

The third consequence from aggressive behavior is a delay in maturation and growth. Mice caged in groups show a delay in estrus in immature females. A complication of these phenomena is the effect of the male alone in accelerating reproduction (Vandenbergh, 1967). Presumably crowding and its attendant aggressive behavior would disrupt the normal sexual behavior and result in a delay in sexual maturity.

In addition some prenatal effects (Kelley, 1962) occur in crowded mice that may well result from the sequence of hormonal changes resulting from aggressive behavior. These defects of motor activity can also occur when corticosterone is given to mice in the postnatal period (Howard and Granoff, 1968).

Though many physiologic repercussions of aggressive behavior are known, knowledge of the pathways of action is meager. Stimulation by electrodes of certain areas in the brain results in an increase in corticoids (Setekleiv *et al.*, 1961), whereas in other areas stimulation has no effect. In particular, the amygdala is necessary for a response (Knigge, 1961). Removal of certain areas in the brain (Egdahl, 1961) results in an increase of ACTH and suggests that the brain tonically inhibits ACTH production. Furthermore, hormones from the posterior pituitary may directly stimulate the adrenal cortex (Smelik, 1960). An unsolved problem is the nature of stimulus to the hypothalamus. A probable stimulus is the secretion of hormones from the adrenal medulla. Innumerable studies (Elmadjian *et al.*, 1958) show that certain behavioral situations result in an increase of adrenalin. Some recent studies may be mentioned in detail. Levi (1961) reports that persons classified by psychologic tests as having high tolerance for stress had low levels of catechol amines. Frankenhaeusser *et al.* (1961) found that the stress of a psychologic task produced an increase in excretion of breakdown products of adrenalin. Further, Melick (1960) examined the urine of medical students before, during, and after examinations. The excretion products of corticoids were significantly increased just before and during the examinations. The catechol amines themselves may produce direct physiologic or pathologic consequences. A number of studies (see McNeil, 1959: 260-264) show correlations between various states or stages of aggression and the occurrence of allergies (Bacon, 1956), constipation, headaches, ulcers, and many other symptoms. These consequences seem to be related to activity of the autonomic nervous system, which has well-known physiologic effects on blood pressure, glycogen in the blood, circulation, and other symptoms. Further, it should be noted that another result of catechol amines is the release of LH (Ginliani *et al.*, 1961), which stimulates aggressive behavior in some species.

Thus, we know that behavior, through a long chain of nervous and hormonal paths, produces an increase in two major types of hormones. We saw above that aggressive behavior produces, through the corticoids, many physiologic changes in reproduction and mortality rates. We also saw that stressful situations resulted in an increase of catechol amines. Some as yet inconclusive evidence suggests that these amines, perhaps acting through the posterior pituitary hormones, cause a release of ACTH, which, in turn, stimulates the adrenal cortex. While much work needs to be done, we have a possible chain of hormonal and nervous actions from the behavior to the physiologic consequences. But the behavior itself is associated with what humans call the "emotions" of fear and anger, which affect aggression.

References

Arvay, A., Balazsy, L., Jakubecz, S., and Takacs, I. 1959. Effect of severe nervous stimulation on the morphology and function of the adrenal cortex. *Acta Physiol. Acad. Sci. Hung.* 16(4): 267-284.

Bacon, C. L. 1956. The role of aggression in asthmatic attack. *Psychoanal. Quart.* 25:309-324.

Birch, H. G., and Clark, G. 1946. Hormonal modification of social behavior, II: The effects of sex-hormone administration on the social dominance status of the female-castrate chimpanzee. *Psychosom. Med.* 8(5):320-331.

Christian, J. J. 1950. The adreno-pituitary system and population cycles in mammals. *J. Mammal.* 31(3):247-259.

____. 1963. Endocrine adaptive mechanisms and the physiologic regulation of population growth. *Physiological Mammalogy*, ed. W. V. Mayer and R. G. van Gelder. New York: Academic Press, pp. 189-353.

____. 1970. Population density and fertility in mammals. *Bull. Sinai Hospital* 47:108.

Davis, David E. 1949. The role of intraspecific competition in game management. *Trans. North Amer. Wildlife Conf.* 14:225-331.

____. 1957. Aggressive behavior in castrated starlings. *Science* 126(3267):253.

____. 1958. The role of density in aggressive behavior of house mice. *Anim. Behav.* 6(3-4): 207-210.

Edwards, David A. 1969. Early androgen stimulation and aggressive behavior in male and female mice. *Physiol. Behav.* 4(3):333-338.

Egdahl, R. H. 1961. Cerebral cortical inhibition of pituitary-adrenal secretion. *Endocrinology* 68(4):574-581.

Elmadjian, F., Hope, J. M., and Lamson, E. J. 1958. Excretion of epinephrine and norepinephrine under stress. *Recent Progr. Hormone Res.* 14:513-554.

Frankenhaeusser, M., Jarpe, G., and Matell, G. 1961. Effects of intravenous infusions of adrenaline and noradrenaline on certain psychological and physiological functions. *Acta Physiol. Scand.* 51(2-3):175-187.

Ginliani, G., Martin, L., Pecile, A., and Foch, M. 1961. Studies on luteinizing hormone release and inhibition. *Acta Endocr.* 38(1):1-12.

Greeley, F., and Meyer, R. K. 1953. Seasonal variation in testis-stimulating activity of male pheasant pituitary glands. *Auk* 70(3):350-358.

Howard, Evelyn, and Granoff, Dan M. 1968. Increased voluntary running and decreased motor coordination in mice after neonatal corticosterone implantation. *Exp. Neurol.* 22(4):661-673.

Kelley, K. 1962. Prenatal influence on behavior of offspring of crowded mice. *Science* 135(3497):44-45.

King, J. A. 1957. Relationships between early social experience and adult aggressive behavior in inbred mice. *J. Genet. Psychol.* 90:151-166.

Kislak, J. W., and Beach, F. A. 1955. Inhibition of aggressiveness by ovarian hormones. *Endocrinology* 56:684-692.

Knigge, K. M. 1961. Adrenocortical response to stress in rats with lesions in hippocampus and amygdala. *Proc. Soc. Exp. Biol. Med.* 108(1):18-21.

Levi, L. 1961. A new stress tolerance test with simultaneous study of physiological and psychological variables. *Acta Endocr.* 37(1):38-44.

MacLean, P. D., Ploog, D. V., and Robinson, B. W. 1960. Circulatory effects of limbic stimulation, with special reference to the male genital organ. *Physiol. Rev. Suppl.* 4:105-112.

Mathewson, S. F. 1961. Gonadotropic control of aggressive behavior in starlings. *Science* 134:1522-1523.

McNeil, E. B. 1959. Psychology and aggression. *J. Conflict Resol.* 3:195-293.

Melick, R. 1960. Changes in urinary steroid excretion during examinations. *Australasian Annals Med.* 9(3):200-203.

Sawyer, C. H. 1959. Nervous control of ovulation. *Endocrinology of Reproduction*, ed. C. W. Lloyd. New York: Academic Press, pp. 1-20.

Scott, J. P. 1958. *Aggression.* Chicago: University of Chicago Press, p. 149.

Selye, H. 1957. *The Stress of Life.* New York: McGraw-Hill Book Co., p. 324.

Setekleiv, J., Skaug, O. E., and Kaada, B. R. 1961. Increase of plasma 17-hydroxy-corticosteroids by cerebral cortical and amygdaloid stimulation in the cat. *J. Endocr.* 22(2):119-128.

Smelik, P. G. 1960. Mechanism of hypophysial response to psychic stress. *Acta Endocr.* 33(3): 437-443.

Snow, D. W. 1961. *A Study of Blackbirds.* London: Allen and Unwin, p. 192.

Thiessen, D. D., and Rodgers, D. A. 1961. Population density and endocrine function. *Psychol. Bull.* 58:441-451.

Vandenbergh, John G. 1967. Effect of the presence of a male on the sexual maturation of female mice. *Endocrinology* 81:345-349.

Welch, Bruce L., and Welch, Annemarie S. 1969. Sustained effects of brief daily stress (fighting) upon brain and adrenal catecholamines and adrenal, spleen, and heart weights of mice. *Proc. Nat. Acad. Sci.* 64(1):100-107.

2

Effects of gonadal hormones on displaced and direct aggression in pairs of rhesus monkeys of opposite sex

Richard P. Michael

There has recently been an increasing number of field and colony studies on the social organization of various species of primates, particularly baboons and macaques. In general, intra-group agonistic behaviour is at a low level under free-ranging conditions where groups are relatively stable and well integrated. Southwick (1967), working with a stable group of captive rhesus monkeys, *Macaca mulatta,* found that social changes, such as the introduction of strange individuals into the group, produced a greater increase in the frequency of aggressive behaviour than did environmental changes such as severe crowding.

There is evidence that changes in the pattern of intra-group aggression, even in stable groups, are associated with changes in sexual activity. The frequency of aggressive episodes between female chacma baboons, *Papio ursinus,* not in full oestrus, was highest during those times of the day when the dominant male was mating most frequently with an oestrous consort; the occurrence

---

SOURCE: *Aggressive Behaviour,* Proceedings of the International Symposium on the Biology of Aggressive Behaviour, S. Garattini and E. B. Sigg, eds., Amsterdam: Excerpta Medica, 1969. This work was supported by grants from the USPHS MH-10002, and the Bethlehem Royal and Maudsley Hospital Research Fund. Reprinted by permission of Excerpta Medica.

of sexual activity was associated with increased agonistic exchanges between those females not directly involved in it (Hall, 1962). There is, in addition, evidence for changes in the levels of male and female aggression in relation to the menstrual cycle of the female. Both rhesus monkeys and baboons were reported to become more aggressive when sexually receptive and actively seeking the vicinity of males (Carpenter, 1942; Chance, 1956; Bolwig, 1959; Altmann, 1962; Rowell, 1963). Before the time of maximum sexual activity, at the stage when females begin to approach males, they appeared to be particularly prone to attacks by males (Carpenter, 1942; Imanishi, 1963; Southwick *et al.,* 1965). In contrast, at the height of oestrus, when consort bonds are well established, the male showed increased tolerance towards his partner (Carpenter, 1942). In a captive group of rhesus monkeys, females were most frequently attacked by males just prior to menstruation (Rowell, 1963); such females would, of course, be able to avoid the close vicinity of males in the wild.

Aggression directed away from the sexual partner has also been reported from both field and laboratory studies. Hall (1966) described threatening at a third individual by sexually interacting patas monkeys, *Erythrocebus patas,* and Altmann (1962) described threatening-away from the partner, either towards a third individual or at nothing in particular, by young rhesus monkeys, more particularly by females, just prior to copulation. In fact, Ball and Hartman (1935) used threatening at an outsider as a criterion of sexual excitability in the female rhesus monkey.

This paper is concerned with both "displaced" and direct aggression occurring between oppositely sexed pairs of adult rhesus monkeys observed under laboratory conditions.

Methods

Mature, intact male and female rhesus monkeys were paired together daily for hourly test sessions in large, glass-fronted observation cages and observed from behind a one-way vision mirror. Between tests, all animals were housed singly and the methods for observing and scoring behaviour, which are routine in our laboratory, have been given elsewhere (Michael *et al.,* 1966; Michael and Saayman, 1967). After periods of observation when the females were intact, they were ovariectomized and given the following hormone replacement treatments: first, oestradiol alone (5 μg/day s.c.) and, then, oestrogen and progesterone (25 mg/day s.c.) in combination. When intact females were studied during the administration of a contraceptive agent (mestranol 50 μg + ethynodiol diacetate 1 mg s.c. per day), this was given in cycles of 21-day treatments with 7 days between treatments over a period of 6 months: a similar regimen to that employed for oral contraception in women. Certain of the ovariectomized females subsequently carried small implants of oestrogen in the hypothalamic region of their brains, the purpose of which was to make them highly receptive sexually; details of these experiments are outside our present scope.

Results

Displaced aggression – threatening away

Three males made vigorous threatening gestures during tests directed away from their female partners. Two males visually fixated on, and threatened at, particular points outside the observation cage, while the third directed his threats upwards or in whatever direction he happened to be facing at the time. Threats consisted of rapid jerks of the head and thorax, often accompanied by the open-jawed gesture (Altmann, 1962), the males sometimes hitting out and even leaping forward as in an attack. While threatening in this manner, males repeatedly glanced backwards towards the female sitting beside or behind him, and the female not infrequently responded by threatening, also, in the same direction as the male so that both were threatening together. This behaviour would quite frequently begin just before the first mount of a mounting series, tended to increase in intensity between mounts, and invariably ceased after ejaculation had occurred. The most notable characteristic of this threatening-away behaviour was that it was directed in any direction *except* towards the partner.

Figure 1 shows data from one male tested with each of two females on alternate days. The upper histograms show the mean number of sexual mounting attempts by the male and the lower histograms show the mean numbers of threatening-away episodes by the male per test, during different hormonal conditions of the females, ovariectomized, ovariectomized with oestrogen, ovariectomized with oestrogen and progesterone, brain implants of oestrogen, brain implants of oestrogen with progesterone s.c. There was a well-marked positive correlation between the number of male mounting attempts upon the female and the frequency of threatening-away behaviour. In essence, when the male was sexually interested in the female he threatened-away more frequently than when his interest in her was low. It seems clear that, in this particular behavioural context, threatening-away was related to the male's sexual interest in the female.

These two females infrequently initiated threatening-away behaviour themselves but joined in with that initiated by the male. It was to be expected, then, that male and female threatening-away would vary together. However, this was not necessarily so.

Figure 2 shows male threatening-away episodes (upper), female threatening-away episodes (middle), and female refusals of male mounting attempts (lower); the latter gives a measure of female receptivity. When the ovariectomized female received 5 μg oestradiol per day, both male and female threatening-away increased as compared with the anhormonal condition of the female. The additional administration of progesterone to the female, which decreased her receptivity (refusals increased), had a differential effect on the threatening-away behaviour of the pair: that of the male was little changed, whereas threatening-away by the female was markedly depressed. It thus appeared that the female's readiness to join in with the male's threatening-away behaviour depended also on her state of sexual receptivity.

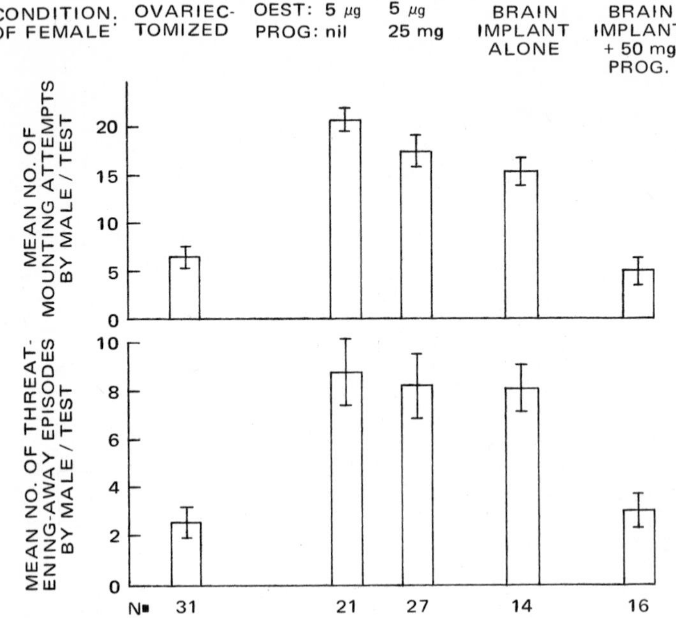

Figure 1. Male sexual mounting attempts and episodes of threatening-away behaviour during 1-hr. mating tests (1 male rhesus monkey and 2 females) were positively correlated, and depended upon the hormonal condition of the female partners: when male sexual interest in the female was high, his threatening-away behaviour increased (109 tests).

Some females, the more dominant ones, sometimes took the lead in this threatening-away activity, and the behaviour in a pair with such a female is shown in Figure 3. Here, the female was experiencing artificial cycles as the result of treatment with an antifertility compound (mestranol 50 μg with ethynodiol diacetate 1.0 mg s.c. per day). Where the female initiated much of the threatening-away behaviour, her frequency, which was changing with her hormonal status over the 6-month period, in large measure determined the frequency of the male's threatening-away behaviour: the female's frequency was always the higher of the two, and the male appeared to be drawn along by it. This contrasted with the female's readiness to join in when the male was the initiator, since this was influenced also by her state of receptivity.

Direct aggression

All forms of aggressive threats (staring, open-jawed gesture, jerking, slapping the ground, and charging) as well as hitting and biting, and all intensities of submissive behaviour (presenting, fear-grimacing, crouching, and fleeing) described from both field and laboratory studies were observed. Normally, however, agonistic behaviour

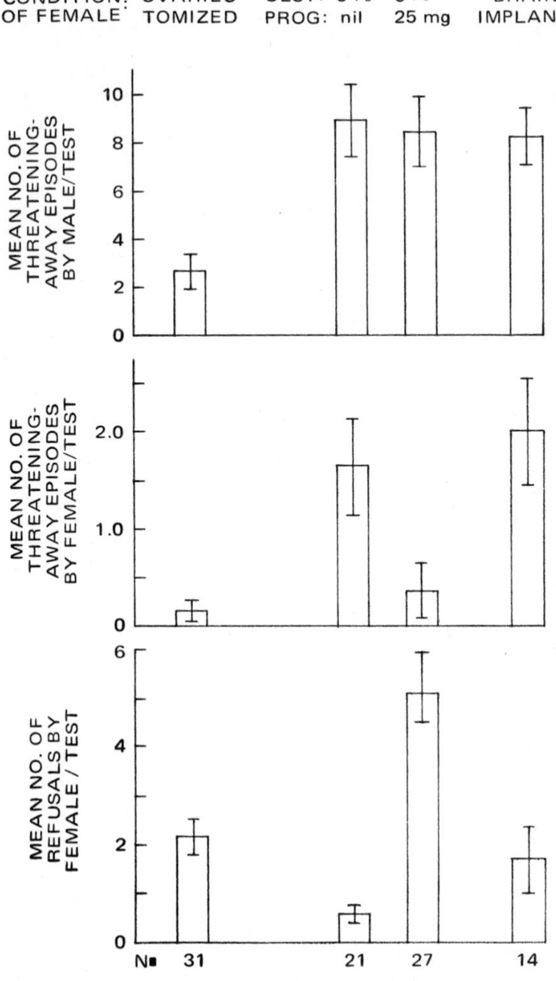

Figure 2. The administration of progesterone to ovariectomized females receiving oestrogen did not influence threatening-away by the male but depressed that of the female partners (2 pairs). The decline in female threatening-away behaviour was associated with a decline in sexual receptivity—increased refusals (93 tests).

was infrequently encountered under our experimental conditions but, nevertheless, was observed sufficiently often in some pairs to study the effects on it of administering ovarian hormones to the female of the pair. Direct aggression by the male usually occurred in response to threats by the female but occasionally occurred apparently spontaneously.

The upper part of Figure 4 shows the mean number of aggressive episodes by the male (above the line) and by the female (below the line – solid) in 3 pairs during 196 tests before and after ovariectomy of the females. The middle part shows the mean number of male mounting attempts, and the lower part, the number of refusals by the females. Although with these particular animals the number of male mounting attempts remained unchanged, there was a marked increase in aggressive exchanges when the female of the pair was ovariectomized. In particular, it can be seen that aggression was being initiated by the male who was doing more than just responding to increased female aggressivity. Aggression by the female may well be related to the increase in her refusals of male mounting attempts consequent upon ovariectomy, but there is no doubt that ovariectomized females are more prone to male aggression than intact ones.

When ovariectomized females were subsequently given oestradiol (5 μg/day s.c.) they became sexually receptive and refusals virtually disappeared. Despite this, the number of aggressive episodes by the female remained unchanged, although the male

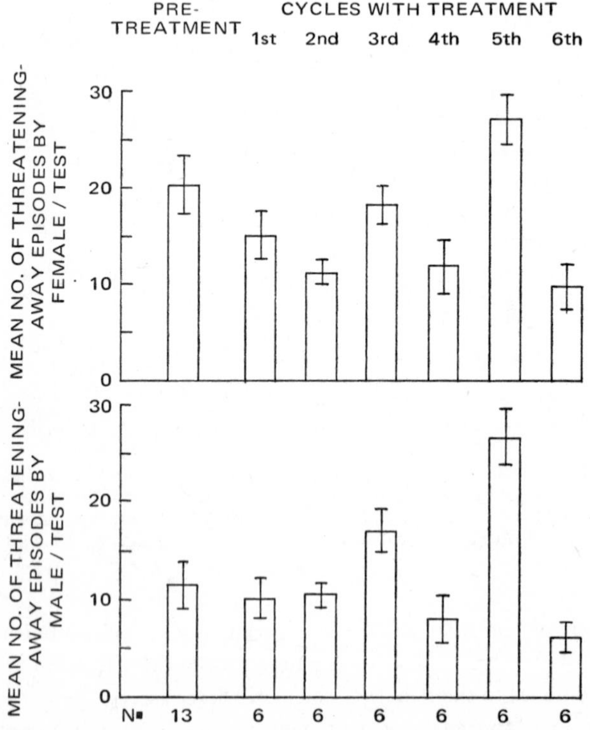

Figure 3. When a female (*Macaca mulatta*) initiated threatening-away during artificial cycles induced by administration of an antifertility agent, male threatening-away generally followed that of the female but at a lower level (49 tests).

became tolerant of the female's aggressivity and his aggression towards her virtually disappeared. When females were then treated with progesterone (25 mg/day s.c.) in addition to the oestrogen, female refusals returned to the same level as in the pre-hormonal treatment condition, but the number of aggressive episodes by the females more than doubled. Despite this dramatic increase in female aggression, the male remained extremely tolerant. The simplest interpretation of these findings would be that oestrogen and progesterone, acting synergistically, greatly enhanced female aggressivity. An alternative, and more attractive, interpretation would be that the refusal behaviour induced by progesterone acts in concert with aggressive behaviour induced by oestrogen to produce the same effect. It would be necessary to study ovariectomized females given progesterone alone in order to discriminate between these alternatives.

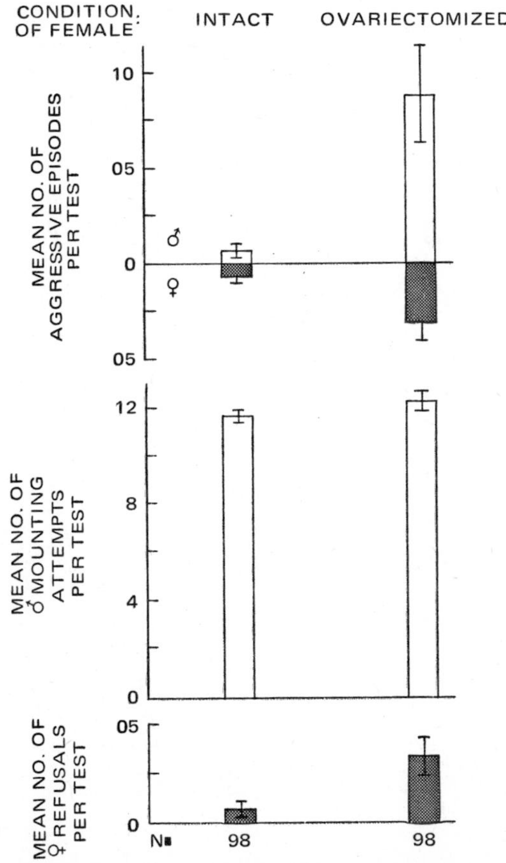

Figure 4. After ovariectomy, aggression between the 3 pairs greatly increased. The males initiated more aggression with ovariectomized females which were more prone to attack. The increased aggression of females may be related to their increased refusals of male mounting attempts (196 tests).

In view of these findings when oestrogen and progesterone were administered to ovariectomized animals, it was considered of interest to study the changes in the aggressivity of the female as her hormonal balance changed physiologically during the course of pregnancy. By controlled mating, the probable time of conception could be determined to within a few days. The upper part of Figure 5 shows the number of aggressive episodes by the female from the 77th day after the probable time of conception, and the lower part, the number of male mounting attempts and of female refusals per test. Here, it was meaningful to distinguish between the number of non-contact threats, hits, and bites. Although the male continued to show considerable sexual interest in the female as pregnancy advanced, the number of female refusals progressively increased and reached very high levels. Female aggression towards the male increased at the same time and towards the latter part of

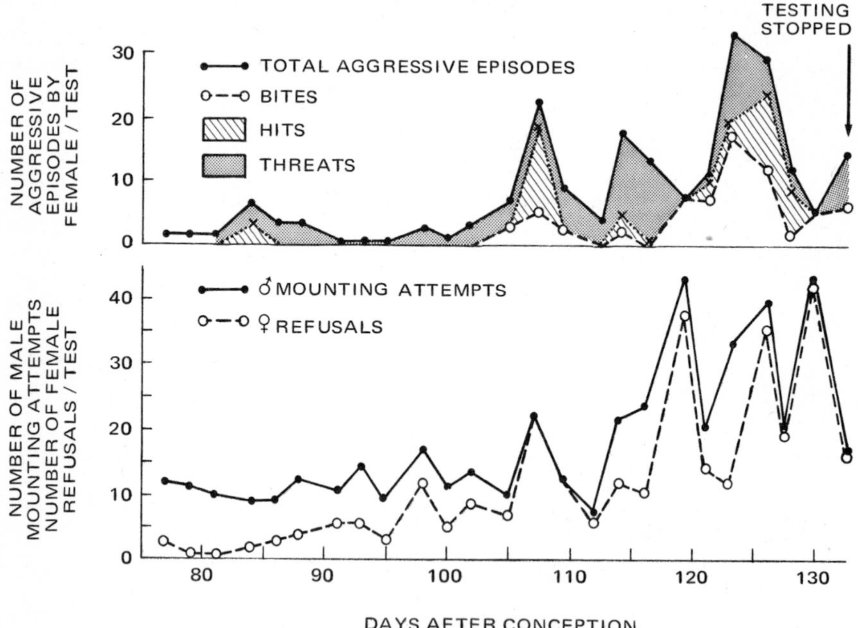

Figure 5. Refusals by the female *Macaca mulatta* of male mounting attempts increased conspicuously as pregnancy advanced. This was also associated with increasing female aggression and actual biting of the male who, nevertheless, remained tolerant.

pregnancy actual hitting and biting of the male occurred. The male remained extraordinarily tolerant until the very end of the period of testing when he began to fight back: the observations were discontinued because of risk to the female and her pregnancy. Thus, the findings in pregnancy closely agreed with those in ovariectomized animals given oestrogen and progesterone.

Conclusions

The threatening-away behaviour described here which was earlier referred to in psychological terms as displaced aggression would, in ethological parlance, be more appropriately termed re-directed aggression. In the male, threatening-away behaviour was frequent when the male was sexually interested in the oestrogenized female, at a time when direct male aggression towards her was low and he was tolerant of her threats. This behaviour may be looked upon as playing a part in the development of consort bonds and pair formation and would, in the wild, serve the additional purpose of warning off potential sexual rivals.

The findings on direct aggression are in agreement with observations from field studies that females are more aggressive at the height of sexual receptivity and, also, that males are more tolerant of receptive than both non-receptive females and those in the early stages of oestrus. These studies also show that there appears to be an endocrine factor underlying these changes in the behavioural interactions of the pair.

References

Altmann, S. A. 1962. A field study of the sociobiology of rhesus monkeys (*Macaca mulatta*). *Ann. N.Y. Acad. Sci.*, 102, 338.

Ball, J. and Hartman, C. G. 1935. Sexual excitability as related to the menstrual cycle in the monkey. *Am. J. Obstet. Gynec.*, 39, 117.

Bolwig, N. 1959. A study of the behaviour of the chacma baboon, *Papio ursinus. Behaviour,* 14, 136.

Carpenter, C. R. 1942. Sexual behavior of free-ranging rhesus monkeys (*Macaca mulatta*). I. Specimens, procedures and behavioral characteristics of estrus. *J. comp. Psychol.*, 33, 113.

Chance, M. R. A. 1956. Social structure of a colony of *Macaca mulatta. Brit. J. Anim. Behav.*, 4, 1.

Hall, K. R. L. 1962. The sexual, agonistic, and derived social behaviour patterns of the wild chacma baboon, *Papio ursinus. Proc. Zool. Soc.* (*Lond.*), 138, 283.

____. 1966. Behaviour and ecology of the wild patas monkey, *Erythrocebus patas,* in Uganda. *J. Zool.*, 148, 15.

Imanishi, E. 1963. Social behaviour in Japanese monkeys, *Macaca fuscata. Primate Social Behavior,* ed. C. H. Southwick, pp. 68-81. London: D. Van Nostrand Company Inc.

Michael, R. P., Herbert, J., and Welegalla, J. 1966. Ovarian hormones and grooming behaviour in the rhesus monkey (*Macaca mulatta*) under laboratory conditions. *J. Endocr.*, 36, 263.

Michael, R. P. and Saayman, G. 1967. Individual differences in the sexual behaviour of male rhesus monkeys (*Macaca mulatta*) under laboratory conditions. *Anim. Behav.*, 15, 460.

Rowell, T. E. 1963. Behaviour and female reproductive cycles of rhesus macaques. *J. Reprod. Fertil.*, 6, 193.

Southwick, C. H. 1967. An experimental study of intragroup agonistic behavior in rhesus monkeys (*Macaca mulatta*). *Behaviour,* 28, 182.

Southwick, C. H., Beg, M. A., and Siddiqi, M. R. 1965. Rhesus monkeys in North India. *Primate Behavior,* ed. I. DeVore, pp. 111-159. New York: Holt, Rinehart and Winston.

3

Internal impulses to aggression

K. E. Moyer

This paper will consider the internal impulses to aggressive behavior and the implications this information has for aggression control. A discussion of the *internal* impulses to aggression necessitates a consideration of the current controversy over whether or not there is an aggressive drive.

Some investigators (Altman, 1966; Hinde, 1967; Marler and Hamilton, 1966) maintain that there is no drive for aggressive behavior in the same sense that there is a drive for eating, drinking, or sex behavior. J. P. Scott, who has done excellent and extensive research on the problem of aggression, is an enthusiastic proponent of this position. In 1965 he said, "All that we know (and this comprises a considerable body of information in certain species) indicates that the physiological mechanisms associated with fighting are very different from those underlying sexual behavior and eating. There is no known physiological mechanism by which spontaneous internal stimulation for fighting arises." (p. 820)

Another group of individuals studying this problem has arrived at exactly the opposite conclusion. Lorenz (1966), on the basis of ethological studies, Lagerspetz (1964), on the basis of behavioral studies with mice, and Feshbach (1964), on the basis of experiments with

SOURCE: *Transactions* of The New York Academy of Sciences, Volume 31, No. 2, pp. 104-114, K. E. Moyer ©The New York Academy of Sciences, 1969. This paper, illustrated with slides, was presented at a meeting of the Section of Biological and Medical Sciences on October 14, 1968, and was supported in part by grant #GB 6652 from the National Science Foundation. Reprinted by permission of the author and the publisher.

humans, have all concluded that there is indeed a drive for aggressive behavior.

Much of this controversy results from the looseness of the various definitions of drive. The concept means very different things to different people. Drive is frequently given the status of an intervening variable which is essentially an expression of ignorance or lack of concern with what is going on inside the organism. However, Dr. Ethel Tobach and others (Scott, 1967) have expressed the view that the term drive, to be useful, must be given a sound physiological basis. However, the more I investigate the physiological basis of behavior, the less need I find for the concept of drive. The difficulties with this construct have been considered elsewhere (Berkowitz, 1965; Bolles, 1958; Cofer and Appley, 1964), so I need not detail them here. In addition to the criticism offered in those sources, it appears to me that there are certain philosophical problems with the term drive as it is sometimes used. I find the implied mind-body interaction neither necessary nor useful in making predictions about behavior. Further, the drive concept frequently implies a hedonistic interpretation of behavior (the pleasure principle of psychoanalytic thinking and the affective arousal of Young are examples) which is also neither necessary nor useful.

It appears to me that the time has come to reject the term drive in order to avoid further confusion. There are certain basic circuits in the nervous system. When they are active, certain complex behaviors occur. The problem for the student of behavior is to determine the variables, both internal and external, which activate and deactivate these circuits. There are certainly differences in the mechanisms for turning the basic neuronal circuits on and off. There are also remarkable similarities. The evidence seems to indicate that there are basic (in a sense, built-in) circuits for aggressive behavior just as there are for consummatory and sex behavior. Some of these similarities will now be considered.

Much of the discussion about the similarity of aggressive behavior to other basic behaviors (Tinbergen, 1968) seems to revolve around whether aggression is endogenously or exogenously determined. Scott and Fredericson (1951, p. 820) have suggested that, "There is no evidence for any sort of spontaneous internally arising stimulation which would cause a 'need for fighting' per se. Instead, we have a mechanism which will produce fighting in response to predictable external stimulation." However, the same statement can be made about all basic behavior patterns. Behavior does not occur in a vacuum. A deprived animal does not make random chewing movements nor does it attempt to eat all available objects. Regardless of the intensity of the internal state produced by deprivation, the animal responds to a very limited set of stimuli with an eating response. It eats only food objects. In the same manner, the aggressive subject behaves aggressively only toward a very limited number of stimulus objects. The converse is also true. An animal will not engage in eating behavior or in aggressive behavior to an appropriate stimulus object unless a certain characteristic physiological state is present. Some of these physiological mechanisms will now be examined.

Facilitation of consummatory and aggressive behavior by brain stimulation

It has been demonstrated repeatedly that when certain areas of the brain are activated an animal will become restless and engage in exploratory behavior. If that behavior brings it into contact with food, the animal, even though satiated, will begin to eat (Akert, 1961). An extensive series of experiments by Miller and his colleagues (1957, 1961) has shown that the eating behavior resulting from brain stimulation has many of the charactersitics of normal deprivation-induced behavior. A rat stimulated in the lateral hypothalamus will eat lab chow or lap milk, but it will not drink pure water. Thus, the response is stimulus bound.

In a similar manner, an animal can be induced to display aggressive behavior by the stimulation of specific brain areas. Cats which normally do not attack rats will do so during electrical stimulation of the hypothalamus (Wasman and Flynn, 1962). If the lateral hypothalamus is stimulated, the cat ignores the experimenter and quietly and efficiently stalks and kills the rat, usually by biting in the neck region as is characteristic of this species. In my own laboratory, Richard Bandler has been able to induce a similar predatory mouse killing in rats by carbachol stimulation of the lateral hypothalamus. If there is no stimulus object available, the animal may explore in a restless manner, but it does not behave aggressively. The cat stimulated in the lateral hypothalamus shows distinct and evidently unlearned preferences in the types of stimulus objects it will attack. An anesthetized rat will be attacked more quickly and persistently than a stuffed rat, and there is little tendency for the cat to attack a foam rubber block about the size of a rat (Levison and Flynn, 1965).

Stimulation of the medial hypothalamus produces a very different kind of aggression. The cat shows pronounced sympathetic arousal and attacks with a high-pitched scream, tearing at the stimulus object with unsheathed claws. It may ignore an available rat but viciously attack a person (Egger and Flynn, 1963).

Just as food is reinforcing to the animal whose "feeding system" is activated, the opportunity to attack is reinforcing to an animal whose "predatory system" is activated. Cats which will attack rats during hypothalamic stimulation will learn a Y maze "to obtain a rat they could attack" (Roberts and Kiess, 1964, p. 187).

One must, of course, be careful about generalizing data obtained from animal research to humans. For obvious reasons, there is a limited amount of data on the effects of brain stimulation in man. Nothing is known about the effects of brain stimulation of humans on eating behavior. However, somewhat more is known about aggression. King (1961) describes a patient with an electrode implanted in the amygdaloid region who became angry, verbally hostile, and threatened to strike the experimenter when stimulated with a current of 5 milliamperes. When the current was reduced or turned off, she again became mild mannered and apologetic for her aggressive behavior.

There is also indirect evidence that spontaneous activity of the neurones in the temporal lobe, as well as other areas of the brain, results in aggressive behavior. In some individuals, spontaneous firing of the cells in the temporal lobe and in the thalamus leads to subjective feelings of rage and the execution of incredibly violent behavior (Gibbs, 1951; Treffert, 1964). A number of studies have shown that aggressive behavior, such as fire setting, aggressive sex behavior, murder, and other acts of violence are associated with 14/second and 6/second positive spikes in the EEG record (Swade and Geiger, 1956, 1960; Woods, 1961). This assaultive aggressive behavior may or may not be associated with epileptic motor seizures. Even when it is, there is reason to believe that the neurohumoral substrates underlying the two behaviors are different in that they are differentially affected by brain lesions and drugs (F. R. Ervin, 1968, personal communication).

It might be suggested that "spontaneous neurological rage reactions" are abnormal and that they have little to do with the bulk of human behavior. However, "abnormal" is a statistical concept, not a neurological one. There seems to be good evidence that some individuals are born with a tendency for certain neurones to fire spontaneously and that the amount of spontaneous firing is on a continuum, occurring more in some individuals than in others. The most relevant question is not whether aggressive behavior *can* occur spontaneously as a result of the internal activation of certain brain areas, but how common is it? A mechanism for internally activated aggressive behavior appears to exist. Perhaps it occurs in many people, but less frequently in most. (See Jonas, 1965, for a further discussion of this point and an excellent review of the literature.)

Reduction of consummatory and aggressive behavior by brain lesions

The above evidence indicates that there exist in the brain of man and of animals well-integrated mechanisms which, when activated, result in complex, well-organized, well-directed behavior. Whether it is consummatory behavior or aggressive behavior depends on the particular circuit involved. Both types of behavior are directed toward particular stimuli. As one might suspect, when these brain mechanisms are damaged, the individual is unable to respond appropriately to the relevant stimuli.

Damage to the lateral nucleus of the hypothalamus produces an animal which does not show the slightest interest in food. It will, if left alone, starve to death in the midst of plenty. If tube fed (in some cases for several months), it may begin to respond to only the most preferred taste stimulation (Morrison and Mayer, 1957; Teitelbaum and Epstein, 1962).

The brain mechanisms for aggression can also be damaged with dramatic reductions in aggressive behavior. It has been shown that bilateral lesions in the amygdala will surgically tame the untameable wildcat *Lynx rufus* (Schreiner and Kling, 1956), the fierce, wild Norway rat (Woods, 1956), and a variety of other innately hostile animals including the agouti, cat, monkey, hamster, and cotton rat (see Moyer, 1968, for details). These normally vicious animals can be handled without gloves immediately after the operation. Lesions in a number of other brain areas will also reduce aggressive tendencies (Moyer, 1968).

In man the data are limited, but do exist. Ursin (1960) summarizes several cases of hostility control through brain surgery. He refers to one of Sawa's patients (Sawa *et al.*, 1958) who reported that after the operation he could not get angry even if he wanted to. Lesions in the temporal lobe (Pool, 1954), dorsomedial thalamus (Speigel *et al.*, 1951), posterior hypothalamus (Sano, 1962; Sano *et al.*, 1966), and the anterior cingulum (Tow and Whitty, 1953) have all been used successfully to reduce uncontrollable hostility in man. Le Beau (1952, p. 315) suggests, "Cingulectomy is specially indicated in intractable cases of anger, violence, aggressiveness, and permanent agitation."

Facilitation of consummatory and aggressive behavior by brain lesions

There are neurological mechanisms in the brain which prevent the manifestation of both excessive eating behavior and excessive aggressive behavior. When these mechanisms, located in well-defined areas of the brain, are destroyed, the individual's reaction to particular kinds of stimuli becomes excessive. Lesions in the ventromedial nucleus of the hypothalamus, for example, frequently result in the well-known syndrome of hypothalamic hyperphagia (Ehrlich, 1964). Soon after recovery from surgery the animal begins to eat voraciously, doubling or tripling its food intake with a resulting weight increase of similar magnitude. However, the animal is "finicky" (Graff and Stellar, 1962) and its excessive eating response is elicited only by certain preferred taste stimuli.

Bilateral destruction of either the basal or central nucleus of the amygdala will convert a friendly, affectionate, domestic cat into one which will attack without provocation (Wood, 1958). Wheatley (1944) has produced extremely vicious cats by lesioning the ventromedial hypothalamus. Increased aggressive behavior has also been produced by destruction of the septal region, frontal lobes, cingulum, and portions of the hippocampus. These aggressive responses are well directed, stimulus oriented, and are not comparable to the sham rage produced by decerebration (see Moyer, 1968, for specific studies).

Specific brain lesions in man will also increase hostile tendencies (Vonderahe, 1944; Wheatley, 1944).

Inhibition of consummatory and aggressive behavior by brain stimulation

The evidence from lesion experiments is sometimes difficult to interpret because of the possibility of resulting irritative scars. However, further evidence on the role of inhibitory mechanisms in the control of both eating behavior and aggressive behavior comes from brain stimulation experiments. Again, there is considerable evidence that the types of physiological mechanisms underlying eating behavior are similar in kind to those underlying aggressive behavior.

Eating can be inhibited by stimulation of the "satiety" center in the ventromedial hypothalamus (Wyrwicka and Dobrzecka, 1960). Septal stimulation can block eating behavior in the deprived monkey (Delgado, 1960).

Brain stimulation can also block aggression without interfering with normal motor responses. Amygdaloid stimulation can block normal mousing in cats as well as predation induced by hypothalamic stimulation (Egger and Flynn, 1963). Stimulation of the caudate nucleus will inhibit continuing aggressive behavior in a dominant male monkey (Delgado, 1963). In humans, Heath (1963) has reported the immediate reduction of agitated, violent, psychotic behavior by stimulation in the septal region. The patient's behavior changes almost instantly from disorganized rage to happiness and mild euphoria. Heath indicates further that this phenomenon has been repeated in a large number of patients.

Influence of blood chemistry changes on consummatory and aggressive behavior

There is a generally held theoretical conviction that eating behavior is regulated by the action of certain components in the blood which in turn act to produce increases in sensitivity in particular brain circuits. Glucose changes have been suggested as important in the short-run control of eating (Mayer, 1953) and lipids in long-run control (Kennedy, 1953).

In light of the available evidence, it is not unreasonable to postulate a similar mechanism in the regulation of aggressive behavior. However, as there may well be various kinds of aggression (Moyer, 1968), there must also be a variety of contributing regulators. Androgens in the blood stream are undoubtedly critical to the development of inter-male aggression (Beeman, 1947; Levy and King, 1953; Seward, 1945; Sigg, 1968; Urich, 1938). There is recent evidence that these androgenic effects may be masked or inhibited by estrogens, at least in isolated male mice (Suchowski, 1968). Female irritability is cyclical and increases during estrus in the shrew (Pearson, 1944), and in the guinea pig (Kislak and Beach, 1955). Further, aggressiveness in the ovariectomized female guinea pig can be inhibited by a series of estrogen injections followed by an injection of progesterone (Kislak and Beach, 1955).

Changes in the hormone balance in the blood stream can also inhibit maternal aggression. The domesticated mother rat will attack and kill a frog that is put into her cage only during the period of lactation. This maternal aggressiveness can be completely abolished without interfering with the care of the young if the rat is given a few days of oestrone therapy (Endroczi *et al.*, 1958). Some of the test rats which did not show the frog-killing response did so when they were administered hydrocortisone. Hydrocortisone injections also overcame the killing inhibition produced by oestrone.

Clinical endocrinology offers further support for the importance of blood components in the regulation of aggressive tendencies. Care must be exercised in the interpretation of these data because they are not from controlled laboratory studies. Certainly, however, the data are suggestive and can result in hypotheses which should be followed up in the laboratory.

Irritability is a frequent component of the premenstrual tension syndrome in the human female and is successfully treated by the administration of progesterone (Dalton, 1964; Greene and Dalton, 1953). It has also been shown that crimes of violence committed by women are related to the menstrual cycle. In a study of 249 women prison inmates, it was shown that 62 percent of the crimes of violence were committed during the premenstrual week and only 2 percent at the end of the period (Morton *et al.*, 1953). Diandrone (dehydroisoandrosterone) increases confidence in adolescents with feelings of inferiority and promotes aggressive responses (Sands and Chamberlain, 1952). In patients with a history of aggressiveness, diandrone is likely to produce excessive irritability and outbursts of rage (Sands, 1954; Strauss *et al.*, 1952). On the other hand, castration reduces the asocial acts of individuals convicted of sex crimes (Hawke, 1950; Le Maire, 1956), and the administration of stilboestrol, in some cases, provides dramatic control of both hypersexuality and irritable aggression (Dunn, 1941; Sands, 1954).

It is generally recognized that frustration and stress, particularly if prolonged, are likely to result in increased irritability and aggressive behavior. It may well be that the frustration-induced irritability results from the sensitization of certain brain areas by the particular hormone balance which characterizes the stress syndrome. Both the adrenal cortex and the thyroid are intimately involved in the stress syndrome, and dysfunctions of either gland result in increased irritability (Cleghorn, 1957; Gibson, 1962).

Influence of learning on consummatory and aggressive behavior

The influence of learning on aggressive responding has received considerable emphasis (Scott, 1958, 1962; Scott and Fredericson, 1951). Scott and Fredericson suggest that training can overcome hereditary predispositions and conclude that, "Training includes by far the most important group of factors which affect agonistic behavior" (p. 306). The implication of these discussions is that aggressive behavior is in some way set apart from other basic behaviors because learning has a strong influence on it. It is obvious, however, that learning has a strong influence on all basic behavior patterns. Psychiatrists' couches are filled with individuals who have learned hypo, hyper, or deviate sexual behavior. Learning also has a potent influence on consummatory behavior (Wright, 1965). Eating behavior reinforced by shock termination results in excessive food consumption with marked obesity (Williams and Teitelbaum, 1956).

It is possible through training to inhibit all consummatory behavior (Lichenstein, 1950; Masserman, 1943). In one study, negative reinforcement in the form of sublethal doses of poison produced a complete inhibition of eating behavior with the result that the subjects (rats) starved to death (Richter, 1950). Since training can completely inhibit consummatory behavior, leading to the death of the organism, one might conclude, as Scott and Fredericson (1951) did about aggression, that training can overcome hereditary predispositions and that training includes by far the most important group of factors which affect consummatory behavior.

Further, while there is good evidence that all eating behavior can be completely inhibited by training, there is some doubt that the same thing is true for all aggressive behavior. Swade and Geiger (1956) conclude that the aggressive behavior which is correlated with the 6 and 14 per second positive spiking on the EEG can no more be controlled by the individual than a grand mal seizure can be controlled by an epileptic. After a study of over 1000 cases, these authors characterize that form of aggressive behavior as follows: "The control by rage is so absolute that parents fear for their lives and those of others. Typical complaints are: extreme rage outbursts, larceny, arson, violent acts without motivation, sexual acts (aggressive), threats to stab, shoot, mutilate, or beat, poor social adjustment (not schizophrenic), rage reactions, mutilation of animals, and total inability to accept correction or responsibility for the act." (Swade and Geiger, 1960, p. 616)

Aggression control

Once the facts are sorted out, it can be seen that, as Tinbergen (1968) suggests, the argument of whether or not aggression is a drive is very much a matter of emphasis and the two theoretical positions are not as far apart as it seems. The entire argument might be purely academic and of little consequence, except for the implications for further research and for the control of aggression. One certainly need not conclude with Scott (1966a) that the instinctual analysis of behavior is a complete explanation of behavior and so offers no new leads for research. The term instinct has a confused history and may not be the best term. However, most authors who postulate instinctive aggression agree that it has a physiological basis (Berkowitz, 1962, Chap. 1). Therefore, there are innumerable leads for research which emanate from this point of view. If there is an "instinctual urge to aggression," there must be a physiological basis for it, and that basis can be delineated experimentally. Further, there are many hypotheses to be tested to determine the specific neural and endocrine mechanisms underlying various kinds of aggressive behavior (Moyer, 1967).

The theoretical position that one takes on the determinants of aggressive behavior strongly influences the kinds of control measures considered. The manipulation of the internal environment is not mentioned by either Scott (1962) or Hinde (1967) when they deal with the problem of aggression control. Lorenz (1966) certainly accepts the idea of internal impulses to aggression, but he conceives of them in terms of the rather vaguely defined energy concept. Since he also considers that "aggressive energy" is closely linked with the energy of ambitions, love, and other socially acceptable attributes, he confines his recommendations for aggression control to suggestions for the redirection of "aggressive energy" and does not consider reducing aggressive tendencies per se.

As indicated in the analysis above, aggressive behavior is determined by both external and internal variables, and aggressive response tendencies can be modified by learning. This should provide us with at least three approaches to the most important problem of aggression control. The external environment can be manipulated to reduce the number of stimuli which instigate aggression; the individual can be taught to inhibit aggressive responses; and finally, the internal environment can be manipulated directly. Although the last approach will be dealt with here, there is no intention to imply that the first two approaches are unimportant.

The physiological control of aggressive tendencies may be accomplished by brain stimulation, brain lesions, hormone administration, and the administration of drugs. As indicated above, continuing aggressive behavior in the monkey can be blocked immediately by direct stimulation of the caudate nucleus (Delgado, 1963). In man, a violent, profane, destructive individual is transformed into one who is calm, friendly, and sociable by direct septal stimulation. At the moment, very little is known about this method of control, but there seems little doubt that it is possible. How practical it will become is a matter of conjecture. Two developments could make it eminently practical: One is the development of a method of pinpoint brain stimulation without opening the skull (Tobias, 1962); the second is the discovery of a drug which selectively stimulates these nuclei. Both of these developments are well within the realm of possibility.

As already mentioned, selective brain lesions may reduce or eliminate aggressive behavior. The reader will recall Sawa's patient who, after the operation, felt that he could not become angry if he wanted to (Sawa *et al.,* 1958). Brain surgery is currently being used effectively for the control of extremely assaultive individuals.

Control of aggressive tendencies can also be achieved through the adjustment of hormone balances. Progesterone is frequently used to reduce the irritability associated with premenstrual tension (Greene and Dalton, 1953). Maternal aggression in the rat has been controlled by the administration of oestrone (Endroczi *et al.,* 1958). Stilboestrol has been used clinically to diminish irritable aggression in the male (Dunn, 1941; Sands, 1954). Further understanding of the role of hormones in aggressive behavior should lead to a rational endocrine therapy for certain kinds of aggressive behavior. Dr. Lerner's work (1964) with androgen antagonists may be particularly important here.

Finally, drugs are a currently useful and practical means of altering the internal environment so that aggressive tendencies are reduced. There are a number of chemical agents that appear to be specific inhibitors of hostility, which reduce aggression without appreciably affecting the individual's alertness or motor coordination. The vast literature on this topic cannot be reviewed here, but a few examples will illustrate the point. The use of Dilantin ®* for the control of aggressive tendencies has

*Registered trademark for diphenylhydantoin, Parke, Davis & Co., Detroit, Mich.

recently received national publicity (Rosenfeld, 1967). Dr. Turner (1967) has presented numerous case studies demonstrating the effectiveness of this drug for that purpose and has presented a theoretical statement which may guide research on this problem. Scheckel and Boff (1966) have shown that chlordiazepoxide and diazepam reduce aggressiveness in squirrel monkeys at doses that do not interfere with other behaviors. Diazepam has been used with "remarkable success" in eliminating the destructive rampages of psychotic criminals (Kalina, 1962).

Research on drugs to control behavior is in its infancy and yet there is good reason to believe that the judicious use of the fruits of this research can help to control the minor, but uncomfortable, irritability of such dysfunctions as premenstrual tension as well as the major assaultive crimes of individuals afflicted with discontrol syndrome.

In summary, we must conclude that aggressive behavior is determined by an interwoven complex of internal, external, and experiential factors. The solution to the multifaceted and critical problem of the control of destructive, aggressive tendencies will only be approached when all of these factors are given adequate consideration.

References

Akert, K. 1961. Diencephalon. *Electrical Stimulation of the Brain,* ed. D. E. Sheer. Austin, Tex.: Hogg Foundation.

Altman, J. 1966. *Organic Foundations of Animal Behavior.* New York: Holt, Rinehart & Winston, Inc.

Beeman, E. A. 1947. The effect of male hormone on aggressive behavior in mice. *Physiol. Zool.* 20:373-405.

Berkowitz, L. 1962. *Aggression, A Social Psychological Analysis.* New York: McGraw-Hill Book Co.

____. 1965. The concept of aggressive drive: Some additional considerations. *Advances in Experimental Social Psychology.* Vol. 2, ed. L. Berkowitz. New York: Academic Press, Inc.

Bolles, R. C. 1958. The usefulness of the drive concept. *Nebraska Symposium on Motivation,* ed. M. R. Jones. Lincoln, Neb.: University of Nebraska Press.

Cleghorn, R. A. 1957. Steroid hormones in relation to neuropsychiatric disorder. *Hormones, Brain Function and Behavior,* ed. H. Hoagland. New York: Academic Press, Inc.

Cofer, C. N. & M. H. Appley. 1964. *Motivation: Theory and Research.* New York: John Wiley & Sons, Inc.

Dalton, K. 1964. *The Premenstrual Syndrome.* Springfield, Ill.: Charles C. Thomas, Publishers.

Delgado, J. M. R. 1960. Emotional behavior in animals and humans. *Psychiat. Res. Rep.* 12: 259-271.

____. 1963. Cerebral heterostimulation in a monkey colony. *Science* 141:161-163.

Dunn, G. W. 1941. Stilbestrol induced testicular degeneration in hypersexual males. *J. Clin. Endocr.* 1:643-648.

Egger, M. D. & Flynn, J. P. 1963. Effect of electrical stimulation of the amygdala on hypothalamically elicited attack behavior in cats. *J. Neurophysiol.* 26:705-720.

Ehrlich, A. 1964. Neural control of feeding behavior. *Psychol. Bull.* 61:100-114.

Endroczi, E., Lissak, K., & Telegdy, G. 1958. Influence of sexual and adrenocortical hormones on the maternal aggressivity. *Acta Physiol. Acad. Sci. Hung.* 14:353-357.

Feshbach, S. 1964. The function of aggression and the regulation of aggressive drive. *Psychol. Rev.* 71:257-272.

Gibbs, F. A. 1951. Ictal and non-ictal psychiatric disorders in temporal lobe epilepsy. *J. Nerv. Ment. Dis.* 113:522-528.

Gibson, J. G. 1962. Emotions and the thyroid gland. *J. Psychosom. Res.* 6:91-116.

Graff, H. & Stellar, E. 1962. Hyperphagia, obesity and finickiness. *J. Comp. Physiol. Psychol.* 55:418-424.

Greene, R. & Dalton, K. 1953. The premenstrual syndrome. *Brit. Med. J.* 1:1007-1014.

Hawke, C. C. 1950. Castration and sex crimes. *Am. J. Ment. Defic.* 55:220-226.

Heath, R. G. 1963. Electrical self stimulation of the brain in man. *Am. J. Psychiat.* 120: 571-577.

Hinde, R. A. 1967. The nature of aggression. *New Society* 9:302-304.

Jonas, A. D. 1965. *Ictal and Subictal Neurosis, Diagnosis and Treatment.* Springfield, Ill.: Charles C. Thomas, Publishers.

Kalina, R. K. 1962. Use of diazepam in the violent psychotic patient: A preliminary report. *Colorado GP* 4:11-14.

Kennedy, G. C. 1953. The role of depot fat in the hypothalamic control of food intake in the rat. *Proc. Roy. Soc.* (*Biol.*) 140:578-592.

King, H. E. 1961. Psychological effects of excitation in the limbic system. *Electrical Stimulation of the Brain,* ed. D. E. Sheer: 477-486. Austin: University of Texas Press.

Kislak, J. W. & Beach, F. A. 1955. Inhibition of aggressiveness by ovarian hormones. *Endocrinology* 56:684-692.

Lagerspetz, K. 1964. Studies on the aggressive behaviour of mice. *Ann. Acad. Sci. Fenn.:* 1-131.

Le Beau, J. 1952. The cingular and precingular areas in psychosurgery (agitated behavior, obsessive compulsive states, epilepsy). *Acta Psychiat. Scand.* 27:305-316.

Le Maire, L. 1956. Danish experiences regarding the castration of sexual offenders. *J. Criminal Law Criminol.* 47:294-310.

Lerner, L. J. 1964. Hormone antagonists: Inhibitors of specific activities of estrogen and androgen. *Recent Prog. Hormone Res.* 20:435-490.

Levison, P. K. & Flynn, J. P. 1965. The objects attacked by cats during stimulation of the hypothalamus. *Animal Behaviour* 13:217-220.

Levy, J. V. & King, J. A. 1953. The effects of testosterone priopionate on fighting behavior in young male C57 BL/10 mice. *Anat. Rec.* 117:562-653.

Lichenstein, P. E. 1950. Studies of anxiety: II The effects of lobotomy on a feeding inhibition in dogs. *J. Comp. Physiol. Psychol.* 43:419-427.

Lorenz, K. 1966. *On Aggression.* London: Methuen.

Marler, P. & Hamilton, W. J. 1966. *Mechanisms of Animal Behavior.* New York: John Wiley & Sons, Inc.

Masserman, J. H. 1943. *Behavior and Neuroses.* Chicago: University of Chicago Press.

Mayer, J. 1953. Glucostatic mechanism of regulation of food intake. *New Engl. J. Med.* 249: 13-16.

Miller, N. E. 1957. Experiments on motivation. *Science* 126:1271-1278.

____. 1961. Implications for theories of reinforcement. *Electrical Stimulation of the Brain,* ed. D. E. Sheer:515-581. Austin, Tex.: Hogg Foundation.

Morrison, S. D. & Mayer, J. 1957. Adipsia and aphagia in rats after lateral subthalamic lesions. *Am. J. Physiol.* 191:248-254.

Morton, J. H., Additon, H., Addison, R. G., Hunt, L., & Sullivan, J. J. 1953. A clinical study of premenstrual tension. *Am. J. Obstet. Gynec.* 65:1182-1191.

Moyer, K. E. 1967. Kinds of aggression and their physiological basis. Pittsburgh, Pa.: Carnegie-Mellon University, Report No. 67-12.

____. 1968. Kinds of aggression and their physiological basis. *Commun. Behavioral Biol.* 2: 65-87.

Pearson, O. P. 1944. Reproduction in the shrew (*Blarina Brevicauda Say*). *Am. J. Anat.* 75: 39-93.

Pool, J. L. 1954. The visceral brain of man. *J. Neurosurg.* 11:45-63.

Richter, C. P. 1950. Psychotic behavior produced in wild Norway and Alexandrine rats apparently by fear of food poisoning. *Feelings and Emotions*, ed. M. L. Reymert: 189-202. New York: McGraw-Hill Book Co.

Roberts, W. W. & Kiess, H. W. 1964. Motivational properties of hypothalamic aggression in cats. *J. Comp. Physiol. Psychol.* 58:187-193.

Rosenfeld, A. 1967. 10,000-to-1 payoff. *Life Magazine* 63(13):121-128.

Sands, D. E. 1954. Further studies on endocrine treatment in adolescence and early adult life. *J. Ment. Sci.* 100:211-219.

Sands, D. E. & Chamberlain, G. H. A. 1952. Treatment of inadequate personality in juveniles by dehydroisoandrosterone. *Brit. Med. J.*:66-68.

Sano, K. 1962. Sedative neurosurgery: With special reference to postero-medial hypothalmotomy. *Neurol. Medicochir.* 4:112-142.

Sano, K., Yoshioka, M., Ogashiwa, M., Ishijima, B., & Ohye, C. 1966. Postero-medial hypothalamotomy in the treatment of aggressive behaviors. Second Intern. Symp. Stereoencephalotomy, *Confin. Neurol.* 27:164-167.

Sawa, M., Ueki, Y., Arita, M., & Harada, T. 1958. Preliminary report on the amygdaloidectomy on the psychotic patient, with interpretation of oral-emotional manifestation in schizophrenics. *Folia Psychiat. Neurol. Jap.* 7:309-329.

Scheckel, C. L. & Boff, E. 1966. Effects of drugs on aggressive behavior in monkeys. *Excerpta Med. Intern. Congr. Ser. 129, Proc. Fifth Intern. Congr. Collegium Intern. Neuropsychopharmacologicum:* 789-795.

Schreiner, L. & Kling, A. 1956. Rhinencephalon and behavior. *Am. J. Physiol.* 184:486-490.

Scott, J. P. 1958. *Aggression.* Chicago: University of Chicago Press.

_____. 1962. Hostility and aggression in animals. *Roots of Behavior,* ed. E. L. Bliss. New York: Harper & Row, Publishers.

_____. 1965. Review of J. D. Carthy and F. J. Ebling, The natural history of aggression. *Science* 148:820-821.

_____. 1966a. Review of K. Lorenz, On aggression. *Science* 154:636-637.

_____. 1966b. Agonistic behavior of mice and rats: A review. *Am. Zool.* 6:683-701.

_____. 1967. The development of social motivation. *Nebraska Symposium on Motivation,* ed. D. Levine. Lincoln, Neb.: University of Nebraska Press.

Scott, J. P. & Fredericson, E. 1951. The causes of fighting in mice and rats. *Physiol. Zool.* 24:273-309.

Seward, J. P. 1945. Aggressive behavior in the rat: I. General characteristics; age and sex differences. *J. Comp. Psychol.* 38:175-197.

Sigg, E. B. 1968. Relationship of aggressive behavior to adrenal and gonadal function of male mice. Paper presented at First Intern. Symp. Aggression. Milan, Italy.

Speigel, E. A., Wycis, H. T., Freed, H. & Orchinik, C. 1951. The central mechanism of the emotions. *Am. J. Psychiat.* 108:426-532.

Strauss, E. B., Sands, D. E., Robinson, A. M., Tindall, W. J. & Stevenson, W. A. H. 1952. Use of dehydroisoandrosterone in psychiatric treatment. *Brit. Med. J.*:64-66.

Suchowski, G. K. 1968. Sexual hormones and aggressive behavior. Paper presented at First Intern. Symp. Aggressive Behavior. May 2-4, 1968. Milan, Italy.

Swade, E. D. & Geiger, S. C. 1956. Abnormal EEG findings in severe behavior disorder. *Dis. Nerv. Sys.* 17:307-317.

_____. 1960. Severe behavior disorders with abnormal electroencephalograms. *Dis. Nerv. Sys.* 21:616-620.

Teitelbaum, P. & Epstein, A. N. 1962. The lateral hypothalamic syndrc ne. *Psychol. Rev.* 69: 74-90.

Tinbergen, N. 1968. On war and peace in animals and man. *Science* 160:1411-1418.

Tobias, C. A. 1962. The use of accelerated heavy particles for production of radiolesions and stimulation in the central nervous system. *Responses of the Nervous System to Ionizing Radiation,* ed. T. J. Haley & R. S. Snider. New York: Academic Press, Inc.

Tow, P. M. & Whitty, C. W. M. 1953. Personality changes after operations on the cingulate gyrus in man. *J. Neurol. Neurosurg. Psychiat.* 16:186-193.

Treffert, D. A. 1964. The psychiatric patient with an EEG temporal lobe focu . *Am. J. Psychiat.* 120:765-771.

Turner, W. J. 1967. The usefulness of diphenylhydantoin in treatment of nonepileptic emotional disorders. *Intern. J. Neuropsychiat.* 3(Suppl. 2):S8-S20.

Jrich, J. 1938. The social hierarchy in albino mice. *J. Comp. Psychol.* 25 373-413.

Ursin, H. 1960. The temporal lobe substrate of fear and anger. *Acta Psychiat. Neurol. Scand.* 35:278-396.

Vonderahe, A. R. 1944. The anatomic substratum of emotion. *The New Scholasticism* 18: 76-95.

Wasman, M. & Flynn, J. P. 1962. Directed attack elicited from hypothalamus. *Arch. Neurol.* 6:220-227.

Wheatley, M. D. 1944. The hypothalamus and affective behavior in cats. *Arch. Neurol. Psychiat.* 52:296-316.

Williams, D. R. & Teitelbaum, P. 1956. Control of drinking behavior by means of an operant-conditioning technique. *Science* 124:1294-1296.

Wood, C. D. 1958. Behavioral changes following discrete lesions of temporal lobe structures. *Neurology* 8(Suppl. 1):215-220.

Woods, J. W. 1956. "Taming" of the wild Norway rat by rhinencephalic lesions. *Nature* (London) 178:869.

Woods, S. M. 1961. Adolescent violence and homicide: Ego disruption and the 6 and 14 dysrhythmia. *Arch. Gen. Psychiat.* 5:528-534.

Wright, J. H. 1965. Test for a learned drive based on the hunger drive. *J. Exp. Psychol.* 70: 580-584.

Wyrwicka, W. & Dobrzecka, C. 1960. Relationship between feeding and satiation centers of the hypothalamus. *Science* 123:805-806.

4

The XYY chromosomal abnormality

Saleem A. Shah

Introduction

During 1968 a special branch of the science of genetics was drawn from the quietude of laboratories and professional journals and exposed to the glare of courtrooms and newspaper headlines. Since 1960 a number of geneticists and physicians had been studying the occurrence and effects of extra sex-determining chromosomes in humans. The first published report of a man with an extra Y, or male-determining chromosome (Jacobs *et al.*, 1968) appeared in August 1961 (Sandberg *et al.*). This individual was of average intelligence, without any physical defects, and had no criminal record. The reason his chromosomes were studied was to learn more about the presence of mongolism and other anomalies among his children.

In most of the reports published in the intervening years the individuals chosen for study had some mental or physical abnormality. Some investigators noted that several males with an XYY chromosomal constitution (Jacobs *et al.*, 1968) had histories suggesting violent and aggressive behavior patterns. In addition, it was noted that such men were rather tall (Casey *et al.*, 1966; Jacobs *et al.*, 1965).

These observations led to numerous studies on chromosomal patterns among tall males institutionalized for mental illness, mental subnormality, or various forms of

---

SOURCE: This material is excerpted, with the permission of the author, from a National Institute of Mental Health publication entitled "Report on the XYY Chromosomal Abnormality," U.S. Government Printing Office, 1970. No copyright may be placed on this excerpted material.

criminal behavior. The number of persons found to have the extra Y chromosome markedly exceeded the prevalence of the XYY pattern roughly estimated, but not yet rigorously confirmed, to exist in the general population.

The above findings led some investigators – and many news writers – to conclude that the extra Y chromosome predisposed such males to violent and aggressive behavior. Other scientists disagreed, arguing that the biased nature of the populations studied and the lack of accurate prevalence data for the general population put any direct causal links in doubt. The controversy remained largely within the scientific community.

The emergence in 1968 of the XYY research into the general public domain of controversy was precipitated by the murder trial in Paris of one Daniel Hugon. The defense attorney claimed his client had an extra Y chromosome and thus was not criminally responsible for his behavior. The Court appointed an expert panel to review the mental condition of the defendant. After trial and conviction, a reduced sentence was imposed, presumably because of the chromosomal defect (*The Georgetown Law Journal,* 1969).

At about the same time the press reported on the murder trial of Lawrence E. Hannell in Melbourne, Australia. Hannell was acquitted by reason of insanity; this verdict was allegedly influenced by testimony concerning his XYY constitution. However, more recent reports indicate that the defendant's chromosomal anomaly may actually have had little bearing on the acquittal since it was mentioned only perfunctorily in the trial transcript, and there was considerable evidence about his mental deficiency, abnormal electroencephalogram, and temporal lobe epilepsy (Bartholomew and Sutherland, 1969).

Again in 1968, Richard Speck, convicted of murdering eight Chicago nurses, was reported in the public press to have XYY chromosomes. It was also suggested that the purported finding of this anomaly might be raised in his projected appeal. Speck's attorney later announced that tests had shown his client's chromosomes to be normal.[1] Nevertheless, news items and professional articles still appear referring to Speck as an XYY type.

During and since these events many press and broadcast stories have appeared about the allegedly antisocial propensities of persons with the XYY chromosome abnormality. In addition, over 160 articles have appeared thus far in various scientific and professional journals (see Borgaonkar, 1968, 1970).

Some segments of the general public and also of the scientific and legal communities seem to have accepted the belief that males with XYY chromosomes are more or less inexorably predisposed toward violent and antisocial behavior. On the other hand, many geneticists and behavioral scientists consider the above conclusions quite premature and seriously doubt that the available evidence can establish a cause

[1] See *Chicago Herald Tribune,* Nov. 26, 1968, 1A at 16, Col. 1. See also *The Georgetown Law Journal,* 1969, 57, n. 3, p. 892.

and effect relationship between the presence of an XYY constitution and criminal or other socially deviant behavior.

The research findings thus far, the publicity, the scientific controversy, and various legal issues have generated some important medical-legal-ethical questions among researchers and those concerned with social policy. Thus, on the one hand there is a scientific as well as societal need to conduct further research to gain more knowledge. On the other hand, there are equally important social values which require that the rights, welfare, confidentiality, and privacy of research subjects be safeguarded in such research endeavors (Shah, 1970). However, since a number of legal and social policy questions have been raised in regard to persons with the XYY chromosome complement, it is most essential that the answers to such questions be based upon sound and well-established scientific facts derived from rigorous and carefully designed studies.

Against this background of need for more precise and definite knowledge concerning the biological, behavioral, and social science contributions toward better understanding of deviant and antisocial behavior, the Center for Studies of Crime and Delinquency of the National Institute of Mental Health decided to give particular emphasis to an assessment of present knowledge in this field and to further research addressed to the subject of individual violent behavior.

On June 19-20, 1969, the NIMH Center for Studies of Crime and Delinquency at Chevy Chase, Md., convened a small group of scientists and researchers from the fields of genetics, medicine, psychiatry, psychology, sociology, and law to discuss the subject.

The primary topics of the meeting were the current state of knowledge concerning the XYY chromosome anomaly, outstanding gaps in such knowledge, and the research methodologies which would permit more meaningful comparison of data from needed further studies. The conference also addressed some of the medicolegal issues involved in research on chromosome anomalies.

. . . .

Incidence and prevalence of the XYY condition

A considerable part of the conference was devoted to discussing the fundamentally important question of the incidence and prevalence of the XYY chromosomal abnormality. Even among this expert group the two terms often were used as if they are interchangeable and thus have the same meaning, but they do not. Since the incidence and prevalence rates for a condition may be quite different, it is important to bear in mind the different meanings of these terms and to use them accurately. For purposes of this report, the following definitions have been applied throughout:

Incidence: The rate at which *new* cases of a condition are added to a given population during a certain period of time or in relation to a particular event; more specifically, as related to the XYY condition or other genetic abnormalities, incidence is the rate of occurrence observed or estimated to exist in a given population at birth.

Prevalence: The total number of cases of a condition that can be counted or estimated in all age groups in a given population at a particular point in time.

The first major deficit in our understanding of the XYY phenomenon pertains to the absence of precise and adequate data on its incidence as well as prevalence in the general population. This deficit prevents clear understanding of the effects upon the individual and society of the XYY condition and also interferes with efforts to mount economically the more precise and detailed investigations that are needed.

Data presently available on the aforementioned topic may be grouped and summarized into two major categories: (1) Surveys of institutionalized populations, and (2) surveys of newborn infants.[2]

Surveys of institutionalized populations

Most of the surveys conducted thus far have been among inmates of various institutions. In many instances the subjects for chromosomal screenings were selected for height, e.g., six feet (183 cm.) or taller. Since some of the earlier studies had suggested a possible association between an extra Y chromosome and aggressive behavior and had also noted that such males were tall (Casey *et al.*, 1966; Jacobs *et al.*, 1965), many investigators began to select tall inmates in mental and penal institutions in efforts to verify the above alleged association. Thus, in most of these surveys males six feet and over in height were screened. In a few instances, tall inmates were further selected on the basis of their "aggressive" and "dangerous" behavior (see Welch *et al.*, 1967).

Table I provides a summary of a number of institutional surveys which have been conducted in the past few years; however, this list is not meant to be exhaustive. It is evident from the studies cited in this table that the majority of these investigations selected only tall males for chromosomal screening. Furthermore, there are numerous variations even in the more obvious features of these studies: a number of different populations has been studied (mentally ill, criminals, sexual offenders, defective delinquents, mentally subnormal, mentally disordered offenders, etc.); juveniles as well as adults have been screened; the sizes of the reference groups surveyed range from 11 to 607; the height selection criteria vary; and the rough percentage figures for the XYY karyotypes discovered range from zero to 18.2.

Table I indicates that 103 subjects with a 47,XYY chromosome constitution (excluding the two 46,XY/47,XYY mosaics) were found among the total of 5,342 persons screened. This would provide an overall prevalence rate of 1:52 among the *specially selected institutional groups.*

It should be emphasized that the selection factors inherent in the aforementioned

[2] Here, as in other sections of this report, the information available at the time of the conference has been updated and revised in light of more recent material.

surveys do *not* permit valid estimates of the XYY prevalence rate for the general institutional populations in the relevant studies.

Table I *Summary of Institutional Surveys Pertaining to the 47,XYY Karyotype*[3]

Investigators	*Reference Group Size*	*Classification*	*Height Selection (cm.)*	*No. XYY*	*Approx. XYY %*
Casey *et al.* (1966)	100	Maximum Security Hospitals, England	183	16	16.0
Jacobs *et al.* (1968)	315	Mentally Disordered Offenders, Scotland	None	9	2.8
Akesson *et al.* (1968)	86	Two Mental Hospitals, Sweden	183	4**	2.3
Baker *et al.* (1970)[4]	86	Juvenile Detention Center (14-16 yrs.), Pa.	183	1	1.2
Baker *et al.* (1970)	42	Juvenile Detention Center (15-17 yrs.), Pa.	183	0	0
Baker *et al.* (1970)	74	State Prisons, Pa.	183	2	2.7
Baker *et al.* (1970)	72	City Prisons, Pa.	183	1	1.3
Baker *et al.* (1970)	58	City Prison (penal & mentally ill), Pa.	183	1	1.7
Baker *et al.* (1970)	82	State Prison (penal & mentally retarded), Pa.	183	0	0
Baker *et al.* (1970)	102	State Hosp. for Criminally Insane, Pa.	183	3	3.0
Baker *et al.* (1970)	230	State & V.A. Hospitals, Pa.	183	0	0
Baker *et al.* (1970)	130	School for Mentally Retarded, Pa.	183	1	0.8
Welch *et al.* (1967)	20	"Defective Delinq." aggress. offenders, Md.	188*	0	0
Welch *et al.* (1967)	35	"Defective Delinq." Offenders (various criteria, e.g., particular aggressivity)	183*	1	3.0
Goodman *et al.* (1967)	52	Caucasian Prison Inmates, Ohio	185.4*	2	4.0
Goodman *et al.* (1967)	100	Caucasian & Negro Prison Inmates, Ohio	185.4*	2	2.0
Griffiths & Zaremba (1967)	34	Wandsworth Prison, England	183	2	6.0
Wiener *et al.* (1968)	34	Adult Prisoners, Australia	175.3*	4	12.0
Hunter (1968)	29	Boys in Approved Schools, England	"tall"	3	10.0
Court Brown (1968)	71	Epileptic Colony, England	None	1	1.4
Court Brown (1968)	605	Hospital for Mentally Subnormal, England	None	0	0
Cited by: Price & Jacobs (1970)	607	New Entrants (1 yr.), Scottish Borstals	None	1	0.2
Price & Jacobs (1970)	302	Allocation Center, Soughton Prison, Edinburgh	None	0	0
Price & Jacobs (1970)	204	Recidivist Criminals, Grendon Prison, England	None	2	1.0
Price & Jacobs (1970)	419	Inmates, all Scottish Prisons	178	1	0.3
Price & Jacobs (1970)	74	Young Offenders' Institution, Scotland	178	1	1.4
Price & Jacobs (1970)	17	Scottish Detention Center	178	0	0
Price & Jacobs (1970)	34	Wandsworth Prison, England	183	2	6.0
Price & Jacobs (1970)	24	Nottingham Prison, England	183	2	8.0
Price & Jacobs (1970)	40	Pentridge Prison, Australia	175	5	12.5
Price & Jacobs (1970)	19	Hospital for Mentally Subnormal, England	183	2	10.0
Price & Jacobs (1970)	11	Hospital for Mentally Subnormal, England	183	2	18.2
Price & Jacobs (1970)	30	Scottish Mental Subnormality Hospital	183	2	6.6
Price & Jacobs (1970)	183	Scottish Mental Disease Hospitals	183	2***	1.6
Price & Jacobs (1970)	40	English Mental Disease Hospitals	183	0	0
Melnyck (1969)	200	Mentally Disordered Sex Offenders & Criminally Insane, Calif.	183	9	4.5
Nielsen (1968)	41	State Hospital, Denmark	180	0	0
Nielsen *et al.* (1968)	37	Institution for Criminal Psychopaths, Denmark	180.3	2	5.4

[3]This list is not meant to be complete or exhaustive of all institutional surveys conducted to date.
[4] Most recent information regarding studies previously cited by Telfer *et al.*

Table I *(continued)*

Investigators	*Reference Group Size*	*Classification*	*Height Selection (cm.)*	*No. XYY*	*Approx. XYY %*
Sergovich (1969)	230	Hospital for Criminally Insane, Canada	None	4**	1.7
Daly (1969a)	210	Maximum Security Hospitals, U.S.A.	183	10	5.0
Marinello *et al.* (1969)	86	Attica State Prison, N.Y.	183	2	2.3
Marinello *et al.* (1969)	76	State Mental Hospital, N.Y.	183	1	1.3
Marinello *et al.* (1969)	57	Juvenile Offenders (Detention Home & Court Psychiatric Referrals), N.Y.	None	1	1.8
Abdullah *et al.* (1969)	18	Criminal Psychiatric Patients (known for violent behavior), N.Y.	183	1	5.5
Abdullah *et al.* (1969)	26	Psychiatric Patients (known for "violent, destructive behavior"), N.Y.	183	0	0

*Height converted to centimeters from inches.
**Includes one mosaic – 46,XY/47,XYY.
***One 48,XXYY is not included in this figure.

In an attempt to obtain a rough prevalence rate for institutional populations generally, the findings from eight surveys (listed in Table I) which did not use any height selection criteria were considered. Keeping in mind the varying nature of these populations and the size of their reference groups, a prevalence rate of 1:140 is obtained.

Again, it needs to be reiterated that in view of the relatively small numbers in the samples surveyed and the very low base rates for occurrence of the XYY chromosome anomaly, rather wide variations in obtained frequencies could and indeed do result. Hence the need to use and interpret the above figures with much caution pending availability of more meaningful and accurate prevalence rates for various institutional populations.

Surveys of newborn infants

A number of surveys of neonates have been undertaken in an effort to systematically determine the incidence rates for the XYY chromosomal constitution. During the conference data from five such neonatal surveys were available for review. Eliminating one study which had done selective screening, i.e., only normal appearing infants, a total of approximately 6,700 infants had been tested and 12 were found to have 47,XYY chromosomes.

These surveys were discussed extensively during the conference and determined to be so variable in techniques, methodology, and other relevant aspects, that firm incidence rates could not be derived from them. Taking account of these difficulties, the group accepted a tentative rate of about one XYY in 550 males at birth (1:550) as a rough working estimate.

In light of the availability of additional and more recent information since the conference, the data used at the time have been updated. Table II provides currently available information on neonatal surveys. If data on only unselected infants are used, an incidence rate of 1:518 is obtained. This rate is extremely close to the rough working estimate of 1:550 determined by the conferees, and within the general range of 1-2 per 1000 discussed in the scientific literature.

Table II *Surveys of 47,XYY Newborn Males in the General Population*[5]

Investigators	*Location*	*No. Screened*	*No. XYY*	*Remarks*
Sergovich *et al.* (1969)	London, Ontario	1,066	4	All liveborn infants
Walzer *et al.* (1969)	Boston, Mass.	1,931	0	Phenotypical normal newborn infants*
Lubs *et al.* (1969)	New Haven, Conn.	2,184**	3	Consecutive newborns in one hospital, over period of one year
Turner (1969)	Pittsburgh, Pa.	1,023	3	Quoted from Marinello *et al.* (1969). No details available.
Ratcliffe *et al.* (1970)	Edinburgh, Scotland	3,496	5	Consecutive liveborn infants–April 1967 to October 1969
	Totals	9,700	15	
	Incidence Rate 1:646			
	Incidence Rate excluding Boston data* 1:518			

*Since only phenotypically normal infants were screened, a bias was introduced in the study.
**Latest figures provided by Lubs. In this study a total of 4482 newborns were included; however, successful cultures were obtained in 4366 (2184 males and 2182 females). The difference between total number of cases included and the total number successfully cultured often confuses such calculations. (Personal communication from Lubs, April 8, 1970.) *See also:* Lubs, H. A. & Ruddle, F. H. Chromosomal abnormalities in the human population: estimation of rates based on New Haven newborn study. *Science,* 1970, 169, 495-497.

In a recent publication Price and Jacobs (1970) present some material pertaining to the frequency of 47,XYY males in the adult community at large. These data, summarized in Table III, encompass rather heterogeneous and somewhat unusual groups which, in many instances, could not be considered as very representative of a general adult male population. Once again, bearing in mind the aforementioned caveats concerning the limitations of such studies, the obtained prevalence rate (1:1036) is within the range generally estimated on the basis of neonatal incidence surveys, viz., 1-2 per 1000.

In summary, it may be noted that the data presented above provide no more than rough approximations of accurate incidence and prevalence rates for the XYY chromosome anomaly. Among the requirements for meaningful and precise frequency rates for chromosomal anomalies are: the careful delineation of well-defined and

[5]Adapted from: Borgaonkar, D. S. & Murphy, E. A. On determining the frequency of chromosomally abnormal persons with particular reference to 47,XYY individuals. (Manuscript submitted for publication, 1970.)

pertinent populations for study, assuring representative and random sampling, avoidance of biasing factors in the samples or populations studied and, preferably, use of large enough samples to minimize vagaries of sampling.[6]

The conferees were generally critical of the lack of information in many of the institutional and neonatal survey reports about the characteristics of the populations studied, criteria used for selection of the subjects, and details concerning various study procedures. In view of such variations and the lack of details concerning the study procedures, the value of pooling such data for estimating prevalence rates for various populations was viewed as being of dubious value. Further, the dangers of using such meager and inadequate data on the occurrence of the XYY karyotype for crucial decisions involving the welfare of individuals and groups or for social policy decisions was a recurrent theme during the conference. It was emphasized that the information needed for such decisions can be obtained only through properly designed and conducted prevalence studies of non-institutional as well as institutionalized populations in sufficient numbers to have statistical validity.

Table III *Survey of "Normal" Adult Male Populations Pertaining to the 47,XYY Karyotype*[7]

Population Studied	*No. of Males Examined*	*No. of XYY Males*
General Population Survey	207	0
Industrial Workers	189	0
Non-blood relatives of persons with a familial chromosome abnormality	87	0
Survey of tall (183 cm. or taller) workers in atomic energy establishments	629	0
Blood donors, randomly selected males, relatives of individuals with a chromosome abnormality, and males with neoplastic disease	1,875	3
Males in community at large	6,340	6
Totals	9,327	9
Prevalence Rate 1:1036		

[6] For further discussion of these issues see: Borgaonkar, D. S. & Murphy, E. A. On determining the frequency of chromosomally abnormal persons with particular reference to 47,XYY individuals. (Manuscript submitted for publication, 1970.)

[7] Based on Table IV and relevant information from Price & Jacobs (1970), p. 33.

The XYY karyotype and social behavior

Some relevant research

It was noted earlier that much of the recent publicity concerning the XYY chromosome complement relates to speculations regarding the increased likelihood for males with this karyotype to engage in aggressive, antisocial, and other socially maladaptive behaviors. In efforts to verify some of the early findings of increased prevalence of this chromosomal anomaly among persons in mental and penal facilities, several studies have focused upon inmates of such institutions. It appears to have been assumed that the information obtained would shed some light, even if rather indirectly, on the relationship of this chromosomal constitution and social behavior.

For example, Welch *et al.* (1967) studied selected samples of inmates in a special institution for "defective delinquents." Men confined in this facility had demonstrated "persistent aggravated antisocial or criminal behavior." In the course of screening 35 males who were 72 inches or taller (some of whom had also been selected for aggressiveness and IQ's below 75), a single XYY individual was found. However, when the investigators had asked the administration of the facility to list the 12 "most aggressive, dangerous or violent inmates" (who were also 72 inches or taller), they did not find a single XYY case in this group. These investigators concluded that their findings did not provide any support for a hypothesis suggesting a strong association between the XYY constitution and mental retardation or aggressive behavior.

Price and Whatmore (1967b) compared nine males with the 47,XYY karyotype with 18 controls (46,XY complement) located in a maximum security hospital at Carstairs, Scotland. Most of the patients in this hospital had convictions for criminal acts. It might be added, however, that the control patients were randomly selected from the hospital population and were *not* matched for length of institutionalization.

The following were the main conclusions drawn from this study:

1. The penal records of the XYY patients showed *significantly fewer* crimes against persons compared to the controls (four out of eight XYY males so convicted with mean number of convictions per man of 0.9 versus 17 out of 18 controls with such convictions, the mean number of convictions per man being 2.6). Moreover, within the hospital environment, the *control patients* were more openly hostile and violently aggressive outbursts were more common, as compared to the behavior of the XYY persons.
2. As a group, the XYY patients showed distinctly earlier manifestations of disturbed behavior than the controls. Mean age of first conviction was 13.1 years compared to 18.0 for the controls; the median age for first conviction was 14 years versus 17 years.
3. Considering criminal conduct among the families of the two groups, the frequency of crime among the siblings of the XYY patients was *significantly lower*. The 31 siblings of the XYY group had only one conviction, whereas there had been a

total of 139 convictions among the 63 siblings for the controls. However, it should be noted that only seven of the 18 control families accounted for the above convictions.

4. The XYY patients were found to suffer from severe personality disorders and their criminal behavior was noted to have been resistant to conventional forms of treatment and corrective training. (In reference to this point it might be pointed out that the great majority, 74 percent, of the patients at Carstairs were considered to be suffering from "severe personality disorders" and thus, quite likely, were equally resistant to treatment and corrective training.)

In another study of the Carstairs patients done by Hope *et al.* (1967), seven XYY males were compared with 11 matched controls in regard to their performance on a number of psychological tests designed to assess hostility, direction of hostility, dependence, over-reactivity, and some other personality traits. Overall, there were very few significant differences between mean test scores obtained by the two groups. The XYY males did *not* differ markedly in either intelligence or in hostility; neither was there any difference in the direction of expression of hostility, i.e., whether hostile feelings were expressed inwards against the self or outwards against other persons. The XYY males were viewed as being somewhat lower in self-esteem, more obsessive or introverted, and described themselves as slower and more cautious in making decisions.

Social definitions and determinants of deviancy

Stress was given during the conference to the importance of recognizing that antisocial behavior is a result of complex interactions between hereditary and environmental influences on the one hand, and behavioral norms established by society on the other. Behavioral patterns deviating from these norms are not absolute, but involve rather complex social interactions which depend upon the person committing the infraction, the social context in which it occurred, and the societal group evaluating the behavior.

It is also important to remember that "delinquency" and "crime" are not exact terms. The breaches of law encompassed by these terms are diverse and include greatly varied patterns of behavior. Furthermore, most successful criminals do not come to official attention, especially those from the upper social classes and better endowed in terms of intellectual, economic, and social advantages. Of those who do come to official attention and are charged with crimes, a majority are not convicted. Offenders who are convicted and sentenced represent a rather small and non-representative sample of all those who come to official attention and are accused of violating criminal laws. Thus, the sample of incarcerated offenders may well tend to be over-represented by those who have relatively greater biological, psychological, social, and economic handicaps, as compared to persons not detected or not convicted of their violations of the law.

A variety of social class factors is similarly involved in reference to persons suffering from mental disorders and institutionalized in public facilities. In view of the fact that prisons and other related public institutions have rather high proportions of persons from the lower social class, and since such groups tend to have higher frequencies of pregnancy and birth complications, nutritional and other health problems, these factors need very much to be borne in mind in studies of such populations. For example, Robinson and Puck (1967) have suggested that sex chromosome anomalies may occur more frequently in families with depressed socioeconomic status.

To reiterate, the complex interactions between hereditary and environmental influences must be considered in understanding behavior. For example, a conference participant having experience with juvenile courts provided an illustration of the interactions between heredity, environment, and societal norms for behavior in relation to the secondary sex characteristic of body size. When confronted with a disorderly group of juveniles, the police often tend to focus their attention on the taller boys, presuming these to be the older and stronger and therefore the ringleaders. Thus, the genetically determined trait of body height may lead to the environmental and social influences implicit in a police record, court rooms, detention homes, and jails, as well as notoriety in neighborhood and school.[8]

An evaluation of available information

While a greater prevalence rate for XYY males among several groups of institutionalized criminals and mentally disordered offenders is not to be disputed, the widely publicized beliefs concerning aggressivity and antisocial behavior as typical characteristics of such individuals are premature and subject to error on at least two counts.

First, institutionalized offenders tend to represent a selected, recidivist, and somewhat more handicapped sub-group. Because of this fact, findings on institutionalized criminals *cannot* be generalized to all persons officially labelled as criminals. For example, XYY males, compared to other criminals, may simply be less adept at evading arrest and conviction.

The second problem pertains to establishing a direct causal relationship between the chromosomal disorder and socially deviant behavior. An association between two traits cannot be established simply by demonstrating their coincidence. The fact that criminal behavior is a complex and multi-determined phenomenon makes it extremely unlikely that the extra Y chromosome is the only, or even the major, causative factor.

---

[8]This subject has been discussed in more detail in Shah, S. A. Recent developments in human genetics and their implications for problems of social deviance. Paper delivered at AAAS Symposium, Chicago, Ill., Dec. 28, 1970. (Symposium to be published by The National Foundation —March of Dimes.)

It would appear that at least some of the interest in the XYY karyotype and criminality may relate to the view that if a single Y chromosome makes a contribution to maleness (the normal complement being 46,XY), then an extra Y will add to behavior traits believed to be associated with maleness, viz., aggressiveness. Indeed, persons with the 47,XYY karyotype have sometimes been referred to as "super-males."

In addition to the other reasons why the above line of reasoning is both overly simplified and faulty, there is a considerable amount of information that various other types of chromosomal abnormalities (e.g.,47, XXY or *Klinefelter's Syndrome*) also have a higher prevalence rate among institutionalized populations than would be expected on the basis of their frequency in the general population. Indeed, in several institutional surveys the numbers of XXY cases have been found to equal or even exceed those with the XYY complements (see Bartlett *et al.,* 1968; Clark *et al.,* 1970; Court Brown, 1962, 1967; Court Brown *et al.,* 1969; Telfer *et al.,* 1968). For example, in their survey of sex chromosome abnormalities in an English hospital for mentally subnormal and psychiatric patients, Close *et al.* (1968) had occasion to study 19 individuals over six feet tall. While two of these tall men were found to have XYY complements, a total of three had extra X chromosomes (XXY, XXXY, and XXYY).

In a recently reported study Clark *et al.* (1970) compared XXY and XYY males located in various institutions in Pennsylvania. They found comparatively little difference in the records of criminal convictions in the two groups. The number of convictions, including crimes against persons and those against property, were quite similar. One striking difference, which is consistent with the earlier finding of Price and Whatmore (1967b), was that the XYY males came into conflict with their families and society at an earlier age. Overall, these investigators concluded that XYY men had been falsely stigmatized and that their involvement in crimes and antisocial behavior might not be significantly different from normal (46,XY) individuals.

In what amounted to a summing up of the conference participants' assessment of the role played by the XYY chromosome constitution as a determinant of behavior, one conferee said:

> It is through complex interactions of all kinds of contingencies and priorities mediated by language, culture, and environment, that the inherited organic characteristics affect behavior. It is extremely speculative to assume there is a high predictability from *genotype* to complex behavior such as committing a crime. Moreover, until large numbers of non-institutionalized XYY males can be studied, generalizations about the behavioral correlates of the extra Y chromosome, e.g., increased aggressivity and antisocial behavior, should be held in abeyance.

A slightly different viewpoint was held by some others at the conference and was voiced along the following lines: It certainly could not be said that all infants with the XYY chromosome complement at birth will be confined in some institution.

However, on the basis of our present knowledge they would appear to have an increased risk of developing socially maladaptive and deviant patterns of behavior.

Overall, from the evidence at hand at the time of the conference, the participants concluded that some association between XYY and atypical socialization appeared to have been established only for excessively tall inmates of penal and related institutions. However, extensive research will be necessary to determine whether there is a similar association in some or most of the XYY individuals who have not been detained in such institutions. If research reveals that XYY men on the "outside" either are not overly aggressive or can more adequately channel aggressive tendencies into socially acceptable behavior, then the popular notion that an extra Y chromosome in some way compulsively drives a person to deviant and aggressive behavior will very clearly have been disproved.

On the basis of available studies, a general statement which could be made is that the individual with an XYY chromosomal anomaly in comparison to XY males, appears to incur some increased risk of developing behavioral problems.[9] However, there is no reason to believe that an XYY male is inexorably bound to develop antisocial traits or behavioral problems.

The XYY karyotype and criminal responsibility

As described in the introduction to this report, rather wide publicity has been given in the news media to several criminal trials in which the XYY chromosome constitution was either considered or was actually included as a defense against criminal responsibility. These events have led to much discussion in legal and scientific circles as to the validity of basing an insanity defense on the presence of the XYY karyotype in the accused.[10]

This is an extremely complex issue because the concepts of mental disease and mental disorder are vague and ill defined and have been undergoing important changes. Furthermore, the terms "mental disease" or "mental disorder" are not used by the law in an exclusively medical or psychiatric sense. As used in reference to tests for determining criminal responsibility, they become legal terms. Thus, the findings of "mental disease" in a defendant constitutes a determination by judge and jury of a *legal* rather than a medical or psychiatric fact.

The criminal law is basically concerned with moral and social value judgments. In the insanity defense, the determination is whether the accused is so different

[9] The increased risk of developing behavioral problems is possibly more clearly substantiated for individuals with the 47, XXY chromosomal constitution (*Klinefelter's syndrome*), even though many such persons make quite satisfactory social adjustments.

[10] See Bartholomew, 1968; Bartholomew & Sutherland, 1969; Baumiller, 1969; Baxter, 1969; Burke, 1969; Court Brown, 1962; Epstein, 1969; Farrell, 1969; Fox, 1969; Hall, 1970; Money, 1969; Russell & Bender, 1970; Wiener *et al.*, 1969; *Annals of Intern. Med.*, 1968; *Aust. & New Zea. Jour. of Crim.*, 1968; *The Georgetown Law Jour.*, 1969; *Med. World News*, 1969; *Okla. Law Review*, 1969; *St. Louis Law Jour.*, 1969. (Complete data on these sources appear in References.)

from the average individual, because of mental disease or defect, that he ought not to be held accountable and blameworthy, i.e., criminally guilty, for his act.

The basic issue is not simply whether an accused does or does not have an XYY or other abnormal chromosomal constitution and whether such abnormality might be classified as a mental disease or defect, but rather the precise manner and degree to which his psychopathology impairs his cognition of what is right or wrong or his capacity to regulate and thus be responsible for his behavior. At this point in our state of knowledge we cannot say how far the XYY complement of any given individual is causally linked with possible behavioral pathology.

On this specific issue, viz., the legal questions pertaining to determining an individual's criminal responsibility, the conferees arrived at a formal consensus:

> The demonstration of the XYY karyotype in an individual does not, in our present state of knowledge, permit any definite conclusions to be drawn about the presence of mental disease or mental defect in that individual. A great deal of further scientific evidence is needed.[11]

In reference to the above statement, a recent appellate court ruling concerning a defense of insanity based on the XYY aberration is very pertinent.[12] The defendant, charged with robbery with a deadly weapon, contended that he suffered from a mental disease or defect and lacked the capacity to appreciate the criminality of his conduct or to conform his conduct to the requirements of the law (Hall, 1970). Convicted of the charge, the defendant appealed his conviction. In its ruling the Maryland Court of Special Appeals stated:

> We do not intend to hold as a matter of law that a defense of insanity based upon the so-called XYY genetic defect is beyond the pale of proof under the insanity statute. We only conclude that in the record before us the trial judge properly declined to permit the case to go to the jury – a determination which, contrary to the defendant's further contention, is not violative of any of his constitutional rights, state or federal.

The conference participants indicated their view that increasing knowledge concerning the genetic and other hereditary contributions to behavior make it obvious that all persons are not equally endowed biologically in terms of regulating and controlling their behavior. Further, it was emphasized that the heredity versus environment or nature versus nurture issue is grossly simplistic and outdated. Modern genetic thinking in no way views genetic or other hereditary influences in an absolute or fatalistic manner. Rather, as noted earlier, very complex and continuous interactions among hereditary, social, and environmental factors determine or influence human behavior. This point has very cogently been expressed by Money (1970) in a recent article:

---

[11] For further discussions of this particular issue the reader may wish to see Bartholomew (1968), Burke (1969), Fox (1969), Money (1969), Russel & Bender (1970), and several comments and editorials in scientific and legal journals (listed in footnote 10), in order to study a variety of views on the subject.

[12] *Hillard v. State,* 38 LW 2401, Md. Court of Special Appeals, Jan. 12, 1970.

> The fact is that the genotype cannot express itself except in interaction with the environment, whether it be the environment created by neighboring cells in the embryo, the environment provided by the mother in the uterus, the perinatal environment, or the environment encountered in the home and community.

In a similar vein the conferees expressed much criticism of the notion that problem behaviors associated with a chromosomal abnormality are untreatable and unchangeable, and that the individual is doomed to remain the way he is. Not only is such a view entirely inconsistent with the above-stated interactions of hereditary and environmental influences, but it also misses some other important points. In reference to deviant behaviors the treatment needs are indicated by the particular patterns of problem behaviors manifested, not by the chromosomal abnormality itself. Treatment and remedial efforts would need to be directed, therefore, at specific behavioral problems and not at the chromosomes.

. . . .

Some gaps in knowledge and some research needs

The XYY anomaly and social behavior

Before reliable conclusions can be drawn as to the direct causal influence of the XYY chromosomal constitution on behavior, a solid base must be established regarding the frequency of occurrence of this anomaly in the general male population, adult as well as infant.

It was emphasized several times during the conference that if one studies the frequency of XYY anomalies among tall males detained in institutions because of mental illness, criminal or violent behavior, then quite obviously all that would be determined would be the prevalence of that anomaly among tall mentally ill, criminal, or violent institutionalized males.

The conferees generally agreed that the institutional surveys had probably established tallness as a common characteristic of the extra Y chromosome. However, some participants were of the view that, in light of the selective nature of most institutional surveys (i.e., screening only of tall males), the trait of tallness as associated with the XYY complement should remain an hypothesis until more thoroughly tested in general population surveys.

It was also noted that we do not presently know whether or not there is a similar frequency of XYY complements in those tall and socially aggressive persons who have attained economic success and made outstanding social adjustments and contributions. Likewise, the aforementioned studies of tall, incarcerated offenders tell us nothing about the tall, aggressive men whose antisocial behavior has escaped official notice and action by the various social control systems in the community.

There was general agreement that even in the case of the many XYY males found in institutions for the mentally disordered or criminals, the question of how the chromosome anomaly exerted its influence upon the individual's behavior was at present unknown. There was information from available studies that many XYY persons have displayed a variety of physical abnormalities including those of the endocrine and central nervous system. Very important questions are raised concerning the role of the chromosomal aberration in terms of influencing physical and psychological development, personality, and behavior.

The discussants felt that carefully controlled studies were needed of children and adults possessing the XYY and other chromosomal aberrations (e.g., XXY) to ascertain specific behavioral and response characteristics. For example, one might initially compare the frequency of deviant aggressive behavior among XYY males with carefully matched groups of males without such karyotypes. If such gross comparisons indicated that XYY males had a significantly higher frequency of antisocial aggressive behavior, then a variety of systematic laboratory studies could be undertaken to compare XYY males and matched controls in regard to their threshold for response to modelling cues and the adequacy of inhibiting capacities for controlling aggressive and other behaviors.

The XYY syndrome?

Numerous reports have appeared in the scientific literature which suggest that there is a syndrome having certain common features which describes XYY males. In regard to behavioral features, it has often been stated that persons with an XYY chromosomal constitution are inclined to be aggressive, antisocial, and to suffer from personality disorders.

However, an extremely wide range of physical and behavioral traits have been found for the more than 200 persons with 47, XYY chromosome complements so far described in the scientific literature. For example, there have been reports of cases with a variety of physical abnormalities involving the genitalia, central nervous system, congenital heart disease, webbing of the neck, and other aberrations.[13] On the other hand, there have also been some reports of physically normal males who have average and even superior intelligence (Borgaonkar *et al.*, 1968; Stenchever & MacIntyre, 1969). While much of the discussion of the XYY aberration refers to phenotypic males, and there may be a general belief that this anomaly is found only among men, there have been several reports of phenotypic females with a 47,XYY chromosome complement (Court Brown, 1968; Vignetti *et al.*, 1964).[14]

From his review of almost 100 cases of males with the XYY complement, Hienz

[13] See Carakushansky *et al.*, 1968; Court Brown, 1968; Daly, 1969a, 1969b; Forssman, 1967; Goodman *et al.*, 1967; Thorburn *et al.*, 1968; Vignetti *et al.*, 1964.

[14] Most of the cases described in the literature of phenotypic females with XYY chromosome complements are demonstrable mosaics (45,XO/47,XYY). In such cases, the XO line of cells dominates and provides the female phenotype. Court Brown (1968) reports on a case of a fertile and normally developed male with a 45,XO/47,XYY complement in whom the XYY line dominated. However, Court Brown also refers to a report of a mentally retarded female where extensive chromosome studies on lymphocytes, marrow cells, and fibroblasts from the skin showed a single line of cells with a 47,XYY complement.

(1969) reports that there appear to be at least four clinical manifestations of this anomaly. On the basis of the five cardinal symptoms which appear to dominate the clinical picture, Hienz suggests the following classification:

1. Overgrowth; normal intelligence; no criminal history; no somatic malformations; normal sexual development.
2. Overgrowth; mental deficiency; criminal history (eventually psychosexual disorders); no somatic malformations; normal sexual development. Most published cases of the XYY karyotype appear to fall into this group, which consists almost exclusively of inmates of mental and maximum security hospitals, and of prisons.
3. Overgrowth; normal intelligence or slight mental retardation; no criminal history; no somatic malformations; hypogonadism and other genital disorders.
4. Overgrowth; normal intelligence or mental retardation; no criminal history; various somatic malformations (resembling in part well-known syndromes which usually are not associated with chromosomal aberrations); genital malformations.

Hienz also notes that it remains to be determined whether the different clinical manifestations of the XYY complement represent varieties of a uniform aberration of sex chromosomes or whether they are caused by underlying structural differences between the two chromosomes.

In light of the rather wide range of physical, psychological, and behavioral variations found among persons possessing a 47,XYY chromosome constitution, it seems somewhat premature and indeed misleading to speak at the present time of an "XYY syndrome."

. . . .

Conclusion

Studies conducted thus far on limited and often selected groups of inmates of penal and mental institutions indicate that the prevalence rates for the XYY chromosome anomaly are much higher among such persons than in the general population. Available data, as well as theoretical considerations, suggest that tallness appears to be a fairly common characteristic of XYY males. However, lacking rigorous prevalence studies in the general population, definite causal links between the XYY chromosome complement and deviant, criminal, or violent behavior cannot be established.

Several XYY cases studied in institutions for criminal law violators do demonstrate a variety of endocrinological, neurological, and other abnormalities which appear related to their deviant behavior. However, many XYY individuals display no such abnormalities. Indeed, it is not yet known whether these persons have a higher frequency of such abnormalities than matched non-XYY cases also drawn from institutionalized populations. Moreover, the widespread publicity notwithstanding, individuals with the XYY anomaly have *not* been found to be more aggressive than matched offenders with normal chromosome constitutions. In this respect, it appears that premature and incautious speculations may have led to XYY persons being falsely stigmatized as unusually aggressive and violent compared to other offenders.

Further research is clearly needed to confirm whether the trait of excess body height is a *genotypic* consequence of an XYY constitution and to determine if there are other inherited markers, such as neurological or endocrinological departures from the norm. Such additional information on a wide range of XYY males would help to characterize the *phenotype* and also to indicate the various pathways (e.g., central nervous system, hormonal, etc.) through which the extra Y chromosome exercises influence on behavior. There is also a critical need for appropriate legislation to protect the confidentiality of certain types of research data in order that the rights and welfare of subjects in such studies suitably be safeguarded.

The preponderant opinion among the conference participants was that the behavioral aberrations implied or documented thus far do not indicate a direct cause and effect relationship with the XYY chromosome constitution. Thus, it would not be possible to say at the present time that the XYY complement is definitely or invariably associated with behavioral abnormalities. Quite clearly, very complex and varied interactions between hereditary and social and environmental influences appear to be involved. Further, it seems unlikely that such variable and socially defined and determined problems as delinquency and crime are primarily and directly linked with possession of an extra Y chromosome. Under certain conditions, the trait of nonconformity and aggressiveness hypothetically ascribed to XYY individuals might earn social acclaim; under other conditions and in other social contexts, such behavior might be judged totally unacceptable by society. It is quite possible, however, that in particular cases this and other chromosomal aberrations (e.g., XXY) and their related genotypic traits can increase vulnerability to the development of socially maladaptive patterns of behavior.

It would be highly questionable logic and poor science, in our present state of knowledge, to assume either that this particular interaction of genotype and highly variable external influences constitutes a preordained, inflexible, and irremediable hereditary determinant of a particular behavioral pattern, or that the XYY genotype does *not* constitute a factor contributing to particular patterns of behavior.

A pervasive note struck throughout the conference was the need for more knowledge obtained through extensive and meticulous research. Until more precise knowledge is available, social judgments about the XYY individual based on his chromosomal constitution are unjustified.

Appendix: Background information on genetics

The second half of the nineteenth century saw rapid advances in the biological sciences. Included in those advances was much new knowledge in the field of genetics – that branch of biology which is concerned with the mechanisms by which traits and characteristics are passed on from one generation of living organisms to the next.

In addition to the landmark observations of Mendel on the inheritance of observable traits in the garden pea, important clues were found concerning the specific mechanisms by which living cells divide and reproduce themselves. Utilizing technological advances in microscopy, and with the application of appropriate staining techniques, the fine structures of cells could be observed at various stages of cell division and reproduction, a process termed *mitosis*.

Very briefly, the following events occur within the cell, more specifically, within the nucleus, during mitosis: (1) The basic genetic material known as *genes* is duplicated; (2) The *chromosomes*, long filaments on which the genes are located, are also duplicated; (3) The chromosome filaments grow shorter and thicker and become segregated into roughly paired segments; (4) The nucleus and the entire cell split into two "daughter" cells, each of which contains within its nucleus one set of the paired chromosomes. In normal circumstances, the entire process now begins all over again.

Early in the 1900's the growing science of *cytogenetics* (microscopic and biochemical study of cells, chromosomes, and genes in particular) found that an association existed between the mitotic transfer of chromosomes and the transmission of cell form and function. Working with plants, fruit flies, mice, and other animals, cytogeneticists were able to identify many specific inherited traits with specific genes and to locate their grouping on the same chromosomes.

Sex chromosomes

In 1891 a German biologist found that during formation of the sperm in certain insects half received a particular structure and half did not. He named it the X structure. Subsequently, other investigators found that the X structure existed also in the egg cells of all females of an insect species. They determined further that eggs fertilized with X-carrying sperm developed into females (XX), and that eggs receiving sperm without the X developed into males.

Soon thereafter, studies made on other insect species showed that a distinctive structure, designated as the Y chromosome, usually occurred in half of the mature sperm and that the familiar X chromosome turned up in the other half. Occasionally, however, a sperm might have neither; this was designated as an O sperm. Further, it was determined that the combination in the fertilized egg of either XX or XO chromosomes produced females, while the XY combination produced males. In other words, both X and Y were sex chromosomes, X being the female determinant and Y the male.

The normal individual in each species of living organisms has the same basic number of paired chromosomes. Man, for example, has matched pairs of 23, totalling 46. The rhesus monkey has 42; horses have 32. Chromosomes are of two kinds: *autosomes* (body forming), and the two sex-determining chromosomes. In the normal individual each parent furnishes one half of the usual complement of 46 chromosomes – 22 autosomes plus one sex chromosome (X) contributed by the egg and 22 autosomes plus one sex chromosome (X or Y) from the sperm, thus forming the normal complement of 46 chromosomes.

Obviously, a form of cell division different from mitosis must be required to insure that only one-half of the chromosomes originally in the egg or sperm are present when fertilization takes place. This special form of cell division in the earlier stages of sexual reproduction is known as *meiosis.*

In meiosis, two cell divisions are required to achieve duplication of the chromosomes in the egg and sperm, which are, of course, the highly specialized cells required for sexual reproduction. This is in contrast to the single stage process by which all other cells are divided. The second division of the egg and sperm results in a reduction by one-half of the 46 chromosomes originally present in the primary stage of the sex cells. In this way, not only the doubling of chromosomes in each new generation is avoided, but also each parent is enabled to contribute 23 – one-half – of the required 46 chromosomes.

However, meiosis does not always proceed normally, and either the egg or the sperm may contain more or less than the normal 23 chromosomes prior to fertilization. Perhaps the most frequent cause of this abnormality is *nondisjunction,* or improper separation of the chromosome pairs during the egg or sperm meiotic processes. When such an abnormal egg or sperm is joined with a normal egg or sperm at fertilization, the resulting individual will have one or more chromosomes in addition to or less than the customary 46.

When the 44 autosomal chromosomes are affected by such errors as nondisjunction, serious and often lethal results can arise. For example, in the condition known as Mongolism, or *Down's syndrome,* the 21st group of the 23 pairs of chromosomes is composed of three instead of the usual two chromosomes. This anomaly occurs in about one of each 700 live births and accounts for about 10 percent of hospitalized cases of mental retardation in the U.S. Other, usually lethal, excess autosomal abnormalities have been noted, leading to the conclusion that the human organism can accommodate excess genetic material only within very limited ranges. A deficiency of genetic material is even more harmful.

In still other individuals, sometimes apparently quite normal, two different kinds of cells may be found in the body – one with the normal complement of chromosomes and one with excess chromosomes. This chromosome pattern is known as *mosaicism.* Generally, the "mosaic" individual is less affected physically than a person having excess chromosomes in all cells.

Nondisjunction involving the sex chromosomes is more germane to this discussion than autosomal nondisjunction. More is known about it, because study of a single pair of chromosomes is easier than of the 22 pairs of autosomes.

In normal *meiosis* the mature egg cells each receive one X chromosome. However, nondisjunction can result in either none (O) or a two X complement (XX). When fertilized by a normal X- or Y-bearing sperm, these abnormal eggs can give rise to individuals having chromosomal constitutions and conditions as follows:

45,XO – *Turner's syndrome:* females with defective development of the reproductive system, short stature, broad chest, and other physical anomalies.

47,XXX – Females, normal physically, but generally believed to have a moderately depressed intelligence.

45,YO – This condition is presumed to be lethal and has never been reported in the scientific literature.

47,XXY – *Klinefelter's syndrome:* males with late onset of puberty, underdeveloped testes, possible breast development, increased frequency of mental retardation, and also believed to be more vulnerable to social and psychological problems.

Similarly, nondisjunction can give rise to mature sperm with: an O complement, that is, neither X nor Y chromosomes; an XX complement; and the YY complement. Fertilization of the normal egg with these sperm can result in the following chromosomal constitutions: 45,XO (*Turner's syndrome*); 47,XXX; 47,XXY (*Klinefelter's syndrome*); and 47,XYY (males who are taller than average and who, according to recent studies, may be prone to antisocial or other behavioral problems)

Identifying the XYY

Several procedures are helpful to the cytogeneticist and the physician in identifying individuals with sex chromosome defects. By far the most important is *karyotyping,* which is the characterization of the size and shape of the chromosomes within stained cells at the stage of mitosis during which the chromosomes divide longitudinally and double in number. The stains used have an affinity for chromatin, a material rich in *DNA* (deoxyribonucleic acid), the chemical substance of the genes which carries the hereditary information.

The cells to be examined generally are obtained from gentle scraping of the lining of the mouth (buccal smears) or by culturing lymphocytes (white blood cells) which have been isolated from a tiny sample of the subject's blood. The latter method is more informative and is necessary for enumerating and identifying the individual chromosomes but is more expensive and time consuming. For preliminary screening and rapid identification of excess X chromosomes, buccal smears are used more often. Promising work is under way to develop electronic, computerized methods for karyotyping from lymphocytes.

References

Abdullah, S., Jarvik, L. F., Kato, T., Johnston, W. C. & Lanzkron, J. 1969. Extra Y chromosome and its psychiatric implications. *Archives of General Psychiatry,* 21, 497-501.

Akesson, H. O., Forssman, H. & Wallin, L. 1968. Chromosomes of tall men in mental hospitals. *Lancet,* 2, 1040.

Annals of Internal Medicine. 1968. Sex chromosomes and crime. Editorial (J.R.E.), 69, 399-401.

Asimov, I. 1970. Introduction to genetics. *Seminars in Psychiatry,* 2, 3-10.

Australian & New Zealand Journal of Criminology. 1968. The defense of insanity and XYY. Editorial, 1, 199.

Baker, D., Telfer, M. A., Richardson, C. E. & Clark, G. R. 1970. Comparative studies of XYY and Klinefelter males characterized by antisocial characteristics. Manuscript submitted for publication.

Bartholomew, A. A. 1968. The extra Y chromosome and criminal behavior. (Editorial annotation). *Australian & New Zealand Journal of Criminology,* 2, 6.

Bartholomew, A. A. & Sutherland, G. 1969. A defense of insanity and the extra Y chromosome: *R* v. *Hannel. Australian & New Zealand Journal of Criminology,* 2, 29-37.

Bartlett, D. J., Hurley, W. P., Brand, C. R. & Poole, E. W. 1968. Chromosomes of male patients in a security prison. *Nature,* 219, 351-354.

Baumiller, R. C. 1969. XYY chromosome genetics. *Journal of Forensic Sciences,* 14, 411-418.

Baxter, R. R. 1969. Genetic factor overruled. *Trial Magazine,* Feb.-March, 2.

Borgaonkar, D. S. 1968. 47,XYY bibliography. *Annales de Genetique,* 12, 67-70.

_____. 1970. XYY bibliography. *Mammalian Chromosomes Newsletter,* 11, 9-18.

Borgaonkar, D. S., Murdoch, J. L., McKusick, V. A., Borkowf, S. P., Money, J. W & Robinson, B. W. 1968. The YY syndrome. *Lancet,* 2, 461-462.

Borgaonkar, D. S. & Mules, E. 1971. Comments on patients with sex chromosome aneuploidy: dermatoglyphics, parental age, Xga blood group. *Journal of Medical Genetics,* 7, 345-350.

Burke, K. J. 1969. XYY syndrome: genetics, behavior, and the law. *Denver Law Journal,* 46, 261-284.

Carakushansky, G., Neu, R. L. & Gardner, L. I. 1968. XYY with abnormal genitalia. *Lancet,* 2, 1144.

Casey, M. D., Blank, C. E., Street, D. R. K., Segall, L. J., McDougall, J. H., McGrath, P. J. & Skinner, J. L. 1966. YY chromosomes and antisocial behavior. *Lancet,* 2, 859-860.

Clark, G. R., Telfer, M. A., Baker, D. & Rosen, M. 1970. Sex chromosomes, crime, and psychosis. *American Journal of Psychiatry,* 126, 1659-1663.

Close, H. G., Goonetilleke, A. S. R., Jacobs, P. A. & Price, W. H. 1968. The incidence of sex chromosomal abnormalities in mentally subnormal males. *Cytogenetics,* 7, 277-285.

Court Brown, W. M. 1962. Sex chromosomes and the law. *Lancet,* 2, 508.

_____. 1967. Genetics and crime. *Journal of the Royal College of Physicians,* 1, 311-318.

_____. 1968. Males with an XYY sex chromosome complement. *Journal of Medical Genetics,* 5, 341-359.

Court Brown, W. M., Harnden, D. G., Jacobs, P. A., McLean, N. & Mantle, D. J. 1964. Abnormalities of the sex chromosome complement in man. *Privy Council Medical Research Council,* Special Report Series No. 305, London: H.M.S.O.

Court Brown, W. M., Price, W. H. & Jacobs, P. A. 1968. Further information on the identity of 47,XYY males. *British Medical Journal,* 2, 325-328.

Court Brown, W. M. & Smith, P. G. 1969. Human population cytogenetics. *British Medical Bulletin,* 25, 74-80.

Daly, R. F. 1969a. Neurological disorders in XYY males. *Nature,* 221, 472-473.

_____. 1969b. Mental illness and patterns of behavior in 10 XYY males. *The Journal of Nervous & Mental Disease,* 149, 318-327.

Epstein, C. J. 1969. Medical genetics: recent advances with legal implications. *Hastings Law Journal,* 21, 35-49.

Farrell, P. T. 1969. XYY syndrome in criminal law: an introduction. *St. John's Law Review,* 44, 217-219.

Forssman, H. 1967. Epilepsy in an XYY man. *Lancet,* 1, 1389.

Forssman, H. & Hambert, G. 1966. Chromosomes and antisocial behavior. *Lancet,* 2, 282.

_____. 1967. Chromosomes and antisocial behavior. *Excerpta Criminologica,* 7, 113-117.

Forssman, H., Akesson, H. O. & Wallin, L. 1968. The YY syndrome. *Lancet,* 2, 779.

Fox, R. G. 1969. XYY chromosomes and crime. *Australian & New Zealand Journal of Criminology,* 2, 5-19.

The Georgetown Law Journal. 1969. The XYY chromosome defense. Note, 57, 892-922.

Goodman, R. M., Smith, W. S. & Migeon, C. J. 1967. Sex chromosome abnormalities. *Nature,* 216, 942-943.

Griffiths, A. W. & Zaremba, J. 1967. Crime and sex chromosome anomalies. *British Medical Journal,* 4, 622.

Hall, G. E. 1970. Criminal insanity and the XYY defect. *The New Physician,* June, 13, 547-548.

Hashi, N., Tsutsumi, S. & Tsuda, K. 1969. The first case report on the XYY syndrome (XYY male) in Japan. *Proceedings of the Japan Academy,* 45, 63-67.

Hienz, H. A. 1969. YY-syndrome forms. *Lancet,* 1, 155-156.

Hope, K., Philip, A. E. & Loughran, J. M. 1967. Psychological characteristics associated with XYY sex chromosome complement in a state mental hospital. *British Journal of Psychiatry,* 113, 495-498.

Hunter, H. 1968. Chromatin-positive and XYY boys in approved schools. *Lancet,* 1, 816.

Jacobs, P. A., Brunton, M., Melville, M. M., Brittain, R. P. & McClemont, W. F. 1965. Aggressive behavior, mental sub-normality, and the XYY male. *Nature,* 208, 1351-1352.

Jacobs, P. A., Price, W. H. Court Brown, W. M., Brittain, R. P. & Whatmore, P. B. 1968. Chromosome studies on men in a maximum security hospital. *Annals of Human Genetics,* 31, 339-358.

Kessler, S. & Moos, R. H. 1970. The XYY karyotype and criminality: a review. *Journal of Psychiatric Research,* 7, 153-170.

Lancet Editorial. 1966. 1, 583-584.

Leff, J. P. & Scott, P. D. 1968. XYY and intelligence. *Lancet,* 1, 645.

Lisker, R., Zenzes, M. T. & Fonesca, M. T. 1968. YY syndrome in a Mexican. *Lancet,* 2, 635.

Lubs, H. A. & Ruddle, F. H. 1969. Major chromosomal abnormalities in 4,000 consecutive newborns. *Clinical Research,* 17, 316. Abstract.

Marinello, M. J., Berkson, R. A., Edwards, J. A. & Bannerman, R. M. 1969. A study of the XYY syndrome in tall men and juvenile delinquents. *Journal of the American Medical Association,* 208, 321-325.

Matthews, M. B. & Brooks, P. W. 1968. Aggression and the YY syndrome. *Lancet,* 2, 355.

Medical World News. 1969. XYY syndrome ruled no excuse for crime. April 11, 23.

Melnyck, J., Derencseny, A., Vanasek, F., Rucci, A. J. & Thompson, H. 1969. XYY survey in an institution for sex offenders and the mentally ill. *Nature,* 224, 369-370.

Money, J. 1969. Editorial: XYY, the law, and forensic moral philosophy. *The Journal of Nervous & Mental Disease,* 149, 309-311.

____. 1970. Behavior genetics: principles, methods and examples from XO, XXY and XYY syndromes. *Seminars in Psychiatry,* 2, 11-29.

Money, J., Gaskins, R. J. & Hull, H. 1970. Impulse, aggression and sexuality in the XYY syndrome. *St. John's Law Review,* 44, 220-235.

Montagu, M. F. A. 1968. Chromosomes and crime. *Psychology Today,* 2, 42-49.

Nielsen, J. 1968. Y chromosomes in male psychiatric patients above 180 cm. tall. *British Journal of Psychiatry,* 114, 1589-1591.

Nielsen, J., Tsuboi, T., Sturup, G. & Romano, D. 1968. XYY chromosomal constitution in criminal psychopaths. *Lancet,* 2, 576.

Oklahoma Law Review. 1969. The XYY chromosome complement and criminal conduct. Comment, 22, 287-301.

Pearson, P. L., Bobrow, M. & Vosa, C. G. 1970. Technique for identifying Y chromosomes in human interphase nuclei. *Nature,* 226, 78-80.

Price, W. H. & Jacobs, J. A. 1970. The 47,XYY male with special reference to behavior. *Seminars in Psychiatry,* 2, 30-39.

Price, W. H., Strong, J. A., Whatmore, P. B. & McClemont, W. F. 1966. Criminal patients with

XYY sex chromosome complement. *Lancet,* 1, 565-566.

Price, W. H. & Whatmore, P. B. 1967a. Criminal behavior and the XYY male. *Nature,* 213, 815.

____. 1967b. Behavior disorders and the pattern of crime among XYY males identified at a maximum security hospital. *British Medical Journal,* 1, 533.

Ratcliffe, S. G., Melville, M. M., Stewart, A. L. & Jacobs, P. A. 1970. Chromosome studies on 3500 newborn male infants. *Lancet,* 1, 121-122.

Robinson, A. & Puck, T. T. 1967. Studies on chromosomal nondisjunction in man. II. *American Journal of Human Genetics,* 19, 112.

Roebuck, J. & Atlas, R. H. 1969. Chromosomes and the criminal. *Corrective Psychiatry,* 15, 103-117.

Russell, D. H. & Bender, F. H. 1970. Legal implications of the XYY syndrome. *Seminars in Psychiatry,* 2, 40-52.

Sandberg, A. A., Koepf, G. F., Ishihara, T. & Hauschka, T. S. 1961. An XYY human male. *Lancet,* 2, 488-489.

Scott, P. D. & Kahn, J. 1968. An XYY patient of above average intelligence as a basis for review of the psychopathology, medico-legal implications of the syndrome and possibilities for prevention. *Cropwood Conference on Psychopathic Offenders,* ed. D. J. West, Univ. of Cambridge, 56-62.

Sergovich, F. R. 1969. Chromosome studies in unselected neonates. *American Society of Human Genetics,* Program and Abstracts, Austin, Texas, 33.

Sergovich, F. R., Valentine, G. H., Chen, A. T. L., Kinch, R. A. H. & Smout, M. S. 1969. Chromosome aberrations in 2159 consecutive newborn babies. *New England Journal of Medicine,* 280, 851-855.

Shah, S. A. 1970. Privileged communications, confidentiality, and privacy: Confidentiality. *Professional Psychology,* 1, 159-164.

St. Louis Law Journal. 1969. The XYY chromosome complement: brief application to criminal insanity tests. Comment, 14, 297-309.

Stenchever, M. A. & MacIntyre, M. N. 1969. A normal XYY man. *Lancet,* 1, 680.

Telfer, M. A., Baker, D., Clark, G. R. & Richardson, C. E. 1968. Incidence of gross chromosomal errors among tall criminal American males. *Science,* 159, 1249-1250.

Telfer, M. A., Baker, D. & Longtin, L. 1968. YY syndrome in an American Negro. *Lancet,* 1, 95.

Thorburn, M. J., Chutkan, W., Richards, R. & Bell, R. 1968. XYY sex chromosomes in a Jamaican with orthopaedic abnormalities. *Journal of Medical Genetics,* 5, 215-219.

Vignetti, P., Capotorti, L. & Ferrante, E. 1964. XYY chromosomal constitution with genital abnormality. *Lancet,* 2, 588-589.

Walzer, S., Breau, G. & Gerald, P. S. 1969. A chromosomal survey of 2,400 normal newborn infants. *Journal of Pediatrics,* 74, 438-448.

Welch, J. P., Borgaonkar, D. S. & Herr, H. M. 1967. Psychopathy, mental deficiency, aggressiveness and the XYY syndrome. *Nature,* 214, 500-501.

Wiener, S. & Sutherland, G. 1968. A normal XYY man. *Lancet,* 2, 1352.

Wiener, S., Sutherland, G., Bartholomew, A. A. & Hudson, B. 1968. XYY males in a Melbourne prison. *Lancet,* 1, 150.

Wiener, S., Sutherland, G. & Bartholomew, A. A. 1969. A murderer with 47,XYY and an additional autosomal abnormality. *Australian & New Zealand Journal of Criminology,* 2, 20-28.

PART TWO

Man's "carnivore psychology"

The following selections have been contributed by five scholars who are among the best known of the school of thought that holds that "man's nature is such that he easily learns to enjoy killing" as a consequence of his long evolutionary history as a hunter.

Far from being naïve, these men nevertheless derive qualified suggestions as to the nature of human behavior from studies on living non-human primates. They hold that intragroup aggression among primates (including man) has been underestimated rather than overstressed. Most of these workers have been influenced by Konrad Lorenz, although they repudiate his concept of a spontaneous or inevitably recurring aggressive impulse in man, arising from historical wellsprings. Hinde sees a human "drive" toward intraspecific conflict that demands channelling into socially constructive pursuits. Tinbergen views man's heritage as a "template" or predisposition to aggression which, again, must be sublimated, preferably in scientific research.

Freeman's paper, now somewhat amended from its original version, has long been admired for its forthright appraisal of the cruel and bloodthirsty creature he recognizes as *Homo sapiens.*

5

Aggressive behavior in old world monkeys and apes

Sherwood L. Washburn and David A. Hamburg

In this essay we hope to use the problem of aggression as an example of evolutionary perspective as a scientific tool. We are interested in the way the behavior of the nonhuman primates may be useful in increasing our understanding of man. Study of the forces and situations that produced man is one way of attempting to understand human nature, of seeing ourselves in evolutionary perspective. Because the use of man's closest relatives in the laboratory is the nearest approach to experimenting on man himself, the use of primates as laboratory animals is increasing rapidly. As in so much of science, there is no boundary between the pure and the applied, and the answers to our questions lie in the domain of many different disciplines. Since no one could possibly master all the relevant information, we wish to clarify our objectives before proceeding to the main topic of the paper. In discussions at the conference a series of general questions emerged, many of which we have encountered before – since the beginning of our collaboration at the Center for Advanced Study in the Behavioral Sciences in 1957. We propose to deal with these recurrent, general questions first.

Field studies in a comparative evolutionary framework do not permit the manipulation of variables and the precision of measurement that are possible in laboratory

---

SOURCE: *Primates: Studies in Adaptation and Variability,* ed. Phyllis C. Jay. Copyright © 1968 by Holt, Rinehart and Winston, Inc. This paper was part of a program on primate behavior supported by the United States Public Health Service (Grant No. MH 08623) and aided by a Research Professorship in the Miller Institute for Basic Research in Science at the University of California at Berkeley. Reprinted by permission of Holt, Rinehart and Winston, Inc.

experiments. They are, however, likely to give new perspectives which suggest fruitful directions for experiments and for deeper analysis of problems of living organisms. Field studies do not replace other methods of investigation, nor do studies on animals substitute for the direct study of man. For example, Prechtl (1965) has pointed out that much of the behavior of the human newborn is understandable only in phylogenetic perspective. This does not mean that comparison is the only way to approach the study of behavior in the newborn but only that inclusion of some comparison enriches the understanding of what is being ovserved. In advocating the use of the evolutionary approach, we are not suggesting that it is the only method or that it is always relevant. We are suggesting, however, that the comparative, evolutionary study of behavior offers many insights that are unlikely to come from other sources. We believe that the combination of the evolutionary perspective with experimental science provides a powerful approach to biological problems including those of behavior, and we echo Simpson's 1964 statement "100 years without Darwin are enough."

A central problem in the study of the evolution of behavior is that contemporary monkeys and apes are not the equivalents of human ancestors. To what extent their behaviors may be used as indicators of the behaviors of long-extinct fossil forms is debatable. Obviously this is not a simple question, and the possibility of reconstruction differs with each particular behavior. Each answer is a matter of probability, and there is great variation in the adequacy of evidence bearing on different questions. For example, in all the nonhuman primates females have brief, clearly limited periods of estrus. Since this state is universal and highly adaptive, it is virtually certain that this condition was present in our ancestors. Although the time of the loss of estrus cannot be dated, the comparison calls attention to the significance of the loss. The physiology of human females is quite different from that of any other primate, and many specifically human customs and problems are directly related to continuing receptivity in the human female. The human family is based upon a female physiology different from that of any other primate, and the physiology may well be the result of selection for stable male-female relations. The close similarity in much reproductive physiology permitted the use of the rhesus monkey as the most important laboratory animal in working out the human female's reproductive cycle (Corner, 1942), but the behavioral approach emphasizes the significance of the differences. Our understanding benefits from seeing the nature of both the similarity and the difference. The problems of reconstructing behavior are discussed more fully in Washburn and Jay (1965).*

*After this paper was in nearly final form we received *Adaptation et Aggressivité* (1965), edited by Kourilsky, Soulairac, and Grapin, and *On Aggression* (1966), by Konrad Lorenz. *Conflict in Society* (de Reuck, 1966) also appeared, although we had access to part of that data in prepublication. We find ourselves in general agreement with these new sources, and only wish that we had had them a year ago. We have found J. Altman's *Organic Foundations of Animal Behavior* (1966) exceedingly valuable, and it too would have been very useful if it had been available earlier. None of these references would have led us to different conclusions, and we hope that the point of view presented in the introduction to this paper may help to bridge the gap between the thinking of the students of animal behavior and the social scientists.

Estrus has been used as an example of a problem of the reconstruction of behavior when there is no direct fossil evidence. The same kind of logical reconstruction from indirect evidence can be applied to many other behaviors. We have indirect evidence, for example, that our remote ancestors probably matured more rapidly than we do, lived in small areas, were very aggressive, and hunted little, if any. Let us consider this first statement: If the infant is to cling to the mother, as does the infant monkey and ape, then the infant must be born able to cling. A human infant born with this ability would need far too large a brain at the time of birth, and the adaptation of the mother's holding the immature infant may be looked on as an adaptation to the evolution of the brain. Monkeys are born with more highly developed nervous and motor capabilities than those of apes at birth. A gorilla mother must help her baby for approximately six weeks before it can cling entirely unaided (Schaller, 1963). In *Homo erectus* (Java man, Pekin man, and comparable forms) the brain was approximately twice the size of a gorilla, and the infant's behavior must have been much more like that of modern man than like that of an ape.

The implication of the clinging of the nonhuman primate infant can be generalized that biology guarantees the infant monkey or ape a far greater chance of appropriate treatment than it does the human infant. So far as early experience is important in determining later performance, man should show by far the greatest variability of all primates. The study of comparative behavior calls attention to the uniqueness of the human condition, the importance of early events, and of the human mother's need to acquire complex skills of child care.

In addition to the reconstruction of behavior, another problem that has arisen repeatedly in discussions of the comparison of behavior is the extent to which behaviors in different groups of animals are comparable. The issue is whether behaviors labeled, for example, "aggression" or "play" are comparable enough so that comparisons are useful, or whether these are simply subjective human words used to symbolize collection of noncomparable behaviors. There are four important considerations.

The first is that the words are least likely to be misleading when animals, whose behaviors are being compared, are closely related. For example, we think there would be little disagreement as to which behaviors should be called "play" or "aggression" in Old World monkeys and apes, but the problem is very different if the behaviors of monkeys and birds are to be compared.

The second point is that in the observation of the behavior we are not limited to the view of a single animal or to one occasion. An observer sees repeated interactions of animals in the social group or groups. The judgment that an action is threatening, for example, is based on the repeated specifiable response of the other animals. The response to biting in play and in aggression is very different, and the difference is unmistakable in the response of the bitten animals, although it would often be hard for the human observer to perceive the difference in the actual bite.

The third point is that in classifying and labeling behavior we are not limited to the external view of the actions. For example, Delgado (1967) has shown that stimulation of certain brain areas elicits threat behavior in rhesus monkeys. Although present evidence is limited, we think it likely that the same brain areas are concerned with rage in man. If it can be shown that the behaviors that are classified together are mediated by comparable structures, then the classification is much more likely to be useful. This is best exemplified by the category "sexual," in which the interrelations of behaviors, nervous system, hormones, and experience have been thoroughly investigated (Beach, 1965). This takes us back to our first point: One reason that labeling categories of behavior is less likely to be misleading when the animals are closely related is that the internal biological mechanisms on which these actions are based are more likely to be similar.

The fourth point is that the human observer is most likely to detect relevant cues when observing the behavior of animals closely related to himself. We do not underestimate the formidable problems of observation and the need for experimental clarification of what is being observed in the behavior of monkeys and apes, but at least the special senses and central nervous system of the observer are highly similar to those of the animals being observed. Even within the primates the interpretation of observations becomes much more difficult with the prosimians. Since the sense of smell is important in prosimians and the animals have special tactile hairs that we lack, in many situations there is no assurance that the human observer has access to information of importance to the animal being observed. The human can see a dog in the act of smelling, but simple observation gives no knowledge of the information received by the dog. Viewed in this way, the human observer is more likely to be able to see and record the actions that are important in the analysis of behavior when studying monkeys and apes than he is when watching any other animal.

This does not mean that observations are necessarily easy or correct, but it does mean that man is potentially able to see, describe, and interpret actions made by a close relative, especially in a mode that approximates the judgments the animals themselves are making. The more distantly the animal is related to man, the less the human perception of the situation is likely to correspond to that of the animal. For example, a human observer can learn the facial expressions, gestures, and sounds that express threat in a species of monkey, with some assurance that the signals are seen in the same way a monkey sees them. It is possible to play back their recorded sound to monkeys and most sounds without gestures produce no response. Some monkey gestures can be learned by man, and the human face is sufficiently similar that a monkey interprets certain human expressions as threats and responds with appropriate actions. Without experiment a human observer would hardly have expected that a male turkey would display to the isolated head of a female (Schein and Hale, 1959; reprinted in McGill, 1965). Even when a bird and a mammal are responding to the same sense, vision, in this case, the internal organization of perception is so different that comparison can be made only on the basis of experiments. In monkey, ape, and man the internal organizations are highly similar, and the use of a word such as aggression carries far more comparable meaning than when the same word is used to describe a category of behavior in vertebrates in general.

We are not belittling the importance of the study of behavior in a wide variety of animals, but we are emphasizing that the problems of comparison in such studies are more complex than they are in these comparing a very few of man's closest relatives.

We are writing on aggression in certain monkeys and apes because we think that there is enough information to make such an essay useful. The word "aggression" only indicates the area of our interest and our use of it does not mean that we think the area is fully understood or precisely defined. Accurate definition often comes at the end of research; initially, definitions serve only to clarify the general nature of the subject to be explored. For the purpose of opening the area for exploration and discussion we find that the definition of Carthy and Ebling (1964:1) is useful. They state that "An animal acts aggressively when it inflicts, attempts to inflict, or threatens to inflict damage on another animal. The act is accompanied by recognizable behavioral symptoms and definable physiological changes." Carthy and Ebling recognize the displacement of aggression against self or an inanimate object, but rule out predation as a form of aggression. For our analysis, it is not useful to accept this limitation; if one is concerned with aggressive behavior in man, the degree to which human carnivorous and predatory activity is related to human aggressiveness should be kept open for investigation and not ruled out by definition.

In discussing aggression it is important to consider both the individual actor and the social system in which he is participating. In the social systems of monkeys and apes evolution has produced a close correlation between the nature of the social system and the nature of the actors in the system. Societies of gibbons, langurs, and macaques represent different sociobiological adaptations, and, as will be developed later, the form and function of aggressive behaviors are different in these groups (Jay, 1965a). Through selection, evolution has produced a fit between social system and the biology of the actors in the system. Aggression is between individuals or very small groups, and individual animals must be able to make the appropriate decisions and fight or flee. Rapoport (1966), in particular, has argued that war between modern nations has nothing to do with the aggressiveness of individuals, but rather is a question of culture, of human institutions. Although agreeing that it is very important to understand the cultural factors in war, we think that it is important to understand the human actors too. It is still individuals who make decisions, and it is our belief that the limitations and peculiarities of human biology play an important part in these decisions. We will return to this issue later; at this point we only want to emphasize that it is necessary, particularly in the case of man, to think both of the social system and the actors. It was not long ago that human war was carried out on a person-to-person basis, and our present customs go back to those times.

Finally, we return to a point of view which we have discussed elsewhere (Washburn and Hamburg, 1965), but which needs emphasis and clarification particularly in the context of aggression. The result of evolution is that behaviors that have been adaptive in the past history of the species, which led to reproductive success, are easy to learn and hard to extinguish. As Hinde and Tinbergen have put it: "This exemplifies a principle of great importance: many of the differences between species do not lie in the first instance in stereotyped behavior sequences but consist in the possession of a propensity to learn" (1958:255; reprinted in McGill, 1965). It is particularly important to consider ease of learning, or the propensity to learn, when we are discussing monkeys and apes. These forms mature slowly and there is strong reason to suppose that the main function of this period of protected youth is to allow learning and hence adaptation to a wide variety of local situations.

There is a feedback relation between structure and function starting in the early embryo. Structure sets limits and gives opportunities. Apes cannot learn to talk because they lack the neurological base. Man can easily learn to be aggressive because the biological base is present, is always used to some degree, and is frequently reinforced by individual success and major social reward. The biological nature of man, now far more amenable to scientific analysis than ever before, is thus relevant to aggressive behavior in ways that include learning and social interaction.

The biological basis of aggression

Collias (1944) in a major review of aggressive behavior in vertebrates concluded that the function of the behavior was control of food and reproduction through the control of territory and the maintenance of hierarchy and that males were responsible for most of the aggressive behavior. Scott (1958, 1962) supported these main conclusions, and emphasized the importance of learning in the development of aggressive behavior. Breeds of dogs differ greatly in aggressiveness, but the expression of these differences is greatly modified by learning and the social situation. Recently, Wynne-Edwards (1965) has stressed the role of social behavior in control of territory, hierarchy, and reproduction as mechanisms of species dispersion and population control. In general, the biological studies indicate that aggression is one of the principal adaptive mechanisms, that it has been of major importance in the evolution of the vertebrates (Lorenz, 1966).

We think that these major conclusions will apply to the primates, although adequate data are available on only a few forms and these will be discussed later. Order within most primate groups is maintained by a hierarchy, which depends ultimately primarily on the power of the males. Groups are separated by habit and conflict. Aggressive individuals are essential actors in the social system and competition between groups is necessary for species dispersal and control of local populations. In view of the wide distribution of these behaviors and their fundamental importance to the evolutionary process, it is not surprising to discover that the biological basis for aggressive behavior is similar in a wide variety of vertebrates. As presently understood, the essential structures are in the phylogenetically oldest parts of the brain, and the principal male sex hormone testosterone is significant for aggression. In general, motivational-emotional patterns essential to survival and reproductive success in mammals find their main structural base in the older parts of the brain, particularly in hypothalamus and limbic system. In the higher primates this mammalian "common denominator" is linked to a remarkable development of newer parts of the brain. These are mainly concerned with increasing storage (learning), more complex discrimination, and motor skills; they function in a complex feedback relationship with the older parts (Noback and Moskowitz, 1963; MacLean, 1963). This interrelation of the older and newer parts of the brain is especially important to remember when monkeys and apes are considered because the expression of the brain-hormone-behavior paradigm may be greatly modified by learning in a social environment. A simple release of a complicated emotion-motor pattern in aggression is not to be expected in such species.

The recognition of a biological factor in aggressive behavior long antedates modern science; stock breeders certainly recognized differences in individuals, in breeds, and in the effects of castration. Comparison of the behaviors of ox and bull, as well as experiments such as those of Beeman (1947) on mice, show that a part of the difference in aggressive behavior between males and females is due to the sex hormones. Testosterone makes it easier to stimulate animals to fight, and aggressive behavior in males tends to be more frequent, more intense, and of longer duration than in females. Experimental studies fully support the conclusions of Collias' (1944) survey of vertebrate behavior, and are in agreement with the field studies of primate behavior. It would be extremely interesting to trap a male baboon from a troop that had been carefully studied, castrate him, and release him back into the same troop. The effects of the operation could then be studied relative to hierarchy, predators, and participation in troop life in general.

However, the relation of the hormone to the behavior is not simple, for androgen stimulates protein anabolism in many animals (Nalbandov, 1964), and this is one of the factors accounting for the greater size of males. Skeletal muscles of castrated males and females grow less rapidly than those of intact animals, and androgen administration increases the number and thickness of fibers. The sex hormones affect the growth of the brain, and appear to act in an inductive way to organize certain circuits into male and female patterns (Harris, 1964; Levine and Mullins, 1966). This effect is comparable to that on the undifferentiated genital tract. There is then an interplay, a feedback, among hormones, structure, and behavior, and the nature of this relation changes during development. Testosterone is first a factor in influencing the structure of the brain (especially the hypothalamus) and of the genitals. Later it is a factor in influencing both muscle size and the more aggressive play of males. Finally, it is important in influencing both aggressive and sexual behavior in adults. We stress the complex interplay between hormones, structures, and behavior throughout the life of the individual. It can be seen at once that the concept of a system of coadapted genes is so important because such a developmental and functional pattern depends on the interaction of many different biological entities; variation in any of these may affect the final result. It is probably the primary methodological difficulty in the science of behavior genetics that even apparently simple behaviors are often built from very complex biological bases.

Two groups of experiments yield what seems to be particularly important information regarding factors influencing male aggression. Harris and Levine have studied the sexual behavior patterns in female rats that had received early androgen treatment; treatment of newborn rats with testosterone results in abolition of estrous behavior combined with an exaggeration of male patterns, particularly in the aggressive sphere. Young, Goy, and Phoenix (1964) and Goy (personal communication) gave testosterone to pregnant rhesus monkeys during approximately the second quarter of gestation. In addition to producing pseudohermaphroditic females, the behavior of the prenatally treated females was modified in the male direction. Rosenblum (1961) has shown that there are marked sexual differences in the play of infant rhesus monkeys. The masculinized females were allowed to play for 20 minutes per day, five days a week, from the age of two months; this continued for more than two years (at the time of writing). They threatened, initiated play, and engaged in rough play more than did the controls. Like the males studied by Rosenblum, the masculinized females withdrew less often than did untreated females from initiations, threats, and approaches of other animals. They also showed a greater tendency to mounting; evidently there is a general tendency toward male behavioral repertoire. Treatment changed the whole brain-hormone-behavior complex, and the results of the prenatal treatment persisted into the third year of life.

However, it should be stressed that the expression of the pattern depended on social learning. The infant monkeys were allowed to play, and Harlow and Harlow (1965) have shown that gross behavioral deficits in behavior result from early social isolation. It is also important to remember that these testosterone-treated monkeys were protected. In a free-ranging troop of rhesus, subject to human harassment, predation, intertroop conflict, and intratroop aggression (Jay, personal communication; Southwick *et al.*, 1965), such an animal would probably be punished for inappropriate behavior. The experimentally masculinized female does not have the large canine teeth, jaw muscles, or body size to be successfully aggressive against males under natural conditions. A similar point is well illustrated in an experiment by Delgado (1967). A monkey in whose brain an electrode had been implanted so that threat behavior could be stimulated at the experimenter's will, was put in a cage with four other monkeys. In the test where the experimental animal was dominant over the other four, stimulation led him to threaten and immediately attack. But when the experimental animal was subordinate to all four of the other monkeys, stimulation led to his being attacked and cowering. Even when there is a restricted biological base for a behavior, the expression of the behavior will be affected by socio-environmental factors.

This brings us to a closer examination of the brain in relation to aggressive behavior. Perhaps, the most thorough work has been done on cats and this is summarized by Brown and Hunsperger (1965). Their experiments show several areas in which electrical stimulation will elicit threat and escape behavior. They have been able to elicit such behavior by stimulation in portions of the midbrain, hypothalamus, and amygdala. Although, just as in monkeys, threat can be elicited from only a very small part of the brain, it is not a single or simple area. The threat behaviors are multiple and it is especially interesting that escape is closely related to threat. Brown and Hunsperger relate the anatomical facts to the behavioral fact that following threat an animal may either attack or escape. Certainly this is frequently seen in monkeys; whether threat ends in attack or flight depends on the participating animal's appraisal of the situation. In the laboratory, the direction and intensity of the attack resulting from stimulation of the brain depends on what is available for attack, and may be changed by offering the cat a dummy or a real rat.

In man the same parts of the brain are believed to be involved in rage reactions. Obviously, the same kind of detailed stimulation cannot be undertaken on man, but clinical evidence including neurological studies suggests that the limbic system and hypothalamus are very important in mediation of emotional experiences, positive and negative, including anger.

Aggression in free-ranging apes and monkeys

Just as the biological basis of aggression that we have been discussing can only be seen and analyzed in the laboratory, so the functions and frequencies of aggressive behaviors can only be determined by field studies. The field studies have recently been reviewed by Hall (1964) and Washburn (1966), and here we will call attention only to a few of the major points of interest from an evolutionary point of view.

Conflict between different species is infrequent, even when the species are competing for the same food. Places where the general situation can be most easily observed are at water holes in the large African game reserves. Particularly at the end of the dry season, hundreds of animals of many species may be seen in close proximity in South Africa, Rhodesia, or Tanzania. The Ngorongoro crater affords magnificent views over vast numbers of animals, and from this vantage point it becomes clear that the human notion of "wild," that is, that animals normally flee, is the result of human hunting. In Amboseli it is not uncommon to see various combinations of baboons, vervet monkeys, warthogs, impala, gazelle of two species, zebra, wildebeest (gnu), giraffe, elephant, and rhinoceros around one water hole. Even carnivores, when they are not hunting, attract surprisingly little attention. When elephants walk through a troop of baboons the monkeys move out of the way in a leisurely manner at the last second, and the same indifference was observed when impala males were fighting among the baboons or when a rhinoceros ran through the troop. On one occasion two baboons chased a giraffe, but, except where hunting carnivores are concerned, interspecies aggression is rare. Most animals under most conditions do not show interest in animals of other species, even when eating the same food – warthogs and baboons frequently eat side by side. The whole notion of escape distance is predicated on the presence of a hunter.

Although the general situation seems to be great tolerance for other species (Hall, 1964), there are exceptions. Gibbons usually drive monkeys from fruit trees (Ellefson, 1968). Goodall has shown remarkable motion pictures of baboons and chimpanzees in aggressive encounters. Baboons have been seen trying to drive vervets (*Cercopithecus aethiops*) from fruit trees in which the baboons had been feeding. There is some deliberate hunting by monkeys and apes. DeVore (personal communication) and Struhsaker (1965) have seen baboons catch and eat vervets. Goodall (1965) records chimpanzees hunting and eating red colobus monkeys. Nestling birds and eggs are probably eaten by most monkeys, but the majority of interspecific encounters among the primates appear to be neutral, causing little or no reaction among the species.

Monkeys and apes certainly take aggressive action against predators, and this has been particularly well described by Struhsaker (1965) for vervets. Vervet alarm calls distinguish among snakes, ground predators, and birds, and the monkeys respond with different appropriate actions. Baboons have been seen to chase cheetahs and dogs. Monkeys and apes make agonistic displays against predators, including man, and these behaviors have been reviewed by Hall (1964) and Washburn (1966). The amount of this agonistic behavior leads us to think that predation and interspecies conflict may have been underestimated in the field studies so far available. The problem is that although the primates may have become conditioned to the observer's presence, he is likely to disturb the predator. A fuller picture of interspecies conflict requires field studies of a nonprimate species involved in conflict with primates.

Relations among groups of the same species range from avoidance to agonistic display and actual fighting. In marked contrast to the normally neutral relations with other species, animals of the same species evoke interest and action. This can be seen when strange animals of the same species are artificially introduced (Gartlan and Brain, 1968; Kummer, 1968; Hall, 1964; Washburn, 1966), on the occasions when an animal changes troops, and when troops meet. We think these behaviors suggest that intertroop conflict is an important mechanism for species spacing. The spacing represents a part of the adjustments of the species to the local food supply. The quantity of food is a very important factor in determining the density of primate populations. It has been shown in both Japan and a small island off Puerto Rico where rhesus monkeys were introduced that population expands at a rate of more than 15 percent per year if food is supplied ad libitum (Koford, 1966). Intertroop aggression either leads to one group's having the resources of an area at its exclusive disposal, or at least creates a situation in which one group is much more likely to obtain the food in one area. The clearest description of extreme territorial defense is Ellefson's account (1968) of gibbons. The relation of food supply to population size is considered by Hall (1964). A very clear case of the relation of food supply to territorial defense is given by Gartlan and Brain (1968): Where food was abundant and there was a high density of vervets, the monkeys showed territorial marking and defense. These behaviors were absent in an area of poor food supply and low population density. From this and other examples (rhesus, langurs) it is clear that one cannot describe a primate species as "territorial" in the same sense the word has been used for species of birds. In monkeys and apes the behavior of a part of a species will depend both on biology (perhaps best shown by the gibbon) and on the local conditions. The intertroop fighting of city rhesus monkeys appears to depend both on high density and on the great overlap of living areas that is a product of the city environment (Southwick *et al.*, 1965). The intertroop conflict of langurs described by Yoshiba (1968) also occurred in an area in which the population is estimated at possibly more than 300 langurs per square mile.

It is our belief that intertroop aggression in primates has been greatly underestimated. No field study has yet been undertaken with this problem as a focus, and no effort has been made to study situations in which conflict is likely to be frequent. More important, the groups of a species are normally spaced well apart, and the observer sees the long-term results of aggression and avoidance, not the events causing it. (In this regard, as in so many others, gibbons are exceptional.) A further complication is that the groups of monkeys which are likely to meet have seen each other before. The relations among groups have been established in previous encounters, and one is exceedingly unlikely to see strange troops meet or some major event change the relative strength of the troops. Carpenter (1964), particularly, has called attention to the importance of sounds in species spacing, and, in species in which this mechanism is important, group avoidance does not even require that the animals see each other. The importance of both sounds and gestures in intertroop relations is discussed by Marler (1968). Lorenz (1964, 1966) has stressed the ritualistic nature of the vast majority of aggressive encounters.

In evaluating the amount of intertroop aggression in Old World monkeys and apes, it is important to keep in mind that the data have increased very rapidly. In Scott's (1962) review on aggression in animals the only major sources of information on primates were Carpenter's studies of the howling monkey (1934) and of the gibbon (1940). In Hall's review of aggression in primate society (1964) the data are chiefly from publications in 1962 or later. We stress the frequency and importance of aggressive behavior more than Hall does, in part because of our greater emphasis on the biological importance of aggression in species spacing, but more importantly because there is much more information available in recent accounts. Aggression in langurs is described by Ripley (1967) and Yoshiba (1968). Many more observations of aggressive encounters in rhesus, including intertroop fighting in forest troops, are now available (Jay, personal communication). Shirek (personal communication) has observed a complex pattern of intertroop fighting in *Macaca irus*. Ellefson (1968) has given a much more complete account of intertroop encounters, including actual fighting, in gibbons. For vervets, Gartlan and Brain (1968) and Struhsaker (1965) have provided descriptions of intertroop encounters and of the settings that increase their frequency.

Aggression within the local group

Conflict between individuals within the local group or aggregation is far more frequent than intergroup or interspecies conflicts. It is impossible to watch monkeys and apes for any long period without seeing conflict over food or in interpersonal relations. Scott (1962) has emphasized the importance of learning in the development of aggressive behaviors and Hall (1964) has shown that most learning in monkeys takes place in a group and is appropriate to the group's social structure, individual biology, and ecology. In the societies of nonhuman primates aggression is constantly rewarded. In baboons (DeVore and Hall, 1965; Hall and DeVore, 1965) the most dominant male can do what he wants (within the limits of the traditions of the troop), and he takes precedence in social situations. As DeVore first emphasized, the dominant male is attractive to the other members of the troop. When he sits in the shade, others come to him to sit beside him and groom him. When the troop moves, it is the behavior of the dominant males in the center of the troop that ultimately decides the direction the troop will follow. The whole social structure of the troop rewards the dominant animal, or animals, and when a dominant animal is sick or injured and loses position the change can be seen in the behavior of the other animals. No longer is precedence granted to him for social position, grooming, food, sex, or leadership. Thus, monkeys not only have the biological basis for aggressive behavior, but also use this equipment frequently, and success is highly rewarded.

There are marked species differences in aggressive behavior and in the dominance hierarchies that result from it. Baboons and macaques are probably the most aggressive of the monkeys, but even here there are species differences. *M. radiata* is far less aggressive than *M. mulatta* (Simonds, 1965). The behavior of *Papio hamadryas* is certainly different from that of other baboons (Kummer, 1968). But *interindividual conflict is important in all species described so far.* Even in chimpanzees with their very open social organization (Goodall, 1965; Reynolds and Reynolds, 1965) some males are dominant. Goodall had to make elaborate arrangements to prevent a few large males from taking all the food when bananas were provided.

The position of the individual animal relative to other animals in the group is learned, and this process starts with the mother and her support of her infant in aggressive encounters (Yamada, 1963; Sade, 1965, 1966). Sons of dominant females are more likely to be dominant. The passing of the infant langur from one female to another may be one of the factors in the lack of development of clearly defined dominance hierarchies in this species (Jay, 1965b).

Since the animals in a local group know one another, the dominance order is understood, is normally maintained by threat, and usually serves to preserve a relatively peaceful situation. For example, a small group of crab-eating macaques (*M. irus*) kept in a runway (16 by 75 feet) at Berkeley was dominated by one male. For more than two years there had not been a single serious bite by any member of the group. When the dominant animal was removed, no change occurred for two weeks; the social habits continued. Then the formerly number two animal asserted his power, and four adult animals received deep canine bites. (These bites are quite different from incisor nipping, which hurts the other animal but does not do serious damage. Incisor nipping is the normal mode of biting when an animal gives mild punishment.) Two infants were killed in the encounters. This incident clearly shows the role of dominance in preventing fighting. It also shows another characteristic of dominance behavior in macaques. In the runway all animals had access to ample food; they had comfortable social position including opportunities for grooming; and the dominant animal, although he copulated more than the others, did not prevent them from access to females. Being dominant appears to be its own reward – to be highly satisfying and to be sought, regardless of whether it is accompanied by advantage in food, sex, or grooming. In the long run, position guarantees reward, but in the short run, position itself is the reward, as this monkey's actions suggest; satisfaction apparently comes from others being unable to challenge effectively, as well as from more tangible rewards.

Evolution of conflict

The aggressive behaviors that are the basis of dominance within the group, that are a factor in spacing groups, and that may result in some predation are rooted in the biology of the species and are learned in the social group. As noted earlier, the biological roots of these behaviors are complex, and the individual animal, which carries out the threat or other aggressive action, must have the necessary structure, physiology, and temperament. For example, males tend to be more aggressive than females, and this difference depends on testosterone and is altered by castration of the male or prenatal treatment of the female. The aggressive actions are practiced and brought to a high level of skill in play. Then, as the male monkey becomes fully adult, the canine teeth erupt. Notice that the whole practiced, skillful, aggressive complex is present before the canine teeth erupt. The really dangerous weapon is not present until the male monkey is a fully adult, experienced member of the social group. As the canine teeth erupt, the temporal muscles more than double in size, and the male changes from a roughly playing juvenile to an adult that can inflict a very serious wound, even death, with a single bite.

All the parts of this aggressive complex evolve, and this is best shown by the differences between species. The differences between baboons and patas monkeys give an example of very different ways of adapting to savanna life (Hall, 1964; DeVore and Hall, 1965; Hall and DeVore, 1965). Differences between *Cercopithecus aethiops* and *C. mitis* are noted by Gartlan and Brain (1968). Since selection is for reproductive success, it is clear that there must be a balance between all the differen structural and physiological factors that make aggressive actions adaptive; although the biological elements seem remarkably similar in primates, the pattern and degree of development may be very different in various species. It is no accident that the differences between male and female monkeys are in body size, tooth form, neck muscles, hormones, brain, play patterns, and adult behavior, and this whole pattern of sexual differentiation may result in sex difference that is extreme (as in baboons and macaques) or very minor (as in *Presbytis rubicunda* or *Cercopithecus nictitans*). But as these species have evolved, the process has been slow enough so that selection has modified the whole complex of the adapting aggressive behaviors and their biological base. In man, however, the whole technical-social scene has changed so rapidly that human biological evolution has had no opportunity to keep pace. Throughout most of human history societies have depended on young adult males to hunt, to fight, and to maintain the social order with violence. Even when the individual was cooperating, his social role could be executed only by extremely aggressive action that was learned in play, was socially approved, and was personally gratifying.

In the remainder of this paper we wish to consider human aggression, and the problems created by the nature of man.

As Lorenz (1964, 1966) has stressed, most conflict between animals is ritualized. Gestures and sounds convey threats and greatly reduce the amount of actual fighting. This is certainly true for the primates, and many structures are understandable only as the basis for displays. Dramatic structures of this kind, such as the laryngeal sac of the siamang gibbon, have long been recognized, but many less noticeable (from a human point of view) should be included – for example, the pads of connective tissue on the head of the male gorilla or those of the male orangutan's cheeks. Motions of the ears, scalp, eyelids, are important in gesture. The posture, or the position of the tail, may signal social status. Hair, particularly on the shoulders and neck, erects, signaling aggressive intent, and the manes of many male primates probably are to be interpreted as structural adaptations for agonistic display. Man lacks the kind of structures that the other primates use in threat and agonistic display. Although the structures used in display may differ to some extent from species to species, it is remarkable that man has none – no erecting hair, colored skin, callosities, or dramatic actions of ears or scalp. The kinds of gesture that communicate threat in the nonhuman primates have been shifted to the hand (freed by bipedalism and made important by tools) and to language. The evolution of language as a more efficient method of social communication, including the communication of threat, changed the pressures on a wide variety of other structures that must have functioned in agonistic display, unless it is postulated that our ancestors were unique among mammals and lacked all such adaptations. For example, only about one-half of the behavioral items that Brown and Hunsperger (1965) list as indicating agonistic behavior are anatomically possible in man. It is particularly the kind of structures that signal threat at a distance that have been lost. But even the structures that serve in close, face-to-face social communication may have been simplified. Human facial muscles have been described as more complex than those of the apes, making more elaborate expressions possible, but this is surely a misreading of the anatomical evidence and there is no evidence that the facial muscles of a chimpanzee are less complicated than those of man. Certainly the chimpanzee's mouth is more mobile and expressive, and a much wider variety of mouth expressions are possible in an ape than in man.

If we read the evidence correctly, in man language replaces the agonistic displays of nonhuman primates, and it opens the way to the existence of a social system in which aggressive behavior is not constantly rewarded. As noted earlier, in the societies of monkeys and apes dominance is the key to social order. Even if the dominance system of a group is not a rigid one, individuals in protecting young, gaining access to food, sex, grooming, or social position often threaten, and the threat – or, rarely, actual aggression – is rewarded with the acquisition of the desired goal. Agonistic behavior is an essential element in the day-to-day behavior of monkeys and apes, and language removes the necessity of rewarding this kind of aggressive behavior.

Just as the changed selection that came with tools led to increase in the parts of the brain controlling manual skills and to reduction in the whole tooth-fighting complex, so the origin of language led to changes in parts of the brain (Lancaster, 1968) and to a reduction or loss of most structures concerned with displays. In this sense the human body is in part a product of language and of the complex social life that language made possible. Similarly, the emotions of man have evolved in a way that permits him to participate in complex social life (Hamburg, 1963). We think it is probable that individuals with uncontrollable rage reactions were killed and that, over many thousands of years, there was selection for temperaments compatible with moderately complex social situations. This process may have been somewhat like the early stages of domestication that involved the removal of socially impossible individuals, rather than the breeding of animals according to any plan. It is a fact that the human adrenals are relatively small compared to those of nonhuman primates and in this way man differs from the ape as domestic rats do from wild rats.

The expression of the emotions in man is more complex than in nonhuman primates, and, although emphasizing the continuity of the biological nature of aggressive behavior, we do not forget the remarkable differences. Compared with the ape or monkey, all the association areas of the human brain have undergone a three-fold increase in size. These are the areas particularly concerned with the ability to remember, to plan, and to inhibit inappropriate action. The increase in these areas is probably the result of new selection pressures that came with the evolution of more complex forms of social life, and is probably highly related to the evolution of language which made the new ways of life possible. Taken together the new parts of the association areas and the parts of the brain making language possible might be thought of as the "social brain" – the parts of the brain that (from an evolutionary point of view) evolved in response to social pressures and the parts that today mediate appropriate social action. This concept is consistent with the fact that degeneration in these parts leads to senile dementia, the inability of some old people to continue normal social life – to remember, to plan, and to keep actions appropriate to time and place. However, the social world in which the human brain and emotions evolved was very different from the present one.

Throughout most of human history (at least 600,000 years, if by "man" we mean the genus *Homo*, large-brained creatures who made complex tools, hunted big animals, and at least some of whom used fire), our ancestors lived in small groups, and (as evidenced by the ethnographic literature, archeology, and the behavior of the nonhuman primates) males were expected to hunt and to fight, and to find these activities pleasurable. Freeman (1964) has given us an anthropological perspective on aggression; the record of war, torture, and planned destruction is exceedingly impressive. Most of the behaviors are so repugnant to our present beliefs and values that people do not want to consider them; in spite of the vast number of courses offered in the modern university, usually there is none on war, and aggression is treated only incidentally in a few courses. As ordinarily taught, history is expurgated, and the historian considers the treaties that were never kept rather than the actual experiences of war.

The situation relative to human aggression can be briefly stated under three headings. First, man has been a predator for a long time and his nature is such that he easily learns to enjoy killing other animals. Hunting is still considered a sport, and millions of dollars are spent annually to provide birds, mammals, and fish to be killed for the amusement of sportsmen. In many cultures animals are killed for the amusement of human observers (in bullfighting, cockfighting, bear baiting, and so forth). Second, man easily learns to enjoy torturing and killing other human beings. Whether one considers the Roman arena, public tortures and executions, or the sport of boxing, it is clear that humans have developed means to enjoy the sight of others being subjected to punishment. Third, war has been regarded as glorious and, whether one considers recent data from tribes in New Guinea or the behavior of the most civilized nations, until very recently war was a normal instrument of national policy and there was no revulsion from the events of victorious warfare, no matter how destructive. Aggression between man and animals, between man and man, and between groups of men has been encouraged by custom, learned in play, and rewarded by society. Man's nature evolved under those conditions, and many men still seek personal dominance and national territory through aggression.

The consequence of this evolutionary history is that large-scale human destruction may appear at any time social controls break down; recent examples are Nazi Germany, Algeria, the Congo, Vietnam. Further, it must be remembered that the customs governing our lives evolved in the era when killing animals for fun, the brutal torture of human beings, and war were opposed by few. It is not only our bodies that are primitive, but also our customs, which are not adapted to the crowded and technical world that is dominated by a fantastic acceleration of scientific knowledge. Traditional customs nurtured aggression and frequently continue to do so.

The view that man is aggressive because of his evolutionary past, because of his biological nature, seems pessimistic to some, but we agree with Freeman that if aggression is to be controlled in a way compatible with survival and the realities of the new world of science, "it is only by facing the realities of man's nature and of our extraordinary history as a genus that we shall be able to evolve methods likely, in some measure, to succeed." (1964:116)

The situation might be compared to that of a bank. It is desirable to have employees who are honest people who will abide by the bank's customs. But no bank would rely solely on the honesty of its employees. The best auditing and accounting devices are used to make it virtually impossible for the human element to disrupt the functions of the institution. But on the international scene no comparable institutions for accounting and auditing exist, and reliance is still placed on the judgment of leaders and the customs of states. But these states have used war as a normal instrument of policy, their customs have glorified war, and all history shows that nothing in the human leader will necessarily restrain him from war if he sees success as probable. There is a fundamental difficulty in the fact that contemporary human groups are led by primates whose evolutionary history dictates, through both biological and social transmission, a strong dominance orientation. Attempts to build interindividual relations, or international relations, on the wishful basis that people will not be aggressive is as futile as it would be to try to build the institution of banking with no auditing on the basis that all employees will be honest.

In summary, in Old World monkeys and apes aggression is an essential adaptive mechanism. It is an important factor in determining interindividual relations; it is frequent; and successful aggression is highly rewarded. It is a major factor in intergroup relations, and the importance of aggression as a species-spacing mechanism means that aggression is most frequent between groups of the same species. Both within groups and between groups aggression is an integral part of dominance, feeding, and reproduction. The biological basis of aggressive behaviors is complex, including parts of the brain, hormones, muscles-teeth-jaws, and structures of display; successful aggression has been a major factor in primate evolution.

Man inherits the biological base, modified by the great development of the social brain and language. Aggression may be increased by early experience, play, and the rewards of the social system. The individual's aggressive actions are determined by biology and experience. But an aggressive species living by prescientific customs in a scientifically advanced world will pay a tremendous price in interindividual conflict and international war.

References

Altman, J. 1966. *Organic Foundations of Animal Behavior.* New York: Holt, Rinehart and Winston, Inc.

Beach, F. A. 1965. *Sex and Behavior.* New York: Wiley.

Beeman, E. A. 1947. The effect of male hormone on aggressive behavior in mice, *Physiological Zoology,* 20(4):373-405.

Brown, J. L., and Hunsperger, R. W. 1965. Neuroethology and the motivation of agonistic behavior. *Readings in Animal Behavior,* ed. T. E. McGill. New York: Holt, Rinehart and Winston, Inc., pp. 148-161.

Carpenter, C. R. 1934. A field study of the behavior and social relations of howling monkeys *(Alouatta palliata), Comp. Psychol. Monogr.,* 10(2):1-168.

_____. 1940. A field study in Siam of the behavior and social relations of the gibbon *(Hylobates lar), Comp. Psychol. Monogr.,* 16(5):1-212.

_____. 1964. *Naturalistic behavior of nonhuman primates.* University Park, Pa.: Pennsylvania State Univ. Press.

Carthy, J. D., and Ebling, F. J., eds. 1964. *The Natural History of Aggression.* New York: Academic Press.

Collias, N. E. 1944. Aggressive behavior among vertebrate animals, *Physio. Zool.,* 17:83-123.

Corner, G. W. 1942. *The Hormones in Human Reproduction.* Princeton, N.J.: Princeton Univ. Press.

Delgado, J. M. R. 1967. Aggression and defense under cerebral radio control. *Aggression and Defense,* ed. C. D. Clemente and D. B. Lindsley. Berkeley and Los Angeles: Univ. of California Press, pp. 171-193.

DeVore, I., and Hall, K. R. L. 1965. Baboon ecology. *Primate Behavior: Field Studies of Monkeys and Apes,* ed. I. DeVore. New York: Holt, Rinehart and Winston, Inc., pp. 20-52.

Ellefson, J. O. 1968. Territorial behavior in the common white-handed gibbon. *Primates,* ed. Phyllis C. Jay. Holt, Rinehart and Winston, Inc., pp. 180-199.

Freeman, D. 1964. Human aggression in anthropological perspective. *The Natural History of Aggression,* ed. J. D. Carthy and F. J. Ebling. New York: Academic Press, pp. 109-119.

Gartlan, J. S., and Brain, C. K. 1968. Ecology and social variability in *Cercopithecus aethiops* and *C. mitis. Primates,* ed. Phyllis C. Jay. Holt, Rinehart and Winston, Inc., pp. 253-292.

Goodall, J. 1965. Chimpanzees of the Gombe Stream Reserve. *Primate Behavior: Field Studies of Monkeys and Apes,* ed. I. DeVore. New York: Holt, Rinehart and Winston, Inc., pp. 425-473.

Hall, K. R. L. 1964. Aggression in monkey and ape societies. *The Natural History of Aggression,* ed. J. D. Carthy and F. J. Ebling. New York: Academic Press, pp. 51-64.

Hall, K. R. L., and DeVore, I. 1965. Baboon social behavior. *Primate Behavior: Field Studies of Monkeys and Apes,* ed. I. DeVore. New York: Holt, Rinehart and Winston, Inc., pp. 53-110.

Hamburg, D. A. 1963. Emotion in the perspective of human evolution. *Expression of the Emotions in Man,* ed. P. Knapp. New York: International Universities, pp. 300-317.

Harlow, H. F., and Harlow, M. K. 1965. The affectional systems. *Behavior of Nonhuman Primates,* Vol. II, ed. A. M. Schrier, H. F. Harlow, and F. Stollnitz. New York: Academic Press, pp. 287-334.

Harris, G. 1964. Sex hormones, brain development and brain function, *Endocrin.,* 75:627-648.

Hinde, R. A., and Tinbergen, N. 1958. The comparative study of species-specific behavior. *Behavior and Evolution,* ed. A. Roe and G. G. Simpson. New Haven: Yale University Press, pp. 251-268.

Jay, P. C. 1965a. Field studies. *Behavior of Nonhuman Primates,* ed. A. M. Schrier, H. F. Harlow, and F. Stollnitz. New York: Academic Press, pp. 525-591.

____. 1965b. The common langur of North India. *Primate Behavior: Field Studies of Monkeys and Apes,* ed. I. DeVore. New York: Holt, Rinehart and Winston, Inc., pp. 197-249.

Koford, C. 1966. Population changes in rhesus monkeys, 1960-1965, *Tul. Studies in Zool.,* 13:1-7.

Kourilsky, R., Soulairac, A., and Grapin, P. 1965. *Adaptation et Aggressivité.* Paris: Presses Universitaires de France.

Kummer, H. J. 1968. Two variations in the social organization of baboons. *Primates,* ed. Phyllis C. Jay. Holt, Rinehart and Winston, Inc., pp. 293-312.

Lancaster, J. B. 1968. Primate communication systems and the emergence of human language. *Primates,* ed. Phyllis C. Jay. Holt, Rinehart and Winston, Inc., pp. 439-457.

Levine, S., and Mullins, R. F., Jr. 1966. Hormonal influences on brain organization in infant rats, *Science,* 152:1585-1592.

Lorenz, K. Z. 1964. Ritualized fighting. *The Natural History of Aggression,* ed. J. D. Carthy and F. J. Ebling. New York: Academic Press, pp. 39-50.

____. 1966. *On Aggression.* New York: Harcourt.

MacLean, P. D. 1963. Phylogenesis. *Expression of the Emotions in Man,* ed. P. Knapp. New York: International Universities, pp. 16-35.

Marler, P. 1968. Aggregation and dispersal: two functions in primate communication. *Primates,* ed. Phyllis C. Jay. Holt, Rinehart and Winston, Inc., pp. 420-438.

McGill, T. E., ed. 1965. *Readings in Animal Behavior.* New York: Holt, Rinehart and Winston, Inc.

Nalbandov, A. V. 1964. *Reproductive Physiology.* San Francisco: W. H. Freeman.

Noback, C. R., and Moskowitz, N. 1963. The primate nervous system: functional and structural aspects in phylogeny. *Evolutionary and Genetic Biology of Primates,* Vol. I, ed. J. Buettner-Janusch. New York: Academic Press, pp. 131-177.

Prechtl, H. F. R. 1965. Problems of behavioral studies in the newborn infant. *Advances in the Study of Behavior,* ed. D. S. Lehrman, R. A. Hinde, and E. Shaw. New York: Academic Press, pp. 75-98.

Rapoport, A. 1966. Models of conflict: cataclysmic and strategic. *Conflict in Society,* ed. A. de Reuck and J. Knight. Boston: Little, Brown, pp. 259-287.

Reynolds, V., and Reynolds, F. 1965. Chimpanzees in the Budongo Forest. *Primate Behavior: Field Studies of Monkeys and Apes,* ed. I. DeVore. New York: Holt, Rinehart and Winston, Inc., pp. 368-424.

Ripley, Suzanne. 1967. Intertroop encounters among Ceylon gray langurs, *Presbytis entellus. Social Communication among Primates,* ed. S. A. Altmann, Chicago: Univ. of Chicago Press, pp. 237-253.

Rosenblum, L. A. 1961. The development of social behavior in the rhesus monkey, unpublished Ph.D. thesis, University of Wisconsin.

Sade, D. S. 1965. Some aspects of parent-offspring and sibling relations in a group of rhesus monkeys, with a discussion of grooming, *Amer. J. Phys. Anthrop.,* 23:1-17.

____. 1966. Ontogeny of social relations in a free-ranging group of rhesus monkeys, unpublished Ph.D. thesis, University of California, Berkeley.

Schaller, G. B. 1963. *The Mountain Gorilla: Ecology and Behavior.* Chicago: Univ. of Chicago Press.

Schein, M. W., and Hale, E. B. 1965. The effect of early social experience on male sexual behaviour of androgen injected turkeys. *Readings in Animal Behavior,* ed. T. E. McGill. New York: Holt, Rinehart and Winston, Inc., pp. 314-329.

Scott, J. P. 1958. *Aggression.* Chicago: University of Chicago Press.

____. 1962. Hostility and aggression in animals. *Roots of Behavior,* ed. E. L. Bliss. New York: Harper, pp. 167-178.

Simonds, P. E. 1965. The bonnet macaque in South India. *Primate Behavior: Field Studies of Monkeys and Apes,* ed. I. DeVore. New York: Holt, Rinehart and Winston, Inc., pp. 175-196.

Simpson, G. G. 1964. *This View of Life.* New York: Harcourt.

Southwick, C. H., Beg, M. A., and Siddiqi, M. R. 1965. Rhesus monkeys in North India. *Primate Behavior: Field Studies of Monkeys and Apes,* ed. I. DeVore. New York: Holt, Rinehart and Winston, Inc., pp. 111-159.

Struhsaker, T. T. 1965. Behavior of the vervet monkey (*Cercopithecus aethiops*), unpublished Ph.D. thesis, University of California, Berkeley.

Washburn, S. L. 1966. Conflict in primate society. *Conflict in Society,* ed. A. de Reuck and J. Knight. Boston: Little, Brown, pp. 3-15.

Washburn, S. L., and Hamburg, D. A. 1965. The implications of primate research. *Primate Behavior: Field Studies of Monkeys and Apes,* ed. I. DeVore. New York: Holt, Rinehart and Winston, Inc., pp. 607-622.

Washburn, S. L., and Jay, P. 1965. The evolution of human nature, unpub. paper presented at the Amer. Anthrop. Assoc. Meeting, Denver, Nov. 19, 1965.

Wynne-Edwards, V. C. 1965. Selfregulating systems in populations of animals, *Science,* 147: 1543-1548.

Yamada, M. 1963. A study of blood-relationship in the natural society of the Japanese macaque, *Primates,* 4:43-65.

Yoshiba, K. 1968. Local and intertroop variability in ecology and social behavior of common Indian langurs. *Primates,* ed. Phyllis C. Jay. Holt, Rinehart and Winston, Inc., pp. 217-242.

Young, W., Goy, R., and Phoenix, C. 1964. Hormones and sexual behavior, *Science,* 143:212-218.

6

Recent evidence on the evolution of aggressive behavior

David A. Hamburg

Why study animals if we wish to understand man? We do this primarily to obtain an evolutionary perspective in which we hope to percieve how man came to be the way he is, and to search for subtle legacies of his ancient past that may be carried with him through both biological and social transmission. We deal mainly with broad trends in evolution – asking whether certain characteristics of vertebrate, mammalian, and primate organisms are maintained or may even become more prominent as we come closer to man. If we find certain characteristics that appear to be especially important in the adaptation of man's closest relatives, then we must look in man to see whether these characteristics are present in him, too, albeit in some complex and obscure way. Such a search also tends to highlight man's distinctive and even unique features, such as language.

Animal behavior may be investigated not only in the laboratory, but also in artificial colonies or in natural habitats. The kinds of information gleaned from each setting are complementary, and all are necessary if the complex roots of behavior are ever to be understood.

Despite recent interest in the subject, very few field studies of primate behavior have focused primarily on aggressiveness. For this reason Eric Hamburg and I undertook a brief field study of aggressive behavior in chimpanzees and baboons in East Africa. We were very fortunate in getting more than 200 hours of close-range observation.

SOURCE: Reprinted from *Engineering and Science* magazine, Volume 33, No. 6 (April 1970). Published at the California Institute of Technology. Reprinted by permission of the author and the publisher.

We also had generous access to the files of the unique chimpanzee study in Tanzania conducted by Jane Goodall since 1960. With help from her and from another experienced field worker, Phyllis Jay Dolhinow of Berkeley working in Kenya, we acquired a good deal of data on aggressive behavior in the two species.

By aggressive behavior, in this context, we mean threat and attack patterns. We try to describe such patterns, the conditions under which they are likely to occur, and the circumstances in which they are likely to be diminished or terminated, particularly by means of interanimal communication. We chose chimpanzees because they are man's closest living relatives. Their social behavior is as close to that of man as we can find in nature.

Goodall's study is already a classic. She has described a remarkable repertoire of closely linked, usually sequential classes of behavior – aggression, submission, reassurance – with a rich variety of patterns within each class. The similarity of many of these patterns to those of humans is more impressive than the similarity of such patterns in any other nonhuman primate species.

What are the conditions under which the threat and attack patterns occur in chimps? From Goodall's observations and our own, I would summarize them briefly this way:

1. Competition over food, especially that which is highly desirable, spatially concentrated, or in short supply;
2. Defense of an infant by its mother;
3. A contest over dominance prerogatives of two individuals of similar social rank;
4. Redirection of aggression – that is, downward in the hierarchy (such as when a low-ranking male, who has been attacked by a high-ranking male, turns to attack an individual in turn subordinate to him);
5. A failure of one animal to comply with a signal given by the aggressor;
6. Strange appearance of another chimp – for example, one whose lower extremities became paralyzed during a poliomyelitis outbreak;
7. Change in dominance status over a period of time, especially among males;
8. The formation of consort pairs at the peak of estrus. In the early part of estrus, when the female first becomes sexually receptive in each cycle, she copulates very freely with many males, including some of the older infants. But as she reaches the peak of estrus, she goes into a consort pair with one of the highly dominant males, and they go off together for some time (a few hours for baboons, about a week for chimps).

Goodall also reported recently on the development of aggressive patterns during the early years of life. For example, a ten-month-old male infant has been filmed by Hugo van Lawick showing typical threatening gestures in a context similar to those of an adult threat. These early aggressive patterns are much more characteristic of males than of females – and this is true of a great many primate species. Kinship is also important in the development of such behavior. A juvenile may threaten or attack chimps older than itself provided that its mother is near and that the mother's rank is higher than that of the victim. Adolescent males are often aggressive toward females when no higher ranking males are present, but they apparently restrain such behavior toward females when dominant males are present. As adolescent males mature, they tend to threaten the lowest ranking mature males and so gain admittance to the hierarchy of adult males. In general, adolescence is a turbulent, aggressive period among these chimpanzees.

The chimp community we studied at the Gombe Stream consists of about 50 animals. They live in a forested valley with open woodland high up. Over the ridges on both sides there are other groups of chimps. Very little is known about their contacts with the communities on the other sides, although such information as is available indicates that contact, when it does occur, is pretty tense.

Our chimp community breaks up in subgroups, most commonly three to eight animals, and sometimes even individual animals for short periods. Composition is rather fluid, although there are certain enduring groups such as the unit of a mother and one or more of her offspring.

One of the characteristics of aggressive display by adult male chimps is that their hair stands out, making the animals look bigger and more impressive. As part of the display a male may drag a palm frond, brandish it over his head as he runs, swing it, or even throw it at somebody.

An adult male who has been away from his particular subgroup for a day usually puts on one of these aggressive displays when he returns. It is very interesting that something like a decay of familiarity seems to occur in many primate species; a brief absence elicits patterns that one sees in more full-blown form with total strangers.

We observed and photographed behavior suggesting that "technical ingenuity" in aggressive displays may be a significant part of dominance behavior in chimps. Three years prior to our study, a large can had been left outside by the research workers. One of the males, named Mike, had at that time incorporated it in his display. He ran at it, hit it, started it rolling, and chased it. This action had a tremendous effect on the other chimps, and he very rapidly became the most dominant male – with much less fighting than is typically the case in dominance changes of this kind. Evidently there was nothing in chimp evolution to prepare them for the kinds of sights and sounds that he created with such displays. Three years later – with no intervening episode – we put the can back outside. We were curious about whether he would respond, and how long it would take him. It took him less than ten seconds from the time the can was put down on the ground to the time he took off after it and put on a similar display. All eight other animals within observation at the time ran off into the forest or went up trees. One young male climbed 40 feet and remained in the tree for eight minutes.

Bananas are made available from time to time as a very attractive dietary supplement for both chimpanzees and baboons in the area. These are tense occasions when a good deal of threatening goes on between males of similar rank. What happens typically is that one of them will break off prior to fighting (usually high-ranking males do not fight each other) and attack a smaller, weaker, or less mobile animal. We saw one of those adult males attacking a mother with a ten-month-old infant clinging to her, giving her a severe beating, mainly with his fists and forearm. He did this to the same mother-infant pair three times within a week in these situations of redirected aggression. On one occasion he actually knocked them out of a tree from a height of about 30 feet. Thus, the infant, though generally treated with great tolerance, is not always immune in these episodes of redirected aggression.

After a dominant male has established his control of the bananas, other chimps may try to get him to share with them. An experienced female, for example, may back up to him in a lowered posture. This is called presenting, and it is common in a number of primates in agonistic situations. After she gets up to him, he may put his arm around her waist and give her a hug or a pat on the head.

In the same situation a female might approach with arm extended, palm up, "fear-face," and making a very distinctive panting sound. The approach is ambivalent – three steps forward, two back, three forward, two back. It may take several minutes to cover about 30 feet. Again, he may pat her, and sometimes permit her to take a bit of banana.

In the middle of the day, even after a very tense, agonistic morning, a group of animals tends to seek proximity. They have the whole valley to choose from, but they seek out each other's company and move in close to each other for a rest.

The most organized hunting pattern known in any nonhuman primate has been described in the Gombe Stream area. Typically, this occurs when an infant baboon (or colobus monkey) gets isolated up a tree. One adult male chimp goes up after it, and two or three other chimps surround the base of the tree to fight off any adult male baboon who tries to defend that infant. If the chimps catch the infant, the male in the tree and the next one up will tear it apart, and two or three of these high-ranking males will begin to eat it immediately. There is enormous excitement as other chimps arrive and beg in the most extreme way for just a tiny bit. But if the same kind of animal is put out – freshly killed for experimental purposes – there is nothing like the excitement induced when they do their own killing, and they do not eat the carcass.

At the same time as chimp-chimp interactions are occurring, the chimps and baboons are contesting too, as for example when we made bananas available after about a week's absence. The two species clearly know each other well; the chimps are generally dominant over the baboons in this setting. Members of both species were anxious to get the bananas. Two highly dominant chimps, Mike and Goliath, got them most often. It was common to see an adult male baboon giving Mike a strong threat – a display of his canine teeth. Other male baboons join in the fray. The baboon technique is one of harassment, and they may keep up the pressure for a couple of hours. Now and again they get a banana peel, but not much more.

Despite a few baboon threats, Mike appeared to be so relaxed that he stretched out with a pile of bananas right by his belly. The baboons, smaller then the chimps but with enormous canine teeth, kept close by, frequently threatening. As they persisted in this menacing behavior, Mike's relaxation disappeared. He gathered up a bunch of bananas, put them on his lap, and sat on one of the banana boxes. (Often, if a banana is put down momentarily, a baboon will dash in close and grab for it and then dash away again.)

Finally, after about five minutes more, a baboon broke off and attacked an adult female chimp rather than one of the male chimps he had been threatening. She went up the tree, as fast as she could, and he went after her. Once in the tree she started striking down with her fist and hit him on the snout; and he came back down bleeding. No male made any effort to defend her, although in similar situations there is a good chance that a male would come to an infant's defense.

Infants, of course, eventually learn to defend themselves, and we observed one way they learn. We saw an older infant chimp (in the company of another chimp) wielding a ten-foot palm frond like a baseball bat against an adult male baboon that could certainly kill the infant in an isolated situation. He hit the baboon with good accuracy, and chased him off into the forest. What's interesting is that for two years this infant observed two older siblings in exactly this kind of behavior. Both older siblings were quite skillful in using palm fronds as weapons. The infant practiced that behavior initially in the most clumsy way after observing them at length, and he eventually perfected the skill at age 4, which is still a very young chimp. (They do not fully mature until 10 or 12.)

It is often said that the cues in all species but man are so clear and sharp that aggressive interactions can be fine-tuned so that serious injury hardly ever occurs. This is largely correct, but there's a tendency to exaggerate the point. When evidence of serious injury has been looked for systematically in recent primate field studies, it has been found to be rather more common. The cues that limit aggression usually work, but not always.

Grooming – taking the fingers and lips and going down through the hair to the skin in a deliberate, repeated way – is an important behavior pattern in limiting aggression. The high-ranking males get groomed a lot, but they tend to groom others rather less. In any case, grooming seems to have some kind of tension-relieving effect, whatever other hygienic functions it may have. Similarly, an experienced female can sometimes calm an excited, aggressive male by touching his scrotum.

Baboons are also present in the forest habitat. We wanted to compare these forest baboons with baboons living in a savanna (plains) habitat.

There are several reasons to study baboons. One is the adaptive process of the closely related baboon-macaque group, which has spread widely through Asia and Africa and a variety of habitats. Another is that the baboons are the largest of all the monkeys. A third reason is that they have a relatively great ground-living capability in a type of habitat, the savanna, that was probably crucial in the emergence of early man. These savanna-dwelling baboons spend much more time in open country at a distance from trees than the chimps do. Based mainly on the extensive field work of Irven DeVore (Harvard), the late K. R. L. Hall, Sherwood Washburn, and Tim Ransom (Berkeley), plus our own observations, we can summarize the conditions under which baboon threat and attack patterns are likely to occur:

1. Protection of the troop by adult males against predators, such as lions and cheetahs;
2. Protection of infants, both by their mothers and by adult males;
3. Resolution of severe fighting within the troop by adult males;
4. Formation and maintenance of consort pairs at the peak of estrus;
5. Attainment of preferred sleeping sites in the trees, particularly in the presence of predators;
6. Acquisition of premium foods, such as figs, nuts, and bananas, especially when these foods are spatially concentrated rather than widely distributed;
7. Dominance interactions, especially in the presence of premium food, or scarcity of sleeping sites, or females in full estrus;
8. Exploration of strange or manifestly dangerous areas, which is a function largely of adult males;
9. Contact between different troops, especially if such contact is infrequent.

The baboons' habitat has tall grass in which predators can readily hide, so the problem of predator pressure is very different there than it is in the forest habitat.

To observe the baboons, we followed a troop of 42 animals of both sexes and all ages, who have spent their lifetimes together. It's largely a closed social system, but there is some transfer of males between troops.

At one point the troop met with a lioness hunting. When she appeared, 39 of the 42 animals broke for the nearest trees – about a half mile away – while three adult males stood their ground. And so, in a moment, there was a phalanx of adult males flashing those impressive canine teeth interposed between the lioness and the rest of the troop. This is a case where social organization clearly meets a survival requirement.

Most of the threat and attack behavior on the part of the female is elicited by some kind of interference with her infant; but both males and females will very stoutly defend an infant, especially if the infant is giving a distress call.

The two most dominant males in the troop, Alpha and Beta, rarely got into real fighting. Ordinarily they stayed 100 yards apart at opposite ends of the troop. Their only serious quarrels arose over premium foods.

An older infant we called Torn Ear spent much of his day observing Alpha, and he enjoyed Alpha's protection. Torn Ear was perfectly free to threaten much larger baboons with impunity as long as Alpha was nearby. Torn Ear was also much bolder about approaching us than any other infant, again with Alpha nearby. He observed, he imitated, and he often practiced what he imitated of Alpha's behavior. This observational learning in a social context seems to be the principal mode of learning for the nonhuman primates.

Since various biological indices suggest a rather close relation of man with chimpanzee and gorilla, it is interesting to note several patterns of aggression that are especially prominent in one or both of these species. We mention three.

First, both chimp and gorilla show more elaborate aggressive displays than any other primate species. This rich repertoire of threatening actions might well be called intimidation display. Patterns of submission and reassurance also seem to be more elaborate in these species than in other primates, and more similar to those of man.

Second, in chimpanzees, technology (if I may call it that) is more advanced than anything observed elsewhere among nonhuman primates. Simple tools are made according to an established tradition and are used effectively. Both spherical and cylindrical naturally occurring objects are used in threat and attack, sometimes with considerable efficacy.

Third, attachments based on kinship strongly influence behavior over a large part of the chimp's life, quite possibly all of it. Among other influences, kinship attachments may well serve to increase threats directed toward animals that are not part of the kinship subgroup, and also protection of the offspring's aggressive ventures in early life by the mother and probably by older siblings as well.

Research workers in the field of bird and rodent behavior have studied various environmental conditions that elicit threat and attack patterns. Among them is the crowding of strangers, especially in the presence of valued resources such as food, sex, or nesting locations.

Is this also true of primates? Does the conjunction of these three conditions become an especially powerful instigation to aggression? Our observations of chimps and baboons lead us tentatively to answer yes to these questions, supporting the recent observations of other workers who have conducted studies of primates in natural habitats and in seminatural settings and laboratory experiments.

At Holloman Air Force Base in New Mexico, the Wilsons have observed chimps in a desert compound. When an animal was taken out of the group for a few days, even though he was quite well integrated into it earlier, he was very likely to be attacked when he was put back.

At Stanford, Patricia Barchas has been studying aggression in newly formed rhesus-macaque monkey groups. She finds that fighting is most likely to occur in the first few minutes of their contact with each other, as the strangers are introduced, and then later when food is made available under these crowded conditions.

Southwick, working in Calcutta, has established baseline frequencies for each of 20 behaviors occurring in a social group of 17 rhesus-macaque monkeys composed of adults, juveniles, and yearlings of both sexes. After the group had stabilized, new animals were introduced from time to time in the 25- by 40-foot enclosure. New juveniles were mainly attacked by the resident juveniles; adult females were most likely to be attacked by resident females; and new adult males were attacked mainly by the adult males. For each class of introduced animals, it was found that the class whose status was threatened most directly was most active in the aggressive responses to the stranger.

Southwick also reduced the space by half to determine if crowding alone, in a familiar setting, increases fighting. It did, but modestly. At least under the conditions he used, the introduction of strangers was a more potent instigation to fighting than crowding, although both had some effect.

Generally speaking, among the baboons and a variety of other species, stable, established groups in nature tend to avoid each other, and there is a good deal of tension when they meet. However, it has recently been found in the monkey islands off Puerto Rico that some males fight their way into other groups, then later – even years later – may help a younger brother to enter that group.

Also from the Puerto Rican monkey islands comes evidence that the size of a monkey group is correlated with its dominance. In general, the smaller groups give way to larger ones. If the disparity is great, there is not likely to be more fighting, unless the resources available to them are very condensed and crowded.

Are there any general aggressive patterns common to primate species that are relatively closely related to man? We can make a tentative list of such patterns, referring not to the threat and attack patterns per se, but rather to the conditions under which they most commonly occur:

1. Dominance-submission transactions;
2. The redirection of aggression downward in the dominance hierarchy;
3. The protection of infants;
4. When sought-after resources are in concentrated or short supply – for example, premium food, or a female at the peak of estrus;
5. The meeting of relatively unfamiliar animals – which may be individuals, subgroups of an established group, or intergroup contact;
6. Defense against predators;
7. Killing and eating young animals of other species;
8. Terminating severe disputes among subordinate animals.

Factors of this sort may well have given selective advantage to aggressive primates over millions of years, providing they could regulate their aggressive behavior. Until now most of the research has focused on the sources and instigation of aggressive behavior; future work will profit from paying as much attention to the regulation and control of aggressive tendencies.

Hormonal influences upon brain organization early in life have been shown to affect later aggressive and sexual behavior. The pioneering work in the area was done with rodents. For example, brief treatment of newborn female rats with testosterone results in a lifelong abolition of female sex behavior and a tendency toward male patterns of aggressive behavior as well. That work was later extended by Young, Goy, and Phoenix to rhesus-macaque monkeys. He gave testosterone in large doses to pregnant monkeys; if the pregnant monkey was carrying a female in utero, that female was to some extent masculinized by the testosterone, both in some anatomical and in some behavioral characteristics – for example, clitoral enlargement.

The females who had been androgenized by testosterone in utero were shifted in a male-like direction: They initiated play more often, they engaged in rough-and-tumble play more often, and they threatened other animals more often than females who had not been exposed to androgens in utero.

Eight such monkeys have been followed into adult life at the Oregon Primate Center in Beaverton. These eight animals show a good deal of threatening behavior as adults, although some other measures of aggression have declined over the years under the laboratory conditions that were employed.

It is plausible that processes of this kind may have continued to operate through the long course of human evolution. But because of the extraordinary learning capacities characteristic of our species, it seems unlikely that the early exposure of brain cells to male sex hormones would establish a fixed complex response pattern for a lifetime. It seems more likely that some general orientation would be influenced by the early male hormone so that aggressive patterns are in some way attractive and readily learned.

Is there any evidence at all of similar effects in human development? John Money and his colleagues at Johns Hopkins studied more than 20 girls who had been exposed to various androgens in utero. They differ from a nonandrogenized control group in several respects. The androgenized girls tend to be described by themselves and others as tomboys; they prefer outdoor sports requiring a great deal of energy and vigor, prefer rough play, and prefer toys ordinarily chosen by boys, such as guns. These observations raise an important question and illustrate how a lot of inquiry from basic research on the biology of sex differentiation applies to an important human problem.

But surely the hormone does not act on some template for guns somewhere in the brain. How, then, could such an effect be achieved?

Recall the emphasis on observational learning in the social environment for nonhuman primates. It may be that if the attention of the young primate is drawn to one sex even somewhat preferentially over another, then a great deal of learning will follow from it, such as what kind of objects are characteristically used by members of that sex.

In nonhuman primates, and maybe in human infants and young children, we might learn something from experimental methods for analyzing the deployment of attention. It is feasible to expose isolation-reared monkeys to different kinds of stimuli to see if they prefer to look at certain kinds of stimuli rather than others. I predict, for instance, that if we gave an isolation-reared monkey the chance to look at various pictures, which included rough-and-tumble play, that males would spend more time looking at rough-and-tumble play at some stage in their early development than females would. In any case, that is testable.

Something similar to that has been done by Sackett in Harry Harlow's Wisconsin laboratory. His experimental setup consisted of isolation-rearing for nine months, during which he showed the monkeys various pictures. The pictures included both monkey and non-monkey stimuli. The first point of interest is that they spend much more time in infancy looking at the monkey stimuli than non-monkey stimuli, including pictures of people. Within the monkey stimuli, one finding is particularly interesting in the context of this discussion. A full-face threat elicited a peculiarly strong response – vocalizations and what is described as emotional disturbance. The response to the full-face threat was particularly strong between two and a half and four months of age. Something about that stimulus complex elicits a very strong, emotionally charged response in the isolation-reared monkey. So it is not difficult to imagine how an infant, once his attention has been drawn powerfully to a certain kind of behavior, would go on to learn a great deal about it.

What can we say about the role of the early social environment in shaping the development of aggressive behavior? I have touched on it already, and Harlow and Suomi (1970)* have presented some relevant material. The isolation-reared animals that he talked about are generally highly fearful and prone to outbursts of violence. Also, the infants who experienced brutality from their motherless mothers were themselves significantly more aggressive during the eight months they were studied than were the infants raised by normal mothers.

Lately the isolation-reared primates have been followed to see what happens several years later – at puberty, adolescence, and adulthood. In at least some of the work coming out of the Wisconsin laboratories, it looks as if the aggressiveness does not spontaneously decline with the passage of years after the monkeys are brought out of isolation. Indeed, for some the aberrant behavior becomes more pronounced later in life. Perhaps the onset of puberty is partially responsible for this later exacerbation in males. It may be no coincidence that the onset of puberty in males is associated with a sharp rise in circulating testosterone levels and with heightened aggressiveness. Several of the recent field studies of primate species have shown striking behavioral changes at adolescence, which presumably depend, at least in part, on the hormonal changes in the males.

Lately developmental psychologists have been calling attention to the importance of observational learning in young children. The child between one and two years of age is a devoted watcher; observation and imitation may well be the principal modes of learning at that age. If the primate ethological studies are going to have a stimulating impact on human research, I think it would be particularly on studies of infancy and early childhood. In fact, McGraw in Edinburgh recently published a study of young children in which he applied quite directly the agonistic categories from field studies of nonhuman primates and found they worked quite well.

There is also the major line of inquiry that Bandura and his colleagues have conducted at Stanford over some years with three- to five-year-old children on susceptibility of children to learning aggressive patterns by viewing models who act aggressively. For example, in one experiment preschool children were exposed to a model attacking a target for only ten minutes in a laboratory situation; a control group

*Harry F. Harlow and Stephen J. Suomi, "Induced psychopathology in monkeys," *Engineering and Science* 33:8-14.

experienced the same situation without an aggressive model. When the children were tested in the same situation six months later, those who had witnessed the attack were much more aggressive toward the target object than were the others. A ten-minute exposure enhanced physical aggressiveness in the same situation six months later.

In general, biological predispositions to learning aggressive patterns and exposure to specific social learning situations may interact to produce great individual differences in aggressiveness during later life. In analyzing such problems, the effective conjunction of biological and psychosocial disciplines, so far rarely achieved, holds much promise for future understanding. It hardly seems necessary to point out the aggressive tendencies of the human species today. Whatever adaptive functions such behavior may have served in man's evolutionary past, there is serious question about its utility in comtemporary society. The risks inherent in such behavior have been greatly amplified within our own lifetime, and yet these problems at present attract only a modest amount of attention in the scientific community. It is difficult to imagine a more important area for research in the future. Let us hope that the biological and behavioral sciences in the next decade will really pursue these problems, which are so poignant in their human impact, so urgently in need of solution, and so pertinent to the concerns of our time.

7

The nature of aggression

Robert A. Hinde

Understanding a society requires knowledge both of how individuals interact with each other to produce it, and also of how the society influences the nature of the individuals developing within it. These are matters on which biologists and comparative psychologists both have something to say. Unfortunately the very diversity of animals and their societies creates a difficulty. It is too easy to select examples from subhuman species to support any particular view of human society; if you put your blind eye to the microscope you can use ant societies to support democracy, totalitarianism, capitalism, communism, or any other system you like. Furthermore, it is easy for the sociologist, the respectability of whose discipline has perhaps not yet gained general acceptance, to forget that biology, and indeed all worthwhile sciences, also still have their problems: not all data are secure, not all interpretations universally accepted.

These dangers are nowhere more marked than in the study of man's aggressiveness; much light can be thrown on it from studies of lower species if – but only if – they are used with humility and discipline. In his recent book, *On Aggression,* Konrad Lorenz – whose familiarity with the behaviour of animals under natural conditions is surpassed by few – used his knowledge of animals to draw conclusions about aggression in man, and to suggest how it can be controlled.

Since his thesis implies acceptance that man's aggressive tendency is virtually unmodifiable, neglects the possibility of improvement in our methods of child rearing,

---

SOURCE: *New Society,* Volume 9, No. 233 (1967). This article was first published in *New Society,* the weekly review of the social sciences, 128 Long Acre, London. Reprinted by permission of the author and the publisher.

and advocates the already popular occupations of sport, art, and science as a solution, it has found a wide audience. Is it well substantiated?

Lorenz's main line of argument is as follows. First, he rejects any equation between aggression and the "non-biological" Freudian death wish. Aggression, he says, is a product of natural selection, bringing increased chances of survival or successful reproduction under natural conditions. The advantage of aggression may lie in the dispersal of individuals so that the available resources are used in the best way possible, or in ensuring that it is the fittest individuals which breed. Fighting may also be useful if it promotes a stable "pecking order" (or social ranking system), and this in its turn may lead to the older and wiser individuals in a group becoming its leaders. The aggression that Lorenz chiefly writes about is "intra-specific" – i.e., it occurs *within* a particular animal species, not between this species and another.

Internal drives

Lorenz argues that aggression, like other "instinctive" patterns of behaviour, is spontaneous. In other words his theory of motivation, like the Freudian one, ascribes the occurrence of behaviour to the building up of an internal drive or drives which must somehow find expression.

If aggressiveness is of adaptive advantage in some contexts, it is disadvantageous in others. The establishment of a territory and aggressiveness directed towards rivals may increase a male's chances of successful breeding, but aggressiveness towards his own mate would decrease them. Devices have therefore been evolved to reduce inappropriate intra-specific aggression. The aggression aroused by a sex partner may be redirected onto a rival male, or inhibited by a submissive posture adopted by the mate. Postures which serve to reduce or deflect aggression in such contexts may, in Lorenz's view, come to be ends in their own right, rituals to be performed for their own sake. In some species they have given rise to complex ritual ceremonies which not only reduce aggression but also enhance personal ties between individuals.

Indeed Lorenz points out that personal ties occur *only* in species which show intra-specific aggression. In many gregarious species, such as shoaling fish and swarming insects, individuals lack aggressiveness towards each other, and also show no particular attachments. Since, in some species, individual bonds seem to arise from the performance of a movement or ceremony whose primitive function was to reduce aggression, Lorenz implies that aggressiveness lies at the basis of personal love.

Man, like most other animals, has evolved a drive towards intra-specific aggression. But since he lacks formidable natural weapons, Lorenz thinks, he has never evolved effective mechanisms for reducing or diverting inappropriate aggressiveness. Almost overnight he has invented the axe, the arrow, and the atom bomb, with no time for natural selection to produce mechanisms similar to those which prevent harmful intra-specific aggression in those lower species which are equipped with claws, canines, or other powerful weapons. And he lives in a society which provides little opportunity for the useful or harmless display of his natural aggressiveness.

Sudden danger

Here, then, in Lorenz's view, lies the problem. Man's spontaneous aggressive drive, evolved through natural selection and originally valuable for survival or reproduction, has suddenly become dangerous. What can be done? Before one can consider the solutions which Lorenz offers, one must ask what support his formulation would gain among biologists.

I don't want to become enmeshed in parochial arguments. Many biologists would require Lorenz to state more precisely what he means by aggression. Often he seems to slide from the narrow biological meaning of aggressiveness, indicating patterns of behaviour associated with attack or a readiness to attack another individual, to a broader, perhaps more psychiatric, meaning which includes competitiveness and self-assertiveness. Biologists would also query his happy leaps from fish to man, and many would certainly wonder at the discrepancies between the authorities cited and the bibliography. But these are perhaps minor matters in the present context, more than outweighed by the vividness of his descriptions and the wealth of his observations. There are, however, other crucial points in Lorenz's exposition on which biological opinion would be at least divided. Since Lorenz claims that his facts are verified, and makes many generalisations with a voice of authority, while ignoring the bulk of the experimental literature on his subject, it is as well to reflect on them.

Man's aggression must indeed have a biological basis, and have evolved earlier in his history through natural selection. Furthermore, in intra-specific fighting man, like other species, uses a repertoire of fairly stereotyped expressive movements. Some of these convey threat, others appease: their significance is understood by other individuals. Comparative evidence suggests that the smile evolved as an appeasement movement, but it can perhaps now usefully be described as an end in its own right. Thus at least one of the expressions used in interpersonal relations probably originated in an aggressive context. On such issues the evidence supports Lorenz's account.

But the pivot of Lorenz's argument is his insistence on the *spontaneity* of aggression. Man's problem, he says, arises in part because his aggressiveness wells up in a world where it has no proper outlet. Now spontaneity is a difficult enough concept in any context, but it usually refers to a change in the output of a system without a corresponding change in input. Lorenz uses it in approximately this kind of way, referring to the occurrence of behaviour in the absence of the stimulus situations normally eliciting it. He implicitly associates with this another property – namely that if a certain type of behaviour is not expressed, the underlying drive can or must find expression by activating another type of behaviour.

This implication is a consequence of Lorenz's energy model of motivation. Now, while models of this kind have been of some value in certain contexts (notably, perhaps, to psychoanalysts), they are not accepted by the majority of students of behaviour. This is in part because behavioural energy is so often covertly confused with physical energy; this leads to false explanations. Perhaps more important is that energy models imply that behaviour comes to an end because energy is discharged in action, instead of through the change which it produces in the stimulus situation. Although the use of an energy model is crucial to his thesis, Lorenz does not even attempt to answer the numerous criticisms of such models which have been made during the last two decades, and seems unaware of the dangers which they have for the theoretician.

Primarily a response?

His own arguments for the spontaneity of aggression do not bear examination. In the first place, many of his examples refer to other types of behaviour. Generalisations about mechanisms which cut across different types of behaviour, let alone across different species, can be at best superficial. Prey-catching, courtship, and intraspecific aggression are organised in different ways. This is particularly so in the extent to which they exhibit spontaneity. Lorenz himself argues in another context that each type of behaviour shows spontaneity to a degree which is adaptive in the circumstances in which that type of behaviour is used. So spontaneity of aggression cannot be established by observing other types of behaviour.

A second type of evidence Lorenz gives for spontaneity concerns animals which, in the absence of members of their own species, attack members of another. Yet, as Lorenz himself points out, the animals attacked are those which most resemble the attacker's own species. This aggression could be a response to characteristics shared by the attacked animal and the attacker's own species. Again, Lorenz cites the males of certain Cichlid fish which, in the absence of rival males, attack and kill their own mates. But this is no evidence for the spontaneity of aggression. Lorenz shows elsewhere that the female fish arouses aggressive behaviour which is normally redirected onto another male. In the absence of another male it is hardly surprising that the female is attacked.

Apart from a trivial anecdote about one of his relatives, and some observations on the Ute Indians, which are open to a variety of interpretations, this is almost the whole of Lorenz's evidence for "the spontaneity of aggression."

Lorenz acknowledges that "many sociologists and psychologists maintain" that aggression is primarily a *response* to external factors, but he cites none of the evidence they have produced. He almost totally neglects the long history of support which this view has had among psychologists. He cites Wallace Craig on the courtship of doves as evidence for the spontaneity of instinctive behaviour in general, but he doesn't mention that Craig thought aggression was an "aversion" rather than an "appetite," and that he said animals fight only to get rid of a rival's presence or interference.

Lorenz similarly neglects the view that aggression comes from a frustration of ongoing activity. Yet this can certainly account for a large proportion of human aggressiveness – precisely how much depends on how frustration is defined. There are certainly also cases in which aggression relates primarily to something other than destruction of the object at which it is directed. It aims at winning a parent's attention or a leader's approval. Another case which cannot easily be ascribed to frustration (defined narrowly) is aggression elicited by the approach of another individual, as when a stranger intrudes into a group. This category is the chief cause of aggression in sub-primates.

Whether fighting is due to frustration or to the proximity of another individual, it derives principally from the situation, and there is no need to postulate causes that are purely internal to the aggressor. Cases in which animals seem to seek fights are much rarer than Lorenz suggests, and they are mostly related to previous fighting experience in the same situation. If a thesis is to be hung on the spontaneity of aggression, this contrary view, expressed in nearly every textbook of comparative psychology, and held by the great majority of students of animal behaviour, should at least be considered.

The emphasis on the spontaneity of aggression, basic to Lorenz's thesis, thus has little support. Even if spontaneous aggressiveness does occur, there is no evidence that it is *important* in any subhuman species. Nor is there any evidence that, if an animal lacks situations that elicit its "spontaneous" aggression, its aggressiveness must find outlet.

Yet aggression certainly occurs, and we must all share Lorenz's concern. How can we avoid the harmful consequences of man's aggressiveness? The exercise of "moral responsibility" seems by itself to be inadequate. "Cultural traditions" seem to be failing or in a process of metamorphosis.

The first step is to know ourselves, to recognise in advance the situations in which destructively aggressive behaviour is likely to occur, and to avoid them. Lorenz emphasises the probability of "militant enthusiasm" when a social group, inspired by a leader, feels itself to be threatened by a danger from outside – a situation which certainly can, but need not, be dangerous.

What to avoid?

Lorenz stresses especially the avoidance of situations which he sees as facilitating the outlet of aggressive energies through undesirable channels. Those who ascribe aggression to frustration would feel that it is the frustration which must be reduced. Frustration is part of living and starts with the mother's breast, but excessive frustration can be avoided.

Another possible solution is genetic. Perhaps, in the course of generations, selective breeding could reduce man's aggressiveness. Lorenz rejects this because he believes that loss of aggressiveness would bring with it also the loss of its socially desirable consequences. Some of his arguments here are invalid. For instance, the argument that aggressiveness is valuable because it leads to the formation of a dominance hierarchy, which in turn provides a stable social system, loses its force if the value of the stable society is to mitigate the consequences of aggression.

Lorenz thinks that aggression is an essential component of personal friendship.

He bases this largely on the observation that species which form bonds between individuals all show intra-specific aggressiveness, and that in many species rituals which play a role in personal bonds have evolved from aggressive movements. This is a non-sequitur. Lorenz also asserts that, without aggressiveness, nearly everything that man does would lose its impetus: "Everything associated with ambition, ranking order, and countless other equally indispensable behaviour patterns would probably also disappear from human life." No evidence is cited for this view, and one is left wondering if it depends on the extension of "aggressiveness" to include "self-assertiveness" and similar qualities. These are distinct characteristics, and psychologists are only just developing tools for studying the causal relationships between them. Furthermore, Lorenz himself argues that traits originally dependent on aggressiveness may become casually independent in the course of evolution. This suggests that if genetic selection could produce a race of man less prone to behave aggressively, he would not necessarily also be less prone to smile.

Yet one must agree with Lorenz that different traits do interact, that as yet we know very little of how they do so, and that the consequences of breeding out aggression are unpredictable. It would be a long business, and is hardly an answer to current problems.

Lorenz places much hope on the redirection of the aggressive drive onto suitable objects, or its sublimation into socially useful channels. Now if redirection is potentially useful in this way, then Lorenz should surely pay some attention to the theoretical and experimental work which has been done on the factors determining the object onto which thwarted aggression is directed. However, if aggression does not force an outlet for itself when denied its usual expression – then redirection is merely the elicitation, by one object, of aggression initially aroused by another, and loses much of its promise as a solution. Like Lorenz, I too have been impelled to kick tins when angry, but I am not convinced that this effectively lowered my aggressiveness.

Indeed, it could be argued that kicking tins is pleasurable and reinforcing, and that it thus renders aggressiveness more probable on the next occasion that similar circumstances arise. Certainly responses which lead to an animal being confronted by stimuli for aggression are likely to be repeated.

Lorenz regards sport and other competitive activities as valuable in providing a "cathartic discharge of the aggressive urge," and sporting contests as providing an "outlet for the collective militant enthusiasm of nations." He gives no evidence in support of this. The only two studies cited in a recent review by L. Berkowitz produced ambiguous results, and certainly did not support Lorenz. Games may also arouse aggressiveness, and we still know little about the factors that determine which process predominates. Perhaps the arousing effect is more likely to predominate in spectators than players. Certainly the riots associated with last year's World Cup football matches, and the recent cricket test matches in India, would suggest this is so.

Lorenz follows Freud in emphasising the role of sublimation in a loose sense, but offers no proof of its efficacy. What precisely *is* the evidence? His suggestion that common goals in art or science may reduce the probability of aggression toward a rival may be true, but this does not mean that these activities can be used to discharge aggression once it is aroused. Operationally, sublimation implies that activity A renders activity B (in this case, aggression) less likely both during the performance of A and in the succeeding period. But this does not prove that A is driven by, and uses up, "motivation" which might otherwise have led to B. Other explanations are possible. One is that the subject learns to show A in the circumstances which would initially have led to B. Lorenz does not even consider such a possibility, yet it deflects attention from the situations in which aggression is aroused, and onto earlier experience.

Effect of experience

It is indeed in the scant attention which he gives to the role of experience that the weakness of Lorenz's prescription lies. For example, he neglects, with little more than a sneer at permissive methods of education, how far the characteristics of individuals can be modified by experience. But many studies of subhuman species indicate that individual experience *can* influence aggressiveness. The social conditions of rearing are known to influence the probability of aggression in intra-species encounters in mice, cats, dogs, monkeys, and other animals. The previous experience of success or failure in combative encounters can influence aggressiveness in subsequent ones. Experience of starvation can apparently influence subsequent aggressiveness over food in chaffinches and probably other species.

In man, also, evidence that aggressiveness is influenced by experience is based on numerous detailed studies. Many of these studies are difficult to interpret. We know little enough about how experience produces its effects. We are not yet in a position to specify conditions of rearing which minimise antisocial aggression. But at least we can help to reduce rewards for aggressiveness, such as social approbation, and be aware of the influence which certain types of leaders or of mass entertainment may exert. It is surely through the control of individual experience that man's aggressiveness can be tamed.

Therefore, while acknowledging that man, like most higher animals, has a potentiality for aggression, let us not accept the inevitability of its full expression, pinning all our hopes on redirection in situations which may in fact be arousing aggressiveness, or on sublimation. The solution lies rather in an endeavour to understand the roots of behaviour, to tease out the aspects of experience which influence aggressiveness and to assess the nature of their effects. We must not be dismayed if some of the attempts which have so far been made to reduce human aggressiveness through early experience now seem bungling and naive. Let us not merely plan a society to cope with man at his worst, but remember that society can influence the nature of its ingredients.

References

Berkowitz, L. 1962. *Aggression: a social psychological analysis.* New York: McGraw-Hill.

Brown, J. S. and Farmer, I. E. 1951. Emotions conceptualised as intervening variables – with suggestions toward a theory of frustration. *Psychological Bulletin,* 48, 465-495.

Craig, W. 1918. Appetites and aversions as constituents of instincts. *Biological Bulletin,* 34, 91-107.

Dollard, J., Doob, L., Miller, N., Mowrer, O., and Sears, R. 1939. *Frustration and Aggression.* New Haven: Yale Univ. Press.

Durbin, E. F. M. and Bowlby, J. 1939. *Personal Aggressiveness and War.* New York: Columbia Univ. Press.

Hinde, R. A. 1960. Energy models of motivation. *Symposia of the Society for Experimental Biology,* 14, 199-213.

Lorenz, Konrad. 1966. *On Aggression.* London: Methuen.

Marler, P. R. 1957. Studies of fighting in chaffinches. 4: Appetitive and consummatory behaviour. *British Journal of Animal Behaviour,* 5, 29-37.

Marler, P. R. and Hamilton, W. J. 1966. *Mechanisms of Animal Behaviour.* New York: Wiley.

McDougall, W. 1926. *An Introduction to Social Psychology.* Rev. ed. Boston: Luce.

Miller, N. E. 1948. Theory and experiment relating psychoanalytic displacement to stimulus-response generalisation. *Journal of Abnormal and Social Psychology,* 43, 155-178.

Seward, J. P. 1945. Aggressive behaviour in the rat. 3: The role of frustration. *Journal of Comparative Psychology,* 38, 225-238.

Thompson, T. I. 1963. Visual reinforcement in Siamese fighting fish. *Science,* 141, 55-57.

8

On war and peace in animals and man

Nikolaas Tinbergen

In 1935 Alexis Carrel published a best seller, *Man – The Unknown.* Today, more than 30 years later, we biologists have once more the duty to remind our fellowmen that in many respects we are still, to ourselves, unknown. It is true that we now understand a great deal of the way our bodies function. With this understanding came control: medicine.

The ignorance of ourselves which needs to be stressed today is ignorance about our behavior – lack of understanding of the causes and effects of the function of our brains. A scientific understanding of our behavior, leading to its control, may well be the most urgent task that faces mankind today. It is the effects of our behavior that begin to endanger the very survival of our species and, worse, of all life on earth. By our technological achievements we have attained a mastery of our environment that is without precedent in the history of life. But these achievements are rapidly getting out of hand. The consequences of our "rape of the earth" are now assuming critical proportions. With shortsighted recklessness we deplete the limited natural resources, including even the oxygen and nitrogen of our atmosphere (AAAS, 1967). And Rachel Carson's warning (1962) is now being followed by those of scientists, who give us an even gloomier picture of the general pollution of air, soil, and water. This pollution is seriously threatening our health and our food supply. Refusal to curb our reproductive behavior has led to the population explosion. And, as if all this were not enough,

SOURCE: *Science,* Volume 160 (1968): 1411-1418.

we are waging war on each other – men are fighting and killing men on a massive scale. It is because the effects of these behavior patterns, and of attitudes that determine our behavior, have now acquired such truly lethal potentialities that I have chosen man's ignorance about his own behavior as the subject of this paper.

I am an ethologist, a zoologist studying animal behavior. What gives a student of animal behavior the temerity to speak about problems of human behavior? Of course the history of medicine provides the answer. We all know that medical research uses animals on a large scale. This makes sense because animals, particularly vertebrates, are, in spite of all differences, so similar to us; they are our blood relations, however distant.

But this use of zoological research for a better understanding of ourselves is, to most people, acceptable only when we have to do with those bodily functions that we look upon as parts of our physiological machinery – the functions, for instance, of our kidneys, our liver, our hormone-producing glands. The majority of people bridle as soon as it is even suggested that studies of animal behavior could be useful for an understanding, let alone for the control, of our own behavior. They do not want to have their own behavior subjected to scientific scrutiny; they certainly resent being compared with animals, and these rejecting attitudes are both deep-rooted and of complex origin.

But now we are witnessing a turn in this tide of human thought. On the one hand the resistances are weakening, and on the other, a positive awareness is growing of the potentialities of a biology of behavior. This has become quite clear from the great interest aroused by several recent books that are trying, by comparative studies of animals and man, to trace what we could call "the animal roots of human behavior." As examples I select Konrad Lorenz's book *On Aggression* (1966b) and *The Naked Ape* by Desmond Morris (1967a). Both books were best sellers from the start. We ethologists are naturally delighted by this sign of rapid growth of interest in our science (even though the growing pains are at times a little hard to endure). But at the same time we are apprehensive, or at least I am.

We are delighted because, from the enormous sales of these and other such books, it is evident that the mental block against self-scrutiny is weakening – that there are masses of people who, so to speak, want to be shaken up.

But I am apprehensive because these books, each admirable in its own way, are being misread. Very few readers give the authors the benefit of the doubt. Far too many either accept uncritically all that the authors say, or (equally uncritically) reject it all. I believe that this is because both Lorenz and Morris emphasize our knowledge rather than our ignorance (and, in addition, present as knowledge a set of statements which are after all no more than likely guesses). In themselves brilliant, these books could stiffen, at a new level, the attitude of certainty, while what we need is a sense of doubt and wonder, and an urge to investigate, to inquire.

Potential usefulness of ethological studies

Now, in a way, I am going to be just as assertive as Lorenz and Morris, but what I am going to stress is how much we do not know. I shall argue that we shall have to make a major research effort. I am of course fully aware of the fact that much research is already being devoted to problems of human, and even of animal, behavior. I know, for instance, that anthropologists, psychologists, psychiatrists, and others are approaching these problems from many angles. But I shall try to show that the research effort has so far made insufficient use of the potential of ethology. Anthropologists, for instance, are beginning to look at animals, but they restrict their work almost entirely to our nearest relatives, the apes and monkeys. Psychologists do study a larger variety of animals, but even they select mainly higher species. They also ignore certain major problems that we biologists think have to be studied. Psychiatrists, at least many of them, show a disturbing tendency to apply the *results* rather than the *methods* of ethology to man.

None of these sciences, not even their combined efforts, are as yet parts of one coherent science of behavior. Since behavior is a life process, its study ought to be part of the mainstream of biological research. That is why we zoologists ought to "join the fray." As an ethologist, I am going to try to sketch how my science could assist its sister sciences in their attempts, already well on their way, to make a united, broad-fronted, truly biological attack on the problems of behavior.

I feel that I can cooperate best by discussing what it is in ethology that could be of use to the other behavioral sciences. What we ethologists do not want, what we consider definitely wrong, is uncritical application of our results to man. Instead, I myself at least feel that it is our method of approach, our rationale, that we can offer (Tinbergen, 1964c), and also a little simple common sense, and discipline.

The potential usefulness of ethology lies in the fact that, unlike other sciences of behavior, it applies the method or "approach" of biology to the phenomenon behavior. It has developed a set of concepts and terms that allow us to ask:

1. In what way does this phenomenon (behavior) influence the survival, the success of the animal?
2. What makes behavior happen at any given moment? How does its "machinery" work?
3. How does the behavior machinery develop as the individual grows up?
4. How have the behavior systems of each species evolved until they became what they are now?

The first question, that of survival value, has to do with the effects of behavior; the other three are, each on a different time scale, concerned with its causes.

These four questions are, as many of my fellow biologists will recognize, the major questions that biology has been pursuing for a long time. What ethology is doing could be simply described by saying that, just as biology investigates the functioning of the organs responsible for digestion, respiration, circulation, and so forth, so ethology begins now to do the same with respect to behavior; it investigates the functioning of organs responsible for movement.

I have to make clear that in my opinion it is the comprehensive, integrated attack on all four problems that characterizes ethology. I shall try to show that to ignore the questions of survival value and evolution – as, for instance, most psychologists do – is not only shortsighted but makes it impossible to arrive at an understanding of behavioral problems. Here ethology can make, in fact is already making, positive contributions.

Having stated my case for animal ethology as an essential part of the science of behavior, I will now have to sketch how this could be done. For this I shall have to consider one concrete example, and I select aggression, the most directly lethal of our behaviors. And, for reasons that will become clear, I shall also make a short excursion into problems of education.

Let me first try to define what I mean by aggression. We all understand the term in a vague, general way, but it is, after all, no more than a catchword. In terms of actual behavior, aggression involves approaching an opponent, and, when within reach, pushing him away, inflicting damage of some kind, or at least forcing stimuli upon him that subdue him. In this description the effect is already implicit: such behavior tends to remove the opponent, or at least to make him change his behavior in such a way that he no longer interferes with the attacker. The methods of attack differ from one species to another, and so do the weapons that are used, the structures that contribute to the effect.

Since I am concentrating on men fighting men, I shall confine myself to intraspecific fighting, and ignore, for instance, fighting between predators and prey. Intraspecific fighting is very common among animals. Many of them fight in two different contexts, which we can call "offensive" and "defensive." Defensive fighting is often shown as a last resort by an animal that, instead of attacking, has been fleeing from an attacker. If it is cornered, it may suddenly turn round upon its enemy and "fight with the courage of despair."

Of the four questions I mentioned before, I shall consider that of the survival value first. Here comparison faces us right at the start with a striking paradox. On the one hand, man is akin to many species of animals in that he fights his own species. But on the other hand he is, among the thousands of species that fight, the only one in which fighting is disruptive.

In animals, intraspecific fighting is usually of distinctive advantage. In addition, all species manage as a rule to settle their disputes without killing one another; in fact, even bloodshed is rare. Man is the only species that is a mass murderer, the only misfit in his own society.

Why should this be so? For an answer, we shall have to turn to the question of causation: What makes animals and man fight their own species? And why is our species "the odd man out"?

Causation of aggression

For a fruitful discussion of this question of causation I shall first have to discuss what exactly we mean when we ask it.

I have already indicated that when thinking of causation we have to distinguish between three subquestions, and that these three differ from one another in the stretch of time that is considered. We ask, first: Given an adult animal that fights now and then, what makes each outburst of fighting happen? The time scale in which we consider these recurrent events is usually one of seconds, or minutes. To use an analogy, this subquestion compares with asking what makes a car start or stop each time we use it.

But in asking this same general question of causation ("What makes an animal fight?") we may also be referring to a longer period of time; we may mean "How has the animal, as it grew up, developed this behavior?" This compares roughly with asking how a car has been constructed in the factory. The distinction between these two subquestions remains useful even though we know that many animals continue their development (much slowed down) even after they have attained adulthood. For instance, they may still continue to learn.

Finally, in biology, as in technology, we can extend this time scale even more, and ask: How have the animal species which we observe today – and which we know have evolved from ancestors that were different – how have they acquired their particular behavior systems during this evolution? Unfortunately, while we know the evolution of cars because they evolved so quickly and have been so fully recorded, the behavior of extinct animals cannot be observed, and has to be reconstructed by indirect methods.

I shall try to justify the claim I made earlier, and show how all these four questions – that of behavior's survival value and the three subquestions of causation – have to enter into the argument if we are to understand the biology of aggression.

Let us first consider the short-term causation; the mechanism of fighting. What makes us fight at any one moment? Lorenz argues in his book that, in animals and in man, there is an internal urge to attack. An individual does not simply wait to be provoked, but, if actual attack has not been possible for some time, this urge to fight builds up until the individual actively seeks the opportunity to indulge in fighting. Aggression, Lorenz claims, can be spontaneous.

But this view has not gone unchallenged. For instance, R. A. Hinde has written a thorough criticism (1967 and this vol.), based on recent work on aggression in animals, in which he writes that Lorenz's "arguments for the spontaneity of aggression do not bear examination" and that "the contrary view, expressed in nearly every textbook of comparative psychology . . ." is that fighting "derives principally from the situation"; and even more explicitly: "There is no need to postulate causes that are purely internal to the aggressor" (1967, p. 303). At first glance it would seem as if Lorenz and Hinde disagree profoundly. I have read and reread both authors, and it is to me perfectly clear that loose statements and misunderstandings on both sides have made it appear that there is disagreement where in fact there is something very near to a common opinion. It seems to me that the differences between the two authors lie mainly in the different ways they look at internal and external variables. This in turn seems due to differences of a semantic nature. Lorenz uses the unfortunate term "the spontaneity of aggression." Hinde takes this to mean that external stimuli are in Lorenz's view not necessary at all to make an animal fight. But here he misrepresents Lorenz, for nowhere does Lorenz claim that the internal urge ever makes an animal fight "in vacuo"; somebody or something is attacked. This misunderstanding makes Hinde feel that he has refuted Lorenz's views by saying that "fighting derives principally from the situation." But both authors are fully aware of the fact that fighting is started by a number of variables, of which some are internal and some external. What both authors know, and what cannot be doubted, is that fighting behavior is not like the simple slot machine that produces one platform ticket every time one threepenny bit is inserted. To mention one animal example: a male stickleback does not always show the full fighting behavior in response to an approaching standard opponent; its response varies from none at all to the optimal stimulus on some occasions, to full attack on even a crude dummy at other times. This means that its internal state varies, and in this particular case we know from the work of Hoar (1962) that the level of the male sex hormone is an important variable.

Another source of misunderstanding seems to have to do with the stretch of time that the two authors are taking into account. Lorenz undoubtedly thinks of the causes of an outburst of fighting in terms of seconds, or hours – perhaps days. Hinde seems to think of events which may have happened further back in time; an event which is at any particular moment "internal" may well in its turn have been influenced previously by external agents. In our stickleback example, the level of male sex hormone is influenced by external agents such as the length of the daily exposure to light over a period of a month or so (Baggerman, 1965). Or, less far back in time, its readiness to attack may have been influenced by some experience gained, say, half an hour before the fight.

I admit that I have now been spending a great deal of time on what would seem to be a perfectly simple issue: the very first step in the analysis of the short-term causation, which is to distinguish at any given moment between variables within the animal and variables in the environment. It is of course important for our further understanding to unravel the complex interactions between these two worlds, and in particular the physiology of aggressive behavior. A great deal is being discovered about this, but for my present issue there is no use discussing it as long as even the first step in the analysis has not led to a clearly expressed and generally accepted conclusion. We must remember that we are at the moment concerned with the human problem: "What makes men attack each other?" And for this problem the answer to the first stage of our question is of prime importance: Is our readiness to start an attack constant or not? If it were – if our aggressive behavior were the outcome of an apparatus with the properties of the slot machine – all we would have to do would be to control the external situation: to stop providing threepenny bits. But since our readiness to start an attack is variable, further studies of both the external and the internal variables are vital to such issues as: Can we reduce fighting by lowering the population density, or by withholding provocative stimuli? Can we do so by changing the hormone balance or other physiological variables? Can we perhaps in addition control our development in such a way as to change the dependence on internal and external factors in adult man? However, before discussing development, I must first return to the fact that I have mentioned before, namely, that man is, among the thousands of other species that fight, the only mass murderer. How do animals in their intraspecific disputes avoid bloodshed?

The importance of "fear"

The clue to this problem is to recognize the simple fact that aggression in animals rarely occurs in pure form; it is only one of two components of an adaptive system. This is most clearly seen in territorial behavior, although it is also true of most other types of hostile behavior. Members of territorial species divide, among themselves, the available living space and opportunities by each individual defending its home range against competitors. Now in this system of parceling our living space, avoidance plays as important a part as attack. Put very briefly, animals of territorial species, once they have settled on a territory, attack intruders, but an animal that is still searching for a suitable territory or finds itself outside its home range withdraws when it meets with an already established owner. In terms of function, once you have taken possession of a territory, it pays to drive off competitors; but when you are still looking for a territory (or meet your neighbor at your common boundary), your chances of success are improved by avoiding such established owners. The ruthless fighter who "knows no fear" does not get very far. For an understanding of what follows, this fact, that hostile clashes are controlled by what we could call the "attack-avoidance system," is essential.

When neighboring territory owners meet near their common boundary, both attack behavior and withdrawal behavior are elicited in both animals; each of the two is in a state of motivational conflict. We know a great deal about the variety of movements that appear when these two conflicting, incompatible behaviors are elicited. Many of these expressions of a motivational conflict have, in the course of evolution, acquired signal function; in colloquial language, they signal "Keep out!" We deduce this from the fact that opponents respond to them in an appropriate way: instead of proceeding to intrude, which would require the use of force, trespassers withdraw, and neighbors are contained by each other. This is how such animals have managed to have all the advantages of their hostile behavior without the disadvantages: they divide their living space in a bloodless way by using as distance-keeping devices these conflict movements ("threat") rather than actual fighting.

Group territories

In order to see our wars in their correct biological perspective one more comparison with animals is useful. So far I have discussed animal species that defend individual or at best pair territories. But there are also animals which possess and defend territories belonging to a group, or a clan (Kruuk, 1966).

Now it is an essential aspect of group territorialism that the members of a group unite when in hostile confrontation with another group that approaches, or crosses into their feeding territory. The uniting and the aggression are equally important. It is essential to realize that group territorialism does not exclude hostile relations on lower levels when the group is on its own. For instance, within a group there is often a peck order. And within the group there may be individual or pair territories. But frictions due to these relationships fade away during a clash between groups. This temporary elimination is done by means of so-called appeasement and reassurance signals. They indicate "I am a friend," and so diminish the risk that, in the general flare-up of anger, any animal "takes it out" on a fellow member of the same group (Tinbergen, 1959b, 1964b). Clans meet clans as units, and each individual in an inter-group clash, while united with its fellow members, is (as in interindividual clashes) torn between attack and withdrawal, and postures and shouts rather than attacks.

We must now examine the hypothesis (which I consider the most likely one) that man still carries with him the animal heritage of group territoriality. This is a question concerning man's evolutionary origin, and here we are, by the very nature of the subject, forced to speculate. Because I am going to say something about the behavior of our ancestors of, say, 100,000 years ago, I have to discuss briefly a matter of methodology. It is known to all biologists (but unfortunately unknown to most psychologists) that comparison of present-day species can give us a deep insight, with a probability closely approaching certainty, into the evolutionary history of animal species. Even where fossil evidence is lacking, this comparative method alone can do this. It has to be stressed that this comparison is a highly sophisticated method, and not merely a matter of saying that species A is different from species B (Tinbergen, 1959a). The basic procedure is this. We interpret differences between really allied species as the result of adaptive divergent evolution from common stock, and we interpret similarities between nonallied species as adaptive convergencies to similar ways of life. By studying the adaptive functions of species characteristics we understand how natural selection can have produced both these divergencies and convergencies. To mention one striking example: even if we had no fossil evidence, we could, by this method alone, recognize whales for what they are – mammals that have returned to the water, and, in doing so, have developed some similarities to fish. This special type of comparison, which has been applied so successfully by students of the structure of animals, has now also been used, and with equal success, in several studies of animal behavior. Two approaches have been applied. One is to see in what respects species of very different origin have convergently adapted to a similar way of life. Von Haartman (1957) has applied this to a study of birds of many types that nest in holes – an anti-predator safety device. All such hole-nesters center their territorial fighting on a suitable nest hole. Their courtship consists of luring a female to this hole (often with the use of bright color patterns). Their young gape when a general darkening signals the arrival of the parent. All but the most recently adapted species lay uniformly colored, white, or light blue eggs that can easily be seen by the parent.

An example of adaptive divergence has been studied by Cullen (1957). Among all the gulls, the kittiwake is unique in that it nests on very narrow ledges on sheer cliffs. Over 20 peculiarities of this species have been recognized by Mrs. Cullen as vital adaptations to this particular habitat.

These and several similar studies (Crook, 1965) demonstrate how comparison reveals, in each species, systems of interrelated, and very intricate adaptive features. In this work, speculation is now being followed by careful experimental checking. It would be tempting to elaborate on this, but I must return to our own unfortunate species.

Now, when we include the "Naked Ape" in our comparative studies, it becomes likely (as has been recently worked out in great detail by Morris) that man is a "social Ape who has turned carnivore" (Freeman, 1964; Morris, 1967b). On the one hand he is a social primate; on the other, he has developed similarities to wolves, lions, and hyenas. In our present context one thing seems to stand out clearly, a conclusion that seems to me of paramount importance to all of us, and yet has not yet been fully accepted as such. As a social, hunting primate, man must originally have been organized on the principle of group territories.

Ethologists tend to believe that we still carry with us a number of behavioral characteristics of our animal ancestors, which cannot be eliminated by different ways of upbringing, and that our group territorialism is one of those ancestral characters. I shall discuss the problem of the modifiability of our behavior later, but it is useful to point out here that even if our behavior were much more modifiable than Lorenz maintains, our cultural evolution, which resulted in the parceling-out of our living space on lines of tribal, national, and now even "bloc" areas, would, if anything, have tended to enhance group territorialism.

Group territorialism in man?

I put so much emphasis on this issue of group territorialism because most writers who have tried to apply ethology to man have done this in the wrong way. They have made the mistake, to which I objected before, of uncritically extrapolating the results of animal studies to man. They try to explain man's behavior by using facts that are valid only of some of the animals we studied. And, as ethologists keep stressing, no two species behave alike. Therefore, instead of taking this easy way out, we ought to study man in his own right. And I repeat that the message of the ethologists is that the methods, rather than the results, of ethology should be used for such a study.

Now, the notion of territory was developed by zoologists (to be precise, by ornithologists [Howard, 1920; Hinde *et al.,* 1956]), and because individual and pair territories are found in so many more species than group territories (which are particularly rare among birds), most animal studies were concerned with such individual and pair territories. Now such low-level territories do occur in man, as does another form of hostile behavior, the peck order. But the problems created by such low-level frictions are not serious; they can, within a community, be kept in check by the apparatus of law and order; peace within national boundaries can be enforced. In order to understand what makes us go to war, we have to recognize that man behaves very much like a group-territorial species. We too unite in the face of an outside danger to the group; we "forget our differences." We too have threat gestures, for instance, angry facial expressions. And all of us use reassurance and appeasement signals, such as a friendly smile. And (unlike speech) these are universally understood; they are cross-cultural; they are species-specific. And, incidentally, even within a group sharing a common language, they are often more reliable guides to a man's intentions than speech, for speech (as we know now) rarely reflects our true motives, but our facial expressions often "give us away."

If I may digress for a moment: it is humiliating to us ethologists that many non-scientists, particularly novelists and actors, intuitively understand our sign language much better than we scientists ourselves do. Worse, there is a category of human beings who understand intuitively more about the causation of our aggressive behavior: the great demagogues. They have applied this knowledge in order to control our behavior in the most clever ways, and often for the most evil purposes. For instance, Hitler (who had modern mass communication at his disposal, which allowed him to inflame a whole nation) played on both fighting tendencies. The "defensive" fighting was whipped up by his passionate statements about "living space," "encirclement," Jewry, and Freemasonry as threating powers which made the Germans feel "cornered." The "attack fighting" was similarly set ablaze by playing the myth of the Herrenvolk. We must make sure that mankind has learned its lesson and will never forget how disastrous the joint effects have been – if only one of the major nations were led now by a man like Hitler, life on earth would be wiped out.

I have argued my case for concentrating on studies of group territoriality rather than on other types of aggression. I must now return, in this context, to the problem of man the mass murderer. Why don't we settle even our international disputes by the relatively harmless, animal method of threat? Why have we become unhinged so that so often our attack erupts without being kept in check by fear? It is not that we have no fear, nor that we have no other inhibitions against killing. This problem has to be considered first of all in the general context of the consequences of man having embarked on a new type of evolution.

Cultural evolution

Man has the ability, unparalleled in scale in the animal kingdom, of passing on his experiences from one generation to the next. By this accumulative and exponentially growing process, which we call cultural evolution, he has been able to change his environment progressively out of all recognition. And this includes the social environment. This new type of evolution proceeds at an incomparably faster pace than genetic evolution. Genetically we have not evolved very strikingly since Cro-Magnon man, but culturally we have changed beyond recognition, and are changing at an ever-increasing rate. It is of course true that we are highly adjustable individually, and so could hope to keep pace with these changes. But I am not alone in believing that this behavioral adjustability, like all types of modifiability, has its limits. These limits are imposed upon us by our hereditary constitution, a constitution which can only change with the far slower speed of genetic evolution. There are good grounds for the conclusion that man's limited behavioral adjustability has been outpaced by the culturally determined changes in his social environment, and that this is why man is now a misfit in his own society.

We can now, at last, return to the problem of war, of uninhibited mass killing. It seems quite clear that our cultural evolution is at the root of the trouble. It is our cultural evolution that has caused the population explosion. In a nutshell, medical science, aiming at the reduction of suffering, has, in doing so, prolonged life for many individuals as well – prolonged it to well beyond the point at which they produce offspring. Unlike the situation in any wild species, recruitment to the human population consistently surpasses losses through mortality. Agricultural and technical know-how have enabled us to grow food and to exploit other natural resources to such an extent that we can still feed (though only just) the enormous numbers of human beings on our crowded planet. The result is that we now live at a far higher density than that in which genetic evolution has molded our species. This, together with long-distance communication, leads to far more frequent, in fact to continuous, intergroup contacts, and so to continuous external provocation of aggression. Yet this alone would not explain our increased tendency to kill each other; it would merely lead to continuous threat behavior.

The upsetting of the balance between aggression and fear (and this is what causes war) is due to at least three other consequences of cultural evolution. It is an old cultural phenomenon that warriors are both brainwashed and bullied into all-out fighting. They are brainwashed into believing that fleeing–originally, as we have seen, an adaptive type of behavior–is despicable, "cowardly." This seems to me due to the fact that man, accepting that in moral issues death might be preferable to fleeing, has falsely applied the moral concept of "cowardice" to matters of mere practical importance – to the dividing of living space. The fact that our soldiers are also bullied into all-out fighting (by penalizing fleeing in battle) is too well-known to deserve elaboration.

Another cultural excess is our ability to make and use killing tools, especially long-range weapons. These make killing easy, not only because a spear or a club inflicts, with the same effort, so much more damage than a fist, but also, and mainly, because the use of long-range weapons prevents the victim from reaching his attacker with his appeasement, reassurance, and distress signals. Very few aircrews who are willing, indeed eager, to drop their bombs "on target" would be willing to strangle, stab, or burn children (or, for that matter, adults) with their own hands; they would stop short of killing, in response to the appeasement and distress signals of their opponents.

These three factors alone would be sufficient to explain how we have become such unhinged killers. But I have to stress once more that all this, however convincing it may seem, must still be studied more thoroughly.

There is a frightening and ironical paradox in this conclusion: that the human brain, the finest life-preserving device created by evolution, has made our species so successful in mastering the outside world that it suddenly finds itself taken off guard. One could say that our cortex and our brainstem (our "reason" and our "instincts") are at loggerheads. Together they have created a new social environment in which, rather than ensuring our survival, they are about to do the opposite. The brain finds itself seriously threatened by an enemy of its own making. It is its own enemy. We simply have to understand this enemy.

The development of behavior

I must now leave the question of the moment-to-moment control of fighting, and, looking further back in time, turn to the development of aggressive behavior in the growing individual. Again we will start from the human problem. This, in the present context, is whether it is within our power to control development in such a way that we reduce or eliminate fighting among adults. Can or cannot education in the widest sense produce nonaggressive men?

The first step in the consideration of this problem is again to distinguish between external and internal influences, but now we must apply this to the growth, the changing, of the behavioral machinery during the individual's development. Here again the way in which we phrase our questions and our conclusions is of the utmost importance.

In order to discuss this issue fruitfully, I have to start once more by considering it in a wider context, which is now that of the "nature-nurture" problem with respect to behavior in general. This has been discussed more fully by Lorenz in his book *Evolution and Modification of Behaviour* (1966a); for a discussion of the environmentalist point of view I refer to the various works of Schneirla (1966).

Lorenz tends to classify behavior types into innate and acquired or learned behavior. Schneirla rejects this dichotomy into two classes of behavior. He stresses that the developmental process, of behavior as well as of other functions, should be considered, and also that this development forms a highly complicated series of interactions between the growing organism and its environment. I have gradually become convinced that the clue to this difference in approach is to be found in a difference in aims between the two authors. Lorenz claims that "we are justified in leaving, at least for the time being, to the care of the experimental embryologists all those questions which are concerned with the chains of physiological causation leading from the genome to the development of . . . neurosensory structures" (1966a, p. 43). In other words, he deliberately refrains from starting his analysis of development prior to the stage at which a fully coordinated behavior is performed for the first time. If one in this way restricts one's studies to the later stages of development, then a classification in "innate" and "learned" behavior, or behavior components, can be considered quite justified. And there was a time, some 30 years ago, when the almost grotesquely environmentalist bias of psychology made it imperative for ethologists to stress the extent to which behavior patterns could appear in perfect or near-perfect form without the aid of anything that could be properly called learning.

But I now agree (however belatedly) with Schneirla that we must extend our interest to earlier stages of development and embark on a full program of experimental embryology of behavior. When we do this, we discover that interactions with the environment can indeed occur at early stages. These interactions may concern small components of the total machinery of a fully functional behavior pattern, and many of them cannot possibly be called learning. But they are interactions with the environment, and must be taken into account if we follow in the footsteps of the experimental embryologists, and extend our field of interest to the entire sequence of events which lead from the blueprints contained in the zygote to the fully functioning, behaving animal. We simply have to do this if we want an answer to the question to what extent the development of behavior can be influenced from the outside.

When we follow this procedure the rigid distinction between "innate" or unmodifiable and "acquired" or modifiable behavior patterns becomes far less sharp. This is owing to the discovery, on the one hand, that "innate" patterns may contain elements that at an early stage developed in interaction with the environment, and, on the other hand, that learning is, from step to step, limited by internally imposed restrictions.

To illustrate the first point, I take the development of the sensory cells in the retina of the eye. Knoll has shown (1956) that the rods in the eyes of tadpoles cannot function properly unless they have first been exposed to light. This means that, although any visually guided response of a tadpole may well, in its integrated form, be "innate" in Lorenz's sense, it is so only in the sense of "nonlearned," not in that of "having grown without interaction with the environment." Now it has been shown by Cullen (1961) that male sticklebacks reared from the egg in complete isolation from other animals will, when adult, show full fighting behavior to other males and courtship behavior to females when faced with them for the first time in their lives. This is admittedly an important fact, demonstrating that the various recognized forms of learning do not enter into the programing of these integrated patterns. This is a demonstration of what Lorenz calls an "innate response." But it does not exclude the possibility that parts of the machinery so employed may, at an earlier stage, have been influenced by the environment, as in the case of the tadpoles.

Second, there are also behavior patterns which do appear in the inexperienced animal, but in an incomplete form, and which require additional development through learning. Thorpe has analyzed a clear example of this: when young male chaffinches reared alone begin to produce their song for the first time, they utter a very imperfect warble; this develops into the full song only if, at a certain sensitive stage, the young birds have heard the full song of an adult male (1961).

By far the most interesting aspect of such intermediates between innate and acquired behavior is the fact that learning is not indiscriminate, but is guided by a certain selectiveness on the part of the animal. This fact has been dimly recognized long ago; the early ethologists have often pointed out that different, even closely related, species learn different things even when developing the same behavior patterns. This has been emphasized by Lorenz's use of the term "innate teaching mechanism." Other authors use the world "template" in the same context. The best example I know is once more taken from the development of song in certain birds. As I have mentioned, the males of some birds acquire their full song by changing their basic repertoire to resemble the song of adults, which they have to hear during a special sensitive period some months before they sing themselves. It is in this sensitive period that they acquire, without as yet producing the song, the knowledge of "what the song ought to be like." In technical terms, the bird formed a *Sollwert* (literally, "should-value," an ideal) for the feedback they receive when they hear their own first attempts (von Holst and Mittelstaedt, 1950). Experiments have shown (Konishi, 1965; Nottebohm, 1967) that such birds, when they start to sing, do three things: they listen to what they produce; they notice the difference between this feedback and the ideal song; and they correct their next performance.

This example, while demonstrating an internal teaching mechanism, shows, at the same time, that Lorenz made his concept too narrow when he coined the term "innate teaching mechanism." The birds have developed a teaching mechanism, but while it is true that it is internal, it is not innate; the birds have acquired it by listening to their father's song.

These examples show that if behavior studies are to catch up with experimental embryology our aims, our concepts, and our terms must be continually revised.

Before returning to aggression, I should like to elaborate a little further on general aspects of behavior development, because this will enable me to show the value of animal studies in another context, that of education.

Comparative studies, of different animal species, of different behavior patterns, and of different stages of development, begin to suggest that wherever learning takes a hand in development, it is guided by such *Sollwerte* or templates for the proper feedback, the feedback that reinforces. And it becomes clear that these various *Sollwerte* are of a bewildering variety. In human education one aspect of this has been emphasized in particular, and even applied in the use of teaching machines: the requirement that the reward, in order to have maximum effect, must be immediate. Skinner has stressed this so much because in our own teaching we have imposed an unnatural delay between, say, taking in homework, and giving the pupil his reward in the form of a mark. But we can learn more from animal studies than the need for immediacy of reward. The type of reward is also of great importance, and this may vary from task to task, from stage to stage, from occasion to occasion; the awards may be of almost infinite variety.

Here I have to discuss briefly a behavior of which I have so far been unable to find the equivalent in the development of structure. This is exploratory behavior. By this we mean a kind of behavior in which the animal sets out to acquire as much information about an object or a situation as it can possibly get. The behavior is intricately adapted to this end, and it terminates when the information has been stored, when the animal has incorporated it in its learned knowledge. This exploration (subjectively we speak of "curiosity") is not confined to the acquisition of information about the external world alone; at least mammals explore their own movements a great deal, and in this way "master new skills." Again, in this exploratory behavior, *Sollwerte* of expected, "hoped-for" feedbacks play their part.

Without going into more detail, we can characterize the picture we begin to get of the development of behavior as a series, or rather a web, of events, starting with innate programing instructions contained in the zygote, which straightaway begin to interact with the environment; this interaction may be discontinuous, in that periods of predominantly internal development alternate with periods of interaction, or sensitive periods. The interaction is enhanced by active exploration; it is steered by selective *Sollwerte* of great variety; and stage by stage this process ramifies; level upon level of ever-increasing complexity is being incorporated into the programing.

Apply what we have heard for a moment to playing children. (I do not, of course, distinguish sharply between "play" and "learning.") At a certain age a child begins to use, say, building blocks. It will at first manipulate them in various ways, one at a time. Each way of manipulating acts as exploratory behavior: the child learns what a block looks, feels, tastes like, and so forth, and also how to put it down so that it stands stably.

Each of these stages "peters out" when the child knows what it wanted to find out. But as the development proceeds, a new level of exploration is added: the child discovers that it can put one block on top of the other; it constructs. The new discovery leads to repetition and variation, for each child develops, at some stage, a desire and a set of *Sollwerte* for such effects of construction, and acts out to the full this new level of exploratory behavior. In addition, already at this stage the *Sollwert* or ideal does not merely contain what the blocks do, but also what, for instance, the mother does; her approval, her shared enjoyment, is also of great importance. Just as an exploring animal, the child builds a kind of inverted pyramid of experience, built of layers, each set off by a new wave of exploration and each directed by new sets of *Sollwerte,* and so its development "snowballs." All these phases may well have more or less limited sensitive periods, which determine when the fullest effect can be obtained, and when the child is ready for the next step. More important still, if the opportunity for the next stage is offered either too early or too late, development may be damaged, including the development of motivational and emotional attitudes.

Of course gifted teachers of many generations have known all of these things (Standing, 1962) or some of them, but the glimpses of insight have not been fully and scientifically systematized. In human education, this would of course involve experimentation. This need not worry us too much, because in our search for better educational procedures we are in effect experimenting on our children all the time. Also, children are fortunately incredibly resilient, and most grow up into pretty viable adults in spite of our fumbling educational efforts. Yet there is, of course, a limit to what we will allow ourselves, and this, I should like to emphasize, is where animal studies may well become even more important than they are already.

Can education end aggression?

Returning now to the development of animal and human aggression, I hope to have made at least several things clear: that behavior development is a very complex phenomenon indeed; that we have only begun to analyze it in animals; that with respect to man we are, if anything, behind in comparison with animal studies; and that I cannot do otherwise than repeat what I said in the beginning: we must make a major research effort. In this effort animal studies can help, but we are still very far from drawing very definite conclusions with regard to our question: To what extent shall we be able to render man less aggressive through manipulation of the environment, that is, by educational measures?

In such a situation personal opinions naturally vary a great deal. I do not hesitate to give as my personal opinion that Lorenz's book *On Aggression,* in spite of its assertiveness, in spite of factual mistakes, and in spite of the many possibilities of misunderstandings that are due to the lack of a common language among students of behavior – that this work must be taken more seriously as a positive contribution to our problem than many critics have done. Lorenz is, in my opinion, right in claiming that elimination, through education, of the internal urge to fight will turn out to be very difficult, if not impossible.

Everything I have said so far seems to me to allow for only one conclusion. Apart from doing our utmost to return to a reasonable population density, apart from stopping the progressive depletion and pollution of our habitat, we must pursue the biological study of animal behavior for clarifying problems of human behavior of such magnitude as that of our aggression, and of education.

But research takes a long time, and we must remember that there are experts who forecast worldwide famine 10 to 20 years from now; and that we have enough weapons to wipe out all human life on earth. Whatever the causation of our aggression, the simple fact is that for the time being we are saddled with it. This means that there is a crying need for a crash program, for finding ways and means for keeping our intergroup aggression in check. This is of course in practice infinitely more difficult than controlling our intranational frictions; we have as yet not got a truly international police force. But there is hope for avoiding all-out war because, for the first time in history, we are afraid of killing ourselves by the lethal radiation effects even of bombs that we could drop in the enemy's territory. Our politicians know this. And as long as there is this hope, there is every reason to try and learn what we can from animal studies. Here again they can be of help. We have already seen that animal opponents meeting in a hostile clash avoid bloodshed by using the expressions of their motivational conflicts as intimidating signals. Ethologists have studied such conflict movements in some detail (Tinbergen, 1964a; Jones, 1960; Sevenster, 1961; Rowell, 1961), and have found that they are of a variety of types. The most instructive of these is the redirected attack; instead of attacking the provoking, yet dreaded, opponent, animals often attack something else, often even an inanimate object. We ourselves bang the table with our fists. Redirection includes something like sublimation, a term attaching a value judgment to the redirection. As a species with group territories, humans, like hyenas, unite when meeting a common enemy. We do already sublimate our group aggression. The Dutch feel united in their fight against the sea. Scientists do attack their problems together. The space program – surely a mainly military effort – is an up-to-date example. I would not like to claim, as Lorenz does, that redirected attack exhausts the aggressive urge. We know from soccer matches and from animal work how aggressive behavior has two simultaneous, but opposite effects: a waning effect, and one of self-inflammation, of mass hysteria, such as recently seen in Cairo. Of these two the inflammatory effect often wins. But if aggression were used successfully as the motive force behind nonkilling and even useful activities, self-stimulation need not be a danger; in our short-term cure we are not aiming at the elimination of aggressiveness, but at "taking the sting out of it."

Of all sublimated activities, scientific research would seem to offer the best opportunities for deflecting and sublimating our aggression. And, once we recognize that it is the disrupted relation between our own behavior and our environment that forms our most deadly enemy, what could be better than uniting, at the front or behind the lines, in the scientific attack on our own behavioral problems?

I stress "behind the lines." The whole population should be made to feel that it participates in the struggle. This is why scientists will always have the duty to inform their fellowmen of what they are doing, of the relevance and the importance of their work. And this is not only a duty, it can give intense satisfaction.

I have come full circle. For both the long-term and the short-term remedies at least we scientists will have to sublimate our aggression into an all-out attack on the enemy within. For this the enemy must be recognized for what it is: our unknown selves, or, deeper down, our refusal to admit that man is, to himself, unknown.

I should like to conclude by saying a few words to my colleagues of the younger generation. Of course we all hope that, by muddling along until we have acquired better understanding, self-annihilation either by the "whimper of famine" or by the "bang of war" can be avoided. For this, we must on the one hand trust, on the other help (and urge) our politicians. But it is no use denying that the chances of designing the necessary preventive measures are small, let alone the chances of carrying them out. Even birth control still offers a major problem.

It is difficult for my generation to know how seriously you take the danger of mankind destroying his own species. But those who share the apprehension of my generation might perhaps, with us, derive strength from keeping alive the thought that has helped so many of us in the past when faced with the possibility of imminent death. Scientific research is one of the finest occupations of our mind. It is, with art and religion, one of the uniquely human ways of meeting nature, in fact, the most active way. If we are to succumb, and even if this were to be ultimately due to our own stupidity, we could still, so to speak, redeem our species. We could at least go down with some dignity, by using our brain for one of its supreme tasks, by exploring to the end.

References

AAAS Annual Meeting. 1967. See *New Scientist*, 1968, 37:5.

Baggerman, B. 1965. *Symp. Soc. Exp. Biol.*, 20:427.

Carrel, A. 1935. *L'Homme, cet Inconnu.* Paris: Librairie Plon.

Carson, R. 1962. *Silent Spring.* Boston: Houghton Mifflin.

Crook, J. H. 1965. *Symp. Zool. Soc. London*, 14:181.

Cullen, E. 1957. *Ibis*, 99:275.

____. 1961. *Final Rept. Contr. AF 61 (052)29*, USAFRDC, 1-23.

Freeman, D. 1964. *Inst. Biol. Symp.*, 13:109.

Hinde, R. A. 1967. *New Society*, 9:302.

Hinde, R. A. *et al.* 1956. *Ibis*, 98:340-530.

Hoar, W. S. 1962. *Animal Behaviour*, 10:247.

Howard, H. E. 1920. *Territory in Bird Life.* London: Murray.

Jones, N. B. 1960. *Wildfowl Trust 11th Ann. Rept.*, 46-52.

Knoll, M. D. 1956. *Z. Vergleich. Physiol.*, 38:219.

Konishi, M. 1965. *Z. Tierpsychol.*, 22:770.

Kruuk, H. 1966. *New Scientist*, 30:849.

Lorenz, K. 1966a. *Evolution and Modification of Behaviour.* London: Methuen.

____. 1966b. *On Aggression.* London: Methuen.

Morris, D. 1967a. *The Naked Ape.* London: Jonathan Cape.

____. (Ed.). 1967b. *Primate Ethology.* London: Weidenfeld and Nicholson.

Nottebohm, F. 1967. *Proc. 14th Intern. Ornithol. Congr.*, 265-280.

Rowell, F. 1961. *Animal Behaviour*, 9:38.

Schneirla, T. C. 1966. *Quart. Rev. Biol.*, 41:283.

Sevenster, P. 1961. *Behaviour, Suppl. 9*, 1-170.

Standing, E. M. 1962. *Maria Montessori.* New York: New American Library.

Thorpe, W. H. 1961. *Bird-Song.* New York: Cambridge Univ. Press.

Tinbergen, N. 1959a. *Behaviour*, 15:1-70.

____. 1959b. *Z. Tierpsychol.*, 16:651.

____. 1964a. In *The Pathology and Treatment of Sexual Deviation*, ed. I. Rosen, pp. 3-23. London: Oxford Univ. Press.

____. 1964b. *Zool. Mededelingen*, 39:209.

____. 1964c. *Z. Tierpsychol.*, 20:410.

Von Haartman, L. 1957. *Evolution*, 11:339.

Von Holst, E. and Mittelstaedt, H. 1950. *Naturwissenschaften*, 37:464.

9

*Human aggression in anthropological perspective**

Derek Freeman

E. J. Dillon (1896), having described in an article in the *Contemporary Review* the savage destructiveness and the terrible cruelties that had accompanied the massacres of the Armenians of Anatolia during the last decade of the nineteenth century, remarked that these happenings revealed "unimagined strata of malignity in the human heart."

History since that time has provided us with much further evidence of man's destructiveness as, equally, to use the words of Sir Carleton Kemp Allen (1958), of "cruelty on a large and hideous scale," with "the

SOURCE: Amended from *The Natural History of Aggression,* Institute of Biology, Symposium No. 13, J. D. Carthy and F. J. Ebling, eds., Academic Press, 1964. Reprinted by permission of Academic Press and the Institute of Biology.

**Author's Note (1970):* This is the slightly amended version of a paper which was originally prepared in 1963. It has already, in various ways, become outmoded, mainly because of advances in palaeo-anthropological research. It should, then, be read in conjunction with more recent papers on hominid evolution and aggressivity, such as Dr. L. S. B. Leakey's "Development of Aggression as a Factor in Early Human and Pre-Human Evolution," in *Aggression and Defence,* edited by C. D. Clemente and D. B. Lindsley, University of California Press, 1967.

It should also be noted that while in this particular paper (which was part of a symposium) I have directed attention to a possible phylogenetic basis to human aggression, I fully recognize that in the overall aetiology of human aggressive behaviour, environmental (including cultural) determinants are also of great importance, and during my recent researches into aggressive behaviour in Samoa, especial attention was given to variables of this kind. I am, then, in full agreement with Professor K. E. Moyer's conclusions (1969, in this volume) "that aggressive behaviour is determined by an interwoven complex of internal, external and experiential factors," and that "the solution to the multifaceted and critical problem of the control of destructive, aggressive tendencies will only be approached when all of these factors are given adequate consideration."

cold-blooded infamy of 'genocide'" and "psychological torments of unprecedented ingenuity" added to all "the crude old physical horrors."

But also, during this same period, the "unimagined strata of malignity" on which Dillon remarked have, for the first time in human history, been systematically explored, and, in particular, by the discipline of psychoanalysis.

Psychoanalytic recognition of the nature of aggression was, however, but gradual. Thus, although Freud (1905) early recognized impulses of cruelty as arising from sources independent of sexuality, these sources were, at first, traced to the self-preservative instincts and, at this period of his researches, Freud (1909) would not accept the existence of "a special instinct of aggression." It was not, indeed, until after the structure of the human psyche had been systematically explored and much additional clinical and historical evidence sifted that Freud came to his final conclusion that "the tendency to aggression is an innate, independent, instinctual disposition in man." This conclusion, which has been confirmed by subsequent research, is now one of the basic postulates of psychoanalytic theory.

What I want to do, as best I can within the limited confines of this present paper, is to survey the historical and anthropological evidence on human aggression, and, in particular, the palaeo-anthropological discoveries of the last two decades which have led to new interpretations of human evolution and to conclusions directly relevant to those reached by Freud.

In recent years there has been much important experimental research on aggression, as summarized, for example, by J. P. Scott (1958). This work has significantly extended our knowledge; however, if we are to understand adequately the realities of human aggression it is imperative that we should also pay close regard to the facts of history, for here we find, in profusion, happenings never likely to be enacted in a laboratory, and these are the phenomena which, in our theories, we must try to comprehend and explain.

Lewis Richardson, in his book *Statistics of Deadly Quarrels* (1960), has amassed some of the historical evidence for the period 1820-1945. Richardson calculates (p. 153) that during these 126 years, 59,000,000 human beings were killed in wars, murderous attacks, and other deadly quarrels. This huge total (which is, almost certainly, an underestimate) is one indication of the magnitude of the natural phenomenon with which we are dealing. However, to comprehend the nature of human aggression, we must go beyond statistics to details of behaviour.

Much aggressive behaviour, I should stress at this juncture, is under ego control; it may, for example, be a reaction to a threat to self-preservation. In such instances, as Waelder (1960) has pointed out, aggression is an accessory to ego activities; here, in other words, destruction and cruelty are not ends in themselves, but rather, incidental to the achievement of ego purposes.

"However," continues Waelder, "there are also destructive manifestations which, through their character or intensity, lie outside of this area; manifestations of aggression which cannot be seen as reactive to provocation because they are so vast in intensity or duration that it would be difficult to fit them into any scheme of stimulus and reaction. . . ."

Much of the evidence for such "essential destructiveness" or "primary aggression" comes from psychopathology. Thus, Waelder refers to the fact that "a psychotic may strike his head with an axe with full force, and . . . repeat the assault if he has the strength left to do so"; and to "the sudden outbursts of catatonics, reaching out without warning from what seemed to be a state of indifference, to a lightning attack. . . ." In disturbed behaviour of these kinds, which are frequently observed among psychotics, aggression is starkly manifest, and provides, in Federn's view, the real basis for the assumption of a destructive drive.

Comparable behaviour is also to be encountered in plentitude in the annals of crime; just as human cruelty is prominently displayed in the tortures, mutilations, and other punishments of exceeding severity which were once a common feature of the judicial process, and which, in some countries, still persist. L. O. Pike, in his *A History of Crime in England* (1873 and 1876), has given a meticulously documented account of one part of the human record in these matters.

Similarly, there is an abundance of pertinent evidence in the facts of political history. For example, T. A. Walker, in his *A History of the Law of Nations* (1899), presents a scholarly survey of the practices that marked warfare from "the earliest times to the Peace of Westphalia, 1648." These practices, with but rare exceptions, exhibit extremes of destructiveness and cruelty, and, indeed, the epochs surveyed abound with happenings that differ scarcely at all from the phenomena of psychopathology.

I cannot, in such a brief paper, give any kind of adequate survey of the historical facts, but some indication of their nature is conveyed in this typical excerpt from Walker's *History* (p. 124), referring to the Middle Ages: "When Basil II (1014) could blind fifteen thousand Bulgarians, leaving an eye to the leader of every hundred, it ceases to be matter of surprise that Saracen marauders should thirty years later be impaled by Byzantine officials, that the Greeks of Adramyttium in the time of Malek Shah (1106-16) should drown Turkish children in boiling water, that the Emperor Nicephorus (961) should cast from catapults into a Cretan city the heads of Saracens slain in the attempt to raise the seige, or that a crusading Prince of Antioch (1097) should cook human bodies on spits to earn for his men the terrifying reputation of cannibalism."

The years that have elapsed since the Peace of Westphalia have not been without progress; but the course of human history has continued to be marked by wars, revolutions, massacres, rebellions, and riots which have been characterized by destructiveness and cruelty no less extreme than that of earlier epochs. I have appended to this paper references which contain details of some of these events; a further listing of sources may be found in Richardson's *Statistics of Deadly Quarrels* (1960).

Any scholar who is prepared to examine objectively the evidence of history will be led, I believe, to the same conclusion as that reached by Durbin and Bowlby (1938), that no group of animals is "more aggressive or ruthless in their aggression than the adult members of the human race."

Indeed, the extreme nature of human destructiveness and cruelty is one of the principal characteristics which marks off man, behaviourally, from other animals.

This point has been cogently expressed by the biologist Adolf Portman: ". . . when terrible things, cruelties hardly conceivable, occur among men, many speak thoughtlessly of 'brutality,' of bestialism, or a return to animal levels. . . . As if there were animals which inflict on their own kind what men can do to men. Just at this point the zoologist has to draw a clear line: these evil, horrible things are no animal survival that happened to be carried along in the imperceptible transition from animal to man; this evil belongs entirely on this side of the dividing line, it is purely human . . ." (Waelder, p. 147).

At this juncture let me remark that, despite the ubiquity of human aggression, we lack anything resembling an adequate history of human cruelty and destructiveness. There is, for example, no kind of scientific compilation of the essential facts, nor, for that matter, has the phenomenology of the behaviour that actually occurs in the course of massacres and other outbreaks of mass violence been fully reported and analysed. The full realities are, indeed, of a kind that cannot be generally published, and those who observe them readily repress much of the horror they have experienced. Dillon, for example, in his account of the Armenian massacres, after giving details of cruelties and mutilations of a gross kind, adds that there were others which "cannot be described, nor even hinted at." Indeed, in accounts of aggressive behaviour one constantly encounters the epithets "unbelievable," "indescribable," "unimaginable." In my view, there is great need for dispassionate research into the phenomenology of the aggressive behaviour of the human animal, for until we have come to see its realities for what they are, we shall not achieve a scientific understanding of these realities nor be able to evolve ways of controlling them.

The history of the more primitive peoples confirms the conclusions I have reached for the partially civilized. Davie (1929), having surveyed the ethnographic evidence, came to the conclusion that "war plays a prominent part in the lives of most primitive peoples, and is usually a sanguinary affair." There are some peoples, it is true, among whom aggressive behaviour and war are relatively rare; such cases are, however, "quite exceptional" in the ethnographic record. Moreover, these cases are, in general, those of puny and technically backward groups living under the dominance of alien, powerful, and overtly aggressive neighbouring societies. In other words, we are here dealing with special forms of submissive adaptation. In the intragroup existence of such submissive peoples, however, as Ginsberg (1934) has noted, "violence and the fear of violence are there, and fighting occurs, though it is obviously and necessarily on a small scale." With these few exceptions, the ethnographic evidence shows warfare among primitive peoples to have been endemic and, on occasion, internecine.

Primitive cultures also exhibit many bizarre expressions of human cruelty and aggression, in sacrificial rites, ceremonies of initiation, ritual mutilations, headhunting and cannibalistic cults, and murderous societies (like those of the thugs of historical India or the "leopard men" of Africa). These diverse forms of symbolic behaviour are paralleled by the highly aggressive fantasies to be found in mythologies throughout the world, and in the frightful torments of the various hells of human religions. Here we are dealing with delusional beliefs which have become shared and traditional; it is certain, however, that they are all, finally, endopsychic in origin and, therefore, products of the human unconscious. The violent character of these fantasies, and the fact that they are so often acted out in ritual behaviour, present graphic evidence of the dynamic nature of the aggressive drive in the human animal.

Comparable evidence (as psychoanalytic research has demonstrated) is to be found in the dreams, fantasies, and play of children. Again, as anyone who cares to study the history of blood-sports or the productions of the film industry can establish, spectacles of violence are a predominant element in the entertainments popular among men. Indeed, field observation shows that expressions of pleasure are basically associated with the witnessing of destruction and the infliction of hurt – the most common of these expressions being that of involuntary and cathected laughter.

William James (1911), in discussing "the rooted bellicosity of human nature," described man as "biologically considered . . . the most formidable of all the beasts of prey, and indeed, the only one that preys systematically on its own species." Here, James was pointing to one of the forms of behaviour, that of cannibalism, by which the human animal may be sharply distinguished from other primates. Cannibalism, which is but one expression of man's carnivorous nature, has been reported for almost all parts of the world, and, on the evidence of palaeoanthropology, was probably once a universal practice. Blanc (1961) has shown that a range of fossil skulls, from the mid-Pleistocene onwards, are characterized by a "careful and symmetric incising of the periphery of the foramen magnum" to produce an opening which, on comparative evidence, was made with the purpose of extracting the brain for eating. Blanc also remarks that ritual theophagy (such as that of ancient Greece in which a goat, symbolizing Dionysus, was eaten), obviously had its origin in former ritual cannibalism, and notes that St. Paul, in his Letter to the Corinthians, stresses with particular strength "the real presence of Christ's blood and flesh in the Eucharistic ritual," this being "a powerful means of promoting the penetration and acceptance of Christianity and its major ritual in Greece where the tradition of the Dionysiac symbolic ritual meal was particularly strong and deeply felt." As a codicil to this commentary on the origin of theophagy and its deep appeal to the human animal, let me direct attention to the age-old association of fanaticism and aggression, and record that in sixteenth-century England, denial of the real presence was one of the offences for which heretics were punished, under statute, by being publicly burnt alive (Pike, 1876). Indeed, human aggression is never more terrifying than when at the service of the dogmatic and delusory group ideologies characteristic of *Homo sapiens:* "When truth kills truth, O devilish-holy fray!" So (Durbin and Bowlby, 1938) will men "die like flies for theories and exterminate each other with every instrument of destruction for abstractions."

I have now sketched, in very summary fashion, some of the principal manifestations of human aggression. In the past these basic aspects of human behaviour have been attributed (as by Rousseau, Eliot Smith, and others) to the state of civilization, it being argued that man was "a being naturally good," and that the "earliest forms of man must have been, in the main, harmless, frugivorous animals" (Eisler, 1951).

The time when such views might be entertained by informed scholars is now, however, past, for the discoveries of palaeoanthropology during the past two decades have, in fundamental ways, transformed our comprehension of the origin of man and of the probable processes of human evolution.

Darwin, in 1871, expressed the view that it was "somewhat more probable" that our early progenitors lived on the African continent than elsewhere"; this speculation has, during the present century, been borne out by the discovery of such fossil primate forms as *Propliopithecus* (of the Oligocene of Egypt), *Proconsul* and *Limnopithecus* (of the Miocene of Kenya), and of the lower Pleistocene hominids of eastern and southern Africa, which I shall refer to collectively as the Australopithecinae.

The first Australopithecine fossil, *Australopithecus africanus,* was discovered at Taungs, in Bechuanaland, in 1924, and described by Raymond Dart. Since then additional major discoveries have been made by Broom, Robinson, and Dart in South Africa, and by Leakey (in 1959) at the Olduvai Gorge, Tanganyika (of *Zinjanthropus boisei,* the skull and other bones of which were found on the living floor of an ancient camping site in association with stone tools, a hammer stone, and flakes).

The limb and pelvic bones of the Australopithecinae indicate that these hominids walked erect. This is an important fact, for, as Darwin and others have stressed, the attainment of bipedal locomotion is a crucial stage in the transition from ape to man, for by freeing the hands it makes possible the evolution of the employment and manufacture of weapons and tools. A concomitant process in this evolutionary development is a reduction in the size of the teeth and of the facial skeleton. This condition we also find in the Australopithecinae, whose teeth are small and of human conformation. Furthermore, the Australopithecinae were typically found (Bartholomew and Birdsell, 1953) in association with mammalian fauna of the open grasslands of southern Africa, on which fauna they carnivorously preyed.

The evidence for the carnivorous adaptation of the Australopithecinae, and of their employment of lethal weapons (despite the relative smallness of their brains, which were in the range 450-600 cc.), was first summarily stated by Raymond Dart in 1953, in his paper *The Predatory Transition from Ape to Man;* and this was followed, in 1957, by the detailed publication by the Transvaal Museum of the archaeological data on which Dart's views were based, in his monograph *The Osteodontokeratic Culture of Australopithecus Prometheus,* in which the weapons of bone, tooth, and horn employed by these hominids of the lower Pleistocene are fully described, illustrated, and discussed, as are their predatory, murderous, and cannibalistic predilections.

The Australopithecinae, then, are an evolutionary innovation, a primate species that, becoming terrestrial, achieved an unprecedented evolutionary advance by a predatory and carnivorous adaptation to their new environment, based on an upright stance and the adoption of lethal, manual weapons.

We are here confronted with events of great consequence for the understanding of man's nature, and of his emergence as a dominant species on this planet.

The predatory adaptation achieved by the Australopithecinae involved, we may infer, "a behavioural transition from a retreating to an attacking pattern" (Freedman and Roe, 1958), and to related changes of a phylogenetic kind. Prehistoric man was a hunter, and may be distinguished from all other living primates by his predatory habits which are well established by the Pithecanthropine evidence as well as that for the rest of the Palaeolithic period. With the discovery of the Australopithecinae and the nature of their highly specialized cultural adaptation to a predatory way of life, the palaeoanthropological evidence presents a prospect of human evolution in which, possibly since the lower Pleistocene, "carnivorous curiosity and aggression have been added to the inquisitiveness and dominance striving of the ape" (Washburn and Avis, 1958).

"Man," Washburn (1959) has recently written, "has a carnivorous psychology. It is easy to teach people to kill, and it is hard to develop customs which avoid killing. Many human beings enjoy seeing other human beings suffer, or enjoy the killing of animals . . . public beatings and tortures are common in many cultures."

It is significant, I would suggest, that palaeoanthropology has, during the last decade, revealed a possible phylogenetic basis for the conclusions about human aggression which have been reached by psychoanalytic research into man's nature. The view taken by these two disciplines is, furthermore, supported by general historical and ethnographical evidence.

I cannot here hope to survey all of the implications for evolutionary theory of the Australopithecine evidence, but I would like to indicate very briefly one or two of the more important of them. The Australopithecinae, we have seen, were hominids with small brains (in the range 450-600 cc.) who, nonetheless, used manual implements. The principal inferences to be drawn from these facts (Washburn, 1959) are that the evolution of the highly competent human hand occurred as a result of the new selective pressures that were initiated by the adoption of weapons and tools, and that the real increase in the brain size of the human species, of approximately three times, which took place during the Pleistocene, was also the result of this new cultural adaptation.

Confirmatory evidence for this hypothesis is to be found in the researches of Penfield and his associates (1952, 1959) on the localization of function in the cerebral cortex of man. In the monkey motor cortex (Woolsey and Settlage, 1950) the area associated with the hand is approximately as large as that for the foot. In the human brain, however, the area for the hand is relatively much larger. This, as Washburn (1959) has noted, supports the view that "the increase in the size of the brain occurred after the use of tools, and that selection for more skilful tool-using resulted in changes in the proportions of the hand, and of the parts of the hand (including primary motor and sense areas, and the areas concerned with the elaboration of skills)."

In broad anthropological perspective then, it may be argued that man's nature and skills and, ultimately, human civilization, owe their existence to the kind of predatory adaptation first achieved by the carnivorous Australopithecinae on the grasslands of southern Africa in the lower Pleistocene.

At the present stage of progress of human civilization, however, the aggressive disposition which served evolutionary development at various times in the past is perhaps man's most basic and difficult problem. It is not my purpose in this paper to discuss the methods by which human aggression may be controlled; let me merely, on this present occasion, state again my conviction that it is only by facing the realities of man's nature and of our extraordinary history as a genus that we shall be able to evolve methods likely, in some measure, to succeed.

From discussion following the presentation of "Human aggression"

J. D. Carthy (Department of Zoology, Queen Mary College, London, England): I wonder whether the development of weapons used at a distance might increase aggression by putting space between the two men so that gestures of submission became ineffective. What evidence is there of the use by the Australopithecinae of weapons which were thrown? I believe it has been suggested that they threw stones at baboons.

Freeman: Dr. Carthy's suggestion is, I think, of great interest. There is good ethological evidence that in many species gestures of submission do tend to inhibit aggression, and the invention of weapons capable of being used at a distance (which has been a constant trend in the evolution of weapons) is certainly counter to any such natural inhibitory process. Here is a problem which might well be taken up by ethologists and anthropologists alike. Stones thrown from the hand are used most effectively by primitive peoples, both in hunting and in war; of the early Hottentots, for example, it is said they used "showers of stones" in war, and that "the most amazing strokes of Hottentot dexterity are seen in their throwing of a stone" (Clark, 1959). Kortlandt and Kooij (1963) have recently surveyed agonistic throwing among infrahuman primates. On this, and other evidence, I would suppose that early hominids, like the Australopithecinae, were capable of such throwing. One of the postcards on sale at the British Museum (Natural History), I recollect, shows Australopithecus rushing forward, threatening, with a stone in his upraised hand. Dart (1957) has argued that some of the long bones found at Australopithecine sites were used as clubs, and almost certainly produced the matching, indented fractures seen on associated baboon skulls. It is not unlikely that stones were also used.

Sir Julian Huxley: It seems probable that a decisive step in recurring hominid dominance was the use of weapons (clubs and especially spears), both for predation and for defence against predators and especially rivals.

Freeman: Yes, I would agree on the decisive importance of weapons, but these included many types in addition to clubs and spears.

Huxley: Spears and clubs, being wooden, would not survive whereas the (non-aggressive) pebble tools characteristic of the Australopithecinae would.

Freeman: It is true that wooden weapons would not survive, but incorrect that pebble tools were characteristic of the Australopithecinae (Clark, 1959). The evidence amassed by Dart (1957) indicates that the weapons of the Australopithecinae were of bone, teeth, and horn, and that these weapons represent an evolutionary stage antecedent to the working of pebbles. It is likely that rudimentary wooden clubs (i.e., branches, etc.) were also used. Kortlandt and Kooij (1963) have recently discussed agonistic clubbing by chimpanzees.

Konrad Lorenz: Animals can be made to behave like men and massacre the fellow members of their own species. If one crowds a dozen roe deer into a pen in a zoo, the most gory massacre is the result. I think that Professor Washburn in the sentence quoted by Dr. Freeman ("Man has a carnivorous psychology") does grave injustice to carnivores. Those that have power to hurt most grievously by using their hunting weapons usually have correspondingly reliable inhibiting mechanisms preventing them from hurting the fellow members of their species. Wolves and lions do not usually commit massacre even under abnormally crowded conditions.

Freeman: I fully accept what Professor Lorenz has said in defence of lions, wolves, and other carnivores. It is not possible for me to answer for Professor Washburn, whose words I have quoted, but I am sure he would, with me, deplore injustice being done to such noble creatures. My own view is that the term carnivorous when it is used to refer to the behaviour of the Hominidae has to give a meaning quite distinct from that which it has when applied to species within the order Carnivora.

Huxley: Carnivorous predators are not aggressive in the customary sense when hunting – only when attacked. Herbivores like rhino, African buffalo, and elephant are among the most aggressive of animals. There is no correlation between diet and aggressivity.

Freeman: Sir Julian Huxley's statements about the carnivores and herbivores known to zoology, I accept, but I would question whether such findings can be automatically applied to the human animal. A snare here is the term carnivorous, which would seem to have a somewhat different meaning for zoologist and anthropologist. For the zoologist it is an epithet he applies to any carnivore. Literally carnivorous means "feeding on flesh," and it is, therefore, a fitting word to describe such feeding by the human animal. Feeding on flesh was a major feature of hominid adaptation during the one or two million years of the Pleistocene, and (in most cultures) it remains the habit of contemporary man, with the innovation that today it is the flesh of domesticated rather than hunted animals on which men feed. However, when as an anthropologist I refer to the Hominidae as being carnivorous I am certainly not classing them with members of the order Carnivora. On present evidence the carnivorous habit characteristic of the Hominidae emerged, during the Pleistocene, with the evolution of manual weapons and an adaptation based on hunting. It is possible, however, that a predilection for flesh-eating and a capacity to capture some kinds of prey may have been in existence before the evolution of actual weapons; and these developments, indeed, may have been among the selective pressures which led to the devising of rudimentary manual weapons by the Australopithecinae, and early members of the genus *Homo,* such as (possibly) *Homo habilis* (Leakey, Tobias, and Napier, 1964). Evidence for this hypothesis is to be found in the recently published researches of Miss Jane Goodall (of Newnham College, Cambridge) on the behaviour of wild chimpanzees (*Pan satyrus schweinfurthi*) in Tanganyika. Miss Goodall reports having observed the capture, killing, and eating of a red colobus monkey by one of these wild chimpanzees (Goodall, 1963b), and, on other occasions, the eating of "a very young bushpig," and "a bushbuck about one month old" (Goodall, 1963a). The predatory adaptations of hominids during the Pleistocene were plainly of a markedly different kind from those which have evolved, by phylogenetically distinct processes, among the Carnivora. Further, in the case of the hominids, we may possibly be dealing with animals which evolved lethal manual weapons and became predatory and carnivorous, but who lacked the efficacious, phylogenetically given inhibitory mechanisms of the Carnivora. So, in the light of recent palaeoanthropological discoveries, the hypothesis has now been advanced that certain aspects of human nature (including possibly aggressivity and cruelty) may well be connected with the special predatory and carnivorous adaptations which were so basic to hominid evolution during the Pleistocene period. This, in my view, is an hypothesis that deserves to be investigated scientifically and dispassionately, for it concerns matters about which we are, at present, most ignorant. . . .

C. J. O. Harrison (British Museum, Natural History, London): Dr. Freeman has suggested that at a certain period in evolution man became much more aggressive in his behaviour. This would seem to have occurred at the time when men were tending to group themselves in larger units and there must have been a need to inhibit aggressive behaviour within the group together with a need for an outlet for such dammed-up aggression. This aggression might then be canalized and an individual outside the group might be the recipient of the redirected aggression of the entire group. In such circumstances there might not be an increase in the amount of aggressive behaviour present in man but a great manifestation of it when it was redirected by an entire group to a single end.

Freeman: I would agree that Dr. Harrison has drawn attention to a basic process in the aggressive behaviour between tribes and nations which has characterized human history. It is also a process, I would add, very much to be found within societies. There is, for example, often considerable inhibition of aggression under parental dominance within the family, and this may lead to the redirection of aggressive impulses within the family, as also on to others beyond the family, but within the same society. The whole question of the redirection of aggression within and by human groups is, I consider, eminently worthy of intensive further study.

References

Allen, C. K. 1958. *Aspects of Justice.* London: Stevens and Sons.

Anon. 1896. The Constantinople Massacre. *Contemporary Review,* vol. 70, pp. 457-465.

Bartholomew, G. A., and Birdsell, J. B. 1953. Ecology and the Protohominids. *American Anthropologist,* vol. 55, pp. 481-498.

Blanc, A. C. 1961. Some evidence for the ideologies of early man. *Social Life of Early Man,* ed. S. L. Washburn. Chicago: Viking Fund Publications in Anthropology No. 31.

Broom, R., and Schepers, G. W. H. 1946. *The South African Fossil Ape-Men, the Australopithecinae.* Pretoria: Transvaal Museum Memoir No. 2.

Clark, J. Desmond. 1959. *The Pre-history of Southern Africa.* Harmondsworth: Penguin.

Clark, W. E. Le Gros. 1958. *History of the Primates: An Introduction to the Study of Fossil Man.* 6th Edition. London: British Museum (Natural History).

Corfield, F. D. 1960. *Historical Survey of the Origins and Growth of Mau Mau.* London: Her Majesty's Stationery Office.

Dart, R. 1925. *Australopithecus africanus:* The man-ape of South Africa. *Nature,* vol. 115, pp. 195-199.

____. 1953. The predatory transition from ape to man. *International Anthropological and Linguistic Review,* vol. 1, pp. 201-219.

____. 1957. *The Osteodontokeratic Culture of Australopithecus Prometheus.* Pretoria: Transvaal Museum Memoir No. 10.

____. 1959. *Adventures with the Missing Link.* New York: Harper and Brothers.

Darwin, C. 1871. *The Descent of Man.* New York: Modern Library Edition (1949).

Davie, M. R. 1929. *The Evolution of War.* New Haven: Yale Univ. Press.

Dillon, E. J. 1896. Armenia: an appeal. *Contemporary Review,* vol. 69, pp. 1-19.

Durbin, E. F. M., and Bowlby, J. 1938. Personal aggressiveness and war. *War and Democracy: Essays on the Causes and Prevention of War,* ed. E. F. M. Durbin and George Catlin. London: Routledge and Kegan Paul.

Eisler, R. 1951. *Man into Wolf.* London: Routledge and Kegan Paul.

Federn, P. 1952. *Ego Psychology and the Psychoses.* New York: Basic Books.

Freedman, L. Z., and Roe, A. 1958. Evolution and human behaviour. *Behaviour and Evolution,* ed. A. Roe and G. G. Simpson. New Haven: Yale Univ. Press.

Freud, Sigmund. 1905. *Three Essays on the Theory of Sexuality.* Standard Edition, vol. VII. London: Hogarth Press.

____. 1909. *Analysis of a Phobia in a Five-Year-Old Boy.* Standard Edition, vol. X. London: Hogarth Press.

____. 1930. *Civilization and its Discontents.* Standard Edition, vol. XXI. London: Hogarth Press.

____. 1932. *Why War?* Collected Papers, vol. V. London: Hogarth Press.

Ginsberg, M., and Glover, E. 1934. A symposium on the psychology of peace and war. *The British Journal of Medical Psychology,* vol. 14, pp. 274-293.

Goodall, Jane. 1963a. Feeding behaviour of wild chimpanzees. *Symposium No. 10, The Zoological Society of London,* pp. 39-48.

____. 1963b. My life among wild chimpanzees. *National Geographic Magazine,* vol. 124, pp. 272-308.

Hogg, G. 1958. *Cannibalism and Human Sacrifice.* London: Robert Hale.

James, W. 1911. *Memories and Studies.* London: Longmans, Green and Co., p. 301.

Klein, Melanie. 1949. *The Psycho-Analysis of Children.* London: Hogarth Press.

Kortlandt, A., and Kooij, M. 1963. Protohominid behaviour in primates. *Symposium No. 10, The Zoological Society of London,* pp. 61-88.

Leakey, L. S. B. 1960. The origin of the genus *Homo. The Evolution of Man,* ed. Sol Tax. Chicago: Univ. of Chicago Press.

Leakey, L. S. B., Tobias, P. V., and Napier, J. R. 1964. A new species of the genus *Homo* from Olduvai Gorge. *Nature,* vol. 202, no. 4927, pp. 7-9.

Lissagaray. 1898. *History of the Commune of 1871.* New York: International Publishing Co.

Menninger, K. 1938. *Man Against Himself.* New York: Harcourt, Brace and Co.

Moon, P. 1962. *Divide and Quit.* London: Chatto and Windus.

Oakley, K. 1957. Tools makyth man. *Antiquity,* vol. 31, pp. 199-209.

Pelham, C. 1887. *The Chronicles of Crime, or The New Newgate Calendar.* 2 vols. London: T. Miles and Co.

Penfield, W., and Rasmussen, T. 1952. *The Cerebral Cortex of Man: A Clinical Study of Localization of Function.* New York: Macmillan.

Penfield, W., and Roberts, L. 1959. *Speech and Brain Mechanism.* Princeton: Princeton Univ. Press.

Phillips, R. 1949. *Trial of Josef Kramer and Forty-four Others (The Belsen Trial).* London: William Hodge and Co.

Pike, L. O. 1873, 1876. *A History of Crime in England.* 2 vols. London: Smith, Elder and Co.

Portman, A. 1942. *Grenzen des Lebens.* Basel: Friederich Reinhardt.

Reel, A. F. 1949. *The Case of General Yamashita.* Chicago: Univ. of Chicago Press.

Richardson, L. F. 1960. *Statistics of Deadly Quarrels.* London: Stevens and Sons.

Russell, Lord (of Liverpool). 1954. *The Scourge of the Swastika.* London: Cassell.

Schilder, P. 1951. *Psychoanalysis, Man and Society.* New York: Norton.

Scott, J. P. 1958. *Aggression.* Chicago: Univ. of Chicago Press.

Sleeman, C., and Silkin, S. C. 1951. *Trial of Sumida Haruzo and Twenty Others (The "Double Tenth" Trial).* London: William Hodge.

Sleeman, W. H. 1836. *Ramaseena.* Calcutta: Military Orphan Press.

Stekel, W. 1953. *Sadism and Masochism: The Psychology of Hatred and Cruelty.* 2 vols. New York: Liveright.

Taylor, M. 1839. *Confessions of a Thug.* London: Oxford Univ. Press. (World Classics, 1916).

Tuker, F. 1950. *While Memory Serves.* London: Cassell.

Turberville, A. S. 1949. *The Spanish Inquisition.* London: Oxford Univ. Press.

Vidal-Naquet, P. 1963. *Torture: Cancer of Democracy, France and Algeria, 1954-62.* London: Penguin Books.

Waelder, R. 1960. *Basic Theory of Psychoanalysis.* New York: International Universities Press, pp. 141-142.

Walker, T. A. 1899. *A History of the Law of Nations,* Vol. I: *From the Earliest Times to the Peace of Westphalia, 1648.* Cambridge: Cambridge Univ. Press.

Washburn, S. L. 1959. Speculations on the inter-relations of the history of tools and biological evolution. *The Evolution of Man's Capacity for Culture,* ed. J. N. Spuhler. Detroit: Wayne State Univ. Press.

Washburn, S. L., and Avis, V. 1958. Evolution of human behaviour. *Behaviour and Evolution,* ed. A. Roe and G. G. Simpson. New Haven: Yale Univ. Press.

Washburn, S. L., and Howell, F. C. 1960. Human evolution and culture. *The Evolution of Man,* ed. Sol Tax. Chicago: Univ. of Chicago Press.

Washburn, S. L., and DeVore, I. 1961. Social behaviour of baboons and early men. *Social Life of Early Men,* ed. S. L. Washburn. Chicago: Viking Fund Publications in Anthropology, No. 31.

Woolsey, C. N., and Settlage, P. H. 1950. Pattern of localization in the precentral cortex of *Macaca mulatta. Fed. Proc. Amer. Soc. Exp. Biol.,* vol. 9, p. 140.

PART THREE

Variability in primate behavior

The following four scientists, in contrast to those of the preceding section, reject generalizations concerning the genetic predispositions of primates, stressing instead their marked behavioral plasticity and dependence upon learning.

Ethologists Crook, Southwick, and Reynolds detail a number of intraspecific variables in life ways and habits by which primate populations have adapted to different ecological settings and food sources. They find some such traits appearing as seemingly spontaneous innovations, or arising in response to stresses involving habitat displacement or captivity, food deprivation, or exposure to threats or frustrations. A few behavioral curiosae (for instance, sweet potato washing among some groups of Japanese monkeys) seem almost to deserve the status of "culture traits."

Holloway, a physical anthropologist, is especially eloquent in his disbelief in the utility of primate field studies and research designs for analyzing the bases of human conflict and violence, which he believes rest rather upon purely cultural, symbolic constructions.

T. A. Rowell's article "Variability in the social organization of primates" (in *Primate Ethology,* edited by D. Morris, Aldine, Chicago, 1967, pp. 219-235) offers further data on intraspecific behavioral differentiation.

10

The nature and function of territorial aggression

John H. Crook

Ethology and mass culture

Within the last few years the young science of ethology has become "popular" with consequences that its more reserved practitioners have yet to comprehend. Television interviews, articles in magazines, comment in the press and books of mass circulation all thrust this rather reticent science increasingly before the public gaze. In addition, when some of its earlier tenets are presented as explanations for human ills in areas seemingly untouched by psychology and social science, it not surprising that the clamour becomes a marketable product.

Mr. Robert Ardrey, in his introduction to *The Territorial Imperative,* eloquently describes his personal discovery of the huge body of attentive readers his book *African Genesis* had disclosed. Mass literacy provides a market for mass products and indeed a new genre of publication on the problems of animal behaviour and their relevance to the "human situation" has come into being; a genre distinguishable in many ways from popular scientific writing of the type presented, for example, by the Pelican books on scientific subjects. In the latter an authority presents a carefully weighted digest of contemporary research and theory for public information and discussion. The new product, burnished and furnished with all the artifice skilled authorship can employ, seeks the simple statement, the dramatic story, and, above all, an essentially sensational account of human troubles that in simple explanation relieves the anxiety born of our

SOURCE: *Man and Aggression,* M. F. Ashley Montagu, ed., Oxford University Press, 1968. Reprinted by permission of the editor.

massive concern with war, aggression, and sex in a disordered world. A good talking point sells better than serious argument.

It would be dangerous, however, for behaviour scientists to think that such works were merely *kitsch,* mass products for a consumer society, for they are informed by extensive reading of the authoritative texts. Furthermore, the viewpoints presented are plausible, entertaining, and appear to instruct. They also reflect, albeit darkly, the contemporary trend towards biological explanation in both psychology and social anthropology largely the result of two main developments. First, the recent conceptual revisions of motivation theory in ethology have allowed a closer relationship with comparative psychology, so long dominated in America by a theoretical framework derived from behaviourism. Techniques of operant conditioning become tools in motivation research by ethologists, and psychologists pay a new respect to ethological experimentation in field and laboratory. Naturally, unresolved conflicts remain, but enough has been achieved for R. A. Hinde (1966) to subtitle his recent important textbook *Animal Behaviour,* with the phrase *A Synthesis of Ethology and Comparative Psychology.* Second, the study of the relationship between behaviour and ecology and the evolution of animal social organization, for long the field of ethology alone, has attracted the attention of certain social anthropologists (e.g., Fox, 1967) looking for a new derivational approach explaining the origins of human behaviour and social structure in terms of those of our nonhuman forebears.

The question that disturbs the practising ethologist is whether the new genre adequately presents the difficulties inherent in the new orientations of behavioural biology or whether it is a glib or one-sided approach which could bring the whole endeavour into disrepute. As M. V. C. Jeffreys (1962) describes in *Personal Values in the Modern World* it is extremely difficult for the individual subjected to a mass culture to discover the basis for views that affect ethical values – even more so when complex doctrines of social and maybe political relevance are purveyed in popular form and become rapidly the stock subjects for after-dinner conversation and assertion. We shall return to this problem in our last paragraphs. Our first concern is with the adequacy of certain of the popular accounts of ethological theory recently published. Do they really inform as much as they may entertain? Our task is to discuss Mr. Ardrey's account of territorial behaviour in man and animals, a task that leads us also to consider some views expressed in Konrad Lorenz's popular book *On Aggression* (1966), which in certain respects bears the same theme.

Instinct, territory, and social engineering

Anyone who has listened to the film script of *Khartoum* will recognise in Robert Ardrey a dramatist of calibre. In *The Territorial Imperative* (1967) the same gifts of authorship are displayed prominently. He has a feel for the beauty of natural environment and the ability to describe the excitement of observing animals at close quarters, be it in the savannahs of Africa or in the plastic dishes of the worm-runner's laboratory, which must be the envy of his less-endowed fellow enthusiasts. He has also read in some depth the detailed studies relevant to his theme. He portrays too with vivid pen the conflicts, joys, disappointments, and the often narrow-minded conformity of practising scientists – a picture of a community of men often far from flattering. For the general reader there is much here to relish and enjoy.

Ardrey is concerned basically with the cause of war and man's unpleasantness to man. His explanation centres upon an account of territorial behaviour. Man, Ardrey tells us, is a species of animal whose natural properties include an instinct of territorial aggression. Territoriality is conceived as an innate character of the human species as a consequence of evolutionary inheritance and, more generally, treated as a genetically determined form of animal behaviour. We find him repeatedly referring to an "instinct" or "force" "called territory" (pp. 59, 62, 166). Territoriality expresses an innate drive to gain and defend property, but, in that animals recognise the rights of ownership and withdraw when threatened by an owner, the behaviour reveals individual restraint which is interpreted by Ardrey as a form of natural morality. The functions of ownership are said to be the provision of nest site (in birds), a territorial periphery at which stimulative interaction with companions may occur, and identity in that an individual becomes part of an interacting community. These three points, derived in part from the work of well-known naturalists, are stressed again in the last chapter, although here the order of importance is reversed. The basic primordial psychological necessities to life are now identity, stimulation, and security, all of which the instinctive drive to gain and preserve a territory provides. The fact that many animals do not appear to be territorial is evidently of scant relevance because it is those that show this similarity to man that are the focus of interest.

Ardrey distinguishes between two types of society – the *noyau* – a term lifted from the French text of a work by J. J. Petter (1962) on the lemurs of Madagascar – and the *nation*. The *noyau* is a society of "inward antagonism" held together, Ardrey claims, by the mutual animosity of its members. In species after species, Ardrey reminds us, natural selection appears to have promoted social mechanisms that seem to function for no other reason than to alleviate boredom through the promoting of antagonism and excitement. Why this should be so he leaves unexplained (p. 162), but considers the *noyau* an "evolutionary step towards societies characterised by mutual aid" (p. 167), one, indeed, that provides a primitive security of mutual hate. The other type of society, the biological *nation*, is a social group which must contain at least two adult males and which is separated from other groups by antagonism. In a *nation* joint defence of territory promotes the emergence of in-group leadership and co-operation. Examples of *noyaux* include herring gull colonies, song sparrow neighbourhoods, the small and solitary groups of *Lepilemur* in Madagascar forests, and the "family" groups of gibbons and *Callicebus* monkeys. Among *nations* may evidently be included baboons, even though territorial behaviour is usually marked by avoidance on the fringes of home ranges rather than aggression, and those diurnal societies of lemurs that live with *Lepilemur* in Madagascar forests. Ardrey leaves the question as to why Petter's six nocturnal species of lemur appear to form *noyaux* while the nine diurnal ones are evidently *nations* unanswered, in spite of the strong ecological clues suggested by Petter himself. Ardrey's distinction between *noyaux* and *nations* is difficult to maintain. His *noyaux* species show very diverse types of social structure from pairs, to colonies, to family parties, to groups; and the reason why a pair of song sparrows, herring gulls, or gibbons collaborating in rearing young and defending their borders should be distinguished in any fundamental way from groups of baboons doing essentially the same thing is unclear. Certainly the "inner antagonism" of baboon troops is considerable, even though overt aggression is reduced through the social role-playing of animals learnt in relation to their individual dominance, age, and sexual statuses. Ardrey's categories indeed overlap so disastrously that the distinction largely disappears on close examination. This is not to say, of course, that major contrasts in social groups cannot be described by using well-defined natural criteria.

The difficulty is magnified when suddenly we read that Italy is a *noyau,* France (in 1939 without deGaulle as alpha male) also, but Germany, Britain, Japan, and the U.S.A. evidently not; nor, we may infer, is the Soviet Union. These are the nations. Greece was a *nation* because the Greeks with notable courage threw out Mussolini's soldiers in 1940. Mussolini thought his soldiers belonged to a *nation* but he was wrong. The Jews finally became a *nation* once the hazards of border defence imposed territory upon them, thereby eliciting those instincts they had forgotten for so long.

Ardrey asks how human territorial defence and war arose when man's most immediate ancestors were apparently nonaggressive apes resembling chimpanzees or gorillas. He provides a more or less orthodox interpretation from the authorities, noting the likely effect of increasing aridity in Africa in the relevant time period and the consequent development of carnivorous habits in protohominids. Armed with weapons and searching for limited protein resources supplied by the animals of the plain, men soon began to compete, formed territories, and this foreshadowed the development of the nation-state.

Modern man thus brings with him basic needs for identity, security, and stimulation, all of which are satisfied by territorial behaviour, through which that greatest stimulant, war, has come upon us. Ardrey's philosophy of real estate thus gains biological approval and the only trouble is that, nowadays, the war-game is too hazardous to play. In a chapter called the "Amity-Enmity Complex" Ardrey predicts that the removal of external hazard should result in the increase of enmity within groups. Above all, the removal of war necessitates a substitute, a ritualisation of aggression. The space race, he suggests, is not so much covert aggression but rather ritualised aggression – a game in which our tensions may be resolved without combat. Ardrey then takes from V. C. Wynne-Edwards the concept of "conventional competition," originally coined in a quite different and thoroughly rigorous context, and suggests that through "conventional competitions" identity and stimulation may be provided without the dangers of destructive conflict. The "natural morality" whereby intruders understand that aggression leads to stronger territorial response has not yet been acquired by men, possibly because his carnivorous propensities emerged late. We must learn to know ourselves and devise conventions. Whether morality without territory is for man a possibility remains for Ardrey the final problem.

Although imbedded in numerous digressions Ardrey's argument comes through the noise clearly enough. His book, published in 1967, resembles in certain details the ideas on human aggression published by Konrad Lorenz in *Das Sogenannte Böse* in 1963, translated into English in 1966. Lorenz, the "father" of ethology in its classical period, is justly considered one of the most distinguished of the older comparative ethologists and he has made major contributions to motivation theory, the study of parent-offspring relations and early learning, behavioural evolution, and the use of behavioural characters in taxonomy. He shares with Ardrey a profound concern with the human predicament and, in his book, seeks to utilise ethological concepts, largely of his own original formulation, in explanation of aggression in man and animals. The book, addressed to the general public, resembles Ardrey's in its style of popular presentation and in its selectivity of argument. Like Ardrey, Lorenz adopts a highly personal approach, writes in the first person and, as in his earlier *King Solomon's Ring,* reveals the joy and delight that any contemplative naturalist has in the study of complex animal behaviour. Lorenz considers aggressive behaviour in man and animals to be the expression of an innate drive; an appetite seeking consummation in its expression upon release by an appropriate stimulus presentation. He provides a chapter on motivational studies concerning the "spontaneity" of innate drives, which he uses as evidence for his particular approach. Aggression is of survival value to its practitioners because it ensures the dispersal of individuals and hence the optimum utilisation of resources. Competition ensures that only the fittest individuals breed. Fighting within groups promotes the formation of hierarchies which allow for the emergence of leadership. Aggressiveness is not, however, directed inappropriately to any member of a species, nor is it biologically advantageous for it to lead to the death of one antagonist and the possible exhaustion of the other. Natural selection has led to the development of postures which signal the submission of one of two opponents thereby reducing the attack drive of the other. Encounters become ritualised into threatening matches – intruders withdraw and owners retain their territories, a tiring opponent signals submission and the fight ceases. Sometimes complex relationships between individuals become based upon such rituals and involve the formation of strong affectional ties. Indeed, strong personal ties appear characteristic of societies within which marked intraspecific aggression occurs. Lorenz thinks that aggressiveness lies at the root of personal affection. Man differs from many other animals in that he lacks major morphological weapons and, in Lorenz's view, has thus never evolved the means of diverting disadvantageous aggressiveness through innate ritual. Man now lives in a society in which there is little acceptable opportunity for the useful or harmless release of his aggressive drive. Furthermore, with the advent of nuclear weapons, man holds the tool for his own extinction in his hands while he is yet unsure of the restraints he can impose on the impulse to attack. Lorenz, like Ardrey, suggests that competitive games provide the outlet for the collective fury of the *nations.* Through ritualisation and sublimation, aggression may be tamed enough to make life tolerable.

Certain assertions occur in both books. First, that man, in common with many other animals, has an innate territorial or aggressive drive seeking consummation in periodic performance. Second, a superficial comparison of animal societies reveals a variety of territorial and social dispersion patterns to which simple survival values are attributed in terms of optimum utilisation of commodities, selective elimination of the least fit, security and stimulation for the survivors. Third, man is defective in his control of his aggression by reason of his recent evolution without concomitant development of innate ritualised restraints. In both books the possibility that the leopard may change his spots through learning is dismissed. The instinct, rather, must be diverted into conventional substitutes for war. The case for social engineering rather than education is complete.

Is the account in these texts a reasonable basis for the inference from animals to man? To find out we must evaluate the key aspects of the story. First, we may pinpoint the main questions.

1. What is the evidence for an innate aggressive drive involving the defence of territory? Is such behaviour really the compulsive, spontaneous, unalterable force it is supposed to be? Or are aggressive animals modifiable, educable?
2. Do biologists really conceive of the survival value of territory in terms of security, stimulation, and identity? Upon what theoretical contributions have these ideas been based?
3. What is the role of territory in man's primate relatives and what may be inferred from this regarding the evolution of his social organisation?
4. Is the Lorenz-Ardrey explanation an adequate account of recent ethological thinking in relation to the problems of human relationship?

Motivation and territoriality

Ardrey repeatedly speaks of a force or instinct called "territory." The meaning of this term requires elucidation. A solitary animal cannot be territorial, for, to show defence of an area, at least one neighbour is needed. The term "territory" cannot, therefore, refer to an intrinsic aspect of the motivation of an individual but, rather, it refers to a relationship between two or more animals with respect to a location. Territory is a "group characteristic" arising out of the cohabitation of individuals in a given locality and which, as a result of their interaction, come to show a particular pattern of dispersion.

Traditionally, ethologists have been concerned with the fixed action patterns common to all individuals of a species population and which are mostly as stable in their manifestation as morphological traits. In many cases there are good reasons for considering such patterns to be more or less directly under genetic influence and their physiological control may be reasonably described as "innate." Lorenz's own work has contributed greatly to the understanding of such movements, the relative stereotyping of which permits their use in the systematics. Similar arguments may perhaps be applied to many of the movements expressive of emotion in primates including man. Species characteristic behaviour attributes such as temperamental traits and other more complicated features cannot, however, always be treated as innate characters. Common conditions of early rearing and parent-child relations throughout a population are now known to account for many regularities. Highly specific modes of learning may account for the elaboration of simple reflex patterns, as in the case of recent studies of bird song. Behaviour observably beneficial to individuals cannot therefore always be attributed, without extensive investigation, directly to the operation of natural selection of genes over many generations. Other processes may be at work. This is a particularly significant viewpoint when "group characteristics" such as "territory" or "dominance" are under consideration. The physical and social environment of a population may impose direct constraints on social structure. A salmonid fish, the ayu, shows territoriality in shallow brooks but moves in shoals in deep pools (Chapman, 1966). Certain rodents may be highly territorial in some environments at certain population concentrations but fail to show such behaviour under different conditions (Anderson, 1961). Populations of vervet monkeys have been found to be territorial in one habitat but to move in groups of contrasting size and behaviour in undefended home ranges in another (Gartlan, 1966). Ecological and social conditions are thus important in determining whether a population does or does not exhibit territorial behaviour. Its inevitability as a species character cannot simply be assumed.

Nevertheless, it is clear that in species which, under given conditions, reveal a population dispersion based on territoriality there must be some behavioural property that induces the members so to distribute themselves. In an important review, Tinbergen (1957) points out that when we are considering the defence of a geographically fixed site or area, territory is the result of two tendencies shown by the owner; first, site attachment and, second, hostility to that class of animals the members of which comprise the rivals or competitors. These two tendencies can occur independently of one another. Thus certain birds make use of regular roosting sites without defending them; and partridges, after pair formation, attempt to prevent the close approach of conspecifics, although this occurs without reference to a particular site. Furthermore, the functions of these two tendencies are commonly different. Tinbergen remarks that Howard's important studies of territorial behaviour (1920) tended to hinder the development of this distinction by focusing attention on their combined effects. "Simply because birds happen to be 'landed proprietors' (Selous, 1933) or, in other words, combine site attachment with hostility, there is a natural disinclination to consider the two aspects separately." Again, in considering territorial maintenance, both attack and escape are involved, and many cases of territorial dispersion result essentially from mutual avoidance rather than from combat. While all these factors combine to produce territorial behaviour, any analysis of its motivational control must consider each facet of the system separately. Several interrelated mechanisms are likely to be at work and susceptible to differential modification under changing conditions of population pressure or environment.

It is clear, however, that the most important element in the complex is the willingness of an individual to fight to maintain ownership when conditions require it to do so. The question is whether an innate drive to aggression of the sort described by Lorenz and assumed by Ardrey accounts for the observed phenomenon.

Lorenz's account of the proximate determination of aggressive behaviour is based upon a formulation of motivation theory largely developed by him in the classical ethology of the 1930's. According to his famous "hydraulic model" of instinctive behaviour (see Lorenz, 1950) the performance of fixed action patterns, such as are shown in sexual behavior or feeding, depends upon the accumulation of energy specific to these activities in centres in the conceptual nervous system. Release of this energy occurs when appropriate stimuli are provided, but in the absence of stimulation the energy must sooner or later find an outlet in relation to an inappropriate stimulus or even "in vacuum." Lorenz has commonly used the apparent spontaneity of behaviour under minimal stimulation as support for this view. However, the occurrence of aggressive behaviour seems rarely to fit such an account even descriptively. Lorenz's ideas were in large measure based upon Wallace Craig's distinction (1918) between the appetitive and consummatory phases of cyclic drives. According to Lorenz's account the action-specific energy appears first as appetitive behaviour and finds outlet in the performance of the consummatory act. In considering aggression Lorenz ignores, however, Craig's (1918, 1928) further and more important distinction between "appetites" and "aversions." Aversive behaviour is a response to undesirable or harmful stimulation and persists until the individual flees or until the stimulation is removed. Aggression, which Craig described as an "aversion," occurs in the social context only on the appearance of an offending individual and continues until one or other of the mutual offenders goes away. According to this account, aggressive behaviour is nonrhythmic and lacks an appetitive phase (see Chapter 5 in Marler and Hamilton, 1966). There is no theoretical requirement for aggressive behaviour to well up spontaneously without prior stimulation; and this appears to accord well with descriptive data. Studies which have revealed persistence in attacking on reduction in stimulation appear commonly to implicate a learning process whereby the repeated performance of aggression has secured beneficial reward and the response has generalised to a wide range of stimuli. Unusual persistence may also be due to changes in physiological conditions imposed by hunger, for example, or the recent performance of other aggressive acts. There is in fact no uncontroversial evidence that in the absence of stimulation, aggressiveness must find a spontaneous outlet. Lorenz's attempt to justify his explanation of the causes of aggression with descriptions of rhythmic behaviour in other contexts is largely irrelevant and fails to convince. In any case, the whole structure of motivation theory in ethology has undergone a major conceptual revision in recent years and even if aggression could be classified descriptively as an "appetite," the simple Lorenz-Ardrey account of its causation would have to be severely modernized. As Hinde (1967) remarked in a critical review: "Since Lorenz claims that his facts are verified and makes many generalisations with a voice of authority, while ignoring the bulk of the experimental literature on his subject, it is as well to reflect on them."

In animal societies, individuals do not fight because they have territories; they have territories because, among other things, they fight. The territorial context is not the only one in which aggression occurs. Individuals of many species, but by no means all, maintain a space around their bodies within which they repel approaching individuals. Individual distance infringements both in wild flocks of certain birds and in caged groups are thus a common cause of aggressive encounters. Marler (1956b) has shown that at sources of food chaffinch males usually either attack or withdraw if a companion approaches within about 20 cms. Females may approach more closely before they are attacked, but if they are experimentally coloured to look like males then they are repulsed at the same distances as other males. The weaver bird *Quelea quelea,* an extremely social species, tolerates approach to about 4 cms., and in caged groups some individuals rapidly come to win encounters more frequently than others so that individual distances are maintained as much by avoidance of attack by relatively subordinate individuals as by actual aggression (Crook, 1961). Repeated encounters give rise to hierarchies, the so-called "peck order" first described from flocks of chicken. Such dominance hierarchies are also found in many mammals living in social groups and, as in baboons, may become very complex with individuals playing elaborate roles resulting from their relative dominance, sex, and age statuses. Locations for sleeping, mating, nesting, or for a whole complex of activities can become an external reference for dominance. The relative dominance of Steller jays at feeding stations placed in winter at various distances from the nesting area of the previous season varied inversely with the distance (Brown, 1963). In great tits, robins, and many other species, interaction occurs primarily at the periphery of a territory within which intruders invariably flee. External reference for inter-male dominance may consist in the temporary location of a male's "family," as in wild geese and among male hamadryas and gelada baboons. Crowding and hormonal states may affect the type of aggressive reference individuals show. In certain fish, birds, and rodents, high population densities produce a shift from the holding of territories to the maintenance of individual dominance. Chaffinches, which show individual distance maintenance in winter flocks, show an increase in the area of intolerance as the gonads enlarge in spring; this enlargement rapidly acquiring topographical reference and leading to the establishment of territories (Marler, 1956a).

Territoriality is thus a special case of spatial defence not easily separable from the maintenance of personal space. It appears that the intolerance of individuals of certain species to the approach of conspecifics may increase under the influence of reproductive hormones, leading to an increase in individual distance. Much experimental work has shown that testosterone administration lowers the threshold for aggressive response, the hormonal effect being mediated via particular areas of the brain. Other hormones are now known to effect aggression. The ranking positions of starlings and queleas in hierarchies can be altered by the administration of luteinising hormone (L.H.) – experimentals improving their status. In *Quelea* the status ranking of individual birds in small groups may differ according to whether the hierarchy is calculated from encounters due to individual distance infringements on perches or based on the results of competitions for nesting material. Individual distance is maintained by L.H.-mediated aggression while testosterone level affects competitiveness for reproductively valent commodities (Crook and Butterfield, 1968). The relative subordination of female *Quelea* appears due to the inhibitory effects of oestrogen. Aggression is thus not an unitary phenomenon but the expression of the effect of the interaction of a number of factors both intrinsic and extrinsic to the performer. As our structural account of the process becomes more complete, the need to discuss it in terms of "instinct" will disappear (Bolles, 1967).

Increased hunger tends to provoke an increase in fighting through food competition. Many such encounters can be attributed to increased crowding at food sources and a high frequency of infringement of personal space. Some authors have, however, attributed such increases in aggressive encounters to frustration – meaning an interference preventing the completion of an on-going goal response. Certainly there is a great deal of psychological evidence supporting this contention for man (Dollard *et al.,* 1939), but experimental studies with animals have not yet clarified the question. Marler (1957) describes a caged male chaffinch of unstable rank in a hierarchy that developed the habit of making infrequent visits to the food source, remaining there longer than normal and fighting vigorously all others that approached him there. After the completion of the experiment this bird continued to show threat and to attack others at considerable distances whenever it became hungry. Although detailed studies remain to be done, it does not appear difficult to relate, at least in principle, the work on frustration and aggression in man to that on fighting in lower organisms. The complex programming of behaviour through the acquisition of cultural norms in both human and nonhuman primates leads to the inception of much inhibition or delay into ongoing behaviour. Whereas aggression in more primitive animals is elicited by a variety of relatively precise stimuli in given social contexts, the more complex interplay of motives within the elaborate societies of higher animals gives rise to greater problems of explication. At present the use of mentalistic terms such as "frustration" suffice to indicate behavioural contexts in which the threshold of aggressive tendencies is reduced. Continuing research will provide the precise details of the environmental and physiological circumstances attending this fact. Frustration was once considered to be the sole cause of hostility. There is no need now to adopt that view. The alternative, however, is not a nativistic explanation of the type presented in the books under discussion but a closer investigation of the precise conditions under which aggression is elicited in higher mammals.

In higher mammals and in man, as well as in more lowly creatures, the hereditary component of aggression consists in the tendency to react with attack or hostility to certain classes of stimulation. There is, however, as we have seen, no effective evidence for a genetically determined appetite for aggressive behaviour. The social organisation of advanced birds and mammals is, furthermore, known to depend upon the adoption of appropriate roles by young animals subject to learning in "socialisation." Ample work with nonprimate and primate mammals testifies to the importance of various types of learning and other nongenetic factors in the determination of individual temperament and behaviour (e.g., Thomson, 1965; Harlow and Harlow, 1965; and others). It is to be expected, therefore, that the tendency to show aggression may be modified by contrasting socialisation procedures. Freudian analysis has shown that in man, contrasts in toilet training during the "anal period" of maturation produce differing effects with regard to children's compliance or resistance to parental demand. Overpunitive methods tend to produce a fixation of defiant characteristics, including petulancy, pedantry, and overassertiveness involving aggressive elements. Conversely, guidance without punishment yields a more compliant character. The work of Robert Sears and others (e.g., Sears, Maccoby, and Levin, 1957) has shown that aggressive children are likely to come from homes where the expression of aggression is not regulated by family rules but rather is heavily punished. By the age of twelve, however, such children show less aggression than those from permissive homes with neither rules nor punishments. The least aggressive children come from homes which confront them from infancy with strong rules to prevent aggression but in which bad behaviour is controlled in a nonpunitive manner. In such homes praise and affection are balanced against the withdrawal of love when the child behaves badly. It appears that such treatment is effective in eliciting a strong conscience. The child's personality is developed through the necessity to consider his behaviour and decide upon his subsequent attitudes. Much depends upon the nature of parental "permissiveness" and the sort of rules used in family control of aggression. Current research has yet to describe fully these relationships and much work remains to be done.

There is no doubt that Ardrey is right to emphasise the fact that human beings like animals show assertion and aggression of many kinds in relation to the ownership of objects and property and also in relation to ethnic or national territory. Attitudes towards in-groups, out-groups, foreigners, other races, and the newspaper accounts of the doings of other governments and nations must nevertheless be determined in large measure by the cultural concomitants of socialisation experienced in childhood and adolescence. To ignore or dismiss important research on these effects is to abandon the most relevant evidence on the subject.

The functions of territory

The problems presented by territorial behaviour in nature remain many and mostly unresolved. Certainly the subject has not received the attention it deserves although current research into both avian and mammalian social organisation is rapidly increasing the information available for analysis. The subject has been reviewed several times; the studies by Nice in 1941, Hinde in 1956, Tinbergen in 1957, and Carpenter in 1958 give a comprehensive account of the history of the concept and state of knowledge up until those years. Recent work has tended to see territoriality as part of a wider conception framed, as it were, within the social system of a species itself considered in relation to population dynamics (Wynne-Edwards, 1962; Crook, 1965; Lack, 1966). Ardrey himself provides many good accounts of the earlier investigations and summarises many of the views current until about 1962.

Animals, particularly birds, have been recognised as holding territories at least since the days of Aristotle. Carpenter (1958) describes the history of the concept from Willoughby's notes on the nightingale in 1678 to the modern definition of the subject by Altum in 1868, Moffat in 1903, and Elliot Howard in 1907-14 and 1920. The descriptive data showed that territoriality involved the defence of an area more or less well-defined spatially and within which intruders normally fled when challenged, the most aggressive encounters occurring on the periphery of the territory bordering that of another individual. In its territory a bird makes itself conspicuous by vocal or visual display as also do, for example, the males of groups of certain lemurs, the vervet monkey, and the howler monkey, which live in territorial areas. Much of the aggression in territorial defence consists of threatening display or ritualised fighting whereby spacing is achieved with little damage done to the protagonists. Real fighting is, however, not always avoided. In early work the prime functions of territory were considered to be the maintenance of an area ensuring a sufficient food supply for the defender and his family and provision of a topographical focus for mating and nesting. Territory was also considered to be a mechanism limiting the number of pairs of birds in an area by spacing them. Fighting was thought to ensure that the strong rather than the weak reproduced.

The main body of information on territory has come from ornithology. In particular, a great diversity of territorial arrangements has become apparent. In his 1956 paper Hinde classified bird territories into four main types. The first consists of a large breeding area within which nesting, courtship and mating, and most food seeking usually occur; as in certain warblers (*Sylviidae*) and the robin, for example. The second type is a large breeding area but one which does not furnish most of the food, as, for example, in the nightjar, reed warbler, and the Euplectine weaver birds. In the third type, the territory is confined to a small area around the nest as in many bird colonies. Colonial polygamous species may build several nests in a territory. Feeding obviously occurs elsewhere and the spacing effect occurs only within the confines of the colony itself. In the last type the defended area, of small extent, is used solely for pairing or for mating. In gulls, pairing territories exist early in the breeding season separately from those locations used later for nesting. In "arena" birds males occupy small sites often placed closely together and to which females come. The males show elaborate displays and complex procedures exist whereby females choose a mate, the most remarkable system so far described in detail being that of the ruff. In addition, work on the birds of paradise and bower birds in Australasia and the manakins in Central America suggests that the tropical forests hide much that will prove remarkable. After mating, the females of "arena" birds go elsewhere for nesting and rear their young alone. In addition to normal territoriality, birds of certain species defend areas around their mates, their families, their young or a number of young irrespective of parentage, and, as we have seen, themselves. Defence of an area by a group is not common among birds but a number of examples are known. Among the *Crotophaginae* the ani lives in groups of 15 to 25 birds and defends an area around a communal nest in which several females lay (Davis, 1940). The Australian magpie (*Cracticidae*) holds group territories throughout the year and fights in teams, cock with cock and hen with hen (Carrick, 1963). In a number of other species, communalism involving the participation of a number of adults and juveniles in the rearing of young in a territory also occurs.

Among mammals, the family home or nest may be the focus of territorial behaviour, as in many rodents. In other cases, areas may be defended by relatively large groups that may spend some or all of their time there. The vicuna, a species of South American llama, has a system in which a male defends an area against other males and keeps his herd within bounds (Koford, 1957). Red deer move within circumscribed areas (Lowe, 1966), and prides of lions may attack other lions trespassing within their range (Schenkel, 1966). Adult male seals hold territories on beaches where a population hauls out for breeding, and the male Ugandan kob, studied by Buechner, whose report is well described by Ardrey, defends a small territory in an arena. The male kob's behaviour there resembles that of blackcock on a lek. The wildebeest in the Ngoro-ngoro crater near Serengeti apparently are territorial but, on the plains nearby, they defend mobile harem groups during long migrations. As with birds, some mammals are "distance" species and resent close approach, whereas others allow close contact.

In a survey of mammalian territories, Burt (1943) made an important distinction between areas that are actually defended and the area over which a group ranges. In many species, actual territorial defence does not occur and the home ranges of groups overlap markedly. Usually such ranges contain a "core area" in which the group centres most of its activities. Such "home range" systems intergrade with territorial ones, as in cases where groups avoid close contact rather than showing aggression. There is thus a gradient between tightly packed territorial groups and groups wandering in more or less undefended ranges often sharing the use of certain environmental commodities such as good feeding grounds or water holes. An important survey of a variety of such systems has recently been published under the editorship of Peter Jewell and Caroline Loizos (1966).

The very diversity of these mammalian and avian dispersion types suggests that any simple statement about the function of territorialism in general is almost bound to be inadequate. Among the many functions attributed to territory holding have been the promotion of dominance, the selective breeding of the strong, the reduction or regulation of sexual fighting, the enforcement of monogamy, the protection of nests and young from predators, the regulation of group size, the preservation of food supplies, the dispersion of populations, the localisation of waste disposal, and the limitation of the spread of diseases. The condensation of this range of possibilities into abstract principles such as identity, security, and stimulation not only appears premature but neglects the diversity of the phenomena; in different species territories may certainly have functions of widely differing kinds.

Although there is a considerable range both in the referents to which territorial behaviour may be shown and in the types of dispersion produced by it, early work suggested that all forms of territorial aggression, in common with other types of agonistic relationship such as dominance or individual distance behaviour, were due basically to the same motivational source (Hinde, 1956). Nevertheless, while all forms of fighting are essentially similar, it is clear that the threshold for the elicitation of aggressive behaviour is dependent upon a complex of physiological conditions which may vary independently and change seasonally. This threshold may be expressed as the distance from a territorially valent object towards which approach will elicit attack. Thus some species of birds become aggressive at greater distances from the nest than others. The sensitivity of individuals to the relationship between defended object and the distance at which aggression occurs appears subject to natural selection and – in that characteristic mean sizes of territory have been described for certain species – may be due to factors based on genetic inheritance. If fighting in territorial defence gives reproductive advantages to breeding male birds, for example, it can be predicted that the genetic basis for the trait will become relatively fixed and transmitted from generation to generation.

The fundamental survival values of aggressive behaviour in social life can be conceived only in relation to intraspecific competition. In addition, however, the holding of space appears to reduce direct competition for a commodity and to allow the development of social competition promoting the evolution of ritualised ceremony. Lockie (1956) pointed out that birds which maintain individual distances in winter flocks keep to an interindividual dispersion that reduces actual combat for food. The more dominant animals defeat subordinates in spatial threat during competition for a food object, but the latter, which remain undamaged, can continue to search. Actual combat could damage the subordinate severely and weaken the stronger bird. Nevertheless, fighting for food does occur when starvation is sufficient to override distance maintenance. The effect of a range of individual dominance values in flocks is thus likely to produce differential starvation during food shortage – the more dominant birds being more likely to survive.

Intraspecific competition is most meaningfully discussed in the context of population dynamics. Most bird species in temperate zones show an annual cycle of numbers with marked winter mortality. Following an unusually severe winter, losses are replaced by spring breeding and numbers increase until breeding individuals are forced more closely together in their chosen habitat. There will come a point at which certain commodities essential for life or reproduction, such as nesting sites, appropriate cover, or food, come into short supply. Clearly the type of commodity most likely to fall into shortage will depend greatly on the ecological niche occupied by a species. The successful defence of such commodities will tend to ensure the perpetuation of an individual's genes through successful reproduction and hence the selection of the traits that gave it advantage. Territorial defence is likely to arise in many species but, in that they tend to experience different types of competitive contingency, the sorts of territoriality displayed will be quite diverse over a wide range of cases.

An explanation of a territorial system may not, however, rely only on the concept of the natural selection of genetic factors. While in some species territory size is markedly stable, in others considerable variation is found. Certain swamp-dwelling weavers breed in large territories in small bushes fringing the swamp, but they may also utilise a large tree islanded in the flood wherein they breed in extremely small territories crowded together and forming a colony. The baya weaver of India commonly breeds in large palm trees in colonies, but in homogenous scrubland relatively isolated nests have been recorded. Here the territory size is highly labile, the individual adapting itself to the apparently optimum circumstances in any given locality. Species that otherwise appear to show stable territory sizes are probably affected to some extent in a similar way. For example several British woodland birds breed at greater densities near housing estates, where their winter survival is higher than in natural woodlands, where it is comparatively low. On Mandarte Island, Canada, a population of song sparrows divided up the habitat into similarly sized territories for several years. Then, suddenly, they increased numbers by half as much again indicating that the territory size was not strictly controlling the number of birds present but was rather an expression of it (Tompa, 1964). A similar increase in the numbers of great tits breeding in a wood near Oxford suggests the same could be true for this species. In all these cases then the dispersion of a species population was largely controlled by ecological aspects and population density. Territories, however, appear to be of limited compressibility and hence provide a species with certain environmental qualities without which its members cannot reproduce.

Unfortunately, relatively little experimental work has been done on the territories of wild animals and hence the relative importance of the different determinants of territorial dispersion in any given case remains to be determined adequately. It seems, however, clear that the information required for an adequate account of a given dispersion pattern must come from at least three sources. The first concerns the hereditary traits of the species governing its tendency to maintain the defence of certain commodities and the distances (thresholds of response to intrusion) from these at which aggression will occur. How far such responsiveness is actually inherited or acquired during some process of imprinting in relation to habitat and parental behaviour requires experimental analysis. The second group of factors concerns the relative availability of commodities essential for survival and reproduction. The third set concerns the density of the population and the type of social community in which the population exists. We have already argued that territoriality cannot be conceived as a species property, like leg length or plumage pattern; rather it is a group characteristic expressing the effects of the interaction of individuals with one another and the environment. Territory is but a single aspect of the social system shown by a species. An understanding of the system as a whole is more likely to inform us regarding territory than will the particular study of territory to the neglect of other social behaviours.

In a recent survey of avian social systems in relation to ecology, Crook (1965) examined correlations between some six types of nonbreeding social-dispersion pattern, four types of breeding-season pattern, and a number of ecological characteristics including habitat and food type, food dispersion, and nest sites of 115 avian taxonomic families in which little variation between species in social organisation had been reported. Seventy-nine showed patterns of dispersion involving the holding of sizeable pair territories for breeding. Of these, territory holding characterised nonbreeding dispersion in some forty families. The remaining thirty-nine families showed gregarious flocking outside the breeding season. Twenty-four families showed colonial breeding involving the holding of small territories in densely occupied sites and flocking behaviour in the nonbreeding period. No families, however, showed a pattern involving out of breeding season territoriality with breeding season flocking. The most persistently territorial birds occurred in some twenty-eight primarily insectivorous families, two carnivorous ones, four fish eating, two nectar feeding, and a few more or less omnivorous ones. Almost all these birds must hunt or search for their food and their success depends on cryptic approach, speed, and skill. The relatively solitary nature of these species is therefore considered an adaptation to this mode of food exploitation for which gregarious flocking would tend to be of little assistance. This is, however, not the whole story. When the territorial breeders which flock in "winter" are considered, an association between territory holding and cryptic nest siting in locations not otherwise naturally protected from the approach of predators is found. Protection of nests and their contents thus emerges as an important function of territorial behaviour. The flocking behaviour in the nonbreeding season is related to the utility of rapid congregation made possible at dispersed food sources and to protection against predators. In certain species such as the kingfisher, the linear shape of the habitat along the river banks, for example, appears to correlate with the holding of sizeable territories. The nest site in holes seems sufficiently protective to allow colony formation should this be advantageous. However, an increase in population density in a restricted breeding site would rapidly deplete food resources in the vicinity and necessitate search at a distance. It would be advantageous for members of a species in such a habitat to disperse themselves more "in order" to work less hard in food finding when rearing young. Territory size in such cases may be related to the food content of the territorial area.

Colony formation commonly develops in correlation with evidence that the chosen sites are in some way protective and prevent the intrusion of predators. Dense breeding is also associated with a large surrounding area from which the colony inhabitants may draw sustenance for their young in common. Within colonies the actual spacing of nests may be related to the incidence of predator intrusion. Tinbergen (1953) showed that the herring gull colonies to which predators had gained access had nests more widely dispersed than usual. Among the species of Euplectine weavers those with nests in the most protected places in swamps tend to nest territorially in colonies but those building nests hidden in homogenous grassland have much larger territories dispersed in "neighbourhoods." In this case the discovery of one nest by a predator would not lead easily to the discovery of another.

The maintenance of territories within dense colonies is evidently related not only to the defence of a nest site but more particularly perhaps to the prevention of interference from rival males or females in the pairing and mating procedure of the owners. In weaver colonies, males may sometimes attempt copulations with neighbouring females in the absence of the territory owner, and females may attempt to occupy already occupied nests and have then to be driven out by the owning pair. In weavers, too, a great deal of nest robbing for nest-building materials occurs. In some species with short breeding seasons, males rarely leave their territories except to obtain materials and food in brief sallies. The development of true communal life involving co-operation between members of a group is rare in birds, and limited research suggests it occurs when parents experience difficulty in rearing broods and the participation of juveniles or other "helpers" becomes of selective advantage both to parents and, in their turn, to their helpers. Complex social interactions involving ritualised ceremonies reducing the incidence of intragroup aggression have evolved in some of these groups. Certainly intragroup aggression tends to be markedly reduced in such groups which have sometimes been referred to as "sisterhoods." Some of these groups appear to be "clans" – closely related individuals of two or more generations living together. Such species may breed at considerable population densities and then, as in the well-studied case of the Australian magpie (*Gymnorhina tibicen*), group territoriality appears, the function of which appears related to food supply (Carrick, 1963).

The complex group territories of certain mammals associate both with the defence of females by a male and with the holding of a relatively well-defined area (i.e., the vicuna) within which the food supply is located. In the "arena" breeders such as the kob, territory holding is related to competition between males for the sexual attention of females, and the holding of space prevents or greatly reduces the likelihood of interference with mating once it starts. Among seals and sea lions, males hold territories that contain their "harems."

While the diversity of cases is considerable and each requires detailed individual analysis, enough has been said to suggest that among the main functions of territory holding are: the maintenance of dispersion, so that individual hunting techniques may be performed without interference; the maintenance of an area providing a food supply requisite for rearing young or maintaining group existence; the reduction of crowding of cryptic nests so as to reduce the likelihood of their discovery by predators; and the prevention of interference with nesting, courtship, mating, and sometimes the rearing of young. We need not quibble with Ardrey over his use of the blanket term "security" to cover all these cases. We should, however, stress that the diversity of functions that territory holding performs is a consequence of adaptive radiation of species into a wide variety of ecological niches. The nature of competition imposed by the adaptations of a species to a given habitat defines the type of territorial behaviour seen.

Ardrey is right to point out that many territories occur in neighbourhoods or colonies and that equally suitable areas may remain unoccupied. He discusses this in terms of the stimulation evoked by the defence of territorial peripheries but he does not treat its probable function. Darling's original suggestion (1938) referred to the possibility that the social stimulation of colonial life helped to synchronise breeding, thereby reducing the length of the breeding period which in turn decreased the period of heavy predation on young. His data did not, however, prove the point unequivocally, and it remains a fascinating hypothesis. The role of behavioural interaction in promoting breeding synchronisation has, however, been accepted by several recent authors with particular reference to colonial birds. Synchronisation may function in at least two ways. First, it may ensure that as many birds as possible start breeding early in a short breeding season and this increases the likelihood of their rearing young in the annual period of optimum food supply. Second, the mass departure of young may reduce the effects of predation. In theory at least, if the young birds were leaving at staggered intervals a greater number would fall foul of the waiting carnivores. Should these hypotheses be tested in further studies such as those by Patterson (1965) and generally confirmed, the survival value of social stimulation will be seen as a consequence of environmental adaptation rather than as providing excitement of value in itself, as Ardrey seems to suggest.

One of the effects of holding a sizeable area of land for breeding is certainly to space out the individuals of a population. V. C. Wynne-Edwards (1962) has suggested that not only is the prime function of territory to produce dispersal but that dispersion itself functions to control population size (see also Moffat, 1903). This hypothesis forms part of a broader theory which holds that social organisation is essentially a mechanism for providing "conventional competition" whereby numbers are regulated by homeostatic dispersal in relation to food resources. Populations are thereby believed to maintain optimum numbers in relation to resources. Competition is said to be conventional in that its putative function is to measure the density of the population present and relate the finding to food supplies. If the indicated numbers are likely to overexploit the actual supply an exodus of the surplus population follows. Territorial competition is treated as a convention having these supposed advantageous effects. It is true that dispersal may result from territorial behaviour but the suggestion that this is a primary survival value is far from proven. Territorial behaviour could have this effect even if the functions for which it was evolved were quite different. In any case our comparative study of the range of territory types shows that only some of them could function in the way Wynne-Edwards' theory requires and none of them need necessarily do so.

Wynne-Edwards' hypothesis regarding the significance of social structure has received much criticism and appears unlikely to prove acceptable in its entirety (Crook, 1965; Lack, 1966; and others). The evidence from field studies relating population dispersion to the natural control of numbers and territorial behaviour is furthermore highly inconclusive. Lack (1966) has recently surveyed the findings of several of the more detailed ornithological reports on the relation between territoriality and population control. For example, each pair of wood pigeons defends an area around its nest and the resultant spacing probably assists the concealment of nests from predators. The birds, however, feed in flocks; the territory cannot therefore conserve a food supply and there is no reason to think it regulates numbers. In other species, population is known to be regulated by actual food shortage rather than by any factors producing dispersion. Again, as we have already remarked, both the song sparrow on Mandarte Island and great tits at Oxford showed numbers of breeding birds that in certain years greatly exceeded the usual population of the study area so that the average territory size seems to have little to do with the control of numbers. In some species, however, such as the red grouse and ptarmigan in Scotland and the population of skylarks studied at Ravenglas, breeding density is related to the holding of territories, and unsuccessful birds are pushed into peripheral habitats and fail to reproduce (e.g., Jenkins, Watson, and Miller, 1963; Watson, 1965; Delius, 1965). Older work on great tits in Holland had also indicated that in a particular habitat territorial behaviour set an upper limit to numbers (Kluijver and Tinbergen, 1953).

It seems, in fact, certain that in contrasting habitat conditions different factors will play the crucial role of key constraints imposing density-dependent mortality (see Cody, 1966; Blank, Southwood, and Cross, 1967; Southwood, 1967). In environments subject to severe winter mortality involving food shortage, the numbers of birds present may rarely reach such proportions that territorial behaviour limits their settlement for breeding. In richly endowed habitats, however, or in particularly stable ones, territorial behaviour may become the prime constraint controlling breeding density. The relative frequency of such cases remains to be determined. Their effective demonstration, however, would not necessarily establish Wynne-Edwards' contention. Territorial competition may be "real" rather than "conventional" in that without the maintenance of space for uninterrupted mating, for example, breeding might not be able to occur at all. Exclusion of some individuals from breeding would then be an effect of competitive social behaviour of a functional value to the successful individuals of the species for reasons unconnected with dispersal. The overall social system is best conceived as an open arrangement controlled by inputs from factors both intrinsic and extrinsic to the structure itself rather than a biotic adaptation especially evolved for population control.

Finally, we should again emphasise that social systems are characteristics of groups. Discussion of their "evolution" poses a number of semantic problems akin to those involved in the treatment of the evolution of ecological communities (Williams, 1966). Social systems develop historically through interactive effects of population size, social behaviour, and environment. Their control is not a "property" of the species in question but rather lies in the relations its members have established with one another and with the features of their habitat. Evolution by the natural selection of the genetic endowment of the population forms only a part of this historical process. If these arguments are found to be sound then Wynne-Edwards' technical use of the term "convention" is of doubtful explanatory value. Its adoption by Ardrey without an adequate examination of Wynne-Edwards' theory adds nothing to current usage. Football matches and the space race may well be "conventions" but the link between them and biological theory is not established.

Primates, man, and territory

Perhaps the most striking feature of those nonhuman primates the behaviour of which is of most relevance to man is precisely their lack of easily defined territorial behaviour. There have been several recent surveys of this material (e.g., Hall, 1965; Washburn, Jay, and Lancaster, 1965; Crook and Gartlan, 1966; Rowell, 1967) and space allows only brief discussion here. Comparative studies of forest fringe, and savannah *Cercopithecus* and *Macaca* monkeys, the baboons of the genera *Papio* and *Theropithecus,* the chimpanzee and gorilla do not provide evidence of rigorously defended territories. On the other hand, populations of several forest primates in Madagascar, Africa, and South America do defend group territories by means of elaborate vocal and visual displays, border skirmishing and olfactory marking in some cases. These species are, however, of less relevance to man than the savannah monkeys and the great apes.

Several kinds of social organisation in the African grasslands and savannah have been reported. All are complex and consist either of troops containing several males and rather more females with attendant juveniles, or of single males with "harems" of females, again with their young. In the latter case groups of nonreproductive and usually subadult males move separately from the reproductive units. The multi-male troop is well known from the research of K. R. L. Hall, S. L. Washburn, I. DeVore, and Thelma Rowell on *Papio ursinus, P. cynocephalus,* and *P. anubis* and from Altmann's and Southwick's studies on the rhesus monkey on Cayo Santiago Island and in India. In addition, detailed studies have been made on the Japanese macaque. The one-male reproductive unit has been reported from *Papio hamadryas,* the patas monkey, and the gelada baboon. In the former the units tend to comprise subunits of large troops which may coalesce to form herds. In the patas they move separately in large home ranges, whereas in the gelada they congregate in large herds over good grazing but tend to scatter and forage separately in the dry season of poor food availability. In *Papio ursinus,* the macaques, and the patas the social units forage within large home ranges which tend to overlap to varying extents. Dispersion is maintained mostly by the withdrawal of the intruders. "Ritualised" border encounters do not occur but, in certain unusually structured environments such as temple precincts in India, rhesus troops coming suddenly upon one another may fight, in which case individuals will inflict severe injury upon one another. In the gelada even the maintenance of home ranges in uncertain. Certainly gelada herds comprise any number of reproductive units and all-male groups each of which is quite free to enter or leave a congregation and to travel separately over several miles. While populations utilise core areas in particularly appropriate parts of their habitat, there seems no behavioral factor preventing their wandering off and joining any other feeding congregation at considerable distances from their usual foraging area. No evidence of avoidance of any kind has been seen.

Gorillas forage within large home ranges that overlap extensively and there is no clear evidence of marked avoidance, although a preference for small group life is evident. Chimpanzees live in "open groups" with considerable interchange of membership and all appear to utilise a common range of sizeable extent (Reynolds, 1965).

All these social groupings are extensively structured owing to complex relations between individuals dependent upon relative dominance, age, sex, the adoption of particular roles, and the formation of friendships. Compared with most nonprimate societies, life for these animals is a particularly rich social experience.

The adaptive significance of these different types of society has received some recent attention, and they can be related quite clearly to different environmental contingencies – the nature and availability of sleeping sites, the abundance and seasonal dispersion of food supplies – and to predation pressures. Precise details, however, remain to be worked out. The process whereby this adaptation of society to environment occurs is clearly complex and appears to depend upon the establishment and maintenance of learnt traditions of a protocultural kind gradually acquired by the phenotypic adaptations of individuals to their home locality and social group repetitively over many generations. Social structure is furthermore apt to differ in subtle or pronounced ways in different localities, thereby emphasising the importance of the direct effect of contrasts in environment. Although innate behaviour patterns play important roles in communication of affect within these groups there appears to be no case for suggesting that "instinct" plays a major role in the moulding of social structure as such. This is probably also the case in other advanced nonprimate mammalian societies, few of which have yet been studied in any detail.

Both Rowell (1966) and Crook (1967) have pointed out that where social structures of a primate species appear relatively specific the ethologist, traditionally a student of innate behaviour patterns, could be misled into making incorrect assumptions concerning the origins of the systems observed. Rowell's detailed studies in field and laboratory have amply demonstrated the importance of social learning in the structuring of groups. Learning is a continuous process and the individual's behaviour is markedly adaptable in relation to changes in natural reinforcement contingencies. Hall (1963) has stressed the importance of observational learning in monkey groups; the experience of one animal is witnessed by others and the information obtained utilised by them on later occasions. Social structures appear to diverge in contrasting or changing ecological conditions owing to shifts in reinforcement contingencies controlled by such factors as the frequency of food finding, hours needed for satiation, spacing of individuals in relation to food dispersion, size of food object, frequency of food antagonism, and time available for playful interaction and social grooming. Life for these animals may be conceived in terms of sets of complex natural learning "schedules," each providing various types of reward. In particular, the time needed for foraging, the patterns of spacing best suited for search, and the rate of movement required for optimum reward will effectively ration the time available in the day for social activities. Crook and Aldrich-Blake (1968) recently related the rather stereotyped behaviour of geladas at a site in Ethiopia to the long hours they had to spend feeding. Doguera baboons in woods nearby obtained food in larger units and spent less time foraging and more time in social interaction. Their more flexible, reflective behaviour in relation to the presence of the observers might be meaningfully related to these contrasts.

It has been argued that the one-male groups of geladas and certain other primates are sociological adaptations to arid environments (e.g., Crook and Gartlan, 1966). One large male is adequate for the fertilisation of several females and exploits a low percentage of the food available to the nomadic group. The reproductively more important sex then tends to get the most food. Large troops with many adult males are typical of richer environments with both more food and more predators. In arid country individual males and females appear to contribute more to the next generation by living in one-male groups than they would in larger social units that would tend to overexploit the resources of the ground over which they ranged. Probably increasingly arid environments impose splits in troops so that small parties wander separately. Indeed, there is evidence from Japanese macaques and African baboons to support this view. Competition between reproductive males for females in small parties would then tend to produce the separation of subordinate and juvenile males into their own parties, leaving single males in reproductive units. The adaptation to environment in this case thus appears essentially phenotypic. Such changes would appear, however, to initiate new patterns of social and sexual selection such that individuals of differing temperament from those in the parent society may gain reproductive advantages. Concomitant shifts in the genetic basis of individual behaviour may occur and have the effect of stabilising the patterns of interindividual interaction and hence the social structure as a whole.

As Ardrey says, the reappearance of aggressive territory holding in man contrasts strongly with the relatively peaceable affairs of other higher primates. The advent of carnivorous habits, use of weapons, and competition between groups for limited sources of animal protection are indeed the most likely original causes. It seems that the emergence of the new territoriality involved shifts in social traditions in relation to ranging and an acquired lowering of the threshold for aggression towards outgroups as a result of repetitive experiences of hunger and ultimately an intellectual appreciation of its cause. Certainly our modern appreciation of the important role of learning and tradition in the maintenance of nonhuman primate societies would lead us to emphasise this kind of historical change rather than the possible development of a territorial instinct of the type Ardrey requires.

This is not to deny, however, the probability that changes in human social organisation and the adoption by man of carnivorous feeding habits may not have affected his aggressive reactivity through the selection of certain inherited traits rather than others. Certainly the necessity for increased control of individual behaviour in relation to hunting and role playing in co-operative social life will have entailed the marked development of the ability to delay responding, to interiorise and reflect on alternative causes of action, and to cope with motivational frustration. Aggression itself would have become increasingly complex in manifestation and often separated in time from the events that lowered the threshold for its expression. The hunter's pleasure in killing prey may also have arisen at this time and the "cruelty" inflicted on the "game" animals thus became available for translocation into a social agonistic context.

The development of ownership of tools, homesteads, and domestic animals would greatly have increased the opportunities for conflict within communities, these things becoming in effect extensions of a person's "individual distance." Complex patterns of conventional behaviour (in the usual sense of the word) would arise, giving way in due course to codified laws concerning property and its exchange. International conduct may be conceived as an extension of this principle to a community and political level.

Early in his book Ardrey remarks that "there will remain always the chance that what we observe in man is a kind of mirror held up to nature; our culture and our learning reflect the natural way without in a biological sense being beholden to it" (p. 103). The likelihood that the motivational control of territorial behaviour in man is at a different level from that of fishes and birds suggests that human resemblances to the lower animals might be largely through analogy rather than homology. Indeed this is certainly the impression given by a careful reading of the several papers comparing man and animals at the 1963 symposium on "The Natural History of Aggression," in London (Carthy and Ebling, 1964). Ardrey fails to recognise that the great advances in learning ability and intelligence in the higher mammals mean that historical change through "cultural" processes is possible among them too and the concept need not be reserved for man alone. Man is indeed an animal – but we should not forget his primate status and the behavioural complexity of his relatives. The idea that "the territorial nature of man is genetic and ineradicable" would appear unnecessarily parsimonious.

Conclusions

By adopting a limited Lorenzian view of the nature of aggression Ardrey ignores most of the experimental ethological literature on the subject. Instead of resulting from an innate and ineradicable force demanding repetitive expression, aggressive behaviour occurs normally as a response to particular aversive stimuli and ceases upon their removal. The prevalence of aggression in modern man may thus be attributed to aversive features in the complex overcrowded, overcompetitive, overstratified social world in which he lives rather then to some unsatisfied vital urge. In man, also, aggression is commonly associated with frustrations born of the delay in responding imposed largely by his learning to play social roles in a community. There is every reason to suppose that individual sensitivity to stimuli likely to evoke aggression is determined during socialisation. The manifestation of aggression in human society is thus largely a cultural attribute.

Ardrey's account of the function of territoriality in terms of identity, security, and stimulation is derived from ethological research reports concerned largely with the adaptive significance of behaviour. He provides little detailed discussion on the evolutionary significance of social behaviour in relation to the adaptations of members of a population to their physical and social environment. In this paper this problem is treated at length to clarify the arguments presented in the sources. In discussing man Ardrey gives his three terms a motivational significance in which they represent needs satisfied by the holding of territory. Reflection brings to mind, however, many individuals, who in their maturity found identity, security, and excitement in activities far removed from real estate of any kind. If an instinct is present in a species it should be apparent in the individual members.

Man's nearest relatives among primates are singularly lacking in simple territorial behaviour. Man's recovery of this attribute may be seen as a continuation of trends already present in protocultural social organisations found in primates and originally influenced by acquired carnivorous feeding and competition for sources of protein. There is no need to explain the behaviour in excessively parsimonious terms based on a misleading and outdated account of aggressive behaviour in lower organisms. The relevant hypotheses lie nearer home.

The behaviour of crowds watching "conventionally" competitive sports often indicates the arousal of aggressive attitudes rather than their happy sublimation. Further, the behaviour of players cannot always be recommended. The wanton destruction of train interiors by British football team supporters on the way to an "away" fixture certainly reveals a release of social tensions in what would appear to be highly convivial surroundings. Indeed, the holding of major sporting events is often manageable only when effective rules of crowd control are operative. As an example of social engineering such conventions alone seem to achieve little in enhancing human conduct. Man's aggressive potential is hardly likely to be controlled solely by attempts at redirection or sublimation. The solution must lie rather in detailed research into those aspects of human experience which influence aggressive reactivity. In particular the problem concerns those patterns of socialisation and education that give rise to hostile feelings towards the stranger and the out-group. The development of attitudes remains an area as yet poorly explored by psychologists, but with an increasing grasp of experimental techniques there seems no reason to abandon hope for the future. Social psychologists are well aware of these problems and strive to find solutions. That their efforts so far may appear academic and slightly naïve is related to the novelty of the research, the complexity of the subject matter, and the youth of this branch of science. The biological basis of human life and its evolutionary history are of great relevance to this enquiry but only when a proper understanding of the advanced level of social organisation and its control in higher primates is taken into account. The promulgation of one-sided and misleadingly simplified doctrine is of no assistance to those concerned and could lead them to neglect those highly relevant contributions that modern ethological theory and experimental method can legitimately supply.

The merit of *The Territorial Imperative* is to have brought an awareness of a major research problem to the attention of many who may not have considered it seriously before. The book nevertheless leaves an unfortunate impression. Apart from its faulty statement of current ethological theory, the view of life – the *Weltanschauung* – portrayed is unhappily pessimistic and for a wrongly conceived reason. Sir Julian Huxley, in a treatment of the relevance of biology to man, once argued strongly against "nothing but-ism" as an unhealthy attitude of unreflective science. Were man indeed "nothing but" a creature of overpowering destructive impulse, hope for the future would be dark. These decades present the advanced technological nations with problems of menacing proportions. Men everywhere are potential victims of an unparalleled background anxiety magnified and reflected at every turn by mass media of communication. The image of man, already demoted from his place near the angels through the popularisation of Darwinian and Freudian ideas, is all too vulnerable to further erosion. The *Zeitgeist* extols the mechanism, and we may perhaps see ourselves as no more than that; but the mechanism is wonderfully complex, its properties poorly understood, and as subjects we remain uniquely self-aware. Although the phenomenon of man cannot be explained by simplistic argument pandering only to the pessimism of an age, the image that most of the people acquire is apt to shape the values of a community. Indeed, a parallel is apparent in the recent past when ideas derived from a misunderstanding of "Social Darwinism" played their part in the history of European fascist politics. Who knows whence a "New Right" may gather a cloak of respectability to condone, perhaps in some new "Report from Iron Mountain," the defence of racial garrisons in the *noyaux* of the near future? The new genre of popular biological exposition neglects the humanity of man. We would do well to meditate upon the reasons.

References

Anderson, P. K. 1961. Density, social structure and non-social environment in house-mouse populations and the implications for regulation of numbers. *Trans. N.Y. Acad. Sci. Ser. II* 23 (5): 447-451.

Ardrey, R. 1967. *The territorial imperative. A personal inquiry into the animal origins of property and nations.* London.

Blank, T. H., Southwood, T. R. E., and Cross, D. G. 1967. The ecology of the partridge. I. Outline of population processes with particular reference to chick mortality and nest density. *J. Anim. Ecol.* 36:549-556.

Bolles, R. C. 1967. *Theory of motivation.* New York.

Brown, J. C. 1963. Aggressiveness, dominance and social organisation in the Steller jay. *Condor* 65:460-484.

Burt, W. H. 1943. Territoriality and home range concepts as applied to mammals. *J. Mammal.* 24:346-352.

Carpenter, C. R. 1958. Territoriality. *Behaviour and evolution,* ed. A. Roe and G. G. Simpson. New Haven.

Carrick, R. 1963. Ecological significance of territory in the Australian magpie, *Gymnorhyna tibicen. Proc. 13th Int. Orn. Congr.* 740-753.

Carthy, J. D. and Ebling, F. J. (eds.). 1964. *The natural history of aggression.* London.

Chapman, D. W. 1966. Food and space as regulations of salmonid populations in streams. *Amer. Nat.* 100:345-356.

Cody, M. J. 1966. A general theory of clutch size. *Evolution* 20:174-184.

Craig, W. 1918. Appetites and aversions as constituents of instincts. *Biol. Bull.* 34:91-107.

____. 1928. Why do animals fight? *Int. J. Ethics* 31:246-278.

Crook, J. H. 1961. The basis of flock organisation in birds. *Current problems in animal behaviour,* ed. W. H. Thorpe and O. L. Zangwill. Cambridge.

____. 1965. The adaptive significance of avian social organisations. *Symp. zool. Soc. Lond.* 14:181-218.

____. 1967. Evolutionary change in primate societies. *Sci. J.* 3(6):66-72.

Crook, J. H. and Aldrich-Blake, P. 1968. Ecological and behavioural contrasts between sympatric ground-dwelling primates in Ethiopia. *Folia Primat.* 8:192-227.

Crook, J. H. and Butterfield, P. A. 1968. Effects of testosterone propionate and luteinising hormone on agonistic and nest building behaviour of captive *Quelea quelea. Anim. Behav.* 16:370-384.

Crook, J. H. and Gartlan, J. S. 1966. Evolution of primate societies. *Nature. Lond.* 210:1200-1203.

Darling, F. F. 1938. *Bird flocks and the breeding cycle. A contribution to the study of avian sociality.* Cambridge.

Davis, D. E. 1940. Social nesting habits of the smooth-billed ani. *Auk* 57:179-218.

Delius, J. D. 1965. A population study of skylarks, *Alauda arvensis. Ibis* 107:465-492.

Dollard, J. *et al.* 1939. *Frustration and aggression.* New Haven.

Fox, R. 1967. In the beginning: aspects of hominid behavioural evolution. *Man* 2:415-433.

Gartlan, J. S. 1966. Ecology and behaviour of the vervet monkey. Lolui Island. Lake Victoria. Uganda. Ph.D. Thesis. Bristol Univ. Library.

Hall, K. R. L. 1963. Observational learning in monkeys and apes. *Brit. J. Psychol.* 54:201-226.

____. 1965. Social organisation of the old world monkeys and apes. *Symp. zool. Soc. Lond.* 14:265-290.

Harlow, H. F. and Harlow, M. K. 1965. The affectional systems. *Behaviour of non-human primates,* Vol. 2, ed. A. M. Schrier, H. F. Harlow, F. Stollnitz. New York.

Hinde, R. A. 1956. The biological significance of the territories of birds. *Ibis* 98:340-369.

____. 1966. *Animal behaviour. A synthesis of ethology and comparative psychology.* New York.

____. 1967. The nature of aggression. *New Society.* 2 March.

Howard, H. E. 1907-14. *The British warblers, a history, with problems of their lives.* 6 vols. Cambridge.

____. 1920. *Territory in bird life.* London.

Jeffreys, M. V. C. 1962. *Personal values in the modern world.* London.

Jenkins, D., Watson, A., and Miller, G. R. 1963. Population studies on red grouse, *Lagopus lagopus scoticus. J. Anim. Ecol.* 32:317-376.

Jewell, P. A. and Loizos, C. (eds.). 1966. Play, exploration and territory in mammals. *Symp. zool. Soc. Lond.* 18.

Kluijver, H. N. and Tinbergen, L. 1953. Territory and the regulation of density in titmice. *Arch. Nethl. Zool.* 10:266-287.

Koford, C. B. 1957. The vicuña and the puna. *Ecological Monographs* 27:153-219.

Lack, D. 1966. *Population studies of birds.* Oxford.

Lockie, J. D. 1956. Winter fighting in feeding flocks of rooks, jackdaws and carrion crows. *Bird Study* 3:180-190.

Lorenz, K. 1950. The comparative method in studying innate behaviour patterns. *Symp. Soc. Exp. Biol.* 4:221-268.

_____. 1963. *Das Sogenannte Böse.* Vienna.

Lowe, U. P. W. 1966. Observations on the dispersal of red deer on rhum. *Symp. zool. Soc. Lond.* 18:211-228.

Marler, P. R. 1956a. Territory and individual distance in the chaffinch (*Fringilla coelebs*). *Ibis* 98:496-501.

_____. 1956b. Studies of fighting in chaffinches. (3) Proximity as a cause of aggression. *Brit. J. Anim. Behav.* 4:23-30.

_____. 1957. Studies of fighting in chaffinches. (4) Appetitive and consummatory behavior. *Brit. J. Anim. Behav.* 5:29-37.

Marler, P. R. and Hamilton, W. J. 1966. *Mechanisms of animal behavior.* New York.

Moffat, C. B. 1903. The spring rivalry of birds, some views on the limits to multiplication. *Irish Nat.* 12:152-166.

Nice, M. M. 1941. The role of territory in bird-life. *Amer. Midl. Nat.* 26:441-487.

Patterson, I. J. 1965. Timing and spacing of broods in the black headed gull. *Larus ridibundus. Ibis* 107:433-459.

Petter, J. J. 1962. Recherches sur l'écologie et l'éthologie des Lémuriens malgaches. *Mém. du Mus. Nat. de l'Hist. Naturelle.* Sér. A, 27. Fasc. I. Paris.

Reynolds, V. 1965. Some behavioural comparisons between the chimpanzee and the mountain gorilla in the wild. *Amer. Anthropologist* 67:691-706.

Rowell, T. E. 1966. Forest living baboons in Uganda. *J. Zool., Lond.* 149:344-364.

_____. 1967. Variability in the social organisation of primates. *Primate ethology,* ed. D. Morris. London.

Schenkel, R. 1966. Play, exploration and territoriality in the wild lion. *Symp. zool. Soc. Lond.* 18:11-22.

Sears, R. R., Maccoby, E. E., and Levin, H. 1957. *Patterns of child rearing.* New York.

Selous, E. 1933. *Evolution of habit in birds.* London.

Southwood, T. R. E. 1967. The interpretation of population change. *J. Anim. Ecol.* 36:519-530.

Thomson, W. R. 1965. The behaviour of offspring. *Sci. J.* August: 45-50.

Tinbergen, N. 1953. *The herring gull's world.* Collins. London.

_____. 1957. The functions of territory. *Bird Study* 4:14-27.

Tompa, F. S. 1964. Factors determining the numbers of song sparrows *Melospiza melodia* (Wilson) on Mandarte Island, B. C., Canada. *Acta. zool. Fenn.* 109:1-68.

Washburn, S. L., Jay, P. C., and Lancaster, J. B. 1965. Field studies of old world monkeys and apes. *Science* 150:1541-1547.

Watson, A. 1965. A population study of ptarmigan (*Lagopus mutus*) in Scotland. *J. Anim. Ecol.* 34:135-172.

Williams, G. C. 1966. *Adaptation and natural selection. A critique of some current evolutionary thought.* Princeton.

Wynne-Edwards, V. C. 1962. *Animal dispersion in relation to social behaviour.* Edinburgh.

11

Sources of cooperation in animals and man

John H. Crook

Introduction

The current public and academic fascination with the implications of animal behavior research for an understanding of human society is in part a consequence of an extraordinary neglect of man's biological roots by social scientists. After vigorously establishing the autonomy of social anthropology, sociology, and other related disciplines the practitioners of these subjects are at last considering the impact of Darwin's thought on humanity as a whole. So far, however, the interest in ethology has focused upon a Darwinism largely dressed in a fashionable Lorenzian form.

Unfortunately, this particular formulation of the subject, based largely on the ethology of the late 1930's, is for the most part inadequate as a tool in the analysis of the complex social processes of higher vertebrates – especially community-living mammals. Many questions posed by ungulate, carnivore, or primate societies simply cannot be answered meaningfully using the limited propositions of an earlier ethology developed in studies of fish, reptiles, and birds. The subject today needs additional or new approaches for an adequate examination of these problems. Thus, while social anthropologists show an increasing interest in ethology, modern ethologists, in

---

SOURCE: *Man and Beast: Comparative Social Behavior,* Wilton Dillon, ed., Smithsonian Institution Press, 1970. This article is a slightly revised version of the paper written for the Smithsonian Institution symposium "Man and beast," held in Washington, D.C., in May 1969. It was prepared during the tenure of a fellowship at the Center for Advanced Study in the Behavioral Sciences, Stanford, Calif., 1968-1969. Reprinted by permission of the publisher.

their turn, are inspecting social psychology and sociology for possible analytical tools.

The phenomenon of cooperation between individuals in producing a behavioral effect poses questions of exactly the kind of complexity that current ethology finds difficult to treat. Indeed, biologists generally have found themselves at a loss in formulating an analytical approach to such cases. In the context of natural selection, of micro-evolution, and of behavioral genetics, the cooperative behavior often shown by higher animals remains an undigested lump that many have evidently preferred to ignore. Yet, for man, perhaps the most fundamental problem of our time is an adjustment between competition and cooperation at every level of human function: the international, the institutional, the township, the familial, and the personal. Possibly an understanding of those processes of cooperation occurring in higher mammals may provide us with an account of the sources from which human cooperative behavior springs and of the forces that prevent its expression.

Our initial problem is to identify those animal analogs of human cooperation that may be useful to such an inquiry. Although of manifest academic interest, the proto-cooperative behavior and contingent environmental conditioning shown by the lower phyla of the animal kingdom (Allee, 1938) will not concern us here; nor will we be interested in behavior that appears programmed purely genetically. The cooperative behavior that concerns us consists rather in the high-order consequences of multifactorial behavioral determination during the ontogeny of advanced mammals and birds. While genetics, child-rearing processes, and social and proto-cultural influences are all involved, it is not in our interest here to attempt a disentangling of such factors. The identification of cases of sufficient complexity and a look at the processes operating at the social level at the time of their occurrence must, for the moment, suffice.

To begin with we need some definition of human cooperation to use as our model in choosing relevant animal examples for study. Cooperation, we may say, is the collaborative behavior of two or more persons in the production of some common behavioral effect. Such behavior is commonly directed toward some goal or to the completion of some preconceived task in which there is common interest, emotional satisfaction, or reward. The collaborative behavior may entail work in common or varying degrees of division of labor to produce the required effect. The motivational sources of the behavior are not likely to be simple and their analysis may require an understanding of the person's history – possibly in psychodynamic terms. Cooperation normally occurs within the context of shared social norms and a common code of conduct. The proximate causal determinants of the behavior lie at several levels including the innate and learned bases of reciprocal action, traditional habits, and contractual obligations. Human cooperation occurs at its most complex in the integrated work schedules of complex institutions – governments, universities, business firms, banks, ships – but, even in such cases, it comprises elements also found in the football match, in assistance given after a road accident, or in domestic washing-up. The term cooperation refers to a characteristic type of intra-group behavior rather than to the specific behavior of an individual participating in it. Cooperation, moreover, occurs within a social structure based in part upon caste and class distinction, status hierarchy, and other products of group and individual competition. Both cooperation and competition exist together in any human organization; they are not simply the opposites of one another. Both belong to the process.

In observing animals we have no means of asking the subject for its "reasons" for doing something, although the past history of an organism and the environmental context may allow us to infer something regarding its motivation. Nevertheless an intensive study allows us to determine the size of an animal's behavioral repertoire and the probability of a cooperative response occurring in relation to a given set of stimuli. There is, in fact, a gradient or range of cases in which the autonomy of the individual in relation to its milieu steadily increases and in which the flexibility of response becomes increasingly pronounced.

At this point it is worthwhile emphasizing an important distinction. We have said that cooperation comprises a type of intra-group or inter-individual behavior rather than denoting simply the behavior of individuals. Cooperation thus refers to a group process – it is a group characteristic. Now in discussing behavioral evolution it is usual for ethologists to argue from a neo-Darwinian viewpoint – that is to say they commonly attribute change solely to the natural selection of the genetic basis of individual behavior. Few ethologists have ever considered whether such an approach is adequate to an analysis of group processes although this is clearly the basis of what social anthropologists would call culture. It seems that in asking what factors act to program the patterns of group behavior, close attention must be paid to the direct intervention of both the physical and the social milieu. The programming of what goes on in a herd – let us say – depends not only on the genetics of the individuals in it but also on the social composition of the herd membership and the frequency of water holes. So also with cooperation. This means that in tracing the emergence of the phenomenon we are not concerned solely with adaptation from the genetic selectionist viewpoint but also with the direct reactivity of a system in relation to its circumstances. Such a system is open rather than closed, adaptive rather than merely homeostatic, and responsive rather than autonomic, Lamarckian as well as Darwinist. It has "history" rather than evolution in the strictest biological sense of that term. The evolution of group processes cannot be reduced simply to a study of the nature of the separate members. Reductionism is not enough. And this seems to be as true of the higher animals as it is obviously true with regard to man.

Cases and contexts of advanced cooperative behavior in animals

Cooperative behavior in nonhuman mammals and in birds crops up quite frequently in many contexts and in a diversity of species. A prime requirement for its occurrence appears to be some structural complexity in the social relations of a population. Mammals that live solitarily in burrow-centered territories for the greater part of the year and whose most complex social unit is the mother-litter family usually have a limited repertoire of patterns of social interaction. The same applies to the more solitary birds usually living in large territories. By contrast, birds and mammals living in densely congregated colonies, in mobile troops or in groups in which long-term monogamous or polygamous pair-bonding has developed commonly show some emergence of group coordination. It is among these species that instances of cooperation are most readily found.

The adaptive significance of living in complex social organizations is receiving an increasing attention at the present time (Crook, 1965, 1970; Wynne-Edwards, 1962; Lack, 1968; Orians, 1968). Briefly, we may say that the emergence of animal societies with complex structures reflects an adaptation of the species in relation to aspects of its ecological niche. Gregarious birds breed in colonies where nesting habitats are relatively inaccessible to predators, large enough to contain nests, and with an adequate food supply near at hand for the rearing of young. In some colonies the reduction of territory size contingent upon crowding has led to the formation of vast fused nests or "lodges," the structure of which may be maintained cooperatively. Communal behavior in birds probably occurs in "clans" arising through the continued association of young with parents. The participation of the young in brood care rather than breeding themselves appears, in certain limiting environments, to be the most likely way to ensure the participants' contribution to the next generation. Such species may show communal nest construction, brooding, care of young, and – in one case – food storage. Among mammals, herd and troop formation appear related to particular conditions of predation and food-resource dispersion in time and space (Eisenberg, 1966).

Cooperative behavior in birds and mammals occurs in a number of contexts but particularly in relation to *food storage, territorial defense, mutual protection against predators, group hunting, parental care and also in child care by animals other than the actual parents, and* – finally, at its most complex – in the *cooperative control of social interaction* in certain primate groups.

In food storage certain group-living species work together to establish stores which are utilized by the communal group as a whole (Ritter, 1938; Morris, 1962). Individuals here work separately, however, and the behavior does not involve either a close interlinking of the behavior of two or more individuals or the reciprocally related response delays of individuals alternating in performance of complex task-oriented cooperation (Crook, 1966a). In several mammals, members of a group territory will act together in its defense against a neighboring group and complex battles sometimes occur (Mykytowicz, 1960; King, 1955; Southwick, Beg, and Siddiqi, 1965). Sometimes certain individuals give vocal and visual signal support to displaying primate males on territorial boundaries (Carpenter, 1965; Gartlan, 1966; Jolly, 1966). Mutual protection against predators is well-known in certain group-living mammals including musk oxen, the water vole, baboons, and rhesus monkeys (Ryder, 1962; Wilson, 1968; etc.). Cooperative hunting in group fishing activities is known from both cormorants and pelicans (Bartholomew, 1942). Many cases of cooperative hunting by wolves and hunting dogs are reported in which some animals trail the prey while others cut corners to shorten the chase.

Assistance at the nests in the care of the young by birds other than the parents is known in a number of species (Skutch, 1935; Davis, 1942), and can be shown to be functional in relation to the ecological niche of the species (Lack, 1968). Instances of assistance in parental care are found among several species of mammals and are the focus of rapidly developing research. Probably the number of species in which it occurs is much larger than is at present known. It happens for instance in mice, also among dolphins where the new-born young has to be taken rapidly to the surface if it is to commence breathing. The group hunting of hunting dogs (Kühme, 1965) includes a complex cooperation between hunters and den-dwelling mothers in the feeding of young. Further cases occur among primates and, because of their complexity and their significance to man, we will examine them in detail.

Parental, "aunt," and "uncle" behavior in primates

An interest in new-born babies by female companions of a mother has been reported in several species – certain lemurs, howlers, langurs, rhesus, Japanese and Barbary macaques, baboons, and gorillas (DeVore, 1965). Studies of such behavior using captive groups has clarified many of the problems involved. In particular R. A. Hinde and his collaborators at Madingley, Cambridge, have analyzed so-called "aunt"[1] behavior within a rhesus group, the members of which had been studied in detail for several years.

"Aunt" behavior arises from the responses of a (usually) childless female to the presence of a mother-baby pair (Spencer-Booth, 1968) and at first may be resented by the mother. It gradually becomes a highly cooperative activity with survival value for the young. Rowell, Hinde, and Spencer-Booth (1964) report that most of the rhesus mothers eventually accepted the attentions of at least one aunt with whom they were willing to leave the babies. The aunt was usually a female that had been a chief sitting and grooming companion. One mother which had allowed her "best friend" (*sic*) to hold the baby when it was only 6 days old subsequently died when the baby was aged 8 months. The aunt adopted the baby with minimum disturbance.

In the wild, aunt behavior probably has great survival value aiding in the protection of the child during the mother's lifetime and leading to its adoption on her death. Macaque troops are apparently structured into castes (Imanishi, 1960) and contain many affiliative subgroups. It is highly likely that a mother's "best friends" are usually those who, if themselves childless at the time, play the role of aunt. Probably, too, the aunts are close kin to the mother. If so, their behavior may well help perpetuate their own genes in the forthcoming generations (Hamilton, 1963, 1970).

Mother-aunt interaction is complex. Mothers of new-born babies at first resist

[1] The term "aunt" as used here does not imply any particular geneological relationship although kinship studies in monkeys suggest that some females showing aunt behavior in nature may be quite close kin to the mothers of the young involved.

the approach of aunts and keep the babies to themselves. Aunts are persistent animals, however, and during the first few weeks of a baby's life they use various cunning devices that enable them to approach baby without upsetting mother: sidling up while pretending to forage, or grooming the mother until her attention is elsewhere and then surreptitiously grooming the baby until she looks again.

As babies become mobile they inevitably interact frequently with the ever-hovering aunts. Aunts carry and cuddle babies, play with them and look after them both in relation to swinging cage doors and to the occasional antagonisms of other companions. Babies sometimes anger the aunt and then, if the mother is not too near, baby gets a cuffing.

Aunt-infant interactions change in type and relative frequency as the infant gets older and they gradually develop into "friendly relations" characterized by adult patterns of mutual grooming. The relations between aunt and mother are affected by the relative dominance of the two animals. The aunts which showed most carrying and cuddling toward infants were all subordinate to the mother. Mothers appeared to prefer attention from subordinate aunts rather than from those dominant to them. High-ranking mothers could control the interactions of others with their babies by low-intensity threat but low-ranking mothers had to "grin" or "present" to potential aunts more dominant than they. The pattern of interactions is thus intimately related to the social position of the participants within the group defined in terms of age status, relative dominance, degree of mutual affiliation, age of baby, and the resultant frequencies of behavioral interactions of specified types.

The long-term effects of the activities of aunts on the behavior of infants remain to be assessed, but Hinde and Spencer-Booth (1967) have shown that their presence affects the frequencies of a number of interaction patterns of infant and mother rhesus. In the absence of aunts and other adult companions mothers are less restrictive and infants wander more. Because these babies lack play and aunt companions, however, they also return more frequently to the mother. This leads to a higher proportion of infant rejections in the behavior of the isolate mother when compared with those living in normal groups.

In the Madingley study, male rhesus macaques were found to show very little behavioral interaction with babies, although males about two years older than the infant tended to show more of such behavior than did others (Spencer-Booth, 1968). Likewise, in the wild, rhesus males do not evidently show much interest in infants (Southwick, Beg, and Siddiqi, 1965), although in some five *Macaca* species a degree of male interest in young animals is known (Gifford, 1967). Particularly notable is the generalized "paternal" behavior of wild male Japanese macaques investigated by Itani (1959). Males behaving in this way may perhaps be called "uncles."[2] Adult male Japanese macaques become interested in juvenile animals when the latter are one year old. At this time females are in the birth season and cease protecting the

[2] Again there is no implication regarding geneological relationship, although some degree of kinship is likely in nature.

young of the previous year. The males appear to restrict their interest in young animals primarily to this period. Their behavior consists in hugging and sitting with the infant, accompanying it on the move, protecting it from other monkeys and dangerous situations, and grooming it. Although Itani found no relationship between dominance, as such, and the frequency of child care, he did find the behavior to be especially developed in middle-class animals of the caste-structured troops. The behavior indeed seemed pronounced in animals that were sociable, not aggressive and oriented toward high-caste animals. Itani suggests that certain monkeys by showing care to high-caste children succeed in being tolerated by leaders and their affiliated females and may therefore rise in rank. Protectors usually behave in a mild manner which may facilitate both their association with infants and their rise in rank. It is not clear, however, whether the effect on rank lasts for more than the birth season. Itani gives no details on permanent changes in social structure so produced. The adult males appear to protect one-year-old males and females equally, but more second-year females than males are protected owing to the peripheral social ranking of young males. Any protected two-year-olds are moreover often poorly grown individuals that were protected by the same male in the previous year. Protection has a further interesting effect in that adults more readily learn to investigate the new foods a progressive infant has discovered than would otherwise be the case.

Itani found cases of paternal care common in only three of 18 troops investigated. It occurred very rarely in seven others and was not observed in the remaining eight. The behavior thus appears to be a local cultural phenomenon. It undoubtedly provides additional chances of survival for young animals likely to be relatives, may improve their social status in the group, increases the rate of spread of new patterns of behavior in the group, and – since its frequency differs between troops – may increase the reproductive success of some monkey groups over others.

Recent observations on the Barbary macaque (*Macaca sylvana*) both in captivity (Lahiri and Southwick, 1966; Gifford, 1967) and in wild groups in the Moyen Atlas of Morocco show that adult males show an extraordinary amount of interest in young babies of the year. An interest in babies this young was relatively uncommon in Itani's study. Furthermore, the wild male Barbary macaque does not seem, on present evidence, to limit his interest to a particular infant. He appears to appropriate babies from females in the group and to groom and care for them for short periods, usually under 15 minutes in length. Babies may, moreover, move away from their mothers to accompany males, commonly riding off on their backs. Babies also move from one male to another. Males carrying babies frequently approach males without them in such a way as to encourage the approached animal to engage in a mutual grooming session with the baby as target. In some of these sequences babies are presented to the second male while on the back of the approacher, the animal turning its rear toward the other male (as it would do in sexual presenting), as it does so. In one case the approached male was seen to mount and thrust an animal that had done this. It appears, too, that most males approaching with babies are relatively juvenile animals. It looks as if relatively subordinate animals may be using the babies in some way to improve their relations with higher-ranking males (Deag and Crook, 1971).

Thus far too little is known about the social structure of the Barbary macaque to show whether there is a caste system comparable to that described from Japan. Whether males are using the babies as a means to increase their social standing and, hence, their freedom to behave without the constraints imposed by low rank, remains unknown. It does seem, however, that in both species not only does the male's behavior increase the chances of survival for young animals but it appears to be closely related to the structure of the monkey group and the pattern of constraints regulating social mobility of individuals within it. We do not know yet whether the behavior of the Barbary macaque male is restricted, as it is with the Japanese macaques, to certain troops and localities or whether it is a general phenomenon found throughout the species.

In the hamadryas baboon behavior by sub-adult males toward juvenile females has effects of the utmost consequence for the social organization of the species. Kummer (1968) describes how such animals steal young females from their mothers and attend them with every semblance of solicitous maternal care. The young female is trained under punishment not to run away. At this stage there is no sexual behavior for the female is as yet too young. Nevertheless this acquisition of females is one of the ways by which the maturing male acquires a harem. Apparent cooperation in child care is thus again seen to have a profound relationship to group structure and social dynamics.

Social control of individual behavior in primate groups

For many years the structure of primate groups was analyzed primarily in terms of dominance. The existence of a status hierarchy was generally thought to stabilize relationships through the reduction of social tension – each animal knowing its place. Often animals were found to cooperate either in the enforcement of existing rank relations or, by contrast, in upsetting them. Cooperation in social control emerges as an important problem area in primate social research. Recently it has become apparent, however, that the simple dominance concept was not only inadequately defined and carrying many unwarranted motivational overtones but that the description of group structure in dominance terminology was in many species not only a difficult task but also an inappropriate procedure (Gartlan, 1968).

In an important discussion of dominance in a captive baboon group Rowell (1966) implies that relative rank depends upon a continuous learning process in relation to rewards in inter-individual competition for environmental or social goals. This occurs, moreover, against a background of differential kinship status and the observational learning of behavioral styles of companions. Relative rank is much affected by health. Dominance ranking is based upon the approach-retreat ratio in encounters between two individuals in a group. Measures of rank by differing criteria do not however, necessarily correlate and Rowell found no single criterion for high rank. Using simpler organisms (weaver birds) Crook and Butterfield (1968) also showed that ranking according to the maintenance of spatial position on perches, ranking according to competitive access to nest-building materials, and ranking by the amount of building done did not necessarily correlate. The rank hierarchies in these birds depend upon different hormonal factors or combinations of such factors in the three cases. The same is probably true in primate behavior.

Rowell also shows that apparent rank is a function of the behavior of the relatively subordinate. Higher rankers evidently feel free to initiate interactions. These initiations commonly lead to some suppression in a continuing activity by a subordinate or to an outright conflict. Subordinates learn to avoid such situations. Avoidance learning leads to behavioral restraint that leaves higher rankers even greater freedom of movement, easy access to commodities, and freedom to initiate behavior with others. In competition for commodities in short supply, low rankers are likely to suffer deprivation (see discussion in Crook and Butterfield, 1970) and, in social relations, repeated constraint may involve physiological "stress" and concomitant behavioral abnormality.

Hall and DeVore (1965) describe the "dynamics of threat behavior" in wild baboon troops. A male's dominance status relative to others is a function not only of his fighting ability but also of his ability to enlist the support of other males. In one group studied, two adult males formed a central hierarchy – the pivot around which the social behavior of the group was organized. When one of these two died, the remaining one was unable to prevent the third-ranking male in cooperation with a newcomer (a subordinate male that had left another troop) from establishing themselves as central. The third male and the newcomer had evidently become affiliated when both had been relatively peripheral in the group structure. Common mutually supporting behavior seems to have been the precondition for their "success" in later assuming high rank. By so doing they gained the freedom to express behavior in the absence of previous constraints and to initiate behavior as and when they wished.

Wilson (1968) provides further information on mutual support in a study of the feral rhesus troops on Cayo Santiago Island. Young males tend to leave the smaller groups and move into the all-male peripheral areas of larger ones. When they do this they are commonly attacked unless they gain the protection of another male already established there. It so happens that males that give support are usually relatives, even brothers, who originated from the same natal group as the "protégé."

The inadequacies of the dominance terminology have led Bernstein and Sharpe (1966), Rowell (1966), and Gartlan (1968) to describe the social positions of individuals in a group in terms of roles. Roles are defined in terms of the relative frequencies (percent of group occurrence, for example) with which individuals perform certain behavioral sequences. When the behavior set of an individual or class of individuals is distinct the animal is said to show a "role."

Bernstein (1966) emphasizes the importance of the role of "control animal" in primate groups and shows that such a role may occur in a group of capuchins, say, in which no clear status hierarchies can be established. The prime responses of a control animal are assuming a position between the group and a source of external disturbance or danger, attacking and thereby stopping the behavior of a group member that is distressing another, and generally approaching and terminating cases of intragroup disturbance. Whether a control animal is also recognizably "dominant" or a "leader" (in the sense of determining direction of march) depends upon the social structure in which he or she is situated.

Control animals in baboon and macaque troops are commonly also either the dominant (at least by certain criteria) or at least a prominent member of a central class. In addition to the properties listed above, the control animal shows a capacity for enlisting aid from affiliated animals in carrying out his activities of social control, in being a recipient for the "presenting" responses of subordinates and in being the focal point of "protected threat" (Kummer, 1957) whereby lower-ranking animals regulate their agonistic encounters by reference to his spatial position. In baboons and macaques it seems that a male maintains his role primarily by gaining the cooperative support of other males, but his often superior physical strength cannot always resist a combination of assertive animals should such a subgroup develop in his troop. In addition, Japanese workers have established that mutual support and affiliation often comes from close kin so that a central hierarchy may, in some troops of Japanese macaques at least, virtually represent a caste or "establishment." This is, however, by no means always the case. Baboons and macaques moving into a troop or group from outside, either directly from another group or after a period of relatively solitary existence, can attain high rank and even control by virtue of establishing affiliation with others. Clearly the social skills involved must relate to the individual personalities of the animals concerned. The process of attaining high rank is unlikely to depend on accidental social conditioning.

In species whose reproductive unit is a one-male group (harem), rather than a multi-male troop, the nature of the hierarchical structure differs. There are usually many males peripheral to the reproductive units or living in separate all-male groups. Kummer (1968) has shown that young male hamadryas baboons in addition to establishing the nucleus of a harem by appropriating juvenile females from the mothers, also manage to enter existing harems and become established there. In this most important field study, Kummer shows that a young male enters by adopting a submissive behavior style that makes him acceptable to the harem male. The two gradually develop a working partnership. As the older male ages the younger animal acquires sexual access to the females but the older animal retains control of group movement and daily routine. A complex system of mutual "notification" is set up between them whereby the possibility of mutual misunderstanding is greatly reduced. As Chance (1967) has emphasized, primates living in groups are constantly watching one another and their mutual attention underlies the control of behavior in a group.

So far we do not know how far the hamadryas "two-male team" is paralleled in other harem-living primates. Geladas certainly live in harems that often contain a large sub-adult male in addition to the adult (Crook, 1966b). How this association is established is not yet known. Among patas monkeys, females appear to play important roles in controlling group behavior for the male spends much time partially withdrawn from the group and behaving as a watchdog in relation to predators (Hall, 1965).

In all these cases cooperative behavior between males ensures the relative stabilization of group behavior, thereby providing optimum social circumstances for the rearing of young. Vandenbergh (1967) records how the absence of a kinship structure and clear male control in macaque groups newly established on a small island apparently accounted for their social instability. Similar effects have been noted in other mammals. Calhoun (1962) has demonstrated that female rats living in groups controlled by the activities of a powerful male were reproductively more successful and such groups more socially stable than others.

It may be that cooperative behavior in social control is biologically advantageous for the practitioners. Cooperation with powerful kin, for instance a brother, may enhance the chances of the passage of some of one's own genes to a later generation. The kinship structure of macaques makes this seem likely even though relatively few males (the dominants) appear to fertilize females in oestrus. Furthermore, for the fathers, it is essential that the social stability of the group is such as to optimize the chances for successful rearing of young by the mothers.

Peripheral males in coordination may, as we have seen, upset a given hierarchy and then play usurped roles. Peripheral males also have the option of leaving the group with affiliated females and setting up a freshly structured unit. In Kummer's hamadryas harems the old male gains the assistance of a physically strong youngster in defense and in social control. While the youngster gradually acquires sexual control of the females the group as a whole can utilize the wisdom of the elder with regard to food foraging in various seasons.

All these cases of cooperation occur, nevertheless, in a highly competitive situation giving rise to the various types of hierarchy, classes, and castes. The motivational sources of cooperation thus appear to be exceptionally complex. Do the animals practice cooperation as a subterfuge for gaining or maintaining rank? Do they perhaps mitigate the disastrous effects of direct competition through aggression by an indirect competition mediated through cooperation? How is the genuine "altruism" of both males and females in relation to young animals in danger related to the complex competitive environment of the group? If we could answer these questions, we would be a long way toward stating in what way nonhuman primate studies are relevant to man.

Competition-contingent cooperation – a working hypothesis

We may try to pull together the existing shreds of evidence into an open-ended working hypothesis that may prove useful in future research direction. Child-care behavior and mutual affiliation are considered the basic behavior systems from which cooperative behavior in higher mammals, particularly in nonhuman primates, emerges.

Parental care of young animals in distress or danger is well-known and is also commonly shown by individuals of the same (occasionally of other) species that are not the actual father or mother of the juvenile concerned. Probably the basis for these responses is genetically programmed. In populations with relatively limited dispersal from natal areas, and also in those societies partly or largely composed of blood relatives, the behavior would appear biologically advantageous to an individual in that it increases the chances of passing on some elements of its own gene complement to the next generation. Selection may thus favor the evolution of child-oriented behavior by some such process as kin-selection (Hamilton, 1963).

Animals brought up in groups of more or less common descent are likely to affiliate more strongly with those nearest to them in the same matrilineal family or reproductive group. Such affiliation is likely to be compounded from the experience of mutual play, supportative behavior in juvenile "protected threat" situations, and a common aversion to a novel animal. The affiliative process also ensures a preference for in-group company. In addition the common experience of males, for example, in the periphery of the same social unit, may lead to an affiliation between animals even though they may not be descended from the same natal group. This seems, however, likely to be a less frequent basis for affiliation than familial relationship and kinship.

Child care behavior and mutual affiliation occur in social contexts commonly marked by high competitiveness in relation to both environmental (food, drink, sleeping ledges) and social commodities (access to oestrus females, opportunities for motivational expression without social constraints). Since some animals are "more equal than others," the stronger will tend to gain access to commodities of both categories more easily. They will also have greater freedom for the expression of behavior advantageous to them in numerous contexts (as in foraging and copulating). Open aggressive conflict in competitive situations is likely to be both painful and harmful particularly to weaker animals, and it will be increasingly avoided by them. In every generation an individual discovers its relative social position in relation to its peers both through real competition and through mock competition, particularly during play. Many behavior mechanisms, such as mutual grooming, are apparently used to lessen the impact of antagonism, to reduce the tension between individuals, and in some cases to maintain sexual bonds outside a mating period. The effect of these interactions will be the emergence of an individual style of behavior for each animal. The style adopted by an individual in encounters with each other member of the group defines the animal's social position. Within this perspective the relative dominance of an individual is seen as an aspect of the individual's social position and not a cause of it.

Social position in primate groups may perhaps be best described in terms of roles but little attention has been given as yet to an appropriate set of descriptive terms. An effective analysis of cooperative behavior requires a means of designating social position precisely and this the categorization that follows may supply. The occurrences of cooperation can then be analyzed in terms of which roles and social contexts are involved in cooperative behavior. We may be able to describe coopera tion not so much as interactions between known individual organisms but as the necessary relations obtaining between any set of individuals occupying particular role categories in a group.

Using concepts derived from writers such as Sarbin (1959) and Nadel (1957), we can describe a primate's social behavior in terms of the individual's *age and sex status, social position, role,* and *group type affiliation.* In any given group each individual shows characteristic patterns of response in relation to others in the group – older animals, dominant animals, subordinates, peers. The variety of an animal's behaviors in relation to others in the group comprises its *social behavior repertoire;* the complete *set of behavior styles* adopted in relation to every possible companion. An observer may prepare a social position network or matrix by allocating the relative frequency of interaction patterns shown by each member to a particular point or cell. In a more general statement each individual may be defined by its proportion of the total of the various interacting patterns shown within the group (Bernstein and Sharpe, 1966; Gartlan, 1968) and allocated a social position.

It so happens that macaque social positions may be categorized into consistent types that recur repeatedly in new groups formed from the division of the old or in separately analyzed independent groups. Such categories may be termed *roles.* There is, for example, the *control animal role,* the central subgroup *secondary male role* (competitive with another in the subgroup, dominant to peripheral males but subordinate to the central animal and commonly supportative of him), and the role of the *peripheral male,* the *isolate male,* the *central female* and the *peripheral female.* We may also bracket together certain types of behavior to describe roles of animals of high-status kinship and low-status kinship respectively. Now, these styles of behavior are called roles because they are not fixed and immutable aspects of given individuals. On the disappearance of a control animal another male typically adopts the same behavior. A male falling in a dominance hierarchy may, however, march out of the group with affiliated females and establish a new group in which he may adopt the behavioral style of a central animal. Isolated males have been known to enter a group and form a central subgroup – one of them perhaps being the control.

While not every conceivable role is necessarily present in any given group, there is an overall consistency that makes this approach meaningful. Furthermore, the basic data consists of quantified reports of individual behavior in relation to companions. Certain roles are usually characteristic of some kinds of groups and not of others – the harem "overlord" occurs in hamadryas, patas, and gelada groups but not in other baboons nor among macaques.

Different sorts of roles occur in groups differentially composed in terms of age and sex categories. Species populations are commonly dispersed in a pattern of groups that is consistent for a given habitat. In some cases the whole species population is dispersed in groups of the same type while in other species there are contrasts across the geographical range. All such contrasts in group composition are intimately related to the ecological adaptations of a species and its social adaptability. These relations have recently been reviewed elsewhere and we need not develop the point further here (Crook, 1970).

The behavior characteristic of a particular role is not the "property" of the individual playing it. Such behavior is not fixed by conditioning so that the individual remains forever the same. Physiological and social changes impel behavioral shifts so that in a lifetime individuals may play many roles in their social structure. Social mobility in the sense of role changing is an important attribute of primate groups. It seems more characteristic of males than of females. Young and sub-adult males go solitarily, live peripherally or in all-male groups, or shift from one reproductive unit to another. Females are more loyal to their natal group and provide the more fixed social positions around which males revolve. This mobility is an expression of a set of tensions or forces characteristic of group life.

At least three types of factors interact in the social sorting process that underlies the dynamics of primate social groups and determines the place of individuals in their respective social positions at any one time. First, periodic shortages of environmental (food and drink shortage in the dry season) and social commodities (mates) provide conditions in which aggressive competition may occur. As in birds, severe damage, particularly to subordinates, is avoided by withdrawal upon threat and the gradual establishment of a social hierarchy giving prior access to commodities to more dominant individuals. The ranking system is maintained primarily by the avoidance behavior of those relatively subordinate and becomes habitual even when actual competition is not involved in an encounter. The behavior of the relatively low-ranking individuals is inhibited whereas high rankers show a free-style confidence that their cringing companions lack. This constraint is liable to place an individual in physiological stress; a behavioral depression that affects comportment, health, chances of survival, and chances of reproduction. The escape from constraint would appear highly rewarding and means of escape are sought and found.

A second factor concerns the aging of individuals. A sexually maturing male will seek a social position wherein he may mate females. If this behavior is denied expression he is likely to enforce a social change or to withdraw. The means whereby young males enter reproduction units may be quite elaborate, particularly in the case of harem species. Likewise, old macaque males may change role. Although their social positions may no longer be defined by threat and mating behavior, they may retain the respect of their companions and remain as control animals almost into senility. The experience of age is valuable in a leader. Dominant animals lacking in local wisdom may perhaps fall rapidly into peripheral status.

The third factor in the sorting process concerns the growth in size of the reproductive unit. In well fed and enlarging groups splits eventually occur with the recreation of old roles in new groups. Some Japanese workers have talked in terms of a fission threshold. In relatively small, cohesive groups of Japanese macaques, high behavioral constraint may force some young males into isolation. Larger groups, comprising mutually affiliated subsections, are liable to split up into branch units – again each with its set of roles. The process of change naturally varies with the species and the social structure concerned.

If this picture is substantially correct, then there appear to be two opposed social forces operating at any one time within a baboon or macaque troop. One consists of the assertive, freely expressed utilization of available physical and social commodities by high status animals which has the effect of constraining the behavior of juveniles and subordinates. The other consists of the adoption of behavioral subterfuge by certain subordinates whereby such behavioral constraint can be avoided (*e.g.*, by temporary solitary living or by splitting up the group into branch groups permitting a greater freedom of expression to the new leaders).

It is not suggested that the subterfuge is conscious or deliberate. It appears to arise from the need of certain subordinates to free themselves from the behavioral constraints to which they have been exposed. There are in fact relatively few social routes along which an aspirant may move. In our review of the evidence we have noted three: *a*) temporary solitude, followed sometimes by take-over of a small branch group; *b*) the use of an affiliated companion to ensure the rise of a dominant animal into a higher or even a centrally located position; *c*) the use of infants and babies as a means of entering high status sub-groups and so to affiliate with them.

In each of these cases individuals closely affiliated with others can combine cooperatively to bring about the liberating effect, an effect which, furthermore, in times of shortage (food, females) would ensure an increased probability of survival and reproductive success in addition to the psychological freedom from the effects of "stress" that undoubtedly accompany in some degree a continuing social restraint on individual behavioral expression. Similarly, by enlisting the cooperation of affiliated animals, often relatives, in their "control" behavior, animals that are already established in social positions of high rank will be able to maintain such positions, and the access to commodities they provide. We have already quoted examples of such behavior.

It seems, then, that cooperative behavior of the high order found in macaque and baboon groups has arisen within the context of competition for access to both physical and social commodities. Both direct affiliative behavior and indirect affiliation through a common interest in child care may provide the basis for common action. As we have seen, such cooperation provides numerous advantages for the participants – and not only for the most dominant animals among them. It also provides the behavioral basis for the complex class-structured society of these animals with its tolerance of individual mobility between roles.

Finally, the stable social structure maintained by a powerful clique around a control animal seems to provide the optimum circumstances for maternal security and child rearing. Females appear to form the more cohesive elements of primate groups and, as a consequence, their affiliative relations and kinship links may play a much greater role in determining who emerges as "control" than is at present known. Males, by contrast, subject to the full force of social competition, are at least in some species more mobile than females, and can transfer themselves, as recent research shows, quite frequently from one group to another.

This outline model of primate group dynamics has some consistency and has been based carefully upon existing field data. Nevertheless, detailed accounts of cooperative behavior are few and still largely anecdotal. Only further field research can clarify its extent and nature. Until we have more data we must also be suspicious of a natural tendency to anthropomorphize. It remains unknown to me how far my explanatory model reflects unconsciously the social tensions clearly present within both Western and Japanese societies during the period of research under review and to which the human observers themselves are exposed. In discussing primate behavior, reflective caution may be vital in preventing the promulgation of misleading interpretations of field reports.

From monkeys to man

Although perennially outsung by the trumpeters of orthodox Darwinism, the idea that a biology of cooperative behavior may be essential for the understanding of man has surfaced periodically ever since Darwin (1871) himself made the point. Kropotkin (1902) provided the significant impetus and he has been followed by Geddes and Thompson (1911), Allee (1938), and Ashley Montagu (1957). The concept of cooperation in all these works was, however, never clearly defined; sometimes meaning little more than reflexive mutuality or a general sociability and occasionally identified with love. In almost all cases cooperation was raised to a "principle" and opposed to "competition." Some passages in these works had a certain missionary intent, and in any case the crucial data from the field studies of wild primates was not yet available. These idealistic ventures may now give place to critical analyses.

The picture of the relationship between cooperation and competition among members of macaque and baboon troops does perhaps suggest an analogy to modern human relations that looks too close for comfort. For example the relationships within the New York law firms described so beautifully by Louis Auchincloss in his *Tales of Manhattan* seem structured in a markedly simian fashion. Were early hominid structures also similar?

Reynolds (1965, 1966) and Goodall (1965) have described the relatively unstructured "open" groups of chimpanzees, and Reynolds (1968) has further argued the case for such a social organization as primordial in man. Both these studies were made, however, in forest or woodland. The available information suggests that baboons, chimpanzees, and men may have all acquired increasingly structured societies in relation to ecological conditions in the savannah (Crook and Gartlan, 1966; Itani and Suzuki, 1967; Crook, 1970). This structural differentiation may be based upon the seasonal shortage of crucial commodities and the resulting competition for them. Learning in relation to competition is a prime factor in the formation of status hierarchies in these animals.

We may infer that far from being a remote analogy to human life the social sorting process in baboon and macaque troops; the emergence of kinship, role, and cooperation as vital to the social organization; and the social mobility of the male players may be a very close homologue of the early social systems of protohominids. Upon such a basis the acculturative and communication processes were added as human society emerged into its primitive forms. Competition-contingent cooperation may thus lie at the root of our behavioral heritage – but it lies there in no simple instinctual sense. It was already the complex, multifactorially governed process such as we have described.

The moral of our story lies in a close focus on socially induced competition in man. Human cooperation, as the studies of Sherif and Sherif (1953) show, is linked closely to the identification of a person with the needs of the group to which he belongs and of which he considers himself a member. Cooperation within such an "in-group" may be high especially if the group is in competition with another. Men, like monkeys, appear to cooperate best when at their most competitive. Nevertheless, human beings, again like monkeys, are socially mobile and may change the frame of reference of their activities from a narrow sectarian concern to broader issues of wider significance. An understanding of the forces controlling the maintenance of social position in relation to human needs in terms of identity, in-group membership, self-esteem, and compassionate empathy would much improve our chances of social control. For example certain group processes such as those involved in sensitivity training can promote high levels of cooperation contingent upon the mutual sense of trust and affiliation that such treatment may induce (Gibb and Gibb, 1967). Ultimately the problem moves to an economic and educational level with a focus on the needs of humanity as a whole (Tajfel, 1966). From this viewpoint local issues may be seen in a more balanced perspective.

References

Allee, W. C. 1938. *Cooperation among animals.* New York: H. Schuman.

Bartholomew, G. A. 1942. The fishing activities of double-crested cormorants on San Francisco Bay. *Condor* 44:13-21.

Bernstein, I. L. 1966. Analysis of a key role in a capuchin (*Cebus albifrons*) group. *Tulane studies in zoology* 13(2):49-54.

Bernstein, I. S. and Sharpe, L. F. 1966. Social roles in a rhesus monkey group. *Behaviour* 26: 91-104.

Calhoun, J. B. 1962. *The ecology and sociology of the Norway rat.* Washington, D.C.: U.S. Department of Health, Education, and Welfare.

Carpenter, C. R. 1965. The howlers of Barro Colorado Island. *Primate behavior,* ed. I. DeVore. New York: Holt, Rinehart and Winston.

Chance, M. R. A. 1967. Attention structure as the basis of primate rank orders. *Man* 2(4):503-518.

Crook, J. H. 1965. The adaptive significance of avian social organisations. *Symposia of the Zoological Society of London* 14:181-218.

____. 1966a. Cooperation in primates. *Eugenics review* 58:63-70.

____. 1966b. Gelada baboon herd structure and movement: A comparative report. *Symposia of the Zoological Society of London* 18:237-258.

____. 1970. The socio-ecology of primates. In Crook (ed.), *Op. cit.*

———. (ed.). 1970. *Social behaviour in birds and mammals.* London: Academic Press.

Crook, J. H. and Butterfield, P. A. 1968. Effects of testosterone propionate and luteinising hormone on agonistic and nest-building behavior of *Quelea quelea. Animal behaviour* 16: 370-384.

———. 1970. Gender role in the social system of Quelea. In Crook (ed.), *Op. cit.*

Crook, J. H. and Gartlan, J. S. 1966. Evolution of primate societies. *Nature* 210:1200-1203.

Darwin, C. R. 1871. *Descent of man and selection in relation to sex.* London: Murray.

Davis, D. E. 1942. The phylogeny of social nesting habits in the Crotophaginae. *Quarterly review of biology* 17:115-134.

Deag, J. M. and Crook, J. H. 1971. Social behaviour and "agonistic buffering" in the wild Barbary macaque *Macaca sylvana L. Folia primatologica* 15:183-200.

DeVore, I. (ed.). 1965. *Primate behavior.* New York: Holt, Rinehart and Winston.

Eisenberg, J. S. 1966. The social organizations of mammals. *Handbuch der Zoologie* 10(7): 1-92 (Vol. 8. 39).

Gartlan, J. S. 1966. Ecology and behavior of the vervet monkey, Lolui Island, Lake Victoria, Uganda. Bristol: Bristol University Library (Ph.D. Thesis).

———. 1968. Structure and function in primate society. *Folia primatologica* 8:89-120.

Geddes, P. and Thompson, J. A. 1911. *Evolution.* New York: Holt.

Gibb, J. R. and Gibb, L. M. 1967. Humanistic elements in group growth. *Challenges of humanistic psychology,* ed. J. F. T. Bugental. New York: McGraw-Hill.

Gifford, D. P. 1967. The expression of male interest in the infant in five species of macaque. *Kroeber Anthropological Society papers* 36:32-40.

Goodall, J. 1965. Chimpanzees of the Gombe Stream Reserve. In DeVore (ed.), *Op. cit.*

Hall, K. R. L. 1965. Behavior and ecology of the wild patas monkey, *Erythrocebus patas,* in Uganda. *Journal of zoology* 148:15-87.

Hall, K. R. L. and DeVore, I. 1965. Baboon social behavior. In DeVore (ed.), *Op. cit.*

Hamilton, W. D. 1963. The evolution of altruistic behavior. *American naturalist* 97:354-356.

———. 1970. Selection of selfish and altruistic behavior in some extreme models. *Man and beast,* ed. W. S. Dillon. Washington, D. C.: Smithsonian Institute Press.

Hinde, R. A. and Spencer-Booth, Y. 1967. The behavior of socially living rhesus monkeys in their first two and a half years. *Animal behaviour* 15:169-196.

Imanishi, K. 1960. Social organization of subhuman primates in their natural habitats. *Current anthropology* 1:5-6, 393-407.

Itani, J. 1959. Paternal care in the wild Japanese monkey, *Macaca fuscata. Journal of primatology* 2:61-93. Also see Southwick, G. H. (ed.). *Primate social behavior.* Princeton, N.J.: Van Nostrand.

Itani, J. and Suzuki, A. 1967. The social unit of chimpanzees. *Primates* 8:355-381.

Jolly, A. 1966. *Lemur behavior. A Madagascar field study.* Chicago, Ill.: Univ. of Chicago Press.

King, J. A. 1955. *Social behavior, social organization, and population dynamics in a black-tailed prairie-dog town in the Black Hills of South Dakota.* Ann Arbor, Mich.: Univ. of Michigan. (Contributions from the Laboratory of vertebrate biology, 67.)

Kropotkin, P. 1902. *Mutual aid. A factor of evolution.* London: Heinemann.

Kühme, W. von. 1965. Freilandstudien zur Soziologie des Hyanenhundes (*Lycaon pictus lupinus* Thomas 1902). *Zeitschrift für Tierpsychologie* 22:495-541.

Kummer, H. 1957. *Soziales Verhalten einer Mantelpavian-Gruppe.* Bern-Stuttgart: Huber.

———. 1968. Social organization of hamadryas baboons. *Bibliotheca primatologica* 6.

Lack, D. 1968. *Ecological adaptations to breeding in birds.* London: Methuen.

Lahiri, R. K. and Southwick, C. H. 1966. Parental care in *Macaca sylvana. Folia primatologica* 4:257-269.

Montagu, M. F. A. 1957. *On being human.* New York: Schuman.

Morris, D. 1962. The behavior of the green agouchi (*Myoprocta pratti*) with special reference to scatter hoarding. *Proceedings of the Zoological Society of London* 139:701-732.

Mykytowicz, R. 1960. Social behavior of an experimental colony of wild rabbits, *Oryctolagus cuniculus* (L), III Second breeding season. *Wildlife research* 5:120. (Commonwealth Scientific and Industrial Research Organization, Australia.)

Nadel, S. F. 1957. *The theory of social structure.* Glencoe, Ill.: Free Press.

Orians, G. 1968. *The study of life.* New York: Allyn and Bacon.

Reynolds, V. 1966. Open groups in hominid evolution. *Man* 1:441-452.

____. 1968. Kinship and the family in monkeys, apes, and man. *Man* 3:209-223.

Reynolds, V. and Reynolds, F. 1965. Chimpanzees of the Budongo Forest. In DeVore (ed.), *Op. cit.*

Ritter, W. E. 1938. *The California woodpecker and I.* Berkeley, Calif.

Rowell, T. E. 1966. Hierarchy in the organization of a captive baboon group. *Animal behaviour* 14:430-443.

Rowell, T. E., Hinde, R. A., and Spencer-Booth, Y. 1964. "Aunt"-infant interaction in captive rhesus monkeys. *Animal behaviour* 12:219-226.

Ryder, S. R. 1962. *The water vole.* London: Sunday Times. Animals of Britain 4.

Sarbin, T. R. 1959. Role theory. *Handbook of social psychology,* ed. G. Lindzey. Cambridge, Mass.: Addison-Wesley.

Sherif, M. and Sherif, C. W. 1953. *Groups in harmony and tension.* New York: Harper.

Skutch, A. 1935. Helpers at the nest. *Auk* 52:257-273.

Southwick, C. H., Beg, M. A., and Siddiqi, M. R. 1965. Rhesus monkeys in North India. In DeVore (ed.), *Op. cit.*

Spencer-Booth, Y. 1968. The behavior of group companions towards rhesus monkey infants. *Animal behaviour* 16:541-557.

Tajfel, H. 1966. Cooperation between human groups. *Eugenics review* 58:77-84.

Vandenbergh, J. G. 1967. The development of social structure in free-ranging rhesus monkeys. *Behaviour* 29:179-194.

Wilson, A. P. 1968. Intergroup relations and individual association in free-ranging rhesus monkeys. University of California (Ph.D. Thesis).

Wynne-Edwards, V. C. 1962. *Animal dispersion in relation to social behavior.* Edinburgh: Oliver and Boyd.

12

Human aggression: the need for a species-specific framework

Ralph L. Holloway, Jr.

Introduction

This paper is being written in a surrounding aura of violence, for it is Summer, 1967. Has there ever been an era without aggression and violence, and are not these a natural penumbra of the human condition? History surely indicates that violence and conflict have been a constant concomitant of the human condition, although the tempos have varied considerably between allegro and adagio.

My task in this article is to compare the aggressive components of man's behavior with those of other animals. There is hardly any question that academic and public interest in this theme is very pronounced – a rash of biologically oriented books has been placed before the public treating this very issue: Konrad Lorenz's *On Aggression* (1966), Robert Ardrey's *The Territorial Imperative* (1966), The Institute of Biology's Symposia, *The Natural History of Aggression* (Carthy & Ebling, 1964) are a few examples. The major issue that comes

SOURCE: *War: The Anthropology of Armed Conflict and Aggression,* Morton Fried, Marvin Harris, and Robert Murphy, eds., Natural History Press, 1967.

[1]Part of the literature research for this paper was supported by the Council for Research in the Social Sciences, whose support is gratefully acknowledged. I also wish to thank Professors Marvin Harris and William Torrey, Columbia University, for reading an earlier version of this manuscript and offering many helpful criticisms and suggestions. Naturally, I am responsible for any inaccuracies or fallacies in this paper.

from these efforts revolves about the very nature of human aggression. Is it innate, an instinct, or is it learned? Do animal studies provide us with illuminating frameworks to further our understanding of human aggression, or not? Do we need a species-specific theory of human aggression? Can anthropology, particularly the study of human evolution, give us any insights into these important questions?

Actually, what is said about human aggression in this paper is somewhat irrelevant to the theme of this symposium. Let me explain. War is, after all, as von Clauswitz wrote long ago, simply an organized extension of politics carried to a different level. It is an organized activity directed by rational decisions by political bodies whose membership is infinitesimal compared to the aggregates involved in actual combat. Abel (1941) showed very clearly in his study of factors operating in several European wars that warfare cannot be understood by recourse to individual psychology. Aggression, outside of how politicians use the term, is an individual act presupposing some emotional basis. Abel showed that rational decisions to make war go well in advance of the emotional, aggressive exacerbations usually thought of as the direct cause of war. (For an excellent discussion of this, see Burton, 1964.) Furthermore, human aggression cannot be discussed without reference to the kinds of socio-economic conditions under which men live, or better, try to live.

This is one of the most disappointing and infuriating aspects of the recent attempts by a few biologists and dramatists to explain human aggression and violence by reference to animal studies, instincts, death drives, and the like. Lorenz (1966) for example, claims that we must understand our animal nature and phylogenetic experience before we are engulfed in a species-wide disaster. Ardrey (1966) re-echoes this line and draws a convenient equation between private property and territorial behavior in other animals. Some writers have called for standardized displacement activities patterned after many ethological examples, e.g., worldwide games, Olympics, et cetera. This is to let the animal aggression in us spill over into nonviolent beneficial activities rather than in harmful aggression. Few have had very much to say about the social and economic conditions confronting most of the human race, and this symposium is not exceptionable in that respect, aside from Professor Alland's contribution.

In other words, if man goes about killing off his own species, let us look to lower animals that show far more biological wisdom in their social habits. Or, let us make sure that private property (free enterprise) stays as it is, since it is obviously distributed justly, according to evolutionary and biological principles. Or, let us institute displacement games for everyone to play to dampen our aggressive overdrive.

To be frank, such lines of reasoning often seem like rationalizations for the status quo. These formulations are, in spite of the possible well-meaning intent, conservative forms of evading the central critical issues concerning the human condition. What faces most humans is poverty, starvation, substandard health, exploitation, increasing relative and absolute deprivations, disease, poverty of self-identification and evaluation, and little if any chance for meaningful self-participation in the "grandeur of human adaptation, civilization."

To put the matter in more simple relief, the problems of human aggression and violence are not up for academic grab-bagging along ethological, psychoanalytic, or displacement lines of research. We know that man has awesome potentialities for aggression and violence, and we know a great deal about the inequities of socio-economic distribution. The real problem facing men is not to better understand lower animals, but to implement drastic social changes throughout the world; to find a way to structure power on a worldwide sharing basis, to prevent the social conditions that lead to violence and war. This problem is a political one, not a biological or psychological one.

Nevertheless, insofar as other authors have made claims about equivalence of human and other animal aggression (and these are few) and its relation to the theme of warfare, there is an academic responsibility to provide a counterreaction against such views. I hope my own academic grab-bagging will be seen in this light. For what I suggest is hardly unique or original, and is only relevant to the major theme of this symposium in the terms I have already discussed. The study of human aggression, like the phenomena itself, is beyond the competence of any one individual or discipline. Psychology, sociology, anthropology, zoology, ethology, anatomy, and physiology, and even political science have contributions to make. Since I am a physical anthropologist, concerned with man's evolution, I will concentrate on this area, and following a brief critique of certain recent biological writings declaring human aggression as instinctual, I will argue for the need for viewing human aggression in the context of a larger framework, and finally present a few ideas concerning man's earliest adaptations (bio-social) and their possible place in the development of a theory of human aggression and violence.

Human aggression: instinctive, innate, or learned?

Most discussions on the nature of human aggression have tended to gravitate between two poles: viewing it as direct (sometimes identical) *instincts* inherited through evolution from other animals; and viewing aggression as learning or cultural conditioning. Neither extreme viewpoint seems to fit the human case, or that for any other vertebrate animal. An enormous amount of zoological, psychological, and sociological literature provides examples of the manipulation of aggression through physiological, psychological, ecological, and social psychological restructuring. Proponents of both extremes have usually ignored the greater weight of evidence from many disciplines that aggression, however defined, has both physiological and learning components involved in its genesis and expression. For reviews on this controversy and empirical findings from different disciplines, the reader is referred to Scott (1958); Berkowitz (1962, 1965); Buss (1961); Lorenz (1966); Ardrey (1966); Carthy and Ebling (1964); Bernard *et al.* (1957); Durbin and Bowlby (1939); McNeil (1965, particularly 14-41); and Masserman (1963). See also Leach (1966, 1967) for critique of ethological positions, and Holloway (1967b). (I am not including the psychoanalytic frameworks of Freud and others in this paper. It should be obvious that these positions are very close to some ethological positions, particularly in terms of instincts, death wishes, and so on.)

Aggression is most often defined as "behavior where goal is the injury of some person or object" (Berkowitz, 1965:302) which stems mainly from the Dollard *et al.* (1939) treatise on aggression and frustration. Scott (1958:1) uses the word to refer to fighting, or the act of inflicting attack. Buss (1961:1) defines aggression as a response that delivers noxious stimuli to another organism. Note that neither Buss' nor Scott's definition includes any explicit or implicit reference to intent. As human beings greatly concerned with aggression, its genesis, and hopefully its control, we are concerned very much with intent. Whether other animals engaged in aggressive actions harbor intents in the manner we are accustomed is an unanswerable question. It seems reasonable that actions may occur that do not harbor aggressive intent in terms of injury, but which are interpreted as such. On the other hand, it seems pointless to deny that much aggressive action has the intent of injury behind it. The reason for discussing this aspect of definition is not to quibble whether or not this or that instance of defined aggression was intended on the part of the actor. The reason is to point out but one tricky aspect of studying aggression: interpreting an action as aggressive depends on an appraisal of the cue functions or environmental stimuli which help to activate an animal to an aggressive action, and also depends on the internal state of the animal in terms of its readiness for action and *its* appraisal of the outside cue or stimulus. To some extent, this is an artificial problem with human beings because we have some basis for sharing our human experiences. When we are talking about nonhuman behavior, however, the cue definitions or appraisal of the environmental stimuli (such as one animal's motor actions toward another), the definition is ours, not the animal's.

This would be a minor quibble were it not for the fact that there appears to be a recrudescence of the idea that humans possess an instinct toward aggression and warfare. Both Lorenz (1964, 1966) and Ardrey (1966) have tried to re-establish this instinct in man.[2] An instinct is generally understood to be a quite specific response pattern, invariant in its development, maturation, and expression, which occurs in the presence of a quite specific cluster of stimuli from the environment. As such, it is regarded as an innate, genetically determined pattern, which comes about without reference to, or in absence of, learning. (See Thorpe, 1963, for a review on the history of this concept; also Lehrman, 1953, for a critique.) The success and increasing sophistication of the ethologist school has focused on the innate and relatively fixed action patterns of numerous animals, and elaborate studies have been attempted to

[2]On the other hand, it is curious to read Lorenz's (1967) remarks concerning ritualization in animals and man. In this publication Lorenz is careful to state that the ". . . role played by genetic inheritance in the evolution and maintenance of phylogenetically evolved rituals is, of course, taken over by tradition in cultural ritualization" (p. 280). For Lorenz (see also Huxley, 1967) the functioning of rituals in human groups are analogous with those occurring in lower animals. I am not sure whether this means that Lorenz is not as adamant about human instincts or whether he regards ritualized behavior patterns as exceptions to human instincts inherited from other animals. For Ardrey (1966) the behavioral dynamics of human adaptation are given as identical homologies with other animal patterns.

demonstrate the almost "key-in-lock" relation between certain stimuli and fixed action patterns of motor sequences. The example of the male stickleback's responses to the red belly of another male is well known. In addition, there has been a great deal of success in interpreting such behavior patterns, in terms of the environmental releasers within the framework of adaptation and natural selection. It is particularly this latter emphasis, that of adaptedness of behavior in the ecological context, that augurs such optimism for the study of animals other than man.

It should be noted that I have been discussing *instinct,* not *instinctual,* which seems so loosely defined (see Huxley, 1967, and Lorenz, 1967) as to include any aspect of behavior involving drive or central states of motivation. If it is this loose, what utility does the concept have, and how does one avoid the Aristotelian fallacy of labeling differently organized processes with the same rubric? If one man attacks another because the latter trespassed on his "territory," and a baboon attacks another because it takes a peanut outside of "prescribed" limits, are we to say that in both cases there is the same *instinctual* basis for aggressive response? Motivational or drive states don't operate in a vacuum: cue stimuli are necessary, and how these are defined by an animal depends on how the animal has organized its experience, and how it has been programmed both biologically and socially. One cannot realistically argue for cue-sameness between man and baboon (or other animals) simply by noting the response. One must know the proximal stimulus for each beast, before one can argue for sameness.

Most of the criticism directed against the ethologists has revolved around the importance of learning in the genesis of fixed action patterns. While there is still debate, there appears to be a greater appreciation that both innate and learning phenomena must be taken into account in the behavior of all vertebrates and possibly those lower in the animal kingdom. Does man have an instinct toward aggression? Does he have any instincts? If understood in the usual sense of a fixed invariant pattern of action directed toward some definite invariant cluster of stimuli, there appear to be precious few (if any) examples of instincts in man, and no evidence for an aggressive instinct.

This does not mean that the human infant, however, does not possess fixed action patterns. The sucking reflex, seeking or head-turning toward a source of stimulation, the smiling response, crying, possible grasping and walking, are examples of relatively fixed action patterns that undergo wide changes as the animal matures (see Eibl-Eibesfeldt, 1967). These types of patterns seem equally applicable to other animals with the exception of smiling, crying, and walking. But the important question is: to what extent are the adult responses the same kind of fixed action patterns? It is precisely here that the anthropologist, and indeed other social scientists and biologists, part company with the more adamant ethological frameworks.

Human aggression shows neither motor nor sensory constancy in the ethological sense. The range of stimuli that can produce acts of aggression for man is enormous, as are the ways in which he can manifest his aggression. What are the critical sign stimuli for the human which act to release stereotypical adaptive responses?

What are the invariances of the cue functions in the human environment not mediated by arbitrary symbols that help to release specific motor patterns built up through evolution by natural selection? Red feathers, blue gewgaws, green turf, butyric acid, white eyelids, the exposed neck, white tails, et cetera, et cetera, have been identified for numerous animals. What are the critical sign stimuli that make up the human "umwelt"? The question is not about human aggressive responses to various stimuli. The sordid history of man attests well to the fantastic plurality of stimuli that can be cooked up to elicit aggression. How natural are they? Skepticism about human instincts is not any attack on the animal nature of man or an arrogant claim that man does not act according to natural and manmade laws. Such skepticism need not blind anyone to the possibility of innate dispositions in man to define certain environmental contexts as inimical to their interests and to act aggressively toward such clusters.

Man, like any other animal, is an evolutionary product. It would be a strange exception indeed if natural selection during the last two million years had not acted on behavior, particularly since man is a highly gregarious animal as are most of his closest relatives, the apes and Old World monkeys. Numerous animal studies on both wild and domesticated forms show conclusively that temperamental variables are operative in all species and can be varied through training, or heightened or lowered through genetic selection (see Hafez, 1962). The biological basis for such variations, as for example between basenji or terrier dog breeds and cocker spaniels have not been demonstrated (see Scott and Fuller, 1965). Indeed the actual biological basis for differences in aggression between wild and domesticated rats, mice, or different species of primates has yet to be demonstrated. This hardly means that biological variables do not exist that help account for the differences. While there has been much fruitful work on the anatomical and physiological underpinnings of behavior, such as rage and attack, there is precious little in the way of relating these in a comparative way to different animals and anchoring these to concrete anatomical and physiological differences.

While we often think of aggression as maladaptive, it is obvious that under certain conditions aggression is an asset to an animal when it prolongs its life and opportunities for passing its genes to the next generation. Animals are up against things from members of their own species as well as from different species, e.g., predators. Man is hardly an exception, and it should occasion no surprise that he is biologically capable of perceiving threat to his existence and reacting to such threats aggressively.

While man evolved in a social context, as did many other animals, his social adaptations were of supreme importance in his evolutionary history, and perhaps unique in their manifold complexity. Selection operated not only on his aggressive potentialities, but on the rest of his social behavior as well. Man is capable of great degrees of cooperation, empathy, sympathy, sacrifice, the deferment of gratification, exceedingly strong bonds to others closely related to him, and extraordinary ties with numerous symbolic constructs involving religious, ideological, and material matters. In other words, man's evolution has involved a number of complex interacting variables, and we cannot hope to understand man or his evolution without reference to his social matrix. One of the major tasks facing the anthropologist is to unravel this matrix and relate the numerous variables to adaptive and selectional processes.

Need for an expanded framework

Looking back at the definitions of aggression mentioned earlier, these are mainly drawn from works that have a highly experimental bent. I think that our understanding of human aggression must encompass more than the laboratory demonstrations compatible with or dependent upon the definitions given. This is hardly meant as any slight to the empirical studies that are able to delimit and vary external and internal variables in their study of human and other animal aggression. It is argued here, however, that we need a species-specific framework[3] of aggression, and such a framework must integrate the aggressive components of man's behavior with the rest of his social and psychological, and biological matrix. Man is the only animal with language and an adaptation based on the sharing and use of arbitrary symbol systems. He is the only animal with plural role responsibilities and the animal who lives under differential power allocations that can be decided arbitrarily, i.e., without reference to biological attributes. His brain is unique as are his behavioral processes, albeit he shares many aspects of his behavioral processes with other animals. The organization and ontogenetic development of his brain is unique – or better – species-specific, as Lenneberg (1967) has so well argued. His development and behavioral expression is species-specific, just as the development of a cat's behavior differs from that of the dog, mouse, chicken, or the chimpanzee differs from the baboon. In addition, man is in constant interaction with his peers, himself, a material world, symbol systems, strangers, enemies, friends, and kin. (See Mead, 1963b, particularly pp. 93-99.)

Nonhuman animal studies show that all animals are capable of aggression. There seems, however, to be fair agreement that animal aggression is not constant but fairly rare and that the stimuli evoking aggressive responses are specific to the animal's habitat and involve discrete cues associated mostly with mating and territorial behavior (see Collias, 1944; Eisenberg, 1966, for reviews; also Schneirla, 1965, for a general theoretical treatment in terms of approach and avoidance; for specific examples relating to primates, see Hall, 1964; DeVore, 1965; and Southwick, 1967). There seem to be no animals who attack purely for attack's sake, the attack being related to the quest for food, as in canids and felids, or when challenged by predatory

[3] I am using *species-specific* in the sense of special characteristics for different animals (see for example Rheingold, 1967, p. 288) to underline the point that not only are the biological attributes of man unique, particularly his brain, but also ontogenesis in terms of interaction with a cultural milieu, and the nature of his social relations are also unique – that is, specific to man. This does not mean that other animal studies cannot be used for purposes of comparison, or that they cannot provide heuristic frameworks with which man may be examined. I do mean that man's behavior, in the holistic sense, cannot be reduced to the same frameworks available for describing nonhuman animals, including primates.

species or by members of their own or different species for territory or mates. As Lorenz and others have pointed out, most animals enjoy the possession of behavior and sometimes structural mechanisms which serve to inhibit further attack that might be injurious, as in the wolf which bares its neck to inhibit the onslaught of its opponents.[4] Perhaps there are postures and vocalizations that have an appeasement function in man, such as the averting of eyes, cringing, tears, et cetera, but it should be equally clear that these do not offer any guarantees against further aggression or injury from an opponent. There are several studies on facial and bodily gestures in different primate species which demonstrate a wide range of adaptations serving to communicate possible aggressive intent and submission on the part of the actors (see Altmann, 1962, 1967; Andrews, 1963; Hall, 1964; Struhsaker, 1967). It does not seem unlikely that we retain, as Darwin suggested, some of these nonverbal communication devices to allay violent actions and reactions, but it also seems certain that there is a heavy cultural or learning component in the genesis of such gestures, and it remains a problem to decide which are universal or specific for different cultures. The fact that they exist in all cultures suggests that conflict is a structural property of human societies. In the human case, the range of stimuli that can evoke aggression is exceedingly varied and complex, and aggressional tendencies can last long beyond the emotional state of anger, and can continue to occur in the absence of the attitude of hostility.

Perhaps analogues to the "displacement activities" of other animals often discussed by ethologists (e.g., Lorenz, 1966) fit in here. Activities such as sports, hobbies, et cetera, probably aid in "draining off" heightened levels of arousal or excitation that involve the degree to which the central nervous system is "tuned up." The state or pitch of excitement can be increased by a fantastic plurality of stimuli (even writing a paper), however, many of an internal symbolic nature, such as in ego-evaluation, paranoia, et cetera. However, even if "displacement activities" do have this function, it is doubtful whether one can claim that they solve the problems of human aggression. Certainly the matter of vicarious substitutes for aggression, as in movies depicting violence, boxing matches, working to decrease aggression is an issue open to question (see Berkowitz, 1965, for review).

The major framework in psychological thought regarding human aggression revolves about the "frustration-aggression" hypothesis offered by Dollard *et al.* in 1939. There seems to be little doubt that frustration is a major stimulus for provoking aggressive responses, but it is debatable whether the original formulation that all aggression stems from frustration, or that aggression always follows frustration is accurate (see Berkowitz, 1962, 1965, for critique).

Several studies of primate behavior (DeVore, 1965; Mason, 1967; Schrier *et al.*, 1965) show that monkey and ape offspring are highly motivated toward play and contact with peers, adults, and inanimate objects, and are highly curious, observa-

[4]This view is, however, open to question (see Scott, 1967, in Symposium on Canine Behavior, in the *American Zoologist*).

tions which apply to man and other young mammals. Through play and mock combat, the young animals learn skills of social interaction, and eventually their position in dominance terms relative to their peers. They enlarge their sphere of knowledge about their environments, and part of this enlargement is the outcome of aggressiveness. The human animal is hardly an exception. In line with the concept of species-specific behavior, the ontogenetic or developmental tendencies (how behavior changes with maturation) offer the best evidence for species-specific patterns of organ development and functioning. The so-called critical periods of birds, sheep, dogs, et cetera, are familiar examples. In the human case, a child acquires different behavioral patterns as it passes from birth to adolescence (see Gesell, 1950). The language abilities, starting at about one to two years, are a good example of species-specific patterns of neural and behavioral development. These also involve a species-specific pattern of social and emotional nurturance for their healthy development. Associated at least in part with the specific neural events that accompany human development, there are patterns of psychological development centering about the construction of the child's ego, his moral sense, his reality picture and abilities for concrete and abstract thought, his pleasure in controlling his body from proprioceptive impulses, and his aggressiveness. The studies of Goodenough (1931), Bender and Schilder (1936), Schilder (1942), and the numerous studies of Piaget (1926, 1929, 1954) are definitive in this regard.

Goodenough (1931) for example, found definite developmental patterns of rage expression and control during the course of child maturation. In general, as the brain grows so does the child's reality picture of the world, his expectations of his parents' and peers' behavior, and his control of rage. In early stages, rage is sudden, explosive yet quick to subside and be forgotten. With maturation the thresholds for such expression rise, but once exceeded, the rage and anger are longer in duration, and subsequent brooding or hostile periods are prolonged. These changes point to neural and ego variables, involving components of inhibition and facilitation, as well as an enlarged capacity for sustaining particular memories. I will return to this aspect later when I discuss the early evolution of man as a set of strategies to promote a longer period of dependence and nurturance so that the enlarged brain had time to mature.

Other authors have studied children's aggression, and there seems to be wide agreement that aggression increases during the early years, reaches a peak, and then tapers off as social control factors and the child's realization of deferment of gratification by the environmental surroundings come into play. It is worth stressing something that Schilder pointed out some time ago: that much of the destructive elements of child playing has natural concomitants of learning and is often accompanied by a constructive aftermath.

Allied with this explorative and constructive aspect, there is yet another realm of species-specific development of the human child – that of his ego structure, his self-concept, his evaluation of self-worth, in an ever-changing external (and internal) environment. *As definitions of the child change through a constantly interacting feedback process of his own development and how adults and other peers perceive and treat him, so do the demands made upon him. It is in this area that frustrations are practically impossible to avoid – they are structured into the process.*

There is another aspect to human species-specific behavioral organization, particularly at the social structural level, which must enter into any framework of human aggression. The cohesion of human societies depends on mutual cooperation in economic tasks, and these require different degrees of role affiliations. A man often has three roles – those of father, husband, and worker. If the social structure has additional complexities, the roles proliferate, and the complexities and contingencies of each role enlarge. Roles depend on tasks, and roles place commitments and burdens upon people. The human animal, because of his social adaptation, is perhaps unique in the fact of plural role responsibilities, each attended by symbolized, arbitrary codes for conduct. These provide a natural structure not only for beneficial adaptation to varying difficult environments, but also for the production of frustrations (see for example: Cartwright, 1950; Coser, 1963; Mead, 1963; Murphy, 1957).[5] As animals, humans are highly egoistic, emotional, and dependent. Their closest relative, the chimpanzee, evokes the greatest amount of empathy among its human observers. Moods, personal attachments to objects and other peers, infants, dominant males, et cetera, seem to be a common theme in the primate literature, and these effects seem particularly heightened and expanded to symbolic stimuli when one deals with man. In other words, there is a matter here of what might be called (to reflect our lack of understanding and ignorance) a "sentiment structure"[6] which figures in the species-specific patterns of human behavior, both socially and individually. The task is to define this structure, understand its components and their interactions, and place this structure in an evolutionary, adaptive framework. This is why our framework of human aggression must be enlarged; why we must reject any simplistic incantation of direct instincts. It is largely through his "sentiment structures" that man is capable of the frantic antics of cathection upon diverse symbol clusters, is able to fan up and maintain hostilities in thought and deed toward symbol clusters and their human associations, and can be manipulated by those who understand too well what men need, and what frustrations are most capable of diminishing the individual evaluation of himself. These considerations lead to the following formulation that the capacity for human aggression is an outcome, in part, of natural selection for heightened sentiment structures focused about self-identity and cooperative social structure. Natural selection for complex and

[5] I am not concerned here with the possible eufunctions of conflict and aggression as derived from Simmel by Coser (1956) and elaborated by other social scientists. For a recent survey into this problem, see Zawodny (1966), Vol. I and II.

[6] Lorenz (1966) uses the concept of "militant enthusiasm" to imply a sort of collective or individual increase of tonicity to the body which can be brought about by certain symbol clusters and which figures so heavily in fanaticism and aggression. I believe this concept is one of the most important topics raised in Lorenz's book and hope that he will pursue this topic further in later publications. My use of "sentiment structure" would include this proclivity or phenomenon.

prolonged cooperation has endowed man with greater degrees of affect interplay than in other animals. These are necessary for other-commitment which develops through self-commitment. But the social and symbolic structures which permit him to perform shared tasks to insure his existence also insure frustration, pain, and group conflict. In short, groups mean conflict. Groups mean figure and ground, where each sees the other sometimes as a figure, sometimes ground. Perceptions are selective and structured, and then become foci for resistance. Conflict, or forays of imposition, are structured into existence by the very fact of group identifications. Aggression may be defined as the imposition of the self (either individual or group identity) or any definition of the self, on another (individual, group, object, abstraction). Imposition may be defined as any statement (speech, motor act, gesture, action) which acts to maintain figure from ground against resistance.

The human brain might be viewed as an organization of tissue and its programming which evolved to cement environmental stimuli into figure-ground anchorages, where symbol systems are the basis for organizing experience into anchorages that facilitate social control through communication. Symbol systems permit arbitrary figure-ground representations to be defined. The adaptiveness of this rests in the fact that power relations can be established which provide social solidarity and implementation of cooperative tasks, *and these can be defined independent of biological variables.*

Human evolution and aggression

It is impossible, however, to do more than speculate about human origins and make educated guesses about the mechanics and dynamics of early human adaptations. This section is thus admittedly speculative, but it is hoped that the speculations might lead to some critical thinking and dialogue about the nature of man and how he came to be.

It is convenient to start with what seem to be reasonable conclusions of some important variables that were involved in the early evolution of man. No attempt is made here to produce a complete list (see Count, 1958; Hockett and Ascher, 1964; Spuhler, 1959).

1. The evolution of the brain, mainly involving an enlargement of the cerebral cortex. The brain enlarged from roughly 500 cc 1.75 million years ago to about 1450 cc at present. (For details, see Holloway, 1966; 1967a; 1968; concerning the significance of this parameter.) It is important to note, however, that this evolution involved more than simple expansion; it also reorganized the different neural tracts and nuclei that make up the brain. While there are no new structures in the human as compared to ape or monkey brains, quantitative shifts between different neural components (i.e., reorganization) resulted in both qualitative and quantitative differences in behavioral processes. This reorganization involved more than the cortex; it also involved the sensorimotor nuclei in the brain stem, the reticular formation,

limbic and septal nuclei. It is probable that the cerebellum, which helps to integrate fine motor movements and proprioception, was enlarged, if not reorganized.

Appreciation of this cannot, of course, be based on appraisal of the cranial capacity alone, but must be based on logical considerations of comparative neuroanatomy and the obvious musculoskeletal changes known from early hominid fossils. Of particular interest is the fact that the major expansion of *cranial capacity* occurred after the Australopithecines, i.e., after stone tools were already being produced according to standardized patterns. This, however, does not mean that brain evolution had not occurred before this; only that cranial capacity was the major change after the appearance of these hominids.

2. The morphological remains of the fossils, particularly the teeth, suggest that sexual dimorphism had decreased significantly in comparison to other terrestrial primates. This decrease must have involved more than simply the structures used aggressively, such as the canines. Other aspects of sexual dimorphism, such as body build and shape and fat deposition, may have increased. Such a change would have involved endocrine-target tissue interactions, probably involving androgens, and it is suggested here speculatively, that behavior was also affected (e.g., raising thresholds to intragroup aggression; see Holloway, 1967b).

3. Associated with the above, full-time sexual receptivity of the female and domestication of the male would have been important behavior adaptations, related both to economic activities, e.g., hunting, and social structure (see Etkin, 1954, 1963, for elaboration). This would have meant division of roles, the male securing added amounts of high protein resources through hunting.

4. To effect an increase in brain growth there was an increase in the dependency period for infants and children. This must again have meant some alteration in endocrine-target tissue interactions suggested in (2) and implied in (3), either involving growth hormone and target tissues, or a synergistic relation between growth hormone interactions and those androgens related to growth of musculoskeletal parts of the body. Such a change or group of changes would have meant concomitant adaptations in terms of nuclear family structure, and very possibly affect-interplay ("sentiment structure") between offspring and parents, and between peers.

5. A cognitive reorganization related to brain growth and organization, resulting in tool-making, and a shift in the nature of social relations involving the use of arbitrary symbols for communication. This last supposition is based on the assumption that stone tools made to a standardized pattern presupposes a cognitive basis in symbol-using, i.e., it is cultural behavior in the peculiarly human sense. Obviously, both tool-making and symbol communication would have been highly adaptive and under intense positive selection. Tool-making alone suggests some basic shift in the nature of social relations to a more cooperative and sustained type.

Thus four main aspects were involved: reorganization of the brain, endocrine relationships (in the broadest sense), and social and individual cognitive behavior. The brain, and its added growth, was the key element in these changes, and its evolution brought on the veritable "revolution" suggested by Hockett and Ascher (1964).

With this basic but incomplete list, it is possible to move to a more detailed consideration of aggressive behavior. The evolution of human social structures was essentially a strategy to engender cooperation for survival. Both intellectual and emotional attributes were involved in human brain evolution and in an integrated fashion. The following discussion makes only an analytic separation for heuristic purposes.

The kind of brain changes leading to increased efficiency of intelligent behavior, e.g., complex stimuli appreciation and task performance are easiest to appreciate. Increases in neuron number, expansion of cortical areas, dendritic branching and possibly neural/glial ratios, can be related to increased adaptive behavior from comparative and experimental neurological evidence (see Holloway, 1967a, for further details and an expanded framework along these lines). Such increases would have facilitated memory storage, recall, communication, and *both* inhibition and facilitation of certain responses of an affective nature.

The fossil record surely attests to an ever-increasing degree of material complexity (e.g., stone tools, shelters, types of animals hunted), and this in turn suggests an attending increase in social complexity. Symbol systems are usually seen as processes to aid in cognitive optimization, allowing for increased communicative facility. It is suggested here, and this is surely not original, that one of the prime functions of the development of symbolization was *social control.* Fearing (1950:455) has suggested that "communication, as a human activity involving the production and utilization of significant symbols, is *always* a part of the process through which the field is cognitively structured and operates to increase or decrease group tensions." (See also Holloway, 1967a, for nonverbal communication as a set of redundancy operations to avoid ambiguities; see also Ekman, 1965.)

Thus, symbolic communication is a device for reducing and/or increasing distortions, ambiguity, and emotions as well as a process that increases memory (amount, storage, permanence), and facilitates recall (see Brown and Lenneberg, 1954, for experimental evidence on how language facilitates cognitive operations). Selection for neural reorganization leading to increased behavioral efficiency would also be selection for *facilitation* of attention and inhibition of second-to-second monitoring of other actors' personal qualities – a condition particularly developed in some of the most aggressive of the terrestrial primates, the baboons and macaques (see Southwick, 1967; Altmann, 1962, 1967, for examples of such constant monitoring of gestures and the penalties paid for inattention by other troop members).

Experimental evidence is very clear that there are optimal levels of arousal of the organism associated with the appreciation of cue complexity and task performance (see Hebb, 1966, for examples). This relationship is known as the "inverted U function" because there exists an optimal state of arousal, mediated through the reticular formation and possibly the limbic lobe, which facilitates intellectual functioning. Too much or too little arousal results in a drop-off in perceiving cue complexity and task performance.

Surely, in the evolution of the human animal, natural selection did not militate against the ability to appreciate cue complexity (the many and ever-increasing attributes of the physical and social environments), or task performance. The increasing complexity and sophistication of stone tools during the Palaeolithic (concomitant with brain size increase) attest to this. This all suggests another possible relationship:

Natural selection favored the development of a large cortex to handle environmental complexity (see Holloway, 1968, for extensive discussion) and task efficiency, at the same time selecting for optimal arousal patterns. Such selection for optimal arousal patterns very likely also meant selection which resulted in temperamental differences, thus adding another sector to the complexity of the environment in social terms. If the adaptation of early man was heavily in the social realm as suggested here, increasing inhibitive controls would have been highly beneficial. In other words, not only was intellect enhanced, but also the ability to get along in groups through positive affects, in part based on more optimal arousal mechanisms which would also have been advantageous for intellective function, e.g., concentration at some task.

Admittedly, the above framework is speculative, but it does allow for a considerable degree of synthesis between neural and behavioral changes and processes at the individual and social-psychological levels. The species-specific attributes discussed earlier involved neural, endocrine (and certainly neuroendocrine), and social structural changes. These processes, taken in concert, produced the human condition.

Let us now ask the question we have been leading up to: would an increase in positive effects or "sentiment structures" help in any way to achieve these improvements through evolution? The argument offered in the early part of this section, and that in the last part of the "need for an expanded framework" suggested that the social nature of man and his social adaptations *were* facilitated by an increase in the emotional sector, associated with what has been loosely termed as "sentiment structure," where these facilitated both the task of cooperative enterprises and care of the long dependency time of the child with its increasing brain growth.

But what of aggression, particularly human aggression? The hypothesis I offer here is as follows:

Human evolution has been the evolution of a paradox. The evolution of the brain and social structure, and symbol systems has also meant an increase in frustration and aggression. The meaning of symbols in the adaptive evolutionary sense is at least two-fold: they aid in cognitive optimization, and also, they mediate the social controls necessary to stem what arises out of the human condition, frustration and aggression. The same symbolism that enhances sentimental bonds between kinsmen, and symbolically defined groups outside of biological relationships (clan, tribe, state, nation, ideology), brings in its wake their antithesis: extra-group aggressional tendencies. Role differentiation and intra-group commitments generate frustration and power allocation. Man is up against himself – he is up against social structure – he is up against culture.[7] *These are his costs as well as his gains. The structures, social*

[7]Freud said much the same thing in *Civilization and Its Discontents.*

and symbolic, which permit his adaptations and the execution of shared tasks to insure his existence, also insure frustration, pain, and conflict.

And what about warfare? Warfare at the level of mass societies cannot be explained by this framework or recourse to individual psychology. (See Abel, 1941, for example.) This framework does provide a basis, however, for understanding how states can utilize the aggressive components of man's nature for their own ends, and how hostilities at all levels can be perpetuated through time. This framework does not explain revolutions either, but does provide a basis for understanding the absolute necessity of providing all with a chance to realize their full human potential, which includes the very important sector of self-evaluation and opportunity for self-participation in any culture.

Animal studies in both the field and laboratory are of great interest and are to be encouraged for their heuristic value. They suggest mechanisms and give us some idea of the range of stimuli that interact with species-specific organizations of genetic and social programming to elicit behavioral patterns. They (animal studies) are not, however, some kind of panacea for human ills. Claims that we need to study lower animals to find out about human aggression seem to me as dangerous as simply attributing human ills to a few instincts or needs for increased displacement activities. It is power, organizations, socio-economic conditions, and symbol systems that need study.

References

Abel, T. 1941. The elements of decision in the pattern of war. *Amer. Soc. Review* 6:853-859.

Altmann, S. A. 1962. A field study of the sociobiology of rhesus monkeys, *Macaca mulatta. Ann. N.Y. Acad. Sci.* 102:338-435.

_____. (ed.). 1967. *Social Communication Among Primates.* Chicago: Univ. of Chicago Press.

Andrews, R. J. 1963. The origin and evolution of the calls and facial expressions of the primates. *Behaviour* 20:1-109.

Ardrey, Robert. 1966. *The Territorial Imperative.* New York: Atheneum.

Bender, L., and Schilder, P. 1936. Studies in aggressiveness IV. *Genetic Psychology* Monograph No. 18:254-261.

Berkowitz, L. 1962. *Aggression: A Social Psychological Analysis.* New York: McGraw-Hill Book Company, Inc.

_____. 1965. The concept of aggressive drive: some additional considerations. *Advances in Experimental Social Psychology,* ed. L. Berkowitz. Vol. 2. New York: Academic Press, Inc., pp. 301-329.

Bernard, J., Pear, T. H., Aron, R., and Angell, R. C. 1957. *The Nature of Conflict.* Belgium: UNESCO.

Brown, Roger, and Lenneberg, E. H. 1954. A study in language and cognition. *J. Abnor. Soc. Psych.* 49:454-462.

Burton, J. 1964. The nature of aggression as revealed in the atomic age. *The Natural History of Aggression,* ed. Carthy and Ebling. London: Academic Press, pp. 145-149.

Buss, A. H. 1961. *The Psychology of Aggression.* New York: John Wiley and Sons, Inc.

Carthy, J. D., and Ebling, F. J. (eds.). 1964. *The Natural History of Aggression.* London: Academic Press.

Cartwright, D. 1950. Emotional dimensions of group life. *Feelings and Emotions:* the Mooseheart Symposium, ed. M. L. Reymert. New York: McGraw-Hill Book Company, Inc., pp. 439-447.

Collias, N. E. 1944. Aggressive behavior among vertebrate animals. *Physiol. Zoo.* 17:83-123.

Coser, Lewis A. 1963. Violence and the social structure. *Violence and War,* ed. J. Masserman, Vol. 7 of *Science and Psychoanalysis.* New York: Grune and Stratton.

Count, E. W. 1958. The biological basis of human society. *Amer. Anthrop.* 60:1049-1085.

DeVore, Irven (ed.). 1965. *Primate Behavior.* New York: Holt, Rinehart and Winston.

Dollard, J., Doob, L., Miller, N., Mowrer, O., and Sears, R. 1939. *Frustration and Aggression.* New Haven: Yale Univ. Press.

Durbin, E. F. M., and Bowlby, J. 1939. *Personal Aggressiveness and War.* New York: Columbia Univ. Press.

Eibl-Eibesfeldt, I. 1967. Concepts of ethology and their significance in the study of human behavior. *Early Behavior,* ed. H. W. Stevenson *et al.* New York: Wiley, pp. 127-146.

Eisenberg, J. F. 1966. The social organization of mammals. *Handbuch Zoo.* 10:1-92.

Ekman, P. 1965. Communication through nonverbal behavior: a source of information about an interpersonal relationship. *Affect, Cognition, and Personality,* ed. T. S. Tomkins and C. Izard. New York: Springer Publ. Co., pp. 390-443.

Etkin, W. 1954. Social behavior and the evolution of man's mental faculties. *Amer. Nat.* 88: 129-142.

____. 1963. Social behavioral factors in the emergence of man. *Human Biology* 35:299-311.

Fearing, F. 1950. Group behavior and the concept of emotion. *Feelings and Emotions,* ed. L. M. Reymert, the Moosehart Symposium. New York: McGraw-Hill Book Company, Inc., pp. 448-451.

Goodenough, F. L. 1931. Anger in young children. *Inst. Child Welfare Mono.* Ser., No. 9. Minneapolis: Univ. of Minnesota Press.

Hafez, E. S. E. (ed.). 1962. *The Behaviour of Domestic Animals.* Baltimore: Williams and Wilkins.

Hall, K. R. 1964. Aggression in monkey and ape societies. *The Natural History of Aggression,* ed. Carthy and Ebling. London: Academic Press, pp. 51-64.

Hebb, D. O. 1966. *A Textbook of Psychology, Second edition.* Philadelphia: W. B. Saunders Co.

Hockett, C. F., and Ascher, R. 1964. The human revolution. *Cur. Anthrop.* 5:135-168.

Holloway, R. L., Jr. 1966. Cranial capacity, neural reorganization, and hominid evolution: a search for more suitable parameters. *Amer. Anthrop.* 68:103-121.

____. 1967a. The evolution of the human brain: some notes toward a general theory. *General Systems* 12:3-19.

____. 1967b. Review of Ardrey: *Territorial Imperative. Pol. Sci. Quart.* 82:630-632.

____. 1968. The evolution of the primate brain: some aspects of quantitative relations. *Brain Research* 7:121-172.

Huxley, Sir Julian (organizer). 1967. A discussion on ritualization of behaviour in animals and man. *Phil. Trans. Roy. Soc. London* 251:247-526.

Leach, E. R. 1966. Don't say "boo" to a goose. *N.Y. Rev. Books.* Dec. 15.

____. 1967. Ritualization in man in relation to conceptual and social development. A discussion of ritualization of behaviour in animals and man, org. J. Huxley. *Phil. Trans. Roy. Soc. London* 251:403-408.

Lehrman, D. S. 1953. A critique of Konrad Lorenz's theory of instinctive behavior. *Quart. Rev. Biol.* 28:337-363.

Lenneberg, E. H. 1967. *Biological Foundations of Language.* New York: John Wiley and Sons, Inc.

Lorenz, Konrad. 1964. Ritualized fighting. *The Natural History of Aggression,* ed. Carthy and Ebling. London: Academic Press, pp. 39-50.

____. 1966. *On Aggression.* New York: Harcourt, Brace and World.

____. 1967. Ritualization in the psycho-social evolution of human culture. A discussion of ritualization of behaviour in animals and man, org. J. Huxley. *Phil. Trans. Roy. Soc. London* 251:278-284.

Mason, W. A. 1967. Motivational aspects of social responsiveness in young chimpanzees. *Early*

Behavior: Comparative and Developmental Approaches, ed. H.W. Stevenson *et al.* New York: John Wiley and Sons, Inc.

Masserman, Jules H. (ed.). 1963. *Violence and War: with Clinical Studies,* Vol. VI of *Science and Psychoanalysis.* New York: Grune and Stratton.

McNeil, E. R. (ed.). 1965. *The Nature of Human Conflict.* Englewood Cliffs, New Jersey: Prentice-Hall.

Mead, Margaret. 1963a. *Sex and Temperament in Three Primitive Societies.* New York: Morrow. (Originally published 1935.)

____. 1963b. Violence in the perspective of culture history. *Violence and War,* ed. J. H. Masserman. New York: Grune and Stratton, pp. 92-106.

Murphy, Robert F. 1957. Intergroup hostility and social cohesion. *Amer. Anthrop.* 59:1018-1035.

Piaget, J. 1926. *The Language and Thought of the Child.* New York: Harcourt, Brace.

____. 1929. *The Child's Conception of the World.* New York: Harcourt, Brace.

____. 1954. *The Construction of Reality in the Child.* New York: Basic Books.

Schilder, P. 1942. *Goals and Desires of Man.* New York: Columbia Univ. Press.

Schneirla, T. C. 1965. Aspects of stimulation and organization in approach/withdrawal processes underlying vertebrate behavioral development. *Advances in the Study of Behavior,* ed. D. S. Lehrman, Vol. I. New York: Academic Press, pp. 1-74.

Schrier, A. M., Harlow, H. F., and Stollnitz, F. (eds.). 1965. *Behavior of Nonhuman Primates,* Vols. I and II. New York: Academic Press.

Scott, J. P. 1958. *Aggression.* Chicago: Univ. of Chicago Press.

Scott, J. P., and Fuller, J. L. 1965. *Genetics and the Social Behavior of the Dog.* Chicago: Univ. of Chicago Press.

Southwick, C. H. 1967. An experimental study of intragroup agonistic behavior in rhesus monkeys. *Behaviour* 28:182-209.

Spuhler, J. N. 1959. Somatic paths to culture. *The Evolution of Man's Capacity for Culture,* ed. J. N. Spuhler. Detroit: Wayne State Univ. Press, pp. 1-13.

Struhsaker, T. T. 1967. Auditory communications among vervet monkeys. *Social Communication Among Primates,* ed. Altmann. Chicago: Univ. of Chicago Press, pp. 281-324.

Thorpe, W. H. 1963. *Learning and Instinct in Animals, Second Edition.* London: Methuen and Co., Ltd.

Zawodny, J. K. (ed.). 1966. *Man and International Relations* (two volumes). San Francisco: Chandler Publishing Company.

13

Open groups in hominid evolution

Vernon Reynolds

In this paper an attempt is made to show that a biological and evolutionary approach to the study of human society can be of value. Humans have species-characteristic behaviour patterns underlying their patterns of social organisation and cultural norms, and these basic patterns have evolved out of the action of environmental selection pressures on the behavioural range of man's ancestral stock. Cultural variability and a range of kinds of social organisation rank among man's outstanding behavioural specialisations and can be seen as the ways in which each society has branched off a basic hominid stem, each society having expanded, modified, or adapted aspects of this stem into particular behavioural norms or institutions. In looking at human societies, therefore, we can see a substratum of universal behavioural tendencies manifesting themselves in different forms according to the tradition and ecology of each particular culture.

It is argued here that the typical hunter-gatherer society evolved naturally out of an ape-like system of nomadism, open groups, wide recognition of relationships, sexual differences in temperament and exploratoriness, lack of territoriality, and the inheritance of behaviour patterns such as tool and weapon use, drumming and dancing, and bed-making, which pre-adapted proto-hominids to evolve in certain directions. In addition, it is argued that many of the features typical of present-day societies, such as territorialism, inter-group aggression, rigid structures of authority, strict sexual mores, as well as advancement in creativity and technology, stem from the stage when permanent settlement began and many social instincts had to be controlled and re-directed for the greater selective advantage of the population as a whole.

SOURCE: *Man,* Volume 1 (1966). Reprinted by permission of the Royal Anthropological Institute of Great Britain and Ireland.

New finds by palaeontologists concerning the fossil histories of apes and man, together with recent detailed primate field studies, make it possible to take a new look at the probable social and behavioural evolution of man. The biological and evolutionary approach to the study of human society takes the viewpoint that both the individual and the social behaviour characteristic of man as a species have evolved as a result of environmental pressures acting selectively on behaviour patterns and range of behavioural variability which are ultimately under genetic control. This does *not* mean that specific items of human cultures, such as marriage ceremonies or tatoo patterns, are inherited direct through the genes: any suggestion on those lines would clearly be unacceptable. It does, however, mean that there is a substratum of inherited behavioural tendencies in man the world over, and that all cultures and systems of social organisation are built on the basis of this substratum. This paper sets out to establish a firm basis for the existence and nature of this substratum, using comparative data drawn from the living Pongidae, and justifies this by reference to man's increasingly well understood fossil history.

The fossil background

The nature of the environmental pressures that must have impinged on the earliest proto-hominids when they began to leave their forest habitat to exploit the savannahs can be readily understood; but we have no direct evidence as to the behavioural inheritance they took with them and which pre-determined them to respond and adapt to those pressures in particular ways. It is possible, however, using data from indirect sources, to build up a probable picture of the kind of creature the forest-dwelling precursor of the first proto-hominids might have been.

In the first place it is necessary to know man's evolutionary position relative to the other primates. Some suggestions based on recent fossil finds by Simons (Simons, 1965; Pilbeam and Simons, 1965) seem to explain hitherto conflicting and unconnected facts. At the mid-Oligocene site in the Fayum, Egypt, has been found a range of small primates. This appears to include the probable very early ancestors of Old World monkeys, gibbons, and the large apes. *Aegyptopithecus,* although it is only the size of a small monkey, is on the line towards the Miocene *Proconsul,* and already has ape-like rather than monkey-like skull characteristics. *Aelopithecus* may be a very early gibbon ancestor. *Oligopithecus* is fragmentary and of uncertain status but could be related to later Old World monkeys. *Propliopithecus,* hitherto assumed to be on the line towards the gibbons, is thought by Simons and Pilbeam to be too generalised for this, and to be probably related to the larger apes or even the hominid line. The existence of these primate species so long ago, very small and unspecialised, but already differentiated according to ape or monkey taxonomic characteristics, suggests that the ape line and the Old World monkey line may have evolved separately from a progressive prosimian stock in the Eocene epoch, in the same way as did the New World monkeys. The relatively short faces of many of these Oligocene primates, which tend to correlate with trunk erectness, indicates that the prosimian ancestor may have been tree-climbing and erect-postured in the manner of present-day tarsiers.

There is no agreement among taxonomists as to when the hominid precursors diverged from the pongid stock. Some, for example Mayr (1963), basing their opinions on recent comparative examinations of the haemoglobin (Zuckerkandl, 1963), the blood proteins (Goodman, 1963), and the chromosome structure (Klinger *et al.*, 1963) of the apes and man, conclude that the orang line left in the Oligocene soon after the gibbon stock diverged, and that man and the two African apes have a common, more recent ancestry. Workers on structural morphology, skull topography, and details of the hands and feet, such as Schultz (1963) and Biegert (1963), are certain that the hominid line separated from the pongid stock soon after the gibbons, in the late Oligocene or early Miocene, certainly before the three large apes became differentiated. This latter view is the one held here. With regard to the differentiation of the three large apes, it is usually assumed that chimpanzees and gorillas are more closely related than either to the orang. Simons and Pilbeam (1965), however, have recently re-examined all the available dryopithecine fossils and have come forward with some unorthodox conclusions. They are of the opinion that *Dryopithecus (Proconsul) major* is in fact an ancestral gorilla, already distinct as long as twenty-three million years ago; and that *Dryopithecus (Proconsul) nyanzae* was probably ancestral to the chimpanzee. Their latest assessment (Pilbeam pers. comm., 1966) is that in the early Miocene the east African proconsuls spread out across the tropical forest belt of Europe into Asia and that one, *Proconsul nyanzae,* probably gave rise to *Dryopithecus (Sivapithecus) indicus,* which they now regard as a possible fossil ancestral orang, hitherto unrecognised. (It is interesting to note here that Biegert explains the peculiarities of the shape of the skull and dental arch of present-day orangs as being due to an extreme specialised development of the laryngeal sacs, which may be comparatively recent, and not due to an earlier evolutionary divergence.) Thus, the view propounded above is that the ancestral stocks of gorillas and chimpanzees were already distinct in the early Miocene, and that chimpanzees and orang utans have a more recent common ancestry – probably late Miocene – than either has with the gorilla. Behavioural data on the three large apes supports this view. For in terms of social behaviour in the wild, intelligence, learning ability, responsiveness in laboratory experiments, temperament, and pattern of juvenile development, orangs and chimpanzees are very similar, whereas gorillas often show marked differences (Reynolds, 1967; Yerkes and Yerkes, 1929).

It would thus seem probable that the divergence of the hominid line had occurred by the Oligocene-Miocene boundary at least. The earliest fossils thought to be on the hominid line belong to the genus *Ramapithecus,* dating from fourteen million years ago in east Africa. The *Ramapithecus* line could have evolved from a proto-ape ancestor towards the end of the Oligocene, prior to the speciation of the proconsul apes.

One criticism of the Pilbeam and Simons hypothesis is that it puts the divergence of the large ape stocks so far back as to antedate the development of those numerous structural specialisations, such as long, brachiating arms, that today seem to be homologous in gorillas, chimpanzees, and orangs. The only dryopithecine for which adequate post-cranial matter exists, *D. (Proconsul) africanus,* had arms and legs of equal length, and the build of a monkey. Its arms, however, showed evidence of being relatively free-swinging, and may have been used for hanging, reaching, and leaping in the manner of some New World monkeys. It has been termed a "semi-brachiator" (Napier, 1963). In the evolution of the apes and man it is possible that *behavioural adaptation* preceded the development of structural specialisations in many instances. Thus, according to Simons (pers. comm. 1966), "The common ancestor of the larger apes and man could have been pre-adapted by behaviour, not morphology, to bipedal branch-walking and to arm-swinging in the trees. From this there are two obvious locomotor pathways, one towards increased arm-swinging as in *Pongo,* and to a lesser extent in *Pan* and *Gorilla,* and the other towards human bipedalism. . . . The numerous similarities . . . may simply be a result of the fact that different stocks, derived from some generalised ancestral hominoid, have had the same basic morpho-system evolved along similar lines because they have the same primary adaptive pattern."

Behaviour of modern apes

If it is assumed that man and the large apes had a common ancestor towards the end of the Oligocene, and that the hominid line branched off only shortly before the chimpanzee-orang and gorilla stocks diverged, then data on the behaviour of the large apes is relevant to a consideration of man's likely behavioural inheritance. All the large apes have remained within the tropical forest habitat and although all have developed specialisations, they have not undergone the great changes and adaptations of the hominid line which emerged on the savannahs. Thus the essential features of the social behaviour patterns of the large apes, which distinguish them from other primates, were probably present in the common ancestor of apes and man, and must have been crucial in determining the modes of adaptation of the emergent hominid line when it left the forest. The following characteristics are common to the societies of gorillas, chimpanzees, and orangs, and are not often found in those of Old World monkeys.

1. Nomadic. There is nothing approaching territory ownership in the large apes. None of them has a fixed range beyond which a group rarely wanders and which may be routinely travelled, as in baboons for example. In the case of chimpanzees (V. and F. Reynolds, 1965) and orang utans (Davenport, 1966), movements of individuals and groups appear to be determined by the availability and distribution of food. Large aggregations gather in areas of abundant fruit while in leaner periods solitary individuals or small groups spread out and travel long distances in their foraging. In the case of gorillas (Schaller, 1965), which have specialised in shoot and pith eating, food is available all over their terrain throughout the year. But they are also nomadic and travel long distances with little routine in their movements. Although they do return from time to time to the same areas they do not have ranges in the sense that baboons or monkey groups do. No gorilla group has the use of any "core area" exclusively; all are free to come and go as they please.

2. **Open groups and sense of community.** In Old World monkeys an individual belongs to a particular group or is an outsider; in the latter case it would not normally be accepted into a group without fighting. Breeding and all social interactions occur within the group, the members of which are normally always within sight or sound of one another. Although aggregations of groups, such as Hamadryas baboon harems or common baboon troops, occur from time to time in some monkey species, when they disperse again membership of the breeding group or troop remains unchanged (Hall and DeVore, 1965). By contrast, all three large apes seem to recognise a far wider nexus of bonds and relationships which could be termed a "sense of community." Chimpanzees and orangs do not live in permanent groups at all. They form temporary associations in which the social bonds appear to be friendship based on like sex or age, sexual attraction, mother-offspring relationships, and possibly sibling relationships (V. and F. Reynolds, 1965). One of the most striking features of chimpanzee society is that though the temporary groups split up, the relationships are recognised by affectionate greeting and re-uniting when the individuals meet again. Thus, although the adult and adolescent offspring of a mother leave her to join in other activities with exploring male bands or in sexual groups, they rejoin her from time to time (Goodall, 1965 and film). Goodall has observed stranger individuals approach local groups and be accepted in local communities after greeting ceremonies and, in the case of adult males, excited displays. Amongst gorillas, which have become terrestrial, there is far greater stability in group membership. Typical groups contain one or more adult males and a number of females and their offspring. But even in gorillas a sense of community is apparent. For example, some adult males seem to prefer a wandering life, attached to no particular group. Such males are temporarily accepted in established groups without hostility. Sometimes two groups happen to be foraging in the same place and they may join up for a day or two; or they may simply stare at each other and go their separate ways. In either case it is clear that gorillas, like chimpanzees and orangs, recognise ties of relationship which extend beyond the immediate group. It is postulated here that this characteristic of open rather than closed group organisation has typified the main pongid-hominid line since the Eocene prosimian stage, and is responsible for the form taken by human society.

3. **Individual choice in sexual relationships.** In most Old World monkeys the hierarchy of dominance which structures the behaviour of group members controls and limits sexual relations between individuals. In the large apes there appears to be free personal choice. A chimpanzee female in oestrus may solicit and mate with a number of males in quick succession without rivalries ensuing. A gorilla group leader may watch uninterestedly while one of the females of his group mates with a male that has only recently joined them.

4. **Exploratory behaviour of adult males.** In some adult male individuals among chimpanzees and gorillas (and among orangs too, judging from what evidence is available) there seems to be an innate urge to roam and explore. Thus, as was men-

tioned above, some male gorillas prefer to travel alone most of the time; on the other hand some seem to prefer the role of "family man" and take on the responsibility of leading a group containing females and juveniles. One can deduce that if new habitats were to become available to gorillas, it would be the roaming males that found them first. A rather similar social pattern is found among chimpanzees. Adult males tend to form small, actively mobile bands of two to five individuals, which travel fast over long distances through the forest and are often to be observed many miles from other chimpanzees. These male bands are real explorers, for they are the first to discover trees newly in fruit, whereupon they call and drum loudly in excitement thus attracting other groups to the area. The exploratory males in this species seem to have evolved a specific function in the social organisation. For in both chimpanzees and gorillas, the females are much less adventurous. Gorilla females are almost never alone, and chimpanzee females, in particular the mothers, are most frequently found in small groups which tend to remain in the same feeding area for days at a time while the adult males are forever moving around. But, as among gorillas, some adult male chimpanzees prefer to remain with the females, and do not seem to move very far. Sometimes these "domestic" males are getting old, but this is not always the case. Among Old World monkey groups there is nothing comparable to the exploratory males found among the large apes. The existence of "bachelor bands" is sometimes reported, but these are usually groups of young males which have retreated from the main part of an organised group as a result of the aggressiveness of the dominant males, and their consequent lack of opportunity for sexual liaisons with the females.

5. Unique behaviour patterns. Certain remarkable habits are found only in the large apes and man and are evidence of great behavioural plasticity and inventiveness at a very early stage of pongid evolution. Such behaviour patterns include use of tools, use of weapons, drumming and dancing, and the making of beds. For example, gorillas in the wild tear up saplings and plants and hurl them about in an intimidation display; in captivity a gorilla has been reported to use a large and heavy object such as a rock or chair or bedstead as a weapon of attack either by direct hitting or by throwing (Hoyt, 1941). Chimpanzees in the wild shake and hurl branches and saplings, and in captivity have been observed to use large sticks as direct weapons against real and dummy leopards (Kortlandt and Kooij, 1963). Orangs deliberately throw broken branches down on human intruders in the forest (Schaller, 1961; Davenport, 1966), and an adolescent, home-raised orang spontaneously grabbed a stick and hit at a live snake (Harrisson, 1963). With regard to tool-using, both chimpanzees and orangs are known to prepare small sticks to poke into insect holes in order to obtain delicacies; chimpanzees have been observed to use rocks to break open palm nut shells, and have even been reported to fashion drinking cups or sponges from leaves; in zoos and laboratories they become adept at many manipulative skills. Orangs in zoos are notorious for their use of the lever system to prise escape holes (Benchley, 1942). Gorillas seem to have almost lost the tool-using propensity, probably as a result of their specialised feeding habits which do not require manipulative skills, but even gorillas have been taught to paint and draw. Drumming as a form of communication is practised by gorillas (on the chest) and chimpanzees (on the ground and on tree buttresses), and all three large apes occasionally engage in repetitive and rhythmic body movements similar to primitive dancing. Finally, although many birds, insects, and mammals build nests, there is no equivalent to the large apes' custom of weaving a nightly bed, except in one or two species of prosimian and, of course, in man, the bed-maker *par excellence*.

Implications for the evolution of hominid society

It is argued that the behaviour patterns listed above, especially the open group system, which are characteristic of present-day large apes and which distinguish their societies from those typical of other non-human primates, were probably present in the common ancestor of apes and man, and that these genetically programmed behaviour patterns determined the social evolution of proto-hominids when they adapted to savannah life. The following is an attempt to reconstruct one logical sequence of hominid social evolution based on the recent fossil chronology and the data on man's ape-like behavioural inheritance.

Out of the proto-ape stock which inhabited the African forests towards the end of the Oligocene a species began to differentiate which specialised in living in the fringes of the forest, where trees are mixed with scrub and grassland. Its members were very adaptable. They were used to bipedal walking and hanging in the trees and were equally at home on the forest floor which they exploited for plants and insects. Curious and exploratory adult males started to increase their amount of animal diet by catching small creatures in the savannah and scrub surrounding the forest, where visibility was better. Sometimes other groups were attracted out of the forest by the excited calling and drumming of the meat-eaters. They had little to fear from predators because they could run fast, quickly climb any nearby trees, and could stand erect to give good visibility over the grass, in addition to being able to intimidate most other animals by their loud calls and hurling of vegetation. Over millions of years this forest-edge species became more distinct in its specialisations and more organised in its social groupings. The male bands began to develop co-operation, and to become more skilled in the use of sticks and stones to kill small animals and to frighten away big cats from their prey. The females and juveniles remained in groups, foraging for fruits and plant foods in the forest and along its fringes. Sometimes such a community of pre-hominids would be widely scattered in and around the forest and out on the savannah. At other times it would be concentrated in areas containing abundant fruit. There were always some adult males, often the older ones, which preferred to remain with the mothers and juveniles in the forest fringes. The roving males normally returned to the trees at night where the community slept in tree nests. Sometimes, when a male band discovered a large source of meat, the fresh carcass of an elephant, for example, they shouted and drummed until other groups, attracted from the forest, joined them. These groups would consist mainly of the younger females and adolescents of both sexes. The noise of the group excitement engendered at these times kept off any potential predators, and some of the groups probably remained on the plains overnight, constructing crude shelters or ground nests of grass and brushwood. Juveniles remained with the mothers on the forest edges and formed playgroups of age mates. Out of these playgroups grew bands of adolescents which attached themselves to adult males and made forays onto the plains. But they always returned to their mothers and siblings from time to time. Communities at this stage may have numbered around fifty individuals frequenting particular stretches of forest and plain. Sometimes members would be scattered, sometimes congregated, at other times following nomadic and seasonal routes to known new sources of food. But a community would never be completely separate from neighbouring communities, for bands of males, sometimes with young females, were always travelling from one to another. There were no closed groups in hominid evolution. The transitory stage between proto-ape and proto-man, between forest and savannah living described above, must have occurred over the Miocene period, at the end of which *Ramapithecus* spread out from Africa through Europe and Asia.

Some time between *Ramapithecus* and *Australopithecus* when, during the pliocene period, the tropical forests were gradually retreating, the proto-hominids became chiefly savannah dwelling. What effects did the ecological pressures of savannah life have on the social behaviour already typical of the new species? Mothers and juveniles were now living on the plains, partially dependent on meat provided by males; with food and water sources more widely spaced, population density decreased. These two facts must have favoured the emergence of more constant groupings than had been the case in the forest and forest edge communities. The most natural grouping to develop was that of a number of friendly or related females and their offspring, accompanied by one or more ageing or domestic-minded males. Gorilla groups may have evolved in the same way when they became terrestrial. These female groups would be scattered around in favourable areas near waterholes, where temporary shelters could be made in clumps of trees or bushes, or among rocky outcrops and caves. Their members would spend most of the time foraging for vegetable foods in the vicinity. Together with neighbouring groups they formed a local community from which juvenile and adolescent age mate bands were drawn. In dry seasons communities were large gatherings around remaining waterholes. In wet seasons the groups were scattered widely, each finding forage in different areas. Adult males in the communities joined together into mobile roving bands for the purposes of scavenging kills from lions and leopards, finding out new areas of vegetation to exploit, discovering fresh waterholes, and making contact with other communities in other areas. These bands might be joined from time to time by young females, and might themselves join up with groups containing sexually attractive females. Males often dragged the carcasses of their finds to a nearby group, or sometimes the groups came out to where the meat was.

***Australopithecus* and *Homo erectus*.** For another few million years the pressures of the savannah habitat developed and structured existing behavioural tendencies. Any increase in the efficiency of inter-individual communication gave advantages to the hunting and scavenging bands, as did any new skill in weapon or cutting tool technology. At this stage it is probable that particular types of stones and sticks and bones were actively sought and retained and primitive fashioning of tools and weapons began. Intelligence was also at a premium as it had always been in primate evolution; for it was advantageous to be able to learn and predict the ways of the other carnivores, the habits of the ungulates, or to remember directions and places previously visited. Development of tools for digging, of receptacles for collecting and of methods of storing plant foods were of survival value; so also were increasingly efficient constructions against wind or rain. The wide ramifications of community ties and relationships and the frequent intercommunications of groups over long distances, encouraged the formation of large co-operative male bands for animal drives and ensured the rapid spread of any new technological development. Already two typically hominid social institutions were clearly in operation: the sexual division of labour, and the basis of the family and tribal systems. The argument here, from our knowledge of ape behaviour, is that the proto-typical hominid family was a matrifocal group of a mother and her offspring, often in association with other friendly or related mothers. The bonds maintaining their cohesion were based on the attraction of the females for each other and each other's young, and not on the common subservience to a dominant male as has often been assumed. While males would act as providers of meat for such a group, the attachment of an individual matrifocal family may have evolved somewhat later. When technology had progressed to the stage where individuals could hunt alone, the smallest economically viable unit at times of maximum dispersion became the nuclear family of a male, a female, and her young. Although males often attached themselves as protectors to these family groups, their role as exclusive sexual partners probably developed much later. The institutionalisation of human tribal systems came at the stage when inter-individual communication in the form of language had evolved to the point where names could be given to designate both the nexus of friends and sex, age, sibling and mother-offspring relationships which were already recognised, and already formed the basis of social interaction over vast areas. It is emphasised that it was the ape-like social organisation of open groups, the network of relationships and the lack of territorial behaviour that caused the evolution of human society with its basic characteristics of extensive kinship systems and inter-group interactions. At no stage did inbreeding, territorial, hominid hordes range the savannahs, being forced to take rational decisions on the subject of co-operation with other hordes – as to whether to marry out or to die out – in order to start human society, as is often assumed. The widespread uniformity of the first stone tool cultures testifies to the truth of this hypothesis. And it interesting that on quite other grounds than the behavioural ones used here, Vallois (1961:229) concluded that "All evidence suggests that the Paleolithic bands were not territorial units, that they were capable of large migrations, and that sexual relations must have existed between them."

Modern man and settled communities

Modern man is territorial and aggressive, hostile to and intolerant of strangers, and lives within an authoritarian social structure in which self-assertiveness and competition for dominance characterises the successful male. If it is true that the essential characteristics of human society evolved naturally out of the adaptation of an ape-like social system to the selection pressures of life on the savannahs, then some additional explanation is needed to account for the advent of inter-group aggression.

As already stated, the evidence indicates that early palaeolithic man was co-operative, not territorial, and had social and sexual relationships over wide areas. Societies still living in a nomadic hunter-gatherer ecology, such as the Bushmen of the Kalahari, or the Hadza of East Africa, show little territoriality or inter-group aggression. Recent studies or re-studies of existing band societies such as the Mbuti pygmies (Turnbull, 1966), the American Indians, and Australian aborigines (Lee and DeVore, 1968) describe continually changing social groupings, often based on simple friendship or common interest as well as on primary kinship ties. There is little organised leadership at any level; it is, in fact, very similar to an ape-like social organisation. On the other hand, the late palaeolithic hunters of Europe depict hostile bands of warriors and indications of hierarchical tribal authorities in their cave paintings. Probably during the later palaeolithic some populations became less nomadic and made semi-permanent settlements in caves and ravines, becoming dependent upon certain stretches of land containing big game for their survival. In Europe the seasonality of the climate with its long cold winters must have necessitated the sheltering of the community in caves with stored animal or vegetable foods. At about much the same time populations in other parts of the world were starting to develop agriculture, or to follow the migratory herds of ungulates, or to start to tame animals to remain with them.

The fact that the populations which took to permanent settlements became the most successful in the history of human evolution indicates the advantages of settled life, conferred in an increased population growth rate. But the necessity of living close together imposed great strains on the ape-like inheritance of behaviour and temperament adapted to nomadism and fluctuating groups. To draw once more from our knowledge of the behaviour of present-day apes, it is clear that groups of captive apes in zoos and laboratories show social patterns which differ from those found in the wild state (Russell, 1966). Social interaction is more frequent and more intense. A hierarchy of dominance is established. Sexual jealousies occur, group structure becomes fixed, individuals may be outcasts, and strangers may not be tolerated. On the other hand it is remarkable that only in captive conditions are the real skills, abilities, and intelligence of apes demonstrated. Great funds of inventiveness, learning power, and ability to acquire new habits are brought out which are never called for in the routine simplicity of their wild lives.

To some extent it is valid to compare the situation of captive apes with that of the successive human populations which took to living in permanent settlements; both are situations of social captivity. As a mode of adaptation such a situation was advantageous in terms of survival and reproduction rate; it fostered the development of unique abilities, too, but it extorted a high price in terms of the social adjustment of the individual with his inherited instincts for quite a different way of life. As a species we have not even yet had sufficient evolutionary time to become adapted to settled living. What were the consequences of settled communities? Chiefly the modifying, institutionalising, and rigidifying of existing social behaviour patterns. Thus, a system of permanent hierarchical political authority probably developed from the older men in the family groups now living permanently in the same settlement. In like manner young males of the community were organised into hunting, and later, warrior bands. Juvenile and adolescent age mates from the community formed sub-communities from which emerged hunting bands and female friendship groups. Hunting bands and adolescent groups would still have innate exploratory and social urges, so that neighbouring communities would have continual interaction, sometimes co-operating for particular projects like animal drives, cattle exchange, festivals, or against a common threat. Breeding would be both within and between communities. However, now that communities were attached to particular territories as an ecological necessity, the advent of other tribes, still nomadic, on their land would be viewed with hostility; or, when a community grew too large for its land, a sub-community might break off and search for new land on which to hunt or to cultivate or to graze its domestic animals. In these circumstances territoriality and inter-group aggression began. Thus, most of the social evils of man have probably stemmed from the point at which he became attached to land as an ecological necessity. On the other hand, as energy previously expended on nomadism and constant foraging was saved, so was more effort put into increasingly complex technological achievements.

Cultural variation

We have so far followed through some of the possible stages in the evolution of human society out of an ape-like, forest-adapted behavioural inheritance; showing how an open-group social organisation in particular may have pre-adapted and predetermined the direction of the development of hominid society under the selection pressures of firstly the savannah environment and secondly the start of permanent settlements.

The development of the argument has concentrated on the evolution of those behaviour characteristics which are typical of humans as a species and which are innate, i.e., genetically programmed. As Tiger and Fox (1966:77) recently stated, "the least variable part of human social behaviour systems has been neglected." In discussing one behaviour pattern – that of the tendency for males to form groups which exclude females – they write: "Cultural transmission and social adaptation are clearly responsible for the variety of forms which such aggregations assume; but while these forms are contingent on external pressures, the internal pressure towards their existence in some form is invariant." (1966:77) Thus it is argued here that other features found in one form or another throughout human societies – such as political authority (actual if not titular) in the hands of males, attraction of mothers into groups, greater exploration activities of adult males, juvenile and adolescent age mate groups, tribal and kinship systems with recognition of a nexus of roles and relationships, sexual division of labour, and incest regulations (Fox, 1962) – are all present in some form or another in all human cultures, and express part of man's genetic behavioural inheritance.

Cultural variations, however, are very real and are also the result of selection pressures. When any indigenous, self-contained culture is studied, it can be demonstrated that the way of life it represents is one possible efficient adaptation to survival within a particular geographical environment. But many factors have prevented even isolated cultures from evolving genetically fixed behaviour patterns specific to the culture. For one thing, measurable cultural variations have been in existence for only hundreds of thousands rather than millions of years. Secondly, for twenty-six or more million years the hominid line has specialised in intelligent, variable response to circumstances rather than a predictable, fixed action pattern. Only this factor has enabled man to colonise new habitats and initiate new behaviour. Thirdly, the typical factors of social organisation, nomadism, and exploratoriness (which *are* genetically programmed) have ensured that throughout the evolution of man no social group has ever been totally isolated for long without some inter-change of members, and have thus kept the gene-pool widely homogeneous. Finally, from the stage when permanent settlements and complex cultural variations began to emerge, another factor, social tradition, operated as efficiently as genetic fixing. With the setting up of permanent authority systems and the attainment of true language, skills necessary for the survival of a particular society have been passed on through learning to each new generation. The genetic variability of the group remains unchanged, but if the environmental circumstances alter, or if a more efficient way of doing things is invented, the behaviour of the whole society can change adaptively. This process achieves the same ends as genetic evolution, only much faster.

References

Benchley, B. J. 1942. *My friends the apes.* Boston: Little, Brown.

Biegert, J. 1963. The evaluation of characteristics of the skull, hands and feet for primate taxonomy. *Classification and human evolution,* ed. S. L. Washburn (Viking Fd Publ. Anthrop. 37). Chicago: Aldine.

Davenport, R. K. 1966. The orang-utan in Sabah. *Folia Primatol.* 4, 247-263.

Fox, J. R. 1962. Sibling incest. *Br. J. Sociol.* 13, 128-50.

Goodall, J. 1965. Chimpanzees of the Gombe Stream Reserve. *Primate behaviour: field studies of monkeys and apes,* ed. I. DeVore. New York: Holt, Rinehart & Winston.

____. film. *Jane and her wild chimpanzees.* New York: National Geographical Society.

Goodman, M. 1963. Man's place in the phylogeny of the primates as reflected in serum proteins. *Classification and human evolution,* ed. S. L. Washburn (Viking Fd Publ. Anthrop. 37). Chicago: Aldine.

Hall, K. L. R. and DeVore, I. 1965. Baboon social behaviour. *Primate behaviour: field studies of monkeys and apes,* ed. I. DeVore. New York: Holt, Rinehart & Winston.

Harrisson, B. 1963. Education to wild living of young orang utans at Bako National Park, Sarawak. *Sarawak Mus. J.* 11, 220-58.

Hoyt, A. M. 1941. *Toto and I.* New York: Lippincott.

Klinger, H. P. *et al.* 1963. The chromosomes of the hominoidea. *Classification and human evolution,* ed. S. L. Washburn (Viking Fd Publ. Anthrop. 37). Chicago: Aldine.

Kortlandt, A. and Kooij, M. 1963. Protohominid behaviour in primates. *Symp. zool. Soc., London* 10, 61-88.

Lee, R. B. and DeVore, I. 1968. *Man the Hunter.* Chicago: Aldine.

Mayr, E. 1963. The taxonomic evaluation of fossil hominids. *Classification and human evolution,* ed. S. L. Washburn (Viking Fd Publ. Anthrop. 37). Chicago: Aldine.

Napier, J. 1963. The locomotor functions of hominids. *Classification and human evolution,* ed. S. L. Washburn (Viking Fd Publ. Anthrop. 37). Chicago: Aldine.

Pilbeam, D. R. and Simons, E. L. 1965. Some problems of hominid classification. *Am. Scient.* 53, 237-59.

Reynolds, V. 1967. *The apes: their scientific and natural history.* New York: Dutton.

Reynolds, V. and Reynolds, F. 1965. Chimpanzees of the Budongo Forest. *Primate behaviour,* ed. I. DeVore. New York: Holt, Rinehart & Winston.

Russell, W. M. S. 1966. Aggression: new light from animals. *New Soc.* 7, 12-14.

Schaller, G. B. 1961. The orang utan in Sarawak. *Zoologica, N.Y.* 46, 73-82.

____. 1965. The behaviour of the mountain gorilla. *Primate behaviour,* ed. I. DeVore. New York: Holt, Rinehart & Winston.

Schultz, A. 1963. Age changes, sex differences and variability as factors in the classification of primates. *Classification and human evolution,* ed. S. L. Washburn (Viking Fd Publ. Anthrop. 37). Chicago: Aldine.

Simons, E. L. 1965. New fossil apes from Egypt and the initial differentiation of the Hominoidea. *Nature* 205, 135-9.

Simons, E.L. and Pilbeam, D. R. 1965. Preliminary revision of the Dryopithecinae. *Folia Primatol.* 4, 81-152.

Tiger, L. and Fox, R. 1966. The zoological perspective in social science. *Man* N.S. 1, 75-81.

Turnbull, C. 1966. *The wayward servants.* London: Eyre & Spottiswood.

Vallois, H. V. 1961. The social life of early man: the evidence of skeletons. *Social life of early man,* ed. S. L. Washburn. (Viking Fd Publ. Anthrop. 31) Chicago: Aldine.

Yerkes, R. and A. 1929. *The great apes.* New Haven: Yale Univ. Press.

Zuckerkandl, E. 1963. Perspectives in molecular anthropology. *Classification and human evolution,* ed S. L. Washburn. (Viking Fd Publ. Anthrop. 37) Chicago: Aldine.

14

*Aggressive behaviour of rhesus monkeys in natural and captive groups**

Charles H. Southwick

Rhesus monkeys (*Macaca mulatta*) are interesting for the study of aggressive behaviour for at least 3 reasons: (1) They show a greater frequency of aggressive behaviour in both natural and captive conditions than most primates; (2) they have an extensive repertoire of aggressive behaviour, ranging from subtle threat displays to violent fighting; and (3) they live naturally in a wide range of habitats varying from forests to crowded urban environments.

Although precisely comparable data on the aggressive behaviour of different species of primates are not readily available, Hall (1964) noted, "It has generally been considered that the baboon and macaque genera contain species which are more overtly aggressive in both within-group and between-group interactions than any other monkey or ape species." Among the macaques, the rhesus certainly ranks as a very aggressive species.

SOURCE: *Aggressive Behaviour,* Proceedings of the International Symposium on the Biology of Aggressive Behaviour, S. Garattini and E. B. Sigg, eds., Amsterdam: Excerpta Medica, 1969. This work was supported by grants from the U.S. Public Health Service (RG-6262, RG-6262 S1, and GM-11326) to Ohio University and the Johns Hopkins University, and a fellowship from the U.S. Educational Foundation in India during the 1959-1960 study period. Reprinted by permission of Excerpta Medica.

*For field assistance, I am indebted to Drs. M. Rafiq Siddiqi, M. Farooq Siddiqi, Mirza A. Beg, and R. P. Mukherjee. For assistance and collaboration in establishing the experimental colony in Calcutta I am grateful to Dr. R. K. Lahiri and his staff in the Calcutta Zoo, and Mlle. Mireille Bertrand. Administrative support and guidance has been provided by Drs. K. F. Meyer, F. B. Bang, J. L. Bhaduri, M. B. Mirza, Carl Frey, Craig Wallace, and Mr. Bernard Wojcik. My wife, Heather Southwick, has been an essential field companion throughout these studies.

Vandenbergh (1966), studying rhesus on island colonies in Puerto Rico, observed, "Fighting between individual rhesus monkeys occurs frequently, perhaps more than in any primate species. . . ."

Several comparisons between rhesus and other species of macaques have been undertaken. Simonds (1965) found that aggression in Bonnet macaques (*Macaca radiata*) was of much lower intensity and frequency than in rhesus. Rosenblum *et al.* (1964) observed in the laboratory that Bonnet macaques have passive social relations with relatively little aggressive behaviour. In most of the studies on the Japanese macaque (*M. fuscata*), social interactions were characterized by more tolerance and avoidance than in rhesus groups, and changes in male dominance structures usually proceeded without serious fighting (Hall, 1964; Imanishi and Altmann, 1965; Miyadi, 1964). Lahiri (1965) observed that captive groups of lion-tailed macaques (*M. silenus*) showed less intense aggressive behaviour than rhesus. Lahiri and Southwick (1966) found that a captive group of Gibraltar macaques (*M. sylvana*) was considerably less aggressive than similar rhesus groups. Kling and Orbach (1963) believed that young stump-tailed macaques (*M. speciosa*) are much less aggressive than rhesus.

On the other hand Bertrand (1968) showed that juvenile and adult *M. speciosa* are highly aggressive, often more so than rhesus. Trollope (1968) has made similar observations. Bernstein (1968) found pig-tailed macaques (*Macaca nemestrina*) to show more contact aggression in captivity than rhesus. Similarly, Mason and Murofushi (1966) found that a captive group of 10 *M. irus* was considerably more aggressive than a similar group of rhesus.

Although several species of macaques have not yet been studied (e.g., *M. sinica,* the toque macaque; *M. assamensis,* the Assamese macaque; *M. cyclopis,* the Formosan macaque), it is apparent that macaques vary in overt aggressive behaviour, with the rhesus probably ranking in the upper half of the scale.

There have been several excellent studies on the forms of aggressive behaviour in rhesus monkeys, particularly by Altmann (1962), Hinde and Rowell (1962), Kaufman (1967), and Sade (1967). These authors have emphasized that most of the repertoire of agonistic behaviour in the rhesus, as in most primates, consists of gestures and displays which communicate status, threat, and aggressive or submissive intent. These signals, which involve facial expressions, pilomotor responses, vocalizations, and entire body postures, usually function to avoid direct fighting. Still the rhesus is not as specialized in these displays as are some macaques. *M. speciosa*, for example, has more elaborate display and presenting behaviour than does the rhesus. Frequent perineal presents of *M. speciosa* regulate many social interactions without overt aggression.

In the comparison of aggressive tendencies between species, it is difficult and often impossible to distinguish species of differences per se from ecologic differences.

Several authors have recently emphasized the major role of ecologic factors in determining the frequency and intensity of aggressive behaviour in primates (DeVore and Hall, 1965; Hall, 1964; Rowell, 1967; Kummer, 1968). DeVore and Hall observed that overt aggression between groups of *Papio anubis* was rare in Nairobi Park, Kenya, where population density was low (10 baboons per square mile in 1959) and average group size was small (41 baboons per group), whereas more overt aggression was seen between groups in Amboseli Park, where population density and average group size were twice as great (25 baboons per square mile; 80 per group). Kummer (1968) observed a higher frequency of male-male aggression in *Papio hamadryas* in eastern Ethiopia where group sizes were considerably larger (averaging 110 to 354 baboons per group) than in western Ethiopia (averaging 54 to 83 baboons per group). Kummer felt that these differences in group sizes were ecologically determined. In the eastern zone, food was more abundant but sleeping rocks were scarce, thus at night up to 750 baboons were forced to squeeze themselves together on a steep river bank. In the west, a great abundance of rocks and cliffs permitted very small groups to have their own private lodging locations.

These observations confirm Hall's statement (1964): ". . . it is now obvious that the characteristic expressions and frequencies of aggression within and between groups cannot be meaningfully considered without detailed reference to their ecological context." Rowell (1967), in reviewing environmental influences on social organization, elaborates on this by stating ". . . there may be no such thing as a normal social structure for a given species . . . a description of social organization is only useful if accompanied by a description of the environment in which it occurs . . . further, we are still only guessing about which features of the environment will be essential in such a description." I think the first part of this statement, that there may be no such thing as a normal social organization for a species, is carrying the environmentalist's position too far; nonetheless, it does emphasize a new awareness in studies of primate behaviour as to the importance of ecology.

Methods

The present data were collected during 6 periods of field study in India from 1959 through 1966. Behavioural studies were made on rhesus groups in temple grounds, villages, rural roadsides, and forests, primarily during the winter and early summer months (December-May). A captive group of rhesus was established in Calcutta during 1964-65 for experimental studies of intragroup aggression.

Observational methods for both the field studies and captive colony have been described previously (Southwick *et al.*, 1965; Southwick, 1967). Behavioural data were obtained primarily in the morning (7 to 10 A.M.) and late afternoon (4 to 6 P.M.). Aggressive interactions were tallied under the following categories:

1. Threat. Any conspicuous aggressive gesture of one animal toward another involving an open-jawed stare gesture, head-bobbing, and ear-flattening; usually accompanied by an aggressive vocalization sounding like a hoarse "ho" or "hough," frequently repeated.

2. Attack. An aggressive chase or lunge, usually involving threat gestures and often terminating in a slap, hit, or bite of one animal upon another.

3. Fight. Mutual rough slaps, hits, and/or bites between two animals; usually with vigorous wrestling.

4. Submissive responses. A fleeing, cowering, or grimacing of one animal away from another, usually accompanied by a high-pitched scream or ". . .eeee . . ." vocalization. The most common form of submission – a simple retreat or quiet withdrawal – was not scored in the data.

In the wild, comparative data were utilized only for groups and circumstances where most or all of the group could be kept under surveillance at the same time. This was particularly difficult for forest groups, and hence the sample size in hours of observation is very small. Only 30 hours of observation out of 2 months study met this criterion. This may have introduced biases into the data that are difficult to evaluate, but without this criterion, the biases would probably have been even greater. Attack scores were chosen as the most reliable comparative measures of overt aggressive behaviour within groups because attacks are discrete, accompanied by sound and motion, and not readily missed in the field.

The Calcutta group consisted of 17 monkeys wild-trapped from different groups in Uttar Pradesh and transported by rail to Calcutta. They were placed in a colony cage of 1,000 square feet provided with perches, climbing bars, walkways, and shelter boxes. The details of this cage and the husbandry procedures have been published previously (Southwick, 1967).

The rhesus monkeys which were introduced into the Calcutta colony were also wild-trapped from Uttar Pradesh, and were maintained in cages until experimental introduction to the colony.

Results

Aggressive behaviour in different habitats

Despite the sampling problem of studying groups of different sizes in different observational conditions, a definite trend in aggressive behaviour in relation to habitat was obvious (Table I).

In the Aligarh farm and temple groups, the attack score was more than 4 times higher (0.009 attack/hr./monkey) than in the Corbett Park forest group (0.002). In the Calcutta captive group, the attack score was more than 50 times higher (0.123) than in the forest group. The highest attack scores of all occurred in the captive group during the period of group formation (0.225 in the first two weeks).

Thus these data show a marked increase in aggressive behaviour associated with crowding and captivity. This is further evidenced by the higher prevalence of wounded and scarred individuals in town and temple groups compared to forest groups (Southwick *et al.*, 1965). Similar observations have been made by other investigators. Neville (1966) noted more aggression in rhesus monkeys living in the town of Haldwani than in forest groups in neighbouring hills. He attributed this to crowding and the concentration of food.

Table I *Frequency of Intragroup Aggressive Behaviour in Rhesus Monkeys: Attack Scores*

Location and type of group	*Group Size*	*Hrs. of observ.*	*Attacks per hr.*	*Attacks/hr. per monkey*
Corbett Park Forest	32	30	0.07	0.002
Aligarh Univ. Farm	12	97	0.11	0.009
Aligarh Temple	42	157	0.395	0.009
Calcutta captivity	17	110	2.091	0.123
Calcutta, group form. (first 4 weeks)	17	83	2.882	0.164
Calcutta, group form. (first 2 weeks)	17	44	3.820	0.225

Rowell (1967a) found in baboons (*Papio anubis*) that aggressive contact was 8 times more frequent in captivity than in the wild. This was attributed to a higher frequency of interaction in the cage, increased social tension, and more "environmental stress." It seems to be generally agreed now that the popular concept of primates as inevitably aggressive and violent has been due primarily to excessive concentration on captive animals.

The rhesus may be characterized as a species with conspicuous tendency toward aggression that is frequently evoked by environmental and social pressures. Its communicative system to regulate this aggression is only partially effective. It has a threat and display system which can function in many normal ecologic and social situations, but this system is not elaborately ritualized and cannot always substitute for overt aggression in difficult circumstances. Its capacity to control aggression can be exceeded by a variety of environmental and social conditions.

Patterns of aggressive behaviour in rhesus groups

The percent attacks initiated by different sex and age groups in various habitats are shown in Table II. In rural groups, adult males, adult females, and juveniles were almost equally responsible for the initiation of attacks (36.5%, 32.7%, and 30.8% respectively); whereas in the temple group, adult males initiated the majority of attacks (63.5%) and juveniles were responsible for relatively few attacks (8.0%).

The captive colony in Calcutta was similar during its period of group formation to the temple group in that adult males initiated most of the attacks (53.4%), and juveniles relatively few (7.6%). The adult females in the Calcutta colony were more aggressive than the temple group, however.

After the Calcutta group had become an established group, adult males and females accounted for approximately the same percentage of attack initiative (46.7% and 44.0% respectively), and juveniles still remained relatively inactive in attack behaviour (9.3%).

In a captive group of 11 rhesus studied by Bernstein and Mason (1963), adult females initiated most of attacks (47.9%), adult males fewer (34.8%), and juveniles the least (17.5%).

These data suggest that crowding aggravates adult aggressive behaviour more than that of juveniles.

Table II *Attack Initiative: Percent Attacks Initiated by Adult Males, Adult Females, Juveniles*

Location and type of group	*Number of Attacks (n)*	*Adult males (%)*	*Adult females (%)*	*Juveniles (%)*
Rural India: Aligarh Univ. Farm and Bareilly	52	36.5	32.7	30.8
Aligarh Temple: Achal Tank	63	63.5	28.5	8.0
Calcutta captivity: group formation	118	53.4	39.0	7.6
Calcutta captivity: established group	75	46.7	44.0	9.3

Tables III-V provide more detailed data on the sex and age groups which initiated attacks and those which received these attacks. In rural groups, adult males directed

Table III *Attack Patterns in Rural Rhesus Groups: Aligarh University Farm and Bareilly (52 attacks)*

Attacker — attacked		*Percent of total attacks: A*	*R*	*Percent of attacker category: R*
Male		36.5		
	Male		7.7	21.1
	Female		11.5	31.6
	Infant		5.8	15.8
	Juvenile		11.5	31.6
Female		32.7		
	Female		13.5	41.2
	Male		3.8	11.8
	Infant		1.9	5.9
	Juvenile		13.5	41.2
Juvenile		30.8		
	Juvenile		28.8	93.7
	Male		0	
	Female		2.0	6.3
	Infant		0	

A = percentage of attacks initiated by
R = percentage of attacks received

most of their attack behaviour toward females and juveniles (31.6% in each case), less to adult males (21.1%), and least toward infants (15.8%). Adult females directed most of their attacks toward other adult females and juveniles (41.2% in each case), considerably less to adult males (11.8%), and least to infants (5.9%). Juveniles directed almost all of their attack behaviour toward other juveniles (93.7%). It is interesting to note that juveniles received 53.8% of the total attack behaviour in the rural groups although they constituted only 37% of the population.

In the temple group, several notable differences occurred (Table IV). The adult males were not only more aggressive, but they directed a greater percentage of their attacks toward other adult males (35% cf., 21% in the rural groups). They were relatively less aggressive toward adult females, but showed approximately the same attack behaviour toward juveniles and infants.

Table IV *Attack Patterns in Aligarh Temple Group (63 attacks)*

Attacker – attacked		*Percent of total attacks:* *A*	*R*	*Percent of attacker category:* *R*
Male		63.5		
	Male		22.2	35.0
	Female		11.1	17.5
	Infant		9.5	15.0
	Juvenile		20.6	32.5
Female		28.5		
	Female		9.5	33.3
	Male		12.6	44.4
	Infant		3.2	11.1
	Juvenile		3.2	11.1
Juvenile		8.0		
	Juvenile		3.2	40.0
	Male			
	Female		3.2	40.0
	Infant		1.6	20.0

A = percentage of attacks initiated by
R = percentage of attacks received

Adult females in the temple were also relatively more aggressive toward adult males, directing 44.4% of their attacks toward males. Considerably fewer were directed toward juveniles.

Juvenile attack behaviour in the temple was less than in the rural groups and it was also directed differently. Only 40% was directed to other juveniles, whereas 40% and 20% was directed respectively to adult females and infants.

The attack patterns in the Calcutta captive group were somewhat intermediate between those of the rural and temple groups (Table V). Adult males directed many attacks toward other adult males (37.1%), adult females (34.3%), and juveniles

(28.6%), but none toward infants. Adult females directed most of their attacks toward juveniles (60.6%), and lesser equal amounts toward adult females, adult males, and infants. Juveniles in the Calcutta group directed most of their attacks toward other juveniles (71.4%), with small amounts toward adult males and infants (14.3% to each).

Table V *Attack Patterns in Calcutta Captive Group: Established Group (75 attacks)*

Attacker – attacked		*Percent of total attacks:* *A*	*R*	*Percent of attacker category:* *R*
Male		46.7		
	Male		17.3	37.1
	Female		16.0	34.3
	Infant		0	0
	Juvenile		13.3	28.6
Female		44.0		
	Female		5.3	12.1
	Male		5.3	12.1
	Infant		6.7	15.2
	Juvenile		26.7	60.6
Juvenile		9.3		
	Juvenile		6.7	71.4
	Male		1.3	14.3
	Female		0	
	Infant		1.3	14.3

A = percentage of attacks initiated by
R = percentage of attacks received

These data show considerable variation in the attack patterns of different rhesus groups. This is not surprising since these groups differed in size, composition, habitat, and personality of the dominant males. In all groups, adult males were responsible for initiating most of the attacks. In only rural groups did juveniles contribute a major part of attack behaviour. The age distributions were approximately the same in all of the groups, particularly in regard to juveniles (37.0% juveniles in rural groups, 37.5% in the temple, 35.3% in Calcutta captive group).

Experimental studies on social and environmental factors influencing aggression in a captive group

The establishment of the captive rhesus group in Calcutta permitted comparisons between captive and natural groups, as well as controlled experiments on ecologic factors influencing aggressive behaviour. It would have been desirable, of course, to capture an intact social group in the wild and place it in captivity, but our attempts to do so were unsuccessful. The group formed in captivity was therefore an artificial one since most of its members had come from different natural groups.

When the animals were first placed together, the level of aggression was very high, averaging 26.0 agonistic interactions per hour in 10 hrs. of observation during the first week (Fig. 1). Of these interactions, 10.3 were threats, 10.3 were submissive responses, 4.9 were attacks, and 0.5 were fights. Total agonistic interactions declined gradually as the group became established, and by the fifth week, the average agonistic interactions per hour dropped to 10.3 (Fig. 1).

Almost half of these agonistic interactions were caused by B male, for when he was removed in week 6 for medical treatment of an intestinal infection, the total agonistic level fell to 5.7 per hr. He was returned in 8 weeks and the agonistic level increased to 13.6.

The experiments conducted on this group consisted of short-term changes lasting from 2 to 7 days in the availability or distribution of food, the amount of space, and various social changes. Between these experimental changes, the group was returned to normal conditions, and these normal periods, which were usually one week in duration, constituted the control or baseline readings on the group. Baseline levels of total agonistic interactions per hour average 13.2 over 8 different baseline periods, and they did not vary significantly.

The first set of experiments involved increasing and decreasing the amount of food available to the group. The standard amount of food was more than adequate to meet the needs of the group. A 25% increase in food resulted in a small but non-

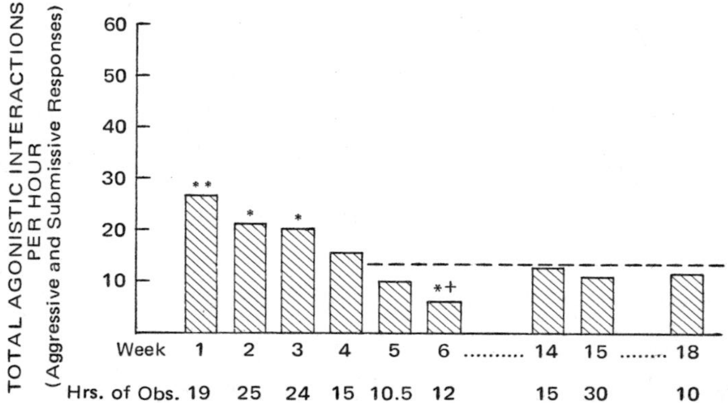

Figure 1. Agonistic behaviour in formation of confined rhesus group. Dashed line represents baseline average after group stabilization. (* = significantly different from baseline, p =< 0.05; ** = significantly different from baseline, p = < 0.01; + = second dominant male removed for medical treatment.)

significant decline in total agonistic interactions to 6.8 (Fig. 2). A 25% reduction in food resulted in a similar low level of agonistic interactions (8.7). A 50% reduction in food produced a significantly lower level of agonistic behaviour (5.9).

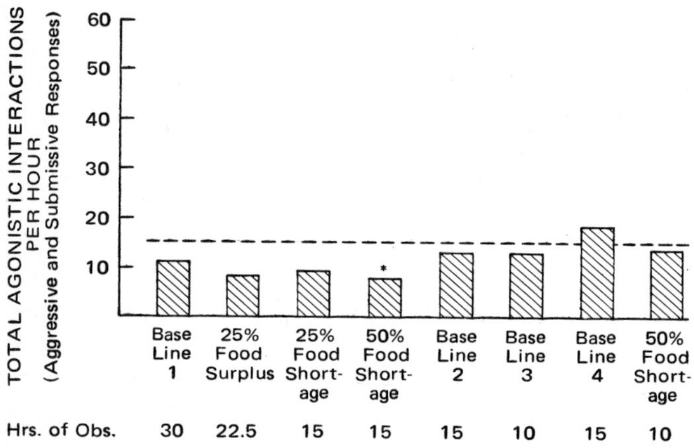

Figure 2. Effects of food shortages on agonistic behaviour of confined rhesus group. Dashed line represents baseline average.

These results came as an unexpected surprise, for I had anticipated that food shortages would increase aggressive behaviour. The 50% food reduction was repeated, and a similar decline in agonistic behaviour occurred (Fig. 2).

Not only was there a reduction in aggressive behaviour during these periods of semi-starvation, but there was also a reduction in sexual behaviour, grooming, and play. These behaviours were all replaced by a slow, lethargic investigation of the entire cage, with tedious and repeated examinations of twigs, leaves, and bits of dirt.

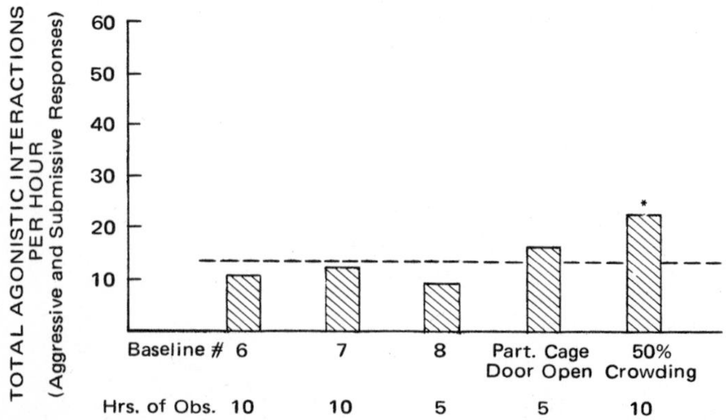

Figure 3. Effects of crowding on agonistic behaviour of rhesus group. Dashed line represents baseline average.

Several references in the literature indicate that depression, lethargy, and behavioural indifferences are common behavioural responses to starvation in both man and animals (Digby, 1878; Keys *et al.,* 1950; Hall, 1964).

A second set of experiments investigated the influence of space on aggressive behaviour. A wire fence partition was built across the cage reducing the available space from 1,000 to 500 square feet. On an initial trial, a door in this partition remained open, permitting the monkeys to use 1,000 square feet, though access to it was reduced. This resulted in a slight, but non-significant rise in aggressive interactions to 16.4 per hr. (Fig. 3). Then the door was closed forcing the monkeys into one-half of the cage. This resulted in a significant increase in agonistic interactions to 22.8 (Fig. 3).

The third set of experiments involved social changes. Two individuals of each major sex and age group were withdrawn at a time, and two strangers of the same type were placed in the group. When two new juveniles were added in place of two removed, the agonistic interactions increased four-fold to 47.2 (Fig. 4). Upon their removal, the agonistic level returned to 11.6.

When two new adult females were added, an even greater increase in aggressive behaviour occurred; a ten-fold increase to 110.0, including 49.9 threats, 29.3 submissive responses, 29.7 attacks, and 1.1 fights per hr.

When two new adult males were added, an eight-fold increase occurred to 84.3 agonistic interactions per hr. (Fig. 4).

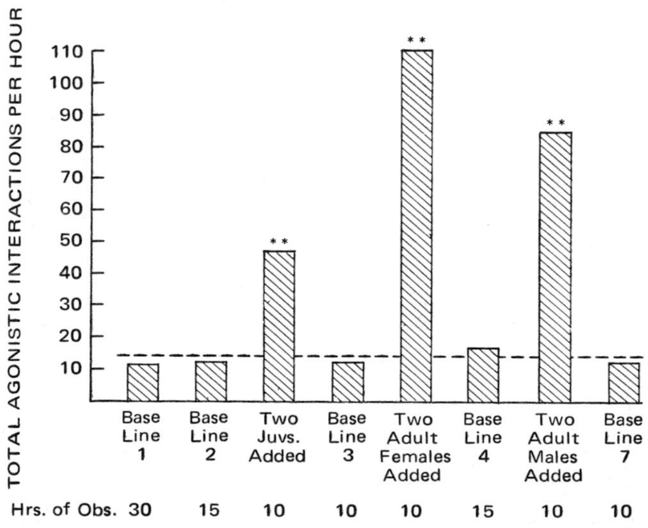

Figure 4. Effect of social changes on agonistic behaviour of confined rhesus group. Dashed line represents baseline average.

Thus, this group was highly intolerant of the presence of social strangers. Field tests of adding 2 new juveniles to a large rural group at Chattari-do-Raho, 12 miles north of Aligarh in northern India, showed a similar increase in threats and attacks. This preliminary field trial suggested, therefore, that this behaviour was not entirely an artifact of captivity, though it was probably exaggerated by confinement.

Another interesting feature of this behaviour was the fact that the attack initiative in each case was led by the sex and age group corresponding to that of the introduced strangers (Table VI). When juveniles were added, 55.3% of the attacks were initiated by the resident juveniles. When new females were added, 66.2% of the attacks were initiated by the resident females on one trial, and 64.5% on a second trial.

When new males were introduced, 80.2% of the attacks were initiated by the remaining resident male.

All of these were significant deviations from normal attack patterns in any of the captive or natural groups. These results suggested that a "social template" existed in the group, so that the sex and age category into which each newcomer had to fit responded aggressively to that newcomer.

Table VI *Attack Initiative: Percent Attacks Initiated by Adult Males, Adult Females, Juveniles*

Location and type of group	*Number of attacks (n)*	*Adult males (%)*	*Adult females (%)*	*Juveniles (%)*
Calcutta captivity: established group	75	46.7	44.0	9.3
Calcutta: introduction of new juveniles	114	3.5	41.2	55.3
Calcutta: introduction of new females (Tr. 1)	353	2.8	66.2	31.0
Calcutta: introduction of new females (Tr. 2)	107	7.5	64.5	28.0
Calcutta: introduction of new males	167	80.2	3.7	16.1

Summary and conclusions

The rhesus macaque is an aggressive species in which the frequency of aggressive behaviour varies with ecologic and social conditions. Rhesus groups in forest habitats showed less aggressive behaviour than those in rural villages and temple areas. A captive group showed the greatest frequency and intensity of aggressive behaviour, significantly above that of any natural group studied in India.

Attack patterns also varied in groups in different habitats. In rural groups, adult males, adult females, and juveniles all contributed significantly to the initiation of attacks. In the temple group, adult males initiated most attacks, and juveniles initiated relatively few. In the captive group both adult males and adult females initiated most attacks and again juveniles relatively few. Attack recipients also varied. In rural and captive groups, juveniles received considerably more attacks than adults. In the temple group, adult males received the most attacks. All of these data indicated that crowding increased primarily the aggressive interactions of adults.

Experimental studies on a captive group in Calcutta showed that social changes in the group increased aggressive behaviour to a much greater extent than did changes in the physical environment. When social strangers were introduced into the group, agonistic interactions increased four- to ten-fold. Attack initiative was led by the sex and age group corresponding to that of the newcomers.

When food shortages were imposed upon the group, agonistic behaviour decreased. Animals became lethargic and depressed with less sexual behaviour, play, grooming, and aggression. Slow, tedious investigation increased. Crowding caused a significant increase in agonistic behaviour, though not as great as that induced by social changes.

References

Altmann, S. A. 1962. A field study of the sociobiology of rhesus monkeys, *Macaca mulatta. Ann. N. Y. Acad. Sci.,* 102/2, 338.

Bernstein, I. S. 1968. Personal communication.

Bernstein, I. S. and Mason, W. A. 1963. Group formation by rhesus monkeys. *Anim. Behav.,* 11/1, 28.

Bertrand, M. 1968. *The behavioral repertoire of the stump-tailed macaque, Macaca speciosa: a descriptive and comparative study.* Ph.D. Thesis, Johns Hopkins University, Baltimore, Maryland.

DeVore, I. and Hall, K. R. L. 1965. Baboon ecology. *Primate Behavior: Field Studies of Monkeys and Apes,* ed. I. DeVore, pp. 20-52. New York: Holt, Rinehart and Winston.

Digby, W. 1878. *The Famine Campaign in Southern India. Vol. 1,* p. 515. London: Longmans, Green and Co.

Hall, K. R. L. 1964. Aggression in monkey and ape societies. *The Natural History of Aggression,* ed. J. D. Carthy and F. J. Ebling. London: Academic Press.

Hinde, R. A. and Rowell, T. E. 1962. Communication by postures and facial expressions in the rhesus monkey *(Macaca mulatta). Proc. zool. Soc. (Lond.),* 138, 1.

Imanishi, K. and Altmann, S. A. 1965. *Japanese Monkeys: A Collection of Translations,* p. 151. Atlanta, Ga.: Yerkes Regional Primate Center.

Kaufman, J. H. 1967. Social relations of adult males in a free-ranging band of rhesus monkeys. *Social Communication Among Primates,* ed. S. A. Altmann, pp. 73-98. Chicago: University of Chicago Press.

Keys, A., Brozek, J., Henscel, A., Michelsen, O. and Taylor, H. L. 1950. *The Biology of Human Starvation. Vol. II,* pp. 767-918. Minneapolis: University of Minnesota Press.

Kling, A. and Orbach, J. 1963. The stump-tailed macaque: a promising laboratory primate. *Science,* 139, 45.

Kummer, H. 1968. *Social Organization of Hamadryas Baboons,* p. 189. Chicago: University of Chicago Press.

Lahiri, R. K. 1965. Social behavior of the lion-tailed macaque, *Macaca silenus.* Unpublished data.

Lahiri, R. K. and Southwick, C. H. 1966. Parental care in *Macaca sylvana. Folia Primatologica,* 4, 257.

Mason, W. A. and Murofushi, K. 1966. Interspecific contrasts in temperament: a comparison of three species of macaque monkeys. *Bull. Ecol. Soc. Amer.*, 47/4, 196.

Miyadi, D. 1964. Social life of Japanese monkeys. *Science*, 143, 783.

Neville, M. 1966. *A study of the free-ranging behavior of rhesus monkeys.* Ph.D. Thesis, Harvard University, Cambridge, Mass.

Rosenblum, L. A., Kaufman, C. and Stynes, A. J. 1964. Individual distance in two species of macaque. *Anim. Behav.*, 12, 338.

Rowell, T. 1967. Social organization of primates. *Primate Ethology*, ed. D. Morris, pp. 219-235. London: Aldine.

_____1967a. A quantitative comparison of the behaviour of a wild and a caged baboon group. *Anim. Behav.*, 15, 499.

Sade, D. S. 1967. Determinants of dominance in a group of free-ranging rhesus monkeys. *Social Communication Among Primates*, ed. S. A. Altmann, pp. 99-114. Chicago: University of Chicago Press.

Simonds, P. E. 1965. The bonnet macaque in South India. *Primate Behavior*, ed. I. DeVore, pp. 175-196. New York: Holt, Rinehart and Winston.

Southwick, C. H. 1967. An experimental study of intragroup agonistic behavior in rhesus monkeys *(Macaca mulatta). Behaviour*, 28, 182.

Southwick, C. H., Beg, M. A. and Siddiqi, M. R. 1965. Rhesus monkeys in North India. *Primate Behavior*, ed. I. DeVore, pp. 111-159. New York: Holt, Rinehart and Winston.

Trollope, J. 1968. Observations on the stump-tailed macaque. *J. inst. anim. Tech.*, 19/1, 11.

Vandenbergh, J. G. 1966. Rhesus monkey bands. *Nat. Hist.*, 75, 22.

PART FOUR

Crowding, stress, and aggression

The problems of unchecked population growth involve not only the projected exhaustion of our traditional food resources, but also a complex of behavioral and physiological responses arising from the loss of personal space, from an existence holding too many face-to-face encounters.

The experience of crowding in non-human animals has been repeatedly observed to result, minimally, in disturbance of normal social interactions including courtship, mating, maternal behavior, and the establishment of dominance-submission relationships: a general failure to maintain stable group organization and viability. Maximally, the unalleviated tensions of prolonged stress due to overpopulation stimulate hormonal (especially adrenal) hyperactivity, a self-maintaining and ever accelerating output culminating in the death of the organism accompanied by several characteristic symptoms (the "stress syndrome"). In the first article Hoagland summarizes a number of these observations and discusses their significance for human welfare.

There is no reason to believe that modern man has eluded these psychological and physiological responses, although the flexibility of his cultural adaptations has certainly succeeded in extending his tolerance for human congestion. For example, the rigorously formalized etiquette with which Orientals interact even at home appears to have had an ameliorating influence in the crowded cities of Asia. Peoples closely confined in large households through long arctic winters or tropical rainy seasons frequently practice personal avoidances with regard to those relationships most prone to friction (sons- and mothers-in-law in residence, siblings). Some writers feel that man's cultural adaptability has proved ecologically catastrophic, and believe that with greater discomfort he might have controlled his numbers like other organisms, as well as coping earlier and more effectively with environmental deterioration.

In a remarkable chapter from their book *Violence, Monkeys and Man,* the Russells interpret many of the events of European history in terms of response to demographic stress. Although admittedly oversimplified, their version seems particularly appropriate to our consideration in view of the current florescence of violence in recreation, in modes of political action (international, national, urban, and academic), and even in our "entertainment" from TV, the theater, movies, and literature.

Ehrlich and Freedman's article sets forth their preliminary observations on sex differences in human subjects under test situations that included a number of confining and high-density environments. They find that under crowded conditions men become more competitive, vindictive, and mutually aggressive, while women become more lenient, tolerant, and cooperative. The presence of women appears to exert an ameliorating effect upon male aggressiveness. If these observations prove accurate, a rationale for the inclusion of a substantial number of women in positions of political influence is certainly evident.

Not reprinted herein, but equally valuable, is Edward S. Deevey's "The hare and the haruspex: a cautionary tale" (*The Yale Review*, Winter 1960).

15

Mechanisms of population control

Hudson Hoagland

It is impossible for the thoughtful man to escape a certain ambivalence of response to the social impact of most great scientific discoveries. The unlocking of nuclear energy promises enormous potential benefits as a source of industrial power and as a servant of the medical sciences. But the rapid multiplication of nuclear bombs in the arsenals of growing numbers of nation states, uncontrolled by enforceable world law, may render man an extinct species. All organisms must adapt to the environments or perish. After Hiroshima, the notable change in our environment is that it now contains nuclear weapons, which have made obsolete not only traditional views of national sovereignty but traditional concepts of how the security of nations can be protected. The hope for man is that he can change his ways of thinking to cope with this new environment before it destroys him.

There are of course many other examples of antithetical applications of science. The automobile and the airplane are of great convenience in transportation, but the automobile kills 40,000 Americans a year, and the airplane overhead may be an enemy bomber. The knife is a tool that can be used as well for murder as for surgery, and most drugs of value in medicine are harmful and even lethal when used inappropriately.

It is especially ironic that the humane practices of medicine and public health, dedicated to reducing physical suffering and prolonging healthful lives, should be the primary cause of a major social disease. This disease is

SOURCE: *Daedalus,* Volume 93, No. 3 (1964). Reprinted by permission of *Daedalus,* Journal of the American Academy of Arts and Sciences, Boston, Massachusetts.

the unprecedented increase in the world population, especially in economically underdeveloped countries least able to afford the increased burden. Prior to World War II, during nearly 100 years following Pasteur and the development of bacteriology and immunology, the European population growth rate accelerated as a result of the conquest of infectious diseases and the improvement in public health measures, which reduced death rates. Since World War II western medicine has administered its sophisticated techniques in underdeveloped countries. Medical missionaries, using relatively inexpensive insecticides, antibiotics, inoculations, and vaccinations applied to masses of people, have drastically reduced the death rate, leaving the birth rate, always large, either unchanged or somewhat increased as a result of improvements in health and longevity. This beneficent process has greatly increased populations in the poverty-stricken countries of Asia, the Near East, Africa, and Latin America, which now contain, according to Kingsley Davis, 69 percent of the world's adults and, through marked decreases in infant mortality, 80 percent of its children.[1]

In most of the underdeveloped countries, the death rate has dropped at a record rate. Davis has pointed out that on the island of Mauritius in the Indian Ocean, within an 8-year period after the war, life expectancy increased from 31 to 51 years, a gain that took Sweden 130 years to achieve. In Taiwan, within two decades, the life expectancy increased from 43 to 63 years. This 20-year gain in life expectancy took 80 years to effectuate in the white population of the United States. These figures are typical of what has happened in most underdeveloped countries. In many countries the population is increasing at the rate of over 3 percent per year, which will result in a doubling in 23 years. The world population as a whole is increasing at 2 percent per year, a rate at which it will double in about 35 years. Oncoming generations of poverty-stricken, economically unproductive young people will increase the birth rate further as they come of age. Already this generation in some places is hungrier and more illiterate than that of its parents, and has fewer job opportunities. This is bad news in those countries with rising expectations, which now contain two-thirds of the world's people, such as China, India, Pakistan, the United Arab Republic, and various Latin American countries, where the average per capita income is less than $100 per year. The increasing numbers of the unproductive make increasingly difficult the accumulation of developmental capital, since most local produce must be consumed to maintain the growing population.

There are only two solutions to the disease of overpopulation. One is to increase death rates, and the other is to decrease birth rates. So far we have manipulated death control by decreasing death rates and so increasing the population. No one that I know of advocates reversing this process, although a nuclear war would certainly do so, and such a war is made increasingly likely by runaway populations. The alternative solution is birth control and family limitation on a rational basis. Man is the only animal that can deliberately direct and control his own evolution.

[1] Kingsley Davis, "Population," *Scientific American,* 209:3 (September, 1963), 62-71.

It will be interesting to see which of these two variables, death or birth, he will manipulate. It must be one or the other, since a 2 percent growth rate will result in one square yard of land area per person 600 years hence, an obvious absurdity.

We may learn something relevant to our problem from a consideration of how animals regulate and control their population problems. Many organisms possess remarkable methods of population control as contrasted with the conscious devices available to man.

In multiplying cultures of micro-organisms the growth rate accelerates exponentially; but as toxic metabolic products, such as acids or alcohol, accumulate, the rate declines and the curve describing numbers of organisms as a function of time ultimately flattens off. These S-shaped growth curves for bacteria and yeasts have been described by equations aimed at elucidating the dynamics of such population growths. Human populations, when relatively isolated by geography, social habits, and cultural factors, also display S-shaped growth curves; in other words, they reach asymptotic levels as a result of Malthusian brakes such as infectious diseases, war and famine, or, more hopefully, by migration or by rational family planning and birth control. The motivation for family planning has historically been a desire for better economic and educational advantages for small families desirous of upward social mobility. It is this factor that is primarily responsible for the small present growth rates of about a half of one percent in the most advanced industrial nations of Europe, rather than the Malthusian factors active in more primitive societies.

There are many studies on the regulation of insect populations. It has been shown that the fruit fly, *Drosophila,* above certain population densities decreases its egg laying, and to an amount proportional to the density. Many investigations have been made of flour beetles. Below a fixed number of grams of flour per beetle, cannibalism occurs in some species, egg production drops off, and in one species crowding results in females puncturing and destroying some of the eggs they have produced. Frequency of copulation also declines with crowding. There are some species of flour beetles with glands that produce a gas, the release of which is increased with crowding. This gas is lethal to larvae and acts as an antaphrodisiac at high densities of population. Flour contaminated with beetle excrement inhibits egg production of one species of beetle investigated, and the mixing of this contaminated flour with fresh flour decreases the rate of population growth, which is entirely reversible in the presence of fresh flour. In these cases, the food supply is ample.

Among populations of mammals other than man, it was long thought that food and predators were the controlling factors in limiting populations of hares, lemmings, and other rodents as well as of deer, caribou, and other forms. The predators might be lynxes, wolves, foxes, and birds of prey, or micro-organisms producing epidemic diseases. It was thought, for example, that the four-year cycles of build-up and decline of lemming populations terminating in their suicidal migrations were due to an increase in predators accompanying population growth, which ultimately caused the panic and decline. But the migrations and deaths appear now not to be caused by the predators. Rather, the predators appear to multiply in response to the multiplying prey. Similarly, for well over a century various observers have reported repetitive wide cyclic variations in the number of fox and lynx pelts taken by trappers in our northern woods. These predators increase in number following cyclic increases in their prey. Lionesses have been reported to bear larger litters, two to four cubs, in environs of plentiful game. When game is scarce, there are only one or two cubs per litter. While the lemming cycles have not been studied as systematically as those of some other species, it seems likely that these four-year fluctuations in population densities are determined by factors now known to regulate population cycles in other mammalian species, and I should now like to say something about these factors.

In past years the snowshoe hare population of Minnesota has been studied extensively. These populations rise and fall through cycles of several years' duration. There is a period of build-up, followed by a dying off. Why do these marked oscillations in numbers of hares occur? It was observed that when the animals died off there was usually plenty of food – they had not starved. There were no evidences of an excessive number of predators. Furthermore, the bodies showed no sign that any specific epidemic had killed them. To quote from a 1939 study of the dead animals:

> This syndrome was characterized primarily by fatty degeneration and atrophy of the liver with a coincident striking decrease in liver glycogen and a hypoglycemia preceding death. Petechial or ecchmotic brain hemorrhages, and congestion and hemorrhage of the adrenals, thyroid, and kidneys were frequent findings in a smaller number of animals. The hares characteristically died in convulsive seizures with sudden onset, running movements, hindleg extension, retraction of the head and neck, and sudden leaps with clonic seizures upon alighting. Other animals were typically lethargic or comatose.[2]

The adrenals were hypertrophied in some cases and atrophied in others. Signs of liver disease, hypertension, atherosclerosis, and adrenal deterioration were typical of what one finds following Hans Selye's acute syndrome resulting from overactivity of the pituitary-adrenal axis.

Since effects of social stress have been found to limit populations of birds and mammals, a brief discussion of its operation is in order. Elsewhere I have defined stress as follows:[3] Any external situation threatening the organism may function as a stress. Situations calling for flight or fight, with their concomitant psychological and physiological expressions of fear and anger, are stressful. Especially in man the processes of inhibiting fight or flight may themselves result in stressful anxiety states. Psychological stress may result from the intensification of our instinctual

---

[2]This quotation is from an unusually interesting review by Edward S. Deevey, *American Scientist,* 48 (September, 1960), 415-430. He does not, however, cite the original paper containing this quotation.

[3]Hudson Hoagland, "Stress," *McGraw-Hill Encyclopedia of Science and Technology* (New York: McGraw-Hill, 1960), pp. 180-182.

drives and of the control of these drives to meet the demands of society. Such stresses may be chronic and produce far-reaching disturbances of a psychosomatic nature, including neuroses, in susceptible individuals. The balancing of one's needs and satisfaction in terms of learned inhibitions and prohibitions occasions stresses of this sort. The same stress situation may have quite different significance, psychologically, for different organisms in terms of their life histories and past conditionings, and therefore attempts to objectify and standardize such stresses meet with difficulty.

The physiologist has a variety of measures of how stress may disturb the body's regulation of the internal fluid environment of its tissues. The maintenance of constancy in this internal environment of blood and lymph is of great importance for proper functioning of the body. Blood and urinary measurements of certain endocrine systems brought into play by stress are particularly useful response indices, and have been used extensively in our laboratories as well as elsewhere. The quantitative analyses of adrenalin, secreted primarily by the medulla of the adrenal gland, and noradrenalin, a neurohumor primarily released at certain synapses and nerve endings of the autonomic nervous system, reflect defense responses especially to acute stress. Blood and urine measurements of the steroid hormones from the adrenal cortex and their metabolites have been used more widely than any other indices in recent years in studies of stress responses in mammals, including man. The adrenal cortex is activated by the pituitary adrenocorticotrophic hormone (ACTH), which, in turn, is released in increased amounts by action of the hypothalamus following bodily damage or threats. The adrenocortical hormones have ubiquitous actions on many tissues involved in response to stress and the maintenance of homeostasis.

Hans Selye has developed the concept of the general adaptation syndrome, which he defines as the characteristic emergency reaction or general stress responses of an animal, developing through three stages: (1) the alarm reaction, in which adaptation is attempted; (2) the stage of resistance, in which adaptation is optimal; and (3) the stage of exhaustion, in which adaptation fails. These various phases of the general adaptation syndrome may be studied in terms of the type of changes in constituents of body fluids, especially those involving activity of the adrenal cortex. In animals, the studies may include determinations, before and after stress, of adrenal size, adrenal ascorbic acid, and adrenal cholesterol as indices of adrenocortical function. Selye has concluded that many diseases are primarily a result of failure of the bodily mechanisms for adaptation to meet chronic stress situations adequately. He considers that disturbed patterns of endocrine secretion following the prolonged application of stressors may result in various chronic diseases and he thus speaks of the diseases of adaptation resulting from prolonged stress.[4]

---

[4]H. Selye, *The Physiology of Stress and Pathology of Exposure to Stress* (Montreal: Acta, Inc., 1950); *Fifth Annual Report on Stress* (New York: MD Publications, 1956); "Stress and Mental Illness," *Lancet*, 275 (1958), 205-208.

Prolonged stressor actions may produce anxiety and chronic behavioral disturbances in man and in experimental animals. The role of life stresses as contributory agents to hypertension, arthritis, ulcers, skin disorders, asthma, and other allergic manifestations has been investigated by many biochemical, physiological, psychological, and psychiatric procedures. Experimentally induced states in animals, closely resembling the neuroses and psychosomatic disturbances seen in man, have been regularly brought about by frustrating conditioned reflex techniques, in themselves mild procedures but productive of highly abnormal and crippling behavior when carried on at regular intervals over periods of time. Life stressors producing neurotic behavior in man are very varied and may be difficult to define or to measure. In the biosciences, stresses for the most part are not directly identifiable, but are measured by the strains they produce as reflected in the above indices, especially those reflecting activity of the adrenal cortex.

In studies of rodents it has been found that, after the severe stress of winter crowding in burrows, there was much fighting among the males, sex drives were at a low ebb, the young were often eaten, and the females produced premature births. Susceptibility to non-specific infections was also found, another by-product of excessive production of adrenal corticoids. After the numbers of such a colony are depleted through the effects of the stress syndrome, the colony then tends to build up again, going through repeated cycles of growth and decline.

There are many other examples. About forty years ago, a pair of deer was put on a small island of about 150 acres in Chesapeake Bay. The deer were kept well supplied with food. The colony grew until it reached a density of about one deer per acre. Then the animals began to die off, and this in spite of adequate food and care. When these dead animals were examined, marked evidence was found that the adrenal stress syndrome had been in operation. Studies made of the crowding of animals in the Philadelphia Zoo disclosed that in some species there was a ten-fold increase in atherosclerosis under conditions of severe crowding, as well as many other symptoms characteristic of stress. John Christian of the Naval Medical Research Institute made population studies in relation to the crowding of mice. In his 1950 paper in the *Journal of Mammalogy* entitled "The Adreno-pituitary System and Population Cycles in Mammals," he wrote in part:

> We now have a working hypothesis for the die-off terminating a cycle. Exhaustion of the adreno-pituitary systems resulting from increased stresses inherent in a high population, especially in winter, plus the late winter demands of the reproductive system, due to increased light or other factors, precipitates population-wide death with the symptoms of adrenal insufficiency and hypoglycemic convulsions.[5]

John Calhoun at the National Institute of Health has studied effects of crowding on rats, and I should like to describe his work in some detail. He investigated colo-

[5] John J. Christian, "The Adreno-pituitary System and Population Cycles in Mammals," *Journal of Mammalogy,* 31:3 (1950), 247-259.

nies of rats kept in pens at critical levels of crowding, and under these circumstances observed high infant mortality, high abortion rates, failures of mothers to build nests. The young were often scattered about and eaten. When the rats were examined, there was also evidence of the stress syndrome, and Calhoun has spoken, most appropriately, of what he calls "pathological togetherness." He has reviewed this work in an article entitled "Population Density and Social Pathology," published in the *Scientific American,* in February, 1962.

Calhoun confined wild Norway rats in a one-quarter-acre enclosure with plenty of food and water. At the end of 27 months the population stabilized itself at 150 adults. From the very low adult mortality rate in uncrowded conditions, one would have expected a population of 5000, not 150 rats. But infant mortality was extremely high. The stress from social interaction disrupted maternal behavior so that only a few of the young survived. Calhoun later studied groups of domesticated white rats confined indoors in observation rooms under better controlled conditions. Six different populations were examined. Each group was allowed to increase to twice the number that his earlier experience indicated could occupy the allotted space with only moderate stress. Pathological behavior was most marked in the females: pregnancies were often not full term; there were many abortions and many maternal deaths; the mothers often could not nurse or care for their young. Among the males there was much sexual deviation, homosexual behavior, and cannibalism, and abnormal behavior ranging from frenetic overactivity to pathological withdrawal, in which some males emerged from their nests only to eat and drink. Patterns of social behavior were thus badly deranged at twice normal crowding.

The experiments took place in four interconnecting pens, each 6 x 6 feet in area. Each was a complete dwelling unit, with a drinking fountain, a food hopper, and an elevated artificial burrow, which was reached by a winding ramp that held five nest boxes. One of these storied rat apartment houses was located in each of the four pens. There was comfortable space in the colony for 12 adult rats in each pen, the size of group in which rats were normally found to thrive. The setup should thus have been able to support 48 rats comfortably without overcrowding. At the stabilized number of 80 to 100, double the comfortable population, which they were allowed to reach by breeding, an equal distribution of the animals would have found 20 to 25 adults in each pen, but the animals did not dispose themselves in this way.

Biasing factors were introduced in the following fashion. Ramps were arranged enabling the animals to get from one pen to another and so traverse the entire four pens in the room. However, the two end pens, numbers 1 and 4, each had only one ramp connecting them with pens 2 and 3 respectively, while the middle pens had two ramps each, one ramp connecting in each direction. The rats had to make a complete traverse of the pens to go from one of the end pens to the other. This arrangement of ramps immediately weighted the probabilities in favor of a higher density in the two middle pens, since pens 2 and 3 could be reached by two ramps, whereas pens 1 and 4 by only one ramp each. With the passage of time strange aspects of the behavior of the group skewed the distribution in an unexpected way.

As a result there developed an unexpected arrangement of the sex ratios of the animals in the various pens. The females distributed themselves about equally in the four pens, but the male population was concentrated almost overwhelmingly in the middle pens, the reason for this being the status struggle which takes place among the males. Shortly after six months of age each male enters into a round robin of fights that eventually fixes his position in the social hierarchy. These fights took place in all of the pens, both the middle and the end pens; but in the end pens, during the period when the social hierarchy was being established, it became possible for a single dominant male to take over the area as his territory.

Calhoun describes how this came about. The subordinate males in all pens adopted the habit of arising early in order to be able to eat and drink in peace. Rats generally eat in the course of their normal wanderings, and the subordinate residents of the end pens, having been defeated by the dominant males there, were likely to feed in one of the middle pens, where they as yet had not had to fight for status. When, after feeding, they wanted to return to their original quarters, they met with difficulty. By this time the dominant male in the end pen would have awakened and would engage the subordinates in fights as they tried to come down the single ramp to the pen. For a while the subordinate would continue his efforts to return to his home pen, but after a succession of defeats he would become so conditioned that he would not even make the attempt. In essence, Calhoun points out that the dominant male established his domination in the end pens and his control over a harem of females, not by driving the other males out, but by preventing their return over the one lead ramp. While the dominant male in an end pen slept a good part of the time, he made his sleeping quarters at the base of the ramp. He was therefore on perpetual guard, awakening as soon as another male appeared at the head of the ramp. He usually had only to open his eyes for the invader to wheel around and return to the adjoining pen. Since there were two ramps for pens 2 and 3, no one male could thus dominate both means of access. The dominant males in pens 1 or 4 would sleep calmly through all the comings and goings of his harem, seemingly not even hearing them. His behavior during his waking hours reflected his dominant status. He would move about in a casual and deliberate fashion, occasionally inspecting the burrow and nests of his harem. But he rarely entered a burrow, as did some other males in the middle pens merely to ferret out the females. A territorial male might tolerate other males in his domain provided they were phlegmatic and made themselves scarce. Most of the time these subordinate males hid in the burrows with the adult females, and only came out onto the floor to eat and drink; they never tried to engage in sex activity with the females.

In the end pens, where population density was thus kept low, the mortality rate among infants and females was also low. Of the various social environments that developed during the course of the experiments, the breed pens – as the two end pens were called – were the only healthy ones, at least in terms of group survival. The harem females generally made good mothers and protected their pups from harm. In the middle pens the pregnancy rates of the females were the same as those in the end pens, but a very much lower percentage of their pregnancies terminated in live births. In one series of experiments 99 percent of the young born in pens 2 and 3 perished before weaning, and in others of the six experiments somewhere between 80 and 95 percent perished.

The females that lived in the densely populated middle pens became progressively less adapted to building adequate nests, and eventually stopped building them at all. Normally rats of both sexes build nests, the females doing so most vigorously around the time of parturition. It is an undertaking that involves repeated periods of sustained activity, with the searching out of appropriate materials, such as strips of paper, and transporting the strips to a nest, which they arrange in cup-like form. In the crowded middle pens, however, the ability of the females to persist in this activity was greatly impaired. The females began merely to pile the strips in heaps, sometimes trampling them into a pad that showed little sign of cup formation. Later they brought fewer and fewer strips to the nesting site, and in the midst of transporting a bit of material often dropped it and engaged in some other activity occasioned by contact and interaction with other rats met on the way. In the extreme disruption of their behavior during the later months of the population's history, they built no nests at all, but would bear their litters on the sawdust in the burrow box. The females also lost the ability to transport their litters from one place to another, a task they would normally accomplish with skill. If they did try to move a litter, they would drop individuals and scatter them about on the floor. The infants thus abandoned throughout the pens were seldom nursed. They would die where they were dropped and be eaten by the adults. In the middle pens, when a female came into heat, she would be relentlessly pursued by all of the males until she was exhausted, with the result that, within a relatively short time, 25 percent of the females in the crowded pens died; in contrast, only 15 percent of the adult males died over the same period in the middle pens. In the end brood pens, however, this sort of thing did not happen. The females there would retire to bear their young in nests they made in a normal fashion, and were protected from the excessive attention of other males by the territorial male.

In the middle pens, a great deal of fighting among the males went on, with now one and now another assuming the dominant position. After a while, most of the males in the middle pens gave up the struggle and simply retired, making themselves as scarce as possible and spending a lot of their time sleeping. In contrast, in pens 1 and 4 one male predominated and peace reigned. These dominant males took care of the females and of the juveniles, never bothering them in any way.

Among the sub-dominant males there was much abnormal behavior. For instance, there was a group of homosexuals. They were really pan-sexual animals, and apparently could not discriminate between sex partners. They made sexual advances indiscriminately to males, juveniles, and females that were not in oestrus. Frequently attacked by their more dominant associates, they very rarely contended for status.

Another type of male emerged in the crowded pens. This was essentially a very passive type, that moved a good deal like a somnambulist, ignoring the other rats of both sexes, and ignored by all of them. Even when the females were in oestrus, these passive animals made no advances to them, and only very rarely did other males approach them for any kind of play. They appeared to be healthy, attractive, and sleek, but they were simply zombies in their conduct as far as the other rats were concerned.

The strangest of all of the abnormal male types described by Calhoun were what he called the probers. These animals, which always lived in the middle pens, took no part at all in the status struggle. Nevertheless, they were the most active of all the males in the experimental population, and persisted in their activities in spite of attacks by the dominant animals. In addition to being hyperactive, the probers were hypersexual, and in time many of them became cannibalistic. They constantly chased females about, entering their nests, having intercourse with them in the nest, a thing that normal rats would never do. These probers conducted their pursuits of oestrus females in a very abnormal manner, abandoning all courtship ritual, which is characteristic of mating rats.

In these experiments by John Calhoun we see the development of serious pathology directly attributable to overcrowding at only twice the number of rats per unit area normally required for a healthy society. It is tempting to draw a comparison of city slums with the crowded middle pens and of prosperous suburbs with the orderly end pens, far-fetched though it may be.

We are, however, justified in asking to what extent the stress syndrome may be a limiting factor in reducing the growth rate of human populations. As far as I know, there are no adequate data on which to base an answer. Studies from a number of laboratories, including our own, have demonstrated that the pituitary adrenal system responds under stress in a way similar to that of other mammals. There is direct evidence that inmates of concentration camps experienced acute forms of the stress syndrome that may have accounted for many deaths. Concentration camps would be more appropriate sources of comparison to highly congested animal populations than city slums, since in crowded cities even the very poor do have some mobility. They can escape from their immediate congestion onto the streets and associate with other members of the population. The high incidence of street gangs and juvenile delinquency is especially characteristic of overcrowded city areas and constitutes a form of social pathology. Several studies have also indicated a higher incidence of schizophrenia and of other psychotic and neurotic behavior in congested urban areas than in more spacious surroundings, but other factors may be involved here. The increased incidence of atherosclerosis and other cardiovascular pathology associated with urban living and its competitive stresses may also be enhanced by crowding, although direct evidence for this effect of population density is lacking. In underdeveloped countries with high birth rates and recently lowered death rates, resulting in population growth rates of 2 to 4 percent per year, any possible decrease occasioned by the stress syndrome would be obliterated through the action of medical and public health measures that are enhancing life expectancies and would mask any small reduction in life expectancies resulting from stress.

There is a large literature on the social behavior of animals in relation to population density. Of especial importance is a book by V. C. Wynne-Edwards entitled *Animal Dispersion in Relation to Social Behavior,*[6] some of whose conclusions I should like to summarize.

In nature, when food supplies are fortuitously removed or fail to materialize, a local overpopulation emergency results; among highly mobile flying animals, such as insects and birds, this can be immediately relieved by emigration. The social hierarchy and code of behavior to which the animal subscribes act as devices to force out whatever surplus of animals exists. The exiles may be condemned to perish, or under other circumstances, they may set up new communities in other localities. In the cold boreal and arctic regions, most of the erupting species are birds. Many birds are adapted to exploit intermittent or undependable crops of food, and are to a large extent nomadic in their search for regions where supplies are temporarily plentiful. Two distinct biological functions appear to be served by emigration. One is that of a safety valve to give immediate relief to overpopulation; the other is a pioneering function to expand and replenish the range of the species as a whole, and provide for gene exchange. Emigration of the safety valve kind is associated with stress and with quickly deteriorating economic conditions (locusts). On the other hand, providing pioneers can be afforded only when conditions are good. In more variable environments, both functions tend to become important and to be exercised on a large scale. The individuals expelled are in either case usually the junior fraction of the hierarchy.

In this connection I am reminded of human colonizing activities – the Greek city states that sent young people off to colonize the Mediterranean area, Italy, Sicily, and Africa, and the lands around the Aegean and the Black Sea. It was the younger sons of British families and the emigrants of Portugal, Spain, and France who established colonies in the western hemisphere, thereby relieving population pressures at home. Like many animal colonies, Australia was originally colonized by a group very low in the British pecking order, namely, prisoners. Ireland is an especially interesting case. In 1670 Ireland had a population of approximately a million people. By 1845 this had increased to eight million. The Irish were heavily dependent upon one crop, the potato, which was grown on small plots sufficient to feed a family. Over a period of six years (1848-1854), a blight destroyed the potato crop. Nearly a million persons starved and another million emigrated. Agriculture reforms were introduced, the small plots being consolidated for purposes of diverse crop farming, and ultimogeniture was established. But the population continued to fall, until it is now about four million, only half of what it was before the potato famine. The reasons for this decline were continued emigration, and a social change characterized by very late marriages, or often no marriage at all. The pattern is for the youngest son to maintain the farm, care for his parents, and usually not marry while

[6] V. C. Wynne-Edwards, *Animal Dispersion in Relation to Social Behavior* (New York: Hafner Press, 1962).

they are alive. The result is that population growth in Ireland is low despite the influence of the Catholic Church.

To revert to animal societies, Wynne-Edwards points out that the same general social machinery that controls safety valve emigrations is involved in regulating such seasonal redispersions of animals as the annual two-way migrations of birds. Among other investigations of mortality promoted by stress, the white stork has been intensively studied. Nestling mortality is often very heavy under crowded conditions; individual chicks may be deliberately killed and sometimes eaten by one of their parents, usually the father. This is most likely to happen where the parents are beginners or young adults, and presumably of lower status in the pecking hierarchy. The killing off of the young in prolific breeding conditions is characteristic of a great many birds that have been investigated, as well as of many mammals, and is a direct result of social stress. Both the killing of the young and cannibalism are known to occur quite widely in mammals: for instance, in rodents, lions, and also in primitive man. Cases of cannibalism are found in fish, spider crabs, spiders, and fratricide in insect larvae of various types. *In all cases experimentally investigated, the mortality is found to be density dependent and to cease below a certain critical population density.*

Mortality from predation, which has also been examined, appears to be density dependent to the extent that the prey cooperates by making its surplus members especially vulnerable to predators. As mentioned earlier, the density elements in predation seem to arise first on the side of the prey and not on that of the predators. Because of lowered resistance to infective agents following prolonged stress, disease as a form of predation may effectively reduce excessive population. In this case a surplus of individuals predisposed to injury by their dominant fellows naturally experiences a variable amount of uncontrolled mortality, which tends to fall most heavily on the young, as yet unprotected by acquired immunity from bacterial and viral infections. Social stress can lead to casualties at all ages, both through direct and mortal combat and through stress-induced disease. The victim of severe stress is likely to develop physiological disorders affecting many organs, especially the lymphatic apparatus, and including the spleen and thymus, the nervous system, circulatory, digestive, and generative organs, the endocrine glands. As we have seen, the effect of stress is especially notable in the adrenal cortex, which serves an intermediary role between the stressor and the organs responding to adrenal cortical hormones. Social stress is sometimes partly physical, as when the exercise of peck-order rights leads to the infliction of wounds, or the withholding of food and shelter. But, as Wynne-Edwards points out, it may also be largely mental, as in man, who in his more unsophisticated states may die from the conviction that he has been bewitched. Instances are known of birds, mammals, and amphibians similarly dying from non-specific injuries apparently induced by social stress.

And now, what about man? What can we do about the world population explosion? We can, of course, do nothing and wait for the stress syndrome or for some new virus to do its work. We can leave our destruction to some trigger-happy dictator with a suitable stock pile of nuclear weapons, or, finally, we can decide on an optimal population for the world and, by education and such social pressure as tax bonuses for small families, try to see that it is not exceeded.

Psychological prejudice, indifference, and downright hostility are the major blocks to planned population limitation. We know many methods of birth control: coitus interruptus, jellies, douches, diaphragms, condums, surgical procedures, and "the pill," and ongoing research will give us more and better methods, but none is of value if people refuse its use. Among the very poor and illiterate, cost and the difficulties of use of contraceptives demand massive government aid, financial, social, and educational. Prudery and politics, myth, superstition, and tradition have so far rendered birth control ineffective in the very countries most in need of it.

There are certain factors that specifically inhibit human population growth. One of these is a rise in the social, economic, and educational level of the people. Thus birth rates in the United States, with the exception of the postwar baby boom, have, in general, fluctuated inversely with economic conditions. Davis has pointed out that in all of the industrialized countries of Europe economic growth always outpaces population growth, thus repeatedly demonstrating that population pressure on the means of subsistence does not operate to lower populations as has often been thought. Other things being equal, the richer the nation the slower the population growth, an observation sharply divergent from the claim that the population explosion is good for business. The decline in birth rates attendant on opulence results from a desire for upward social mobility on the part of parents, who know that their incomes will go further to advance the welfare of a small family and will make possible a better education for a few children and higher standard of living for themselves than for a big family. Within a single country and at a given time, one can see this principle in operation. Thus, in northern industrial Italy, the birth rate is low compared to that in the poor agricultural regions of the south, and this despite the influence of the Catholic Church and cash bonuses paid by the Italian government to encourage large families.

Decrease in birth rates with opulence has led some to the erroneous conclusion that an increase in food supplies decreases birth rates. It has therefore been argued that all we need to do to control the population explosion is to feed people well, as if there were an inverse correlation between food intake and fertility. As a matter of fact, the opposite appears to be the case. We have already pointed out that predatory animals increase in numbers and may have larger litters in the presence of ample prey. This fact has been established for a number of species, although its basis is obscure. A parallel situation also appears to exist for man. William Langer has presented an interesting and well documented discussion of what he calls "Europe's Initial Population Explosion."[7] Before the mid-eighteenth century Europe's population increases were slow and spasmodic. He points out that a population of 140 million in 1750 rose to 188 million in 1800 and to 266 million by 1850. A careful consideration

William L. Langer, "Europe's Initial Population Explosion," *American Historical Review,* 69: 1 (October, 1963), 1-7.

of death rates demonstrates that they did not decrease significantly over this period. The increase appears to be due to fertility increases, and the question is why?

Langer points out that historically it has been established that there are correlations between harvest conditions and marriage and birth rates. In Sweden, where careful statistics go back to the seventeenth century, the annual excess of births over deaths in the eighteenth century was only 2 per thousand after a poor crop, but 6.5 after an average harvest, and 8.4 after a bumper crop. As late as the mid-nineteenth century high wheat prices resulting from scarcity were reflected in low marriage rates and to some extent in low birth rates.

Langer attributes the European population increase between 1750 and 1850 to the introduction of potato culture. The potato, introduced from South America via Spain in the late sixteenth century, within a hundred years had spread widely over Europe. It furnished a food yield per acre of two to four times that of grain, and an acre of even poor soil could feed a large family. Langer points out that under the feudal system the seigneur frequently denied marriage to able young people he had selected for special service, and guild masters also blocked or delayed marriages of apprentices and artisans. Thus during the seventeenth and early eighteenth centuries marriages were late and few compared to a later period after the old regime had broken down, with a resulting increase in marriages and birth rates.

Potato cultivation contributed to the decline of great feudal estates. It facilitated early marriages and made possible the nourishment of larger families. Thus in Ireland, with no industrial revolution and no war and no change in patterns of famine or disease and despite terrible poverty, the population increased from 3,200,000 in 1754 to 8,174,000 in 1846, just before the potato famine, the disastrous consequences of which we have seen. These figures do not include some 1,500,000 who migrated before the famine.

Thus both human and animal populations tend to increase with increasing food supplies, other things being equal. On the other hand, human populations decrease their growth rates with opulence, for in the opulent society economic and social advantages other than food make for small families and usually constitute more effective agents for reducing birth rates than improved food supplies are in increasing them.

Grenville Clark has argued that the population explosion probably cannot be controlled until the world has accepted universal and complete disarmament under world law, and devotes a substantial part of the 120 billion dollars now being spent on weaponry to raising the living standards of have-not peoples. He bases his view on the often demonstrated fact that birth control procedures are used extensively only by literate and prosperous people, with hope and ambition for bettering their own lots and those of their children. The take-off point for family planning and limitation requires a critical level of education and prosperity not now found in the very poor countries.

The completely gloomy view would be that if we do not manage to disarm within a decade or two we may solve the population problem by nuclear extermination. In any case, the two major problems of our time – nuclear war and the population explosion – are closely linked together. The physical sciences and the medical sciences have given mankind these two world-wide challenges never dreamed of by previous generations. Only by fundamental changes in our ways of thinking can they be solved.

16

The natural history of violence

Claire Russell and W. M. S. Russell

1

We have attempted to unravel a web of social inequality, perversion and violence. All these cruel distortions in monkeys, however, are clearly confined to the zoo. The ample evidence of the field observers has shown us the peaceful life of monkeys in the wild, and finally disposed of the view that aggressiveness, whatever the conditions, is an innate and inherent vice of monkeys and man. The question naturally arises, why should violence ever occur in any circumstances? What possible function could it serve, and why are monkeys and human beings capable of aggression at all? The question is far from academic, for if we can discover this function we may be able to perform it by humane and peaceful means, and one day eliminate violence for ever. In our search for an answer to the question, we have one important clue: the effect of crowding.

From our comparison of wild and zoo monkeys, it became clear that the most obvious source of monkey violence is crowding, the forcing of monkeys into closer proximity with each other than they normally tolerate.[1] That violence occurs only under crowding has now been

SOURCE: Abridged from *Violence, Monkeys and Man*, Claire Russell and W. M. S. Russell, eds., Macmillan & Co., Ltd., 1968. Reprinted by permission of David Higham Associates, Ltd.

[1] Very recently, C. H. Southwick has reported experiments made at the Calcutta Zoo, which confirm the comparative evidence. Aggressive behaviour (threat, submission, attack, fighting) was studied and scored in 17 rhesus monkeys kept in a cage area of 1000 square feet. Partitioning the cage in two, with a door open between the two halves, had relatively little effect; but when the door was closed, restricting the monkeys to an area half as great (500 square feet), the amount of aggressive behaviour was roughly doubled (60).

established for a great many mammal species. In 1963 at a Symposium on Aggression held by the Institute of Biology, the then Scientific Director of the London Zoo, L. Harrison Matthews (12), surveyed the field literature and his own considerable field experience for instances of fighting in mammals. He could not find any cases of fighting to the death, except under crowded conditions. The same principle appears in birds (for instance, chickens and doves) and fishes (for instance, sticklebacks) (71).

Allowing for the simpler structure of their societies, mammals other than monkeys show the same tendency to brutal inequality under crowding. In the general terms of Paul Leyhausen, the privacies of territory and the courtesies of relative hierarchy disappear, and absolute hierarchy prevails in its most unrelieved form, as a natural consequence of shortage of space. As the difference between ranks becomes steeper, subordinates eventually become desperate, and violence becomes endemic, with mass redirection and the persecution of outcasts. Leyhausen has vividly described the symptoms of a group of cats caged together in a small space; the parallels with the zoo monkey community are obvious. "The more crowded the cage is, the less relative hierarchy there is. Eventually a despot emerges, 'pariahs' appear, driven to frenzy and all kinds of neurotic behaviour by continuous and pitiless attacks by all the others; the community turns into a spiteful mob. They all seldom relax, they never look at ease, and there is continuous hissing, growling and even fighting." (37, 38)

To produce this dangerous proximity, it is not always necessary to confine mammals in a cage or enclosure. If their food, instead of being widely dispersed, is concentrated at a point, they may be forced to invade each other's social space, and all the symptoms of crowding appear. In an area of woodland near the Flag River in Bayfield County, Wisconsin, white-tailed deer have gathered in winter for many years. They have seriously depleted the trees on which they depend for their food supply. To keep them in the neighbourhood, hay has been supplied in recent years at fixed feeding-stations by the Wisconsin Conservation Congress. In the winter of 1952 three American scientists, C. Kabat, N. E. Collias and R. C. Guettinger, were able to observe the behaviour of the deer as they clustered in the small areas of the feeding-stations. They quickly established absolute hierarchies, with bucks at the top, does in the middle and fawns at the bottom. A high-ranking deer would approach a subordinate, and if he failed to retreat, would strike at him with his hooves. Sometimes the victim would redirect, attacking a still lower-ranking deer nearby. The amount of quarrelling depended on the number of deer in the fixed area of the station, and hence on their *density*. When only 5-7 deer were present, only one quarrel was seen per deer per hour. When 23-30 deer were present, the rate was 4.4 quarrels per deer per hour. Aggressiveness was thus clearly related to the degree of crowding, though the deer were forced together only by their common need to use the artificial food supply (33). The fixed feeding-stations on Cayo Santiago are no doubt partly responsible for the relative aggressiveness of the rhesus monkey colony on the island.[2]

Similar situations can arise without deliberate human intervention of this kind. The concentrated abundance of food in villages, towns and other human-occupied areas has led an estimated 88 percent of the rhesus monkeys of northern India to congregate there. In or near the villages and towns, rhesus monkeys, and also bonnet macaque monkeys and langurs, live at much higher density than they do in the forest, and we have seen that these urban monkeys are correspondingly more aggressive (23, 41, 56). On Barro Colorado populations of howler monkeys are much denser in some areas than others, because the former areas naturally yield more fruits or (for howlers are choosy) more of the fruits they specially prefer. In these densely populated areas, the volume of howling indicates a relatively high degree of tension between bands, though there is no definite evidence of lethal fighting (23). In the Upper Semliki region near Lake Edward the Belgian zoologist R. Verheyen (12) counted the hippopotamus populations. He found they varied in density from one hippo per fifteen metres of river to one per five metres. He examined the corpses of five hippos killed in fights in the more densely populated part of the river. Hans Kummer made a comparison of wild bands of hamadryas baboons in an extensive strip of land in Ethiopia (36). As he went from east to west along this strip, he found an actual increase in the supply of food for the baboons, but a decrease in the number of sleeping-ledges. The western baboons were thus affluent but short of "housing" (sleeping-space), and, as we might by now expect, they showed appreciably more aggression.

Clearly animals quarrel more and begin to fight fiercely when they are crowded at high population density. It is natural to wonder whether the resulting violence does anything to correct the conditions that brought it about: does it, in fact, reduce the local population? This suggestion has been experimentally verified in fast-breeding animals, which can be easily observed over several generations in time. The Australian zoologist John Clarke bred two populations of voles (small, mouse-like animals) in open-air cages, each 67 square metres in area, and observed them for eighteen months (20). One population was raised from a single Adam and Eve, the other from six males and five females. Both were supplied with "a surplus of oats, available at all times." The populations naturally increased, but not nearly up to their full breeding potential. The initially larger population began its second year with three times as many voles as it started with, but the maximum number it reached that year was only sixty-one, compared with fifty-eight in the first year, and at the end of the experiment it was declining. The demographic details suggested that something was limiting the growth of both populations, and that this something was hitting the initially larger population harder. Fighting was seen in both populations, including two lethal fights in the larger one, whose members also had far more scars, and the death-rate of infant voles was high. The evidence strongly suggested

[2] In Southwick's experiments (see footnote 1), aggressive behaviour of the rhesus monkeys was also significantly increased when food was provided in one basket, instead of on eight different feeding-boards. To feed from the basket, the monkeys obviously had to come close together (60).

that violence, chiefly by its effects on the females and young, was checking the growth of both populations. The larger population developed a brutal absolute hierarchy, with a well-marked class structure. The upper-class males were heavy, healthy and had glossy coats; their scars were only from small wounds on their heads, known to result from last-ditch retaliation by desperate subordinates. They moved freely around the enclosure. The middle-class males were almost as heavy and free-moving, but their fur was tattered and their rumps scarred from unprovoked attacks. The lower-class males weighed about half as much and cowered in corners; their fur was tattered and they had scars all over their bodies. The middle classes were liable to be chased and bitten on the rump, but the lower classes tended to be caught and bitten all over; though perhaps "class" is hardly the appropriate term in so disordered and violent a society. Significantly, most of the females showed "lower-class" symptoms; and the effect of the fighting on females and young was almost certainly the factor that kept the population down.

Equally impressive are the results of the American biologist J. B. Calhoun (63). He bred a colony from a few wild rats, in a pen of 10,000 square feet, and he also provided them with an ample food surplus at all times. During the twenty-eight months of the experiment, if the rats had bred all they theoretically could, they would have produced a population of 50,000. In fact the population stabilised at less than 200. The rats split into sub-colonies, with buffer zones between their territories. In each sub-colony, ranks were unstable and quarrels were frequent; the weaker rats were under such stress that they lost the normal rat capacity for hoarding food. Above all, the adult rats mercilessly attacked the young, causing such high juvenile and infant death-rates that the population was kept down throughout the experiment.

From these and similar observations it appears that violence breaks out in an animal society when the population density is high, and that it serves to bring down the population and spread the survivors out again. It begins to look as if we have found the function of violence in animals. It is a device for limiting the growth of populations, called into play only when it is needed for this function. But this is only a formula. We need to understand the function in greater detail, if we are to find a civilised substitute for what Leyhausen has called "the old, cruel methods by which nature balanced our numbers." (38)

2

Just over two centuries ago, in 1766, a son was born to a wealthy land-owner of Surrey. The boy was called Thomas Robert Malthus. When he grew up he was encouraged to take Holy orders, but an active clergyman needed a good voice, and Malthus had a cleft palate. So he adopted an academic career, eventually becoming a professor of history and economics at Cambridge (58, 65). Undergraduates, instead of church congregations, had to grapple with the professor's speech defects;

but it must have been worth it, for Malthus produced, in his *Essay* of 1798 and his later works, the first really systematic treatment of the problem of population growth in its widest aspects. His work had a very wide influence, and it was the clear thinking expressed in the *Essay* that started both Darwin and Wallace, independently, on the train of thought that led them to the idea of evolution by natural selection (5, 7).

Population is a complicated subject, but it has its simple aspects. Migration apart, the rise or fall of a population depends simply on the difference between birth-rate and death-rate, both usually reckoned as numbers percent or per thousand per year. If the birth-rate is higher than the death-rate, the population rises. The trouble is that the rise is by compound interest, since the more people (or animals) there are, the more offspring they can breed. If a population increases by the same percentage every year, it increases by a constantly greater absolute number. A calculation (18) has been made which shows the fantastic implications of this. If mankind had sprung from a single couple living about 12,000 years ago, shortly before the coming of agriculture, and if there had been one more birth than deaths per hundred per year (a one percent increase per year), then today the world population would form a sphere of living flesh many thousand light years in diameter, expanding with a radial velocity many times faster than the alleged speed of light.

In real life, as opposed to the wonderland of mathematics, nothing of the kind can happen. So in real life the growth of a human or animal population is subject to checks or controls, and these were the subject of Malthus' exploration (47, 65). He did not go into detail about animals, though he did remark, with characteristic insight, that "the great check" to their increase is "the want of *room* and nourishment" (our italics). But he made a systematic study of the controls limiting human population growth. The materials available to him were meagre, but he made brilliant use of them. For instance, he saw in the United States, where there was still unlimited food and land, the opportunity to measure the natural, uncontrolled increase of mankind. He decided that this natural increase should be a doubling of the population every twenty-five years, and he proceeded to test this hypothesis. Fortunately, by the 1820s, the results of three censuses were available; for the Americans, concerned with the fair representation of the States in Congress, were the first to count heads with modern completeness and accuracy. By ingenious methods Malthus estimated the increase in American population due to immigration from Europe, and, allowing for this, he concluded that the American population growth agreed with his hypothesis. He published his analysis in the *Encyclopaedia Britannica* in 1824. In 1965 the British economist J. Potter published a careful study (25) of early American population growth. After similar allowances for immigration, he concluded that the natural rate of increase was only "slightly below" the estimate of Malthus.

It was clear to Malthus that the controls on population growth could be classified into two groups. First, there were "preventive checks," operating before birth. Such factors as late marriage, or a high proportion of people remaining single for life, would reduce the birth-rate. Second, there were "positive checks," operating after birth, which Malthus summed up succinctly as the effects of "misery and vice." These would increase the death-rate. Malthus saw clearly that in the long run, if the preventive checks were not working, "misery and vice" were inevitable. For, since indefinite uncontrolled natural increase is absurdly impossible, in the long run mankind must choose between low birth-rates and high death-rates. When he made a careful comparative study, he was surprised to find that the balance between the two kinds of control varied considerably between different countries and periods. Some had high death-rates and high birth-rates; others had low death-rates and low birth-rates. Malthus concluded that there was a real possibility of escape from "misery and vice" by controlling the birth-rate of mankind. Among his preventive or "prudential" checks, he did not explicitly include contraception: as we shall see, a possible reason for this reticence emerged only in 1966. But, in essence, he proposed control of birth-rates as a solution for the troubles of mankind; and he undoubtedly thought of violence as a population problem. Above all, he envisaged social behaviour as playing a key part in population control. His preventive checks were entirely social, and under "misery and vice" he included not only famine and disease but the consequences of human violence (47, 65).

In the two centuries since the birth of Malthus, much has been learned about populations of animals and their regulation, and, as usual, they provide relatively simple situations, which give us clues for unravelling the enormous complexity of human population growth and social behaviour. The year 1962 gave us a new look at the affluent societies; it also saw the publication of a monumental book by the British zoologist V. C. Wynne-Edwards, called *Animal Dispersion in relation to Social Behaviour* (71). From an overwhelming mass of evidence, gathered over a period of seven years, Wynne-Edwards showed that much of animal social behaviour has been evolved as a means of avoiding overpopulation, which could irretrievably destroy the food supply of a species. Indeed his work suggests that the whole of animal social behaviour, while of course it has other functions, is geared to fit in with this vitally important requirement. The structure and ceremonies of animal societies are designed by natural selection to control birth-rates and/or death-rates, by affecting mating behaviour, care of the young and social relations in general. They are in turn closely geared to the actual abundance or scarcity of natural resources. Sometimes these arrangements have an elegant simplicity. A nice example of what Malthus would have called a prudential check can be found in the large, generally seafaring birds called skuas. The courtship ceremony of the Arctic skua, which lives around the Shetland Islands, includes a little ritual in which the male obtains a fish and presents it to the female. This is always repeated a number of times in the course of courtship, so it is probable that, unless a male skua takes his girl-friend out to dinner, he gets no joy, and no breeding occurs. In this case little is known about the changes in abundance of the fishes on which the birds feed. But in northern Sweden there lives another species of skua, which has abandoned the sea to breed on a mountain, preying upon small land animals. Their main food is a small rodent, the lemming, which has an elaborate population cycle of its own. On this mountain, lemmings are abundant in some years, and scarce or absent in others. It is known that the birds do not breed in the years of lemming scarcity. In 1965 the Dutch zoologist Piet Sevenster visited the mountain. That year there were no lemmings around at all, and Sevenster found only two pairs of birds, hanging about the mountain but showing no signs of breeding. Sevenster suspected that they might have a ceremony like that of the Arctic skua, with lemming instead of fish dinners, and that the trouble was, the males had no offerings that year. He tried to come to the rescue of one of the males by supplying ersatz lemmings, in the form of sausages. The sausages disappeared, there were marks of skuas at the spot where he had left them, and the pair concerned stayed on when the other pair gave up and left the mountain. Unfortunately, even sausages were scarce that year in the local store. If, as seems very likely, the remaining pair was engaged in courtship, Sevenster's supply of sausages gave out before the female had been dined often enough to overcome her resistance. So it was impossible to prove that the ceremony occurs and is necessary for breeding. But if we put the facts from the two species together, it is probable that the dinner-ceremony, so necessary for breeding, is only possible when there is actually plenty of food. Obviously this would be a perfectly designed control: the birds will only breed when there is plenty of food for their young.

There are many special devices of this kind, but by far the most important and general is the organisation of social space, and the tendency of higher social animals to fight when they are crowded. As Wynne-Edwards points out, unrestricted competition for food is liable to lead to irretrievable destruction of food resources. In the twentieth century the harpoon-gun and the factory ship opened up the Antarctic to the whaling fleets of mankind. In these extra-territorial waters, nations competed unsparingly for the whales, and as each stock was depleted there was even keener competition to get the lion's share of the last survivors. The formation of the International Whaling Commission in 1946 could not save the situation: the member nations could not even agree on the quota for 1964-5. As a result, the humpback whale had been drastically depleted by 1913, and the blue whale by 1931; by 1960, 80 percent of the world catch consisted of fin whales, the last survivors, and in the same year survival curves already indicated that, at this rate of exploitation, the fin whales were dying out (54, 71). Such is the result of unrestricted competition for natural resources.

Wynne-Edwards pointed out (71) that this danger could be averted for an animal species if its members competed for space, which could in turn be made to respond very sensitively to change in the food supply. The whole competition would thus work in *advance,* giving the precious time necessary for a population of food plants or animals to recover. This is essentially what is achieved by the systems of individual territory, band territory and hierarchy within bands, all closely related to reproduction, and hence to the growth of the feeding population. The starting-point of the system, in mammals, birds and fishes, seems to be an intense resistance by the individual to close contact or near approach. This may be helped by the fact that, in all these highly social groups of animals, the surface of the body is liable to be disturbed by contact (disordering of fur or plumage, removal of scales). Anyway the fact of resistance is certain. The Swiss zoologist and zoo director H. Hediger discovered that most birds, when they congregate, maintain a definite "individual distance" (28) between them – as anyone can verify by looking at birds on a telegraph wire. Contact or close approach is only tolerated when necessary, chiefly in parental care and in mating. Mates, parents and young commonly develop special ceremonies to overcome the fear and/or rage that would otherwise be aroused by close proximity. These ceremonies are, in fact, ritualised conflict activities. Mutual preening in birds (similar to mutual grooming in monkeys) is a case in point, studied recently by the British zoologist C. J. O. Harrison (27). He showed that it was in fact a ritualised conflict activity, and then examined its incidence in the different groups of birds. He found that it was present in species obliged for various reasons to tolerate prolonged close proximity – for instance, when pairs stay together for long periods, or when the nature of the terrain forces a pair to stay very close together at the nest-site, or neighbouring pairs to nest very close together.

This general intolerance of proximity is expressed in the formation of individual territories and band territories, and in the hierarchical structure of social space within a band, which is so acutely sensitive to crowding (71). These systems are closely related to natural resources on the one hand, and breeding on the other. In some oddly named Alaskan birds called pomarine jaegers, the territories of breeding pairs have been seen to fluctuate with the food supply, so that the breeding density varied from four to eighteen pairs per square mile, in years of scarce and abundant food respectively. Birds who had just become adult were able to breed in the "dense" year, but in the "sparse" year they were kept out by the competition for territory: so the production of young was geared in a sensitive way to the availability of food for them. In this case, some individuals in the "sparse" year were forced to remain celibate. Sometimes they may merely be forced to spread into less lush areas, thus preventing exhaustion of the food resources on the more productive sites. Great tits and blue tits have been studied in two woods in the Netherlands, one more attractive, with more plentiful food, than the other. Territory size in the more attractive wood fluctuated; when the territories were large, only a few birds occupied the area, and others had to make do with the less happy hunting-ground. Hierarchy and social space in a band of monkeys may produce similar results in a different way. When natural resources begin to run short (but before there is serious danger of depletion), a band in its territory will begin to incur the tensions of crowding. Under tension, individuals are liable to leave and become solitaries, or, as has been shown in langurs and other monkey species, males may leave and form all-male bands (11, 59). In this way the breeding stock may be reduced; and this adjustment is reversible, for the emigrants may be able to rejoin the band later.

All these controls may be operated without violence as "preventive checks," regulating the birth-rate in a smooth manner in each generation to cope with minor fluctuations in the food supply. If violence does break out, its effects are much more drastic, and it may be seen as an emergency measure. Not only does it raise the death-rate, but it reduces the birth-rate, and can product effects over several generations.

There is by now abundant evidence that the tensions of extreme overcrowding, accompanied by violence, produce physiological effects on the survivors, marked by the enlargement of certain glands and a disruption of normal mechanisms of physiological regulation (17, 19, 63). The effect on the females is not only to reduce their own fertility but to stunt the growth and impair the fertility of those of their young which survive at all. The evidence for these long-term effects was first assembled in 1962 by the British psychologist D. H. Stott, and further surveyed in 1964 by the American physiologist J. J. Christian. Evidence of this kind is available for mice, rats, voles, woodchucks, rabbits, dogs and Sika deer. Stress diseases and pregnancy stress in man are closely related to these stress effects in animals. Stott has studied in particular the incidence of births of malformed babies in human societies (63). As early as 1812 a doctor, Jacob Clesius, had noticed that these malformations are specially prevalent in times of war. They seem to have been widespread in the Thirty Years War in seventeenth-century Germany, and in Paris during the siege and revolution of 1870-71. In the maternity wards of fifty-five German hospitals, the malformation rate nearly doubled after Hitler's accession to power; it rose still further during the Second World War and amidst the shambles of immediately-post-war Germany. Monstrous conditions literally produce monsters. All this suggests that violence is a key component of a complex machinery for drastically reducing a population over an appreciable period of time.

The manner in which this emergency device is used varies between different animal species. Some of them accept crowding and violence as a recurrent situation, and populations of these animals have regular cycles of rise and decline, with crises that cut them down to size every four or five generations. These species include voles (4, 16, 19, 63), studied by the Canadian zoologist Dennis Chitty, and muskrats (17, 63), studied by the American zoologist P. L. Errington. At the beginning of the cycle, the population builds up rapidly, in an uncontrolled way. When a certain density is reached the animals become extremely aggressive. At the same time the physiological effects of crowding increase their need for salt, and each pair needs a larger territory from which to obtain it. Each territory eventually becomes ten times as large, so that many pairs are forced into poor feeding-grounds; but this reduction in density is only attained at the cost of savage fighting, including lethal attacks on the young. The stresses affecting the mothers cause many of the surviving young to be physiologically weak and susceptible to disease, so that many of them die before the following breeding-season. The after-effects of violence thus persist after the density has been lowered, and it takes some time before the population recovers and begins a new cycle of growth. During this interval, the food plants and animals can also recover, so that the population's natural resources are never completely depleted.

Voles and muskrats are highly territorial animals. When forced into each other's company, like Clarke's voles, they evidently arrange themselves into ranks or classes. But, equally evidently, from Clarke's experiment, there is no true hierarchy, only a gradation of terror and scars in a community constantly engaged in fighting. There are other animal species which are territorial at low density, but react to a certain level of crowding by forming true rank hierarchies, in which priorities are allotted without this perpetual violence. These species include moles, studied by the British zoologists Gillian Godfrey and Peter Crowcroft and the German zoologist G. H. W. Stein, wild mice, also studied by Crowcroft, and laboratory mice, studied by the British zoologist John Mackintosh. In laboratory mice, Mackintosh (14) found that caging individuals in isolation gradually switches them into the territorial phase, so that they are more aggressive when again caged with other mice. Isolation for eight days produces three times as much aggressive activity as isolation for one day. Once the hierarchical phase sets in, however, it can become stable. In wild mice, and probably moles, this two-phase system seems to work in the following way (26). Surrounding conditions may at times give rise to a shortage of space, while there is still plenty of food (for instance, mole tunnels may be temporarily flooded). The population is not immediately stampeded into reducing itself by violence, and this is useful, for when space conditions improve again there may still be plenty of food for a large population. In normal circumstances, family territories are large (10-20 square feet in mice, separate tunnel assemblies in moles). In crowded conditions, a hierarchy forms. Subordinate animals have no territories of their own, but they can use the foraging territory of a dominant animal in shifts while he sleeps off his meals, in the manner of Cox and Box. But this only works when there is plenty of food; otherwise the owner will spend most of his time foraging, and when he is awake trespassers will be prosecuted, and the schemes of other mice and moles gang aft a-gley. The result is immediate emigration, or, if that is impossible, violence. The hierarchical phase is set on a hair-trigger for an unusually rapid and sensitive response to a food crisis, with immediate reduction of the population. Moreover, if crowding itself becomes too extreme, the hierarchical phase will not work even if food is plentiful. The American zoologist C. H. Southwick (71) used mice for an experiment like those of Clarke and Calhoun. He let them breed in a pen of limited size, supplying them with unlimited food. When crowding reached a certain point through population increase, fighting became frequent and severe, and was accompanied by desertion, destruction or cannibalism of the young. By the time crowding reached the point where there was one fight per adult mouse per hour, survival of the young fell so low that population growth was slowed or ceased altogether. Mice, therefore (and probably moles), retain the emergency measure of crowding and violence; but, unlike the voles and muskrats, they can adjust to a temporary crisis of *moderately* high density.

Monkeys, with their long generation span, their elaborate care of young, and their educative play-groups, have been able to make permanent use of a hierarchical system within each band, with enough regard for individual rights in social space to eliminate violence altogether in normal times. They owe much of their evolutionary success to their exceptionally low fertility. Nevertheless, if the environment smiles upon them, wild monkey populations do grow. When a band becomes too big for the hierarchical system to work smoothly, it simply splits into two, by a process of peaceful fission. This process has been studied among Japanese monkeys, and in the rhesus bands of Cayo Santiago (59). In 1957 the rhesus colony on the island numbered 155, divided into two bands of 55 and 100 members respectively. By 1960 the total population was 420. The originally smaller band had reached 140 without splitting; the originally larger band had split, by successive fissions, into five bands, containing 140, 50, 40, 30 and 20 members. When a band divided, the current president usually continued to lead one part of it; the other fell to the leadership either of an originally second- or third-rank leader or of a former solitary. Once separated, the new bands adopt each its own territory, and relations between them are regulated in the usual way.

It seems likely that monkey societies normally regulate the relations between population and resources in a peaceful way. Preventive checks and the basically low fertility keep population within bounds, and when a favourable environment permits population growth the monkeys maintain their normal band size, splitting repeatedly to allow "daughter" bands or colonies to spread out, much as did the Danubian villages or the ancient Greek cities that planted "daughter" colonies all over the Mediterranean and Black Sea. It is true that their generation span is much longer than that of voles or muskrats, so that a regular population cycle would be more difficult to observe. But if they did have regular, periodic collapses into violence, at least one of the wild populations studied by the field observers would almost certainly have been in the "violent" stage of the cycle; whereas in fact all of them were found living in peace. Nevertheless, the zoo observations show unmistakably that monkeys have retained the whole system of violence under crowding as a means for drastic reduction in numbers. Changes in the environment of monkeys could occur even before the activities of man, and such changes could result in more or less sudden depletion or limitation of resources. A number of bands could be cut off in an isolated area by some change in the terrain. When this happened, the bands would begin to feel the space shortage before the food supply ran out. They would then have the alternative of going to war with each other for the remaining territories, or contracting their territories so that each band became an affluent crowd. The second alternative is probably more usual, for whenever monkey populations have been seen to decline (howlers on Barro Colorado, rhesus monkeys in parts of India) the number of bands has remained constant but the number within each has dropped, suggesting high mortality *within* each band (23). Clearly, if each band began to behave like a crowded zoo colony, violence would drastically reduce its numbers, before the food resources were irretrievably depleted. If the population continued to be cut off in a limited area, such outbreaks of violence might become recurrent. It is tantalising that we have suggestive evidence that something like this has actually happened when no human observers were there to see it. On Barro Colorado (cut off by the construction of the Panama Canal), the howler population rose from 398 in 1932 to 489 in 1933, the number of bands rising from 23 to 28. By 1951, however, when the next census was taken, the population had sunk to 239, divided among 30 bands: the average band size had shrunk from about 17 to 8. It has been suggested that the howlers were hit by an epidemic. But even if this happened, crowding, violence and stress may well have made them more vulnerable to disease. In support of this, there is evidence of another approaching crisis. By 1959 there were 814 howlers, divided between 44 bands of average size about 18. Between 1951 and 1959 the amount of howling had increased tenfold, and the din could be heard throughout the day. This suggests that howler bands were constantly coming into conflict on the edges of their territories (which are larger than needed strictly for food, because howlers like to have enough of their *favourite* foods) (11, 23, 59). From all this, it seems likely that monkeys retain the whole system of violence under crowding, not as a regular cyclical procedure, but as a means of dealing with a *population crisis,* caused originally by changes in the environment, in such a way as to reduce the population enough to give the food resources time to recover.

Any serious disturbance in the environment or the society might well signal the onset of a population crisis. So we must expect violence to result from severe stress of *any* kind. This indiscriminateness of response becomes important in human societies, which have been subject to kinds of stress which hardly arise in monkeys – for instance, the disturbances in social order which result from technical change. Nevertheless, from the nature of the whole system, the proper or natural stimulus for the whole crisis complex would be *crowding,* either by itself or as a by-product of food shortage. From all the animal evidence, we can by now form a definite picture of the response as a whole. There is a sharp increase in inequality, with insecurity among the higher and real hardship among the lower ranks. Then a whole series of switches is automatically thrown. Our study of monkey societies in particular (*Violence, Monkeys and Man,* Chapters 2-4) showed an extraordinary economy in social organisation. There is a whole set of social devices which act to *reduce* violence in spacious conditions, and to *increase* it under crowding. These include threat, cut-off, pseudosex, intervention by leaders, contagion and redirection, each of which relieves momentary tensions or stops incipient disputes in the wild, and provokes or amplifies quarrels in the zoo. This curious double function at last makes sense in the light of population control. It secures all the benefits of peace (and hence progress) when population and resources are in balance, while providing a terrific boost for the complex of tension and violence once the switches are thrown by crowding, to ensure an immediate, drastic and prolonged fall in numbers.

A key part of the whole response to crisis is the switch in attitude and behaviour towards females and young, the crucial agents of population growth. Chivalrous protection of the females is transformed into brutal domination over them, the imposition of severe stress, and finally the kind of slaughter of females observed among the baboons of Monkey Hill. Even more dramatically, care and protection of the young is transformed into indifference, neglect, competition, domination and ultimately murder (sometimes followed by cannibalism). The fawns took the lowest ranks among the white-tailed deer at the feeding-stations (33); in bad years, before the stations were installed, the fawns had "suffered the greatest loss from starvation when food supplies were inadequate." In all the mammal species studied under intense crowding, the young suffered most severely and showed the highest casualty rates from violence – in voles, rats, muskrats and mice, for instance. The reversal is most dramatic of all in monkeys, which show such elaborate care and education of the young in good conditions, and such brutal cruelty under crowding. The young are both the innocent victims of heedless fighting between adults, and the object of deliberate (often redirected) attack and murder. Birds tell the same story as mammals; deliberate killing of young has been observed in gulls, terns, frigate-birds, pelicans, herons, wagtails, magpies, shrikes and white storks (71). Only the storks have been investigated in detail in this connection; it was found that they throw most nestlings out of their nests (to die) in years of population crisis. In short, when crowding spells that conditions are wrong for rearing them, mammals and birds neglect, desert, accidentally or deliberately kill their young. It is the extreme symptom of violence in the community, the last resort of redirection, and the most crucial device by which violence brings down the population.

We have now found a coherent explanation for the occurrence of violence under stress in higher animal societies. How far does all this apply to man? We might begin by considering individuals and families. We have just seen that the cornerstone of the whole system is the reversal from care and protection to neglect and ill-treatment of the young. Man has carried parental care even further than monkeys, and his children are normally cared for over a much longer period. This in itself may have somewhat distorted the system of population control; the reversal is more difficult in man. Cases are frequent of human mothers feeding their children at the expense of their own health in hard times (for instance, during the Depression in Britain), and of human parents making many other sacrifices under terrible conditions. In many an emergency, the principle of "women and children first" has been genuinely practised. Nevertheless, there is equally no doubt that human adults are capable of neglecting, ill-treating and even killing their children; and this seems to be least infrequent when crowding and/or other stresses are affecting them, such as might impress on the individual the presence of a crisis and the unsuitability of conditions for rearing children. With a very large family, and without exceptional economic resources or help from other relatives, some measure of neglect is particularly likely. In modern societies, there is a close relationship between large families and poverty: they are responsible to a large extent for the number of British children – nearly a million in 1960 – living below the basic national assistance rates. Studies in 1966 by Abel-Smith and Townsend suggest that something like 25 percent of all families with more than five children each may have incomes below the basic national assistance rates (1, 66). Children of such families are small in weight and height and have lower educational opportunities than others; some of them eat little or no meat, and some have diets inadequate for health by the standards of the British Medical Association. Miss Maureen Canning has told us that she has visited large families in the North of England, in the course of social work, where the father cannot remember his children's names. In a court case in England in 1965 one couple counted on their fingers and finally worked out they had twelve children

(75). The previous day they had told their defence counsel they had ten. The couple were convicted of neglecting their one-year-old daughter, who had been taken to hospital suffering from malnutrition and weighing as much as a three-month-old child. Along with ten other children, she had been left in charge of a sixteen-year-old daughter while the parents went to work. (The mother blamed this teenager for the disaster.) By the time the case came up, the father was unemployed and the family was threatened with eviction. Some of the children had been seen scavenging for food in dust-bins. This appalling situation seems a natural enough consequence for a poor family of having so many children literally to lose count of them. But neglect is by no means the only thing children have to fear in conditions of poverty and crowded housing.

The year 1962 was full of discoveries relevant to our theme. In July of that year five American doctors startled the medical profession with an article (34) entitled "The Battered Child Syndrome." They had discovered that large numbers of small children (generally under three years old), taken to doctors for allegedly accidental bruises and bone fractures, had actually been savagely attacked by one or both parents. They were able to give detailed instructions for recognising this "syndrome," or pattern of symptoms. They made a survey of seventy-one hospitals, which reported 302 such cases in one year; 33 children had died and 85 had suffered permanent brain injury. In only one-third of the 302 cases had there been legal action; the others were presumably diagnosed as accidents. They also circulated questions to seventy-seven district attorneys, who reported that 447 cases had come to their attention in the same year; 45 of these children had died, 29 had suffered permanent brain damage. Naturally enough, since district attorneys are more prone than doctors to suspect illegal activity, there had been court action in 46 percent of these cases. In their article, the investigators described two cases as typical; in both cases the child had been unwanted. "Not infrequently," they reported, "the beaten infant is a product of unwanted pregnancy, a pregnancy which began before marriage, too soon after marriage, or *at some other time felt to be extremely inconvenient*" (our italics) – just the sort of unreasoned feeling that might afflict any mammal under conditions of population crisis. Surveying the medical literature for odd published cases of this kind, they found that most of them came from "borderline socioeconomic groups," that is, from poor people at the bottom of the social hierarchy, always the first to feel all these pressures. The urgency of correctly diagnosing these cases was shown by a case where one battered child, discharged after treatment to the care of its parents, died of unexplained causes four weeks later. Since this discovery, cases of battered children have been found to be widespread in Britain (77). In April 1965 Home Office pathologists Francis Camps and Keith Simpson gave press interviews on the subject. They also emphasised the factor of unwanted pregnancies, and a London psychiatrist indicated that such cases were most likely when the parents had economic difficulties and were overworked and overtired.

In 1964 the British social scientists Terence Morris and Louis Blom-Cooper published a valuable summary (42) of all the murder cases (involving 764 men and women) in England and Wales between 21 March 1957 and the end of 1962. Their book was written to provide evidence relevant to capital punishment, and their case-accounts sometimes lack the detail which would be relevant for our present purpose. However, we have analysed these cases (51, 52), and the figures provide evidence that human beings are liable to kill their children in conditions when they feel incapable of rearing them, conditions which might indicate a population crisis. During this period, there were 118 cases of child-killing. Eighty-two of these cases involved killing by the child's own parent or parents; this is the usual proportion, though killing by strangers normally receives much greater publicity. In twenty-six of these cases, one or more of the following factors was present: unwanted child, large family, very young parents, unemployment, money troubles (such as hire-purchase debts), concern about the possibility of caring for the children. Thus nearly one-third of the child-killings were done under conditions where normal parental care seemed or was difficult, where the parents could not cope: this is certainly a much higher proportion than that of parents in the whole population (who do not kill their children) living under these conditions. In eleven cases, a father (in one case a mother) killed when feeling desperate about coping with a crying baby. In another eleven cases, the parent killed because of real, suspected or imaginary disease, deformity or suffering, as a kind of euthanasia. Some of these cases fell in more than one category; together they made up forty-one, or nearly half the total. Most of the remaining child-killers were severely mentally disturbed, sometimes echoing the same theme in insane terms (for instance, fear of bringing up children under the rule of invading Russians).

The cases of battered children make horrifying reading: there must sometimes be an element of pseudosexual (sadistic) involvement, and the grossly unequal status of the victims is prominent. It is true that the assaults sometimes seem to be made in moments of aberration, which the parent genuinely cannot recall afterwards. Sometimes the battering culminates in murder, as in the American case just mentioned and in an English case where the eight-month-old victim had suffered a fractured thigh-bone some months before the murder, and ten broken ribs the previous month. Many of the actual child-killings, however, are not preceded by deliberate ill-treatment: often the parent or parents had done their very best until their problems became too much for them. Most of the child-killing cases make pathetic and tragic, rather than horrifying, reading; some of them are heart-rending. In sixteen of the forty-one cases we have just specified, the killer attempted suicide. Except in the one category of inability to cope with a crying child (eleven cases), about half the killers were mothers and about half fathers. The total impression is not of parents callously abandoning their parental attitudes, but of real parental concern distorted under stress. Mrs. M. D., aged twenty-three, decided to gas herself "when distraught with worry over financial difficulties and in a severe depression following the birth of her second child" (eleven months old at the time). She "decided also to gas her son, Robert (2½), since she was afraid to leave him alone with no one to care properly for him." The gas killed the boy, but the mother was rescued. Mrs. M. M., aged twenty-five, killed her twins and tried to gas herself. She had four children and "was depressed by another pregnancy." Judges and juries generally responded humanely to these tragic situations. Mrs. L. M., aged twenty-eight, a widow in part-time work, "became very depressed and worried about her financial prospects and about the prospects for the children"; she turned on the gas and killed all five of them, but survived herself. Mr. Justice Salmon observed, "this is one of the most terribly sad cases which I have ever had to deal with." The acquittals sometimes indicate other ways in which large families lead to the deaths of children. In the case of Mrs. P. H., aged twenty-nine, the court accepted that she gave her three-year-old son a fatal kick when trying to push him away from the fire "while she was dressing another child, while another was crying out for food" – there were five children altogether (72).

Like other murders, child-murders in England and Wales show a very stable rate. Child-killings by parents numbered 12 in 1957 (last nine months only), 12 in 1958, 13 in 1959, 16 in 1960, 15 in 1961, 14 in 1962. For the whole period, they made up a little over 10 percent of all murders. In the United States in 1964 the percentage was about twice as high. There is, however, evidence that violence against children increased in the 1950s. This appears from analysis of crimes of violence actually dealt with legally in England and Wales during 1950 and 1957: in the second year, the number of attacks on children had doubled (39). This was before the discovery of the battered child syndrome, which will certainly lead to more prosecutions. In the interview given by the Home Office pathologist Keith Simpson (77), he is reported to have said: "I see the problem of battered babies as part of the larger problem of violence which is on the increase in every sphere." He is almost certainly right, but the battered child discovery has been too recent for conclusive direct evidence yet for a continuing increase in private violence against children.

Whatever is eventually established about rates, the evidence we have just considered suggests very strongly that man, like the higher animals, *does* show a reversal of parental behaviour under stress, in all degrees from neglect to killing. It remains to consider whether human violence does indeed fluctuate with conditions, reaching major outbreak proportions in times of population crisis. Our first question concerned the response of the individual, our second the response of societies as wholes. To answer this, we need to use a longer time-scale, and examine the most formidable symptom of human violence – the relative ferocity of wars, and their destructiveness of men, women and children.

Like every other imaginable situation, war offers opportunities for the display of human intelligence and human feelings. But war in itself is, and has always been, a sickening business. The idea that spears and arrows are less horrible than napalm or nuclear missiles is a romantic fallacy. Anyone who doubts this may go to the Landesmuseum in Zürich, stand in front of the life-size tableau of medieval Swiss pikemen, and imagine himself in the opposing front line. Or he can read the account, in Plutarch's *Life of Crassus* (21), of the Battle of Carrhae between Romans and Parthians in 53 B.C. (When Crassus's son urged the Romans to charge the heavily armed Parthian knights, "they showed him their hands nailed to their shields, and their feet stuck to the ground" by the enemy's arrows.) There was still enough fighting with the bayonet in the Second World War to drive home this lesson. Wounds and violent death, however inflicted, are shocking and nauseating. A woman who had been in the Kentucky forts, in the pioneering days of fierce conflict between Indians and white settlers, described her experiences some years afterwards (67). She said that, during her first two years in Kentucky, "the most comely sight she beheld was seeing a young man dying in his bed a natural death." She and some other people had sat up with the corpse all night, "gazing upon him as an object of beauty."

But while war is always horrible, wars do vary in ferocity. A despatch from the British journalist Arthur Cook, dated 19 January 1966, describes one child victim in South Vietnam, and mentions "the constant floating population of 1500 to 2000 child victims" (of American bombing raids) "who reach the provincial hospitals in taxis, bullock carts, on shoulders or on stretchers." (73) Children have not suffered on this scale in every past war. We have seen that in the present century the involvement of civilians in wars has steadily increased, from 5 percent of the (violent) casualties in the First World War, to at least 50 percent in the Second World War and 84 percent in Korea. The proportion of civilians killed is obviously a measure of the slaughter of women and children, and hence of the intensity of the whole violence outbreak, as a means of reducing population. In the Second World War, even this measure is not adequate, for the Russians used women and the Germans used children as front-line fighting troops. But in some quite obvious sense, the First World War was evidently more restrained and less ferocious than the conflict in Korea (62, 70).

This mounting tide of violence is sometimes ascribed to technological advance in weapons or to increasingly total mass conscription in wartime. Neither of these factors, however, will explain the results of a survey of wars between European powers over the last four centuries. To measure these wars is much more difficult, but attempts have been made to do so, and the results are summarised and surveyed in the text and tables of the American sociologist Quincy Wright's monumental *Study of War* (70), first published in 1942 and reissued in a revised edition in 1965 (1679 pages). The problem has been approached in various ways, for instance by assessing numbers of casualties in relation to total populations engaged, and by estimates of the relative involvement of civilians. On all the criteria used, one conclusion is clear. The wars of the eighteenth and nineteenth centuries were more restrained and less ferocious than those of the twentieth *and the seventeenth.*[3] Of the largest-scale wars in this series, by far the most cruel, destructive and unrestrained were the Second

[3]The atrocities of the Napoleonic Wars in Spain (nineteenth century), as depicted in the cartoons of Goya, look just as horrible as those of the Thirty Years War (seventeenth century) pictured by Callot. But there is, almost by definition, little to choose between individual atrocities. The difference between the centuries was one of *scale.*

World War in the twentieth century and the Thirty Years War in the seventeenth (51, 52).

Weapons were far more destructive in the nineteenth century than they were in the seventeenth, and mass conscription far more prevalent. Yet the nineteenth-century wars were the most restrained and least ferocious of the whole series. Why, then, was the seventeenth century a period of such dreadful violence? What does it have in common with the twentieth? The answer lies in the history of European population. Both these centuries were times of acute population crisis. The population of Europe was rising through all four centuries, though there was a slowing-down or halt in this growth in the late seventeenth and early eighteenth centuries. But in the eighteenth, and still more the nineteenth centuries, the surplus was funnelled off by massive emigration of Europeans (18) to temperate regions outside the Continent, especially to North America: more than forty million had left by the onset of the First World War. At the same time, during the eighteenth and nineteenth centuries, the Europeans left in Europe could ease their problems by the massive exploitation of colonial empires outside it. In the nineteenth century, in particular, the invention of the steel plough (54, 64) made it possible to plough up the tough sod of the great North American grassland, and of the Eurasian steppe, for the growing of cereals to feed the hungry mouths of Europe. Hence, during these two centuries, especially the nineteenth, Europe was cushioned against a population crisis by the export of people and the import of food and raw materials. In the seventeenth century no such mitigations were available: the flow of emigration was still only a trickle, the exploitation of the rest of the world was only beginning. In the twentieth century, the flood of emigration was abruptly dammed, especially when the United States, with its lands rapidly filling up, was obliged to put up immigration barriers. The countries of central Europe were short of colonies to exploit. A new population crisis began, first in Germany and Italy, later in the colonial countries as their empires shrank. In short, our own age, like the seventeenth century, is an age of population crisis, and the crisis is growing, just as the ferocity of our wars is on the increase.

It is sometimes argued that war alone is inadequate for significantly reducing the huge populations of modern Europe. But so is the violence in an animal population, considered purely in terms of killing. We have seen that in animals the crisis response works not only through the violence itself, but through the stress it causes, which renders the population vulnerable to disease. And if we survey the history of war, we find that the ages of great violence in the past have indeed been ages when populations rapidly declined, not simply from the wars but from the famine and pestilence for which wars create the ideal conditions, disrupting food production, dislocating trade, weakening public health and transporting crowded bodies of men in unsanitary conditions. We saw that the great advances in modern medicine had reduced this effect by the Second World War, but that nuclear weapons would restore it with a vengeance.

With all that we have learned by now about mass redirection, we need have no difficulty in seeing war as a response to the stresses of a population crisis in each of the contending countries. Indeed it was in this more specific way that Stanislav Andreski formulated his view of civil disturbance and war (2, 3), as "alternative . . . releases of population pressure, as they are alternative methods of organizing emigration to hereafter." Alike at the level of the individual and that of the whole society, the case seems clear that mankind has indeed retained the whole system of violence as a means for drastic population reduction in face of population crisis, and that this, and this alone, is the ultimate significance of human violence. The conclusion is full of hope for mankind, and we may well agree with Andreski that "limitation of the growth of population," and "a determined attempt to bring the majority of the population of the world out of its present condition of misery, offers the best hope of abolishing war." Equipped with this general conclusion and this powerful incentive, we are now ready to consider the characteristics of population crises in the huge societies of civilised man. In studying population crises, we can approach an understanding of the age we live in today.

3

While man practised food-gathering and scavenging, hunting, and even shifting cultivation, his situation was not fundamentally different from that of monkeys, from the point of view of population control. Gradually improving techniques of food-getting enabled his populations to grow, and the control of fire gave him access to a wide variety of climatic regions. But his communities seem to have remained small; he spread over the world by the ordinary "monkey" process of band-splitting. Fundamental changes did occur, however, when man began the practise of *settled* agriculture, which enabled him to continue indefinitely growing crops on the *same* plot of land, by means of irrigation and silt, or rotations and animal manure. One result was the appearance of attachment to a fixed territory, evident in the peasant's passionate concern with the bit of land where he makes his livelihood. Another result was the formation of communities enormously large by monkey standards. The vastly greater amounts of food produced by settled agriculture made possible a large population in a small area. Since each peasant could produce more than he and his family could consume, the surplus supported craftsmen, priest-bureaucrats and other full-time specialists. The new, large communities built towns to live in, and these rapidly increased in size; the increase can be seen, for instance, in the succession of settlements on the site of Jericho from about the eighth millennium B.C. By the fourth millennium B.C. sizeable cities had developed in ancient Iraq; at least by the second millennium B.C., they had attained populations of several hundred thousand (15, 43, 64, 69).

We naturally have no direct evidence about this crucial transition. But, surprisingly, we have a clue to what may have happened in the observations of the Japanese zoologist Hiroki Mizuhara on the band of Japanese monkeys at Mount Takasaki (40, 53). In this "open zoo," where visitors as well as scientists were providing food on the spot, the attractions of a fixed feeding-ground made the monkeys curtail their normal foraging trips in the forest. As their numbers grew, the normal band-splitting process was delayed, creating a kind of population pressure which had dramatic results. When scientists began to feed this band in 1953, the total population was less than 200. There were six leaders and ten sub-leaders, all other males being cadets, By 1956 the population had increased to 440, but there were still only six leaders and ten sub-leaders. It was not until 1959 that the band finally split. Until this occurred, there was considerable tension. The six leaders were Jupiter, Titan, Pan, Monk, Bacchus and Boor, in that rank order. In 1956-7, Monk took a long vacation (180 days) and Pan abdicated; both eventually became solitaries. It is possible that, although not initially driven out, they could not stand the increasing tension in the band. In the summer of 1956, Bacchus took a short holiday (80 days); on his return, he was accepted back into the leader class, but demoted below Boor in rank. So by the start of 1957, the effective leaders were, in order, Jupiter, Titan, Boor and Bacchus.

In the period 15-19 January 1957, some of the sub-leaders attempted a *coup d'état*. Jupiter had disappeared for a day, and came back wounded and shaken, perhaps after a fight with a solitary male. Immediately after his return, his lieutenant, Titan, quarrelled with him. There was a free-for-all, which Mizuhara could unfortunately not observe closely, since dusk was falling; but when it was over, Jupiter was closely accompanied by Uzen and Kuro, the fourth-rank and fifth-rank sub-leaders, while Titan was isolated and "estranged, as if he were a solitary male in the central part." It appears that the sub-leaders had taken advantage of the unwonted tension between Jupiter and Titan to infiltrate the leadership. On the 16th, they appeared to be dominant over Titan, and Mizuhara suggests that they had combined with Jupiter against Titan in the unobserved battle. After submitting to Uzen and Kuro, Titan redirected his resentment against the first-rank sub-leader, Achilles, chasing and attacking him. The demarcation between leaders and sub-leaders was by now so blurred that Achilles, redirecting in his turn, attacked and dominated Bacchus, currently the lowest-rank leader.

By the 17th, however, normal relations had been restored between Jupiter and Titan, and Uzen and Kuro were decisively driven out of the central circle. With monkey opportunism, Bacchus had helped Titan to punish these presumptuous sub-leaders, and this restored his own position; by the 19th he was definitely dominant over Achilles, and had even recovered his own old rank among the leaders, dominating Boor. Jupiter tolerated all these proceedings. It was one thing for him to use the middle classes to teach Titan a lesson; it would have been quite another to let these upstarts stay indefinitely in the boss circle. In the long run, the solidarity of the leaders made it quite impossible for sub-leaders permanently to rise out of their own class.

A similar barrier was evident between the sub-leaders and cadets. In 1955, the first-rank cadet, Soba, seemed to be ripe for promotion to sub-leader; he was ten years old, very active, and regularly herded females who had strayed into the periphery. But during this year, he gradually lost his influence even there, and by the end of the year he had left to become a solitary. Between 1955 and 1959, two other cadets, Gen and Don, went through the same experience in succession, each reaching first cadet rank, occasionally penetrating the court, gradually losing influence, and finally leaving. Two more cadets became solitaries without even reaching first cadet rank. When the band finally split, the next three cadets, after Soba, Gen and Don, became leaders of the "daughter" band, but even they had already suffered from a similar discouragement, and in the new band they were subordinate in rank to much younger males. Mizuhara has aptly called this group of cadets a lost generation, and the first rank in such a group the "jinx" position, where the discouraging effects of totally blocked ambition were most keenly felt. Unable to obtain employment for their obvious gifts as potential sub-leaders, these cadets had no alternative but to emigrate.

The Japanese monkeys have all the ingredients (including family influence) for developing a true class system, that is, one in which some individuals remain in a lower class all their lives. But at Mount Takasaki they proved unable to tolerate the tensions of such an arrangement – the band finally did split, resolving the tensions in the traditional monkey way. Man must have been more flexible: he succeeded in settling in towns, and enduring the division into classes which at once appeared in these large communities (53). Differences in housing in the Indus cities, differences in the richness of early Egyptian graves, attest the appearance of true classes in the earliest civilisations. In ancient Iraq, by the early third millennium B.C., the reforming leader Urukagina of Lagash was indignantly listing the gross inequalities between the priests and the lower classes. He tried in vain to restore the old order "as it had existed from the beginning." Class division was here to stay (15, 69). What we have said of hierarchies can, of course, be applied to classes. With ample mobility between them, with no serious inequality of privilege, classes could be simply a convenient basis for public order and leadership functions. In fact, throughout history they have nearly always been more or less rigid and more or less grossly unequal in rights. Against this persistent background of tension, which only modern technological resources could eliminate forever, the sharp barriers and glaring inequalities of the population crisis periods stand out luridly. Just as mice can shift from territorial to hierarchical systems, but are then extremely sensitive to food shortage, so human societies have shown a muttering ground level of tension ready to swell into a roar of violence whenever resources ran short.

The individuals in a hierarchy recognise each other as individuals, and respond accordingly. Class status, on the other hand, may be signalled without individual recognition, by insignia of rank, by costly robes, armour, wigs, swords, and, even today, by the persistent status symbol of speech accent. It was clear in our comparison of monkey zoo colonies with human societies that all the inequalities produced by crowding between monkey individuals translate, in terms of human history, into inequalities between classes. Moreover, in the huge communities of man, class division is complicated by labour division and the fact that members of one class may employ and/or exploit members of another. Traces of this relationship may indeed be observed even in monkey bands. Subordinate monkeys may obtain tolerance and even protection from superiors by grooming their fur, in a client-patron relationship involving personal service. On the islet of Kōshima, Japanese scientists once buried some food in the sight of a monkey band. The president made a perfunctory scratching at the surface, and withdrew. Immediately, the other monkeys set to work and cleared the trench. The president now returned, and the others scattered, leaving him to select the best of the food at his leisure. This suggests a potentiality for labour exploitation, but of course it is unlikely to be realised in the natural surroundings of monkeys, where food is obtained without this kind of labour. In man, relations of employment and exploitation produce a much more complex situation; yet, as we shall see, the basic principles of the population crisis remain much the same.

Except in northwestern Europe after about 1600, and elsewhere in the twentieth century, the settled civilisations of mankind have generally had high death-rates (3-4 percent) but even higher birth-rates (3.5-5 percent), made possible by the food production of settled agriculture (18, 25, 51, 54, 57). Populations therefore have generally increased by up to 1 percent each year. They have not ended up as a sphere of living flesh, etc., because every so often they have been cut down to size by a catastrophic death-rate of 15-50 percent. History everywhere thus consists of population cycles, which again and again reach a crisis. In certain cases, crowding and bad housing have become important before food shortage. But whether a population outran its food supply or other resources, many of the features of the crisis have been similar, and these we shall consider first. The crisis period begins when population growth begins to outstrip production. Public health is weakened by malnutrition, the stresses of social tension and the effects of increasing violence. The end of every past crisis has been a drastic lowering of the population by epidemics of disease. These are not necessarily especially virulent in themselves, but kill large numbers because they attack a population in poor health, just as among animals. Modern medicine, not without continual struggle and vigilance, is keeping this final killer at bay; but of course a nuclear war would instantly unleash the ultimate horrors of the continent-wide epidemic, or pandemic.

To get a perspective on the modern crisis in the "affluent" societies, it will be enough at this stage to consider in outline the population cycles of European history. These are unusual in that an exceptional amount of creative advance was made in the *non*-crisis periods, when population was growing but still in step with production, and tensions and violence were at a minimum. The resulting momentum of progress has been able to carry Europe forwards even through the crises, in an advance interrupted only when violence and the other disasters were at their worst.[4] Hence the extraordinarily confused and ambivalent nature of the age we live in. The momentum of technical progress is carrying us forward at an unprecedented rate, with continual technical advances which can have profoundly valuable social results

[4]The reasons for the phenomenal success of Europe have nothing to do with any kind of "racial superiority"; they can ultimately be related to factors of soil and climate. These reasons are too complex to be discussed here; the whole problem has been explored by W. M. S. Russell in a recent book, *Man, Nature and History* (1967).

(for instance, the potential educative effects of television, which can arouse and in part satisfy an increasing thirst for facts on the part of the whole public). Meanwhile we are experiencing all the growing tensions of what could be the worst population crisis in history. This is the predicament we have to understand; for the first time in history, we have scientific resources which could release us forever from the problems of violence and population crisis.

For the ancient Mediterranean world, evidence about population is naturally scanty and inexact. It is enough, however, to give us an outline picture of the cycles (54). European civilisation began in Greece, which was almost continuously subject to population pressure on its meagre food resources. In the early first millennium B.C., the pressure was relieved (monkey fashion) in a great surge of migration, which planted Greek colonies all over the coasts of the Mediterranean and Black Sea. Meanwhile a few Greek cities (notably Athens and Corinth) began to specialise in industry and commerce, importing their food from Sicily or southern Russia. Athens was assisted by the possession of the most productive silver mines of that age. The result was the flowering of Greek civilisation in the sixth to fifth centuries B.C. But by this time the migration was being blocked by a similar movement based on the coast of the Lebanon, the migration of the Phoenicians. Also, inevitably, industries began to spread to areas outside Greece, which lost its bargaining position. In the late fifth and fourth centuries, Greece experienced a major population crisis. Further relief came when Alexander the Great conquered the Near East and planted Greek cities all over it, but by this time the civilisation had been seriously affected, and the crisis continued in mainland Greece. Civilisation and population pressure came somewhat later to Italy. The Italians dealt with it in part by migration but chiefly by the military conquests which created the Roman Empire. The wealth and culture of this empire were not based on adequate food production at home, but on the possession of military power and looted capital in precious metals; most of the food came from colonial exploitation of the Near East and North Africa. Archaeological evidence (for instance, from aerial survey, which shows the extent of cultivated land at various periods [64]) suggests that the population of the Roman Empire was growing, with periodic retreats, right up to the sixth century A.D. But there was a chronic imbalance of payments, and the precious metals inevitably drained East, where the food they symbolised was actually produced. The result was an unusually protracted and dreadful population crisis, which extended from the third to the sixth centuries A.D. The crisis ended with the pandemic of the sixth century (mainly bubonic plague), which lasted sixty years and killed between one-third and one-half the populations of the Empire. The western part of the Empire had already declined and fallen; according to the German historian Fritz Heichelheim, the enormous deathrate of the pandemic so disrupted society that Latin and classical Greek "ceased to be living languages." (64)

Before they went under, Greece and Rome had prepared, and bequeathed, two of the ingredients of the final technological breakthrough: fundamental science, a way of organising technical research; and contract law, a way of organising business transactions. The third ingredient was supplied in the early Middle Ages by the peoples of northwestern Europe: a new and passionate interest in the technology of power and machines, coupled with a new and boundless confidence in the technical progress of mankind. By the twelfth century A.D. they had begun work on the Gothic cathedrals, an enterprise as daring for its time (and as rich in technical by-products or "fall-out") as the space programmes of their spiritual successors today. From this century on, Europe was committed to the technological way of life which has transformed the world. Most of the great creative developments occurred in the intervals between crises, when population pressure was relieved. The north Italian Renaissance bloomed in the fifteenth century; the marvels of modern science emerged in that incredibly creative period from the late seventeenth to the early twentieth century, on whose achievement our present technical advances are based. But from the twelfth century onwards the momentum was so great that technical progress continued throughout the frightful population crises that followed; and with technical progress there came, in the long run, progress in the organisation of society (54, 57, 68).

The population growth of Europe was based on a series of technical improvements in agriculture. These began in the seventh century A.D., with special spurts of advance in the non-crisis periods – the eleventh century, fifteenth century, eighteenth and, above all, nineteenth century. But population repeatedly grew faster than food production, and every time it outstripped production a crisis developed. We can dimly discern a crisis in the ninth century A.D., but know very little about it. The first major crisis occurred in the thirteenth and fourteenth centuries (54, 57, 64). Under the pressure of population growth, crop cultivation spread to areas of poor soil, for which its techniques were still inadequate; by the end of the thirteenth century, these marginal areas were beginning to show crop failures, and the extent of cultivation began to shrink; hundreds of pioneer settlements in Germany were abandoned. In 1315-17 there was a catastrophic famine. By this time millions of people were short of protein, and when the Black Death (bubonic and pneumonic plague) struck in 1347, the death-rate was colossal (46, 57). The plague was not, in itself, terribly virulent. The northern Dutch, who continued to raise plenty of stock and to eat meat, and who maintained an independent peasant republic, and had no large towns to attract invaders, were little affected by the pandemic. The majority of Europeans, weakened by malnutrition and the stresses of social tension and war, died in the millions. In five years the Black Death killed between one-third and one-half of the population of Europe. The death-roll drawn up by Pope Clement VI's statisticians came to 42,836,486.[5] The transitional languages of medieval times gave way to the national languages of modern Europe.

---

[5] This medieval estimate is probably not as wildly exaggerated as it looks. A careful modern study, by the British historian M. K. Bennett (1954), gives the following estimates for the population of Europe at different dates (**A.D.**):

1200 A.D. 61 millions   1300 A.D. 73 millions   1400 A.D. 45 millions

It is true that there were serious epidemics in the fourteenth century besides the Black Death, both before and after it.

The fifteenth century was an age of relief, when nutrition and living standards improved and violence was less devastating. By the sixteenth century, the populations had again begun to grow too big, and another crisis set in, to last until the second half of the seventeenth century. The people's diet worsened again; on the manor of Gripsholm, in Sweden, the number of calories (energy supply from food) dropped by about a third between 1555 and 1653 (57). Violence became appalling; this time it led, not to a pandemic, but to an endless succession of epidemics. Germany suffered worst this time; on the most cautious estimates, her population dropped from 21 to 13.5 millions during the Thirty Years War (10, 57). The population of Europe as a whole does not seem to have fallen much, but population growth virtually stopped for a long time. By the mid-eighteenth century it started again, but in a changed situation. From the sixteenth century onwards, northwestern Europe began to have somewhat lower death-rates and birth-rates in normal years (25). The natural increase even so, from the mid-eighteenth century onwards, was enormous; it has been estimated that Europeans (at home and abroad) made up about 22 percent of the world population in 1800, and about 35 percent in 1930. But northwestern Europe was no longer depending on its own food production. From the sixteenth century, it imported grain from eastern Europe. At this stage it was still vulnerable to the unusual event of a bad harvest at both ends of the Continent. But in the eighteenth, and above all the nineteenth century, it began to import from the newly exploited temperate regions of the world outside Europe, especially from the great grassland belts opened up by the steel plough. In addition, it was exploiting other world regions on a massive scale, and thus preserving, on the whole, the standards of living of Europeans. Finally, as we have seen, more than 40 million Europeans emigrated. Europe was still pursuing the old colonial methods of Greece and Rome. The result of all this was a temporary relief from population crisis in its worst forms, leading, as we have seen, to a measure of restraint even in warfare (18, 25, 54, 57, 64).

The twentieth century has seen the end of both mass migration and colonial empires, and a gradual build-up to the full-scale crisis in which we are now involved. Except in Germany and Italy (which had no adequate empires), the crisis was somewhat delayed by a considerable fall in the European birth-rate. After the Second World War, the birth-rate in northwestern Europe and the United States began to rise again. At first this was believed to be the usual temporary consequence of return to peace (soldiers reunited with their wives, marriages of people who had had to wait). But by the early 1950s it became evident that the rise in the birth-rate of the "affluent" societies was continuing, creating a more and more alarming situation, for by now our normal death-rates are lower than ever before in history. In all the "affluent" societies, populations have been increasing at a frightening rate, since about the year 1950, that year which we have already seen as such a turning-point in our affairs (18, 51, 54, 65). The latest European crisis period has begun. What happens in this kind of epoch?

There are some characteristics of excessive population growth that can only appear in the complex societies of human civilisation, though they, too, play a part in bringing about all the responses of an animal population crisis. To begin with, we must notice one simple principle. If anything grows faster than the population, the result is a glut or congestion; if anything grows slower, the result is a shortage. The most outstanding lags occur in the production of food and housing, but the basic principle of relative growth rate applies to many other things. Sometimes a relative rate can change. A case in point is the growth in cities in the early stages of industrialisation. When a critical point is reached, more and more country people flock to the cities. In the United States, country and city people increased in numbers at about equal rates until around 1850; from then onwards, every rise in total population meant a greater proportional rise in city population: hence bigger and bigger cities (44). The same thing is now happening in the developing countries. Leopoldville (Kinshasa) in the Congo increased by 13,000 people per year in 1950-60; in the same period, the population living in towns in India rose by 42.8 percent. (One consequence is an alarming spread of certain diseases, such as filariasis [22], also called elephantiasis, carried by a species of mosquito that breeds in polluted drain-water.) After a certain stage of industrialisation is reached, however, people begin to move out of the larger cities to suburbs and/or the smaller towns (65). In modern Britain and the United States, it is these units that are swelling most rapidly.

Where most things are concerned, however, relative rates are fixed, at least within certain limits, so that rapid population growth results inevitably in certain gluts or shortages.

. . . .

Shortage of skilled, glut of unskilled labour: the obvious answer is more education and training. This is, indeed, a necessary step in the transition to the marvellous civilisation we could have by means of complete automation. But unfortunately, teachers themselves need prolonged and intensive education and training. And just as a medieval farmer, in a bad year, might have to eat some of the grain he needed for next year's seed, so, when skilled man-power is short, some potential teachers have to be used in their generation for other skilled purposes. In the present population crisis, the lag between the production of pupils and the production of teachers is making a more and more serious shortage. Imaginative use of television may ease the problem, but it has its limitations: the students at Berkeley (California) literally revolted against the impersonal quality of amateurishly produced closed-circuit teaching programmes. In the county of Surrey alone, at the present rate of population growth, places will have to be found by 1972 for more than 30,000 additional pupils. In 1965 there were more than two million British primary school children in classes of thirty-six or more (78); this degree of crowding is itself conducive more to violence than to education. In order to reduce classes to thirty or less, Britain will need, within the next ten years, almost double the present teaching force of approximately 300,000 (78). In the Federal Republic of Germany, a leading educationalist, Dr. Hildegard Hamm-Bruecher, forecast in 1965 that within five years the country would be short of 300,000 teachers for an estimated eleven million children. Automation needs a smaller *total* labour force than the present one, so even training all the semi-skilled would not eliminate unemployment if the present rate of population growth continues. But, far from achieving this, the continuation of the crisis can only lead to a *decline* in education and cultural levels. A steady decline of this kind was a prominent feature of the protracted population crisis of the Roman Empire.

That Empire also provides a good example of another effect of population pressure. In the course of the dreadful third century A.D., when the crisis was in its worst phase, the price of bread rose to more than 12,000 times the amount it cost in the second century (49). In effect, the value of money completely collapsed, and society was reorganised on a totalitarian basis, with serfs on the land and everyone compelled to follow the trade of his father. In this particular crisis, precious metals were flowing out of the region. But a rise in prices has been a feature of every population crisis in the history of Europe. Where the society has retained its currency, the effect has been a price revolution, or permanent fall (without complete collapse) in the value of money. The effect is due to two things. First, rising population increases the demand, and therefore the price, of essentials such as cereal grain, flour and bread; other goods gradually rise in price by a chain reaction. Second, the tensions of the crisis lead to increased wastage of real resources on "defence" expenditure.

. . . .

Unemployment, shrinking education and price revolutions are all obviously liable to increase real inequality between classes, and we have seen that inequality is increasing in modern Britain (24) and (steeply) in the modern United States (76). With this effect, we are back in the world of animal population crises, and all the complexities in human societies add up to the same fundamental consequences. The non-crisis periods in European history have regularly seen relatively free movement between classes and the birth or rebirth of democratic institutions; the crisis periods have seen the hardening of class barriers, the growth of serious inequality between classes, and the suppression of older liberties. The supreme expression of inequality is sadistic pseudosex, and legal torture has been abolished and reimposed several times in the history of Europe: it was restored in sixteenth-century Germany, for instance, by the Holy Roman Emperor Charles V. In the long crisis of the Roman Empire, cruel methods of execution, originally restricted to slaves, were gradually extended to the whole population.

. . . .

Along with social inequality, the crisis periods have brought a suppression of individual freedom and privacy, the fundamental territorial rights. In Leyhausen's terms, in man as in cats, relative hierarchy is converted to absolute hierarchy. Leyhausen himself has expressed this well (38):

> Overcrowded conditions are thus a danger to true democracy. . . . Tyranny is the almost inevitable result, whether it be exercised by personal tyrants or

> by an abstract principle like the Common Good, which is no longer any good at all to the mass of individuals. *For this is an unalterable law:* as long as density is tolerable, sacrifices made for a common cause will, one way or another, pay dividends to the individual and contribute to his own fulfilment. Beyond this point, however, the demands of the Common Good rise steeply, and what is taken away from the individual is gone for good; he cannot even see that it goes in any sizeable amount to others, for they are likewise robbed without reward (his italics).

. . . .

Growing social inequality and loss of individual rights are, as we have abundantly seen, features of animal population crises. Whether monkeys, under crowding, become less tolerant of departures from the cultural traditions of a given band, is an interesting research problem yet to be studied. In the human societies of Europe, the population crises have always brought increased intolerance and increased censorship of minority thought, practices and communications. The crisis in ancient Athens brought with it a fierce intolerance of criticism, real or imagined, of the state religion, typified by a savage witch-hunt in 415, and by the conviction of Socrates in 399 B.C. Similar trends can be observed in the Roman Empire, sixteenth-century Europe (in both Catholic and Protestant states), and the modern United States, where Senator Joseph McCarthy was able to ruin a great many people by accusing them of Communist sympathies and "un-American" activities. In the United States, indeed, the trend is opposed by new factors, such as television, as well as by robust traditions of free speech, which sometimes take delightfully piquant forms. Harvey Matusow, one of the Senator's paid informers, eventually repented of his work, and wrote a book about it, called *False Witness,* which was accepted by a publisher. A court order was made for the confiscation of the manuscript. The publisher defied the order at a television and press conference, and the order was withdrawn. A succession of New York printers were browbeaten into refusing the book by agents of the Federal Bureau of Investigation: in one case the work was actually taken off the press. Finally, however, one sturdy printer, a staunch conservative Republican, "having forced an admission from the F.B.I. agents that nothing in the book was illegal, turned them out of his office, saying . . . that their governmental interference with private business was socialistic and un-American." (32) Conservatives (in the general sense of the word), who always take some earlier period as their reference-point, may of course favour or oppose movements of freedom and equality: it depends whether their reference-point lies in a non-crisis or crisis epoch.

The European Middle Ages offer a striking example of the gradual destruction, as the crisis developed, of a really remarkable level of freedom of thought and speech. In the twelfth century virtually anything could be freely discussed and written about. Public debates between Catholics and the more organised heretics continued until 1204, the proceedings being controlled by a jury of twenty-six, on which each side was equally represented. The University of Paris retained its freedom rather a long time; there, as late as the mid-thirteenth century, Siger of Brabant was openly teaching a frankly atheist view of the universe; he denied the creation of the world and the immortality of the soul, and argued that religion was needed only to control the masses, and superfluous for educated people. There are universities today (for instance, in the southern states of America) where Siger could hardly teach as he did. This wide tolerance naturally gave opportunities to those who were trying to reabsorb, via the scholars of Islam, ancient Greek principles of fundamental science. Christians, Moslems and Jews worked freely together in scientific information bureaux under royal patronage, in Spain and Sicily and Provence.

In the course of the thirteenth century, as population pressure rose, all this was drastically changed (29, 54). Siger's own views were condemned by the Church in 1270, and he himself was murdered, while in the custody of papal officers, in 1282. The century witnessed a whole series of such condemnations of leading thinkers and writers, together with the founding of the Inquisition by Pope Innocent III, and the ferocious crusade against Provence, where organised heresy was especially prevalent, though there were Catholic nobles on the Provençal side, including some from Spain who had been fighting the Moslems. This war raged from 1208 to 1229, and destroyed the magnificent Provençal civilisation. In 1231 and 1232 Pope and Emperor, respectively, introduced into their dominions the penalty of burning at the stake for heretics. By the fourteenth century, almost any kind of saying or writing outside the very narrow (and constantly changing) orthodoxy approved at the papal court became heresy, or, as we might call it today, revisionism.

Growing intolerance of this kind formed the background for mass redirection of resentment to minority groups who were more vulnerable than the upper classes. Once again we are on familiar monkey ground; but of course, in these human societies, the scale of cruelty and killing was enormously greater. In the thirteenth century, the victims were chiefly heretics, accused of beliefs and practices contrary to Catholic orthodoxy. The massacre began in Provence, and continued over the rest of Europe. Mass redirection in human societies is liable to get out of hand, and lynchings often went further than the authorities desired. In 1233 Conrad of Marburg (29) was made Chief Inquisitor of Germany. Assisted by his sinister colleagues, Conrad Dorso and John the One-handed and One-eyed, he stirred up the masses into an orgy of lynchings, in which men and women of all social classes were often accused and burned on the same day. This medieval Hitler reduced all Germany to terror for two years. The local bishops were completely intimidated, but the local nobles declined to put up with this indiscriminate campaign; some of their knights assassinated Conrad in 1233. Only then did the Archbishop of Mainz dare to report to Pope Gregory IX, who was deeply shocked. The persecution of heretics nevertheless continued fiercely throughout the century. In the following (fourteenth) century, the chief victims were the Jews, assailed by the most terrible *pogrom* before Nazi times (29, 46), and the "witches," people accused of the enigmatic crime of witchcraft. A second appalling wave of witch-hunting developed from the late fifteenth to the early seventeenth centuries, during the next crisis. In the course of the mass redirections against heretics, Jews and witches, many thousands of people perished.

The Jews were, of course, completely innocent of the various charges brought against them (usually poisoning wells and spreading plague). The more intelligent fourteenth-century chroniclers were perfectly aware of this: the money of the Jews, wrote one of these chroniclers, was "the poison which brought their death." "If the Jews had been poor, and rulers of the countries had not been in their debt," wrote another, "they would never have been burnt." Growing financial activity by Christian bankers, who saw the Jews as rivals, was another obvious factor in steering the redirection this way. Thousands of victims accused of heresy were probably "innocent" of even this "crime," succumbing to personal enmities or the ravings of other victims under torture, or, of course, like the Jews, to debtors or those who coveted their wealth. The actual heretics themselves seem to have been rather decent, if somewhat priggish people, to judge from the desperate plea of one poor wretch to the Inquisitors of Toulouse in 1230. "Lords: hear me," he implored, "I am no heretic; for I . . . lie and swear, and am a faithful Christian." (31)

In the conditions of the witch-hunts, where torture was unsparingly used and no ordinary legal rights were conceded to the accused, thousands of totally innocent people undoubtedly also perished. At Bamberg, on 24 July 1628, the Burgomaster smuggled a heart-rending letter to his daughter from his prison cell. The executioner, himself appalled by the tortures he was inflicting on the Burgomaster, had begged him to confess "something, whether it be true or not," and he had finally admitted to being a witch. "For whoever comes into the witch prison must become a witch or be tortured until he invents something out of his head." The writer begged his daughter to conceal the letter, which asserted his innocence, "else I shall be tortured most piteously. . . . Good night, for your father Johannes Junius will never see you more." On the margin, he added a note, stating that six other victims had accused him, "all false, through compulsion, as they have told me, and begged my forgiveness in God's name before they were executed." (31)

. . . .

We have already seen that increased ferocity in war, with fewer restraints and greater civilian involvement, was characteristic of the seventeenth- and twentieth-century crisis periods. In earlier ages, accurate figures are, of course, much harder to come by, but the general impression bears out the main principle. The wars between Greeks in the late fifth and fourth centuries were certainly much less restrained than those before and after this period: in the third century, there were all sorts of "rules of war," providing a certain protection for both soldiers and civilians (13). In thirteenth-century Europe, the Swiss (48) introduced not only horrible new weapons but the principle of killing all prisoners; this kind of atrocity at first shocked all the other states, but naturally spread. Historians of military technology have noticed an alternation between the predominance of weapons of defence and attack. This cycle roughly but imperfectly coincides with non-crisis and crisis periods. A survey of all the crises leaves little doubt that warfare in these periods pulled no punches and knew few rules or restraints. An interesting and quite regular feature of the crisis periods was that their earlier wars were ideological; their later wars, perhaps through a greater efficiency in organising mass redirection, were between geographical units.[6] The Peloponnesian War of the late fifth century B.C. was a fierce ideological conflict between Democrats and Oligarchs: the fourth-century wars were between shifting combinations of states with no ideological dividing lines. The wars of the thirteenth century were ideological: the crusade against Provence, and the ferocious conflict between Guelphs and Ghibellines (supporters of the Popes and the Hohenstaufen Emperors, respectively); the wars of the fourteenth century were national wars, like that between England and France. The same transition was evident in the sixteenth and seventeenth centuries, where Protestant-Catholic conflict gave way to wars between national combinations irrespective of religion. We seem to be at a turning-point in a similar transition, after the Communist-Capitalist conflict of the Cold War: France is withdrawing from the American alliance, China and the Soviet Union are becoming increasingly hostile to each other. It is sometimes suggested that ideological wars are particularly cruel, but this is doubtful. By the middle of the particularly appalling Thirty Years War in the seventeenth century, there were plenty of Catholics in the armies of the Protestant states, and vice versa.

Every time the population of Europe rose, the event was marked by a great extension of cultivated land, driving into the great forest that once covered all Europe. Every time a crisis developed, cultivated land retreated and the forest returned: there are places in Europe which were probably more densely populated in the thirteenth century than they are today. During these retreats floods and erosion damaged the land in some places. But these disasters were minor and easily reversible, and each time, as the population rose again, the clearing of the forest was resumed. The special climatic conditions of Europe permitted a rapid recovery of areas lost for a time to cultivation. Hence the violence of the crisis periods did no permanent damage to the natural resources of Europe (54, 57, 64). If we ignore the frightful load of suffering and the interruption of technical and social progress, then we can say that the violence of the population crises fulfilled its old animal function. It dealt with excessive population growth in such a way that no resources were permanently damaged, and there was always food available for the recovering populations. But this has not been so in all regions of the world. We have seen how in one vast belt, stretching from Morocco to Turkestan, the violence of crisis periods eventually destroyed the resources of the land, making the whole belt a region of poverty today. Nuclear war could have the same disastrous effect over the whole earth, even in the most favoured and temperate regions. Hence violence in man can no longer serve the fundamental function for which it was evolved in animals – the conservation of the natural resources of a species. On the contrary, it threatens to do the

---

[6]Differences in ideology are connected with differences in levels of economic development; patterns of development may change considerably in the course of decades, within and between regions.

exact opposite, destroying irretrievably the food resources on which our species must depend in the future. Even if we could tolerate the cruelty and waste of violence, we can no longer afford its terrible destructiveness. Instead, we must find a way to control our population growth by other means, to bring the present crisis peacefully to an end, and to ensure that it is the last in human history.

References

1. Abel-Smith, B., and Townsend, P. 1965. *The Poor and the Poorest.* London: Bell & Sons.
2. Andreski, S. 1964. *Elements of Comparative Sociology.* London: Weidenfeld & Nicolson.
3. ____. 1966. *Parasitism and Subversion: the Case of Latin America.* London: Weidenfeld & Nicolson.
4. Aumann, G. D., and Emlen, J. T. 1965. Relation of Population Density to Sodium Availability and Sodium Selection in Microtine Rodents. *Nature,* 208, pp. 198-9.
5. Barlow, N. (ed.). 1958. *The Autobiography of Charles Darwin, 1809-1882.* London: Collins.
6. Barnett, B. 1965. Witchcraft, Psychopathology and Hallucinations. *British J. Psychiatry,* 111, pp. 439-45.
7. Beer, Sir Gavin De (ed.). 1958. *Evolution by Natural Selection: Darwin and Wallace.* Cambridge University Press.
8. Berelson, B., and Freedman, R. 1964. A Study in Fertility Control (in Formosa). *Scientific American,* 210, 5.
9. Bloch, M. 1965. *Feudal Society,* trans. L. A. Manyon, 2 vols. London: Routledge & Kegan Paul.
10. Bruford, W. H. 1965. *Germany in the 18th Century: the Social Background of the Literary Revival.* Cambridge University Press.
11. Carpenter, C. R. 1964. *Naturalistic Behaviour of Non-Human Primates.* University Park, Pa.: Pennsylvania State University Press.
12. Carthy, J. D., and Ebling, F. J. (ed.). 1964. *The Natural History of Aggression.* London and New York: Academic Press.
13. Cary, M. 1932. *A History of the Greek World, from 323 to 146 B.C.* London: Methuen.
14. Chance, M. R. A., and Mackintosh, J. H. 1962. The Effects of Caging. *Laboratory Animals Centre Collected Papers,* 11, pp. 59-64.
15. Childe, V. G. 1942. *What Happened in History.* Harmondsworth: Penguin.
16. Chitty, D. 1954. Tuberculosis and Wild Voles: with a Discussion of Other, Pathological Conditions among Certain Mammals and Birds. *Ecology,* 35, pp. 227-37.
17. Christian, J. J. 1964. Physiological and Pathological Correlates of Population Density. *Proceedings of the Royal Society of Medicine,* 57, pp. 169-74.
18. Cipolla, C. 1962. *The Economic History of World Population.* Harmondsworth: Penguin.
19. Clarke, J. R. 1953. The Effect of Fighting on the Adrenals, Thymus and Spleen of the Vole (*Microtus agrestis*). *J. Endocrinology,* 9, pp. 114-26.
20. ____. 1955. Influence of Numbers on Reproduction and Survival in Two Experimental Vole Populations. *Proceedings of the Royal Society B,* 144, pp. 68-85.
21. Clough, A. H. (ed. and trans.). 1910. *Plutarch's Lives* (vol. 2). London: Dent.
22. Collins, P. 1965. Urbanization and Filariasis. *Span,* 8, pp. 169-71.
23. Devore, I. (ed.). 1965. *Primate Behaviour, Field Studies of Monkeys and Apes.* New York: Holt, Rinehart & Winston.
24. Gibson, T. 1965. *Breaking in the Future* (on British housing prices). London: Zenith Books.
25. Glass, D. V., and Eversley, D. E. C. (ed.). 1965. *Population in History.* London: Arnold.

26. Godfrey, G., and Crowcroft, P. 1960. *The Life of the Mole (Talpa europea* Linnaeus). London: Museum Press.

27. Harrison, C. J. O. 1965. Allopreening as Agonistic Behaviour. *Behaviour,* 24, pp. 161-209.

28. Hediger, H. 1955. *Studies of the Psychology and Behaviour of Animals in Zoos and Circuses.* London: Butterworth's Scientific Publications.

29. Heer, F. 1963. *The Mediaeval World. Europe 1100-1350,* trans. J. Sondheimer. New York: New American Library.

30. Hemphill, R. E. 1966. Historical Witchcraft and Psychiatric Illness in Western Europe. *Proceedings of the Royal Society of Medicine,* 59, pp. 891-901.

31. Hughes, P. 1965. *Witchcraft.* Harmondsworth: Penguin.

32. Joesten, J. 1964. *Oswald – Assassin or Fall Guy?*(on Joseph McCarthy). London: Merlin Press.

33. Kabat, C., Collias, N. E., and Guettinger, R. C. 1953. Some Winter Habits of White-Tailed Deer and the Development of Census Methods in the Flag Yard of Northern Wisconsin. *Technical Wildlife Bulletin,* 7, Madison, Wisconsin Conservation Department.

34. Kempe, C. H., Silverman, F. N., Steele, B. F., Droegemuller, W., and Silver, H. K. 1962. The Battered Child Syndrome. *J. American Medical Association,* 181, pp. 17-24.

35. Kolko, G. 1962. *Wealth and Power in America.* London: Thames & Hudson.

36. Kummer, H. 1967. *Social Organization of Hamadryas Baboons.* Basle: Karger.

37. Leyhausen, P. 1965. The Communal Organization of Solitary Mammals. *Symposia of the Zoological Society of London,* 14, pp. 249-63.

38. ____. 1965. The Sane Community – a Density Problem? *Discovery,* 26, 9, pp. 27-33.

39. McClintock, F. H. 1963. *Crimes of Violence.* London: Macmillan.

40. Mizuhara, H. 1964. Social Changes of Japanese Monkey Troops in Takasakiyama. *Primates,* 5, pp. 27-52.

41. Morris, R., and Morris, D. 1966. *Men and Apes.* London: Hutchinson.

42. Morris, T., and Blom-Cooper, L. 1964. *A Calendar of Murder. Criminal Homicide in England since 1957.* London: Michael Joseph.

43. Mumford, L. 1961. *The City in History.* London: Secker & Warburg.

44. Naroll, R. S., and Bertalanffy, L. Von. 1956. The Principle of Allometry in Biology and the Social Sciences (on urbanisation in nineteenth-century U.S.A.). *General Systems,* 1, pp. 76-89.

45. *New Scientist.* 1964. (correspondence on shortage of skilled labour in British industry), 419, pp. 594-5.

46. Nohl, J. 1961. *The Black Death.* London: Allen & Unwin.

47. Notestein, F. W. (ed.). 1960. *Three Essays on Population* (includes Malthus' last work). New York: New American Library.

48. Oman, C. W. C. 1960. *The Art of War in the Middle Ages.* Ithaca: Cornell University Press.

49. Rostovtzeff, M. 1926. *The Social and Economic History of the Roman Empire.* Oxford: Clarendon Press.

50. Russell, C., and Russell, W. M. S. 1963. Primate Behaviour and the Concept of Pseudosex. *Internat. Mental Health Research Newsletter,* 5, pp. 7-8.

51. ____. 1967. Population and Behaviour in Animals and Man. *Mem. and Proc. lit. philosoph. Soc. Manchester,* 109, 5, pp. 1-16.

52. Russell, W. M. S. 1966. Arms, Rules and Man. *BBC Third Programme,* 23 March.

53. ____. 1967a. The Animal Society. 2: Hierarchies. *Listener,* 77, pp. 487-8.

54. ____. 1967b. *Man, Nature and History.* London: Aldus Books.

55. Shanks, M. 1961. The Stagnant Society (extract) (shortage of skilled labour in British industry). *Times and Tide,* 42, pp. 1390-1.

56. Singh, S. D. 1965. The Effects of Human Environment upon the Reactions to Novel Situations in the Rhesus. *Behaviour,* 26, pp. 243-50.

57. Slicher Van Bath, B. H. 1963. *The Agrarian History of Western Europe, A. D. 500-1850.* London: Arnold.

58. Smith, R. 1966. Some Sociomedical Aspects of the Population Explosion (on career of Malthus). *Proceedings of the Royal Society of Medicine,* 59, pp. 1149-53.

59. Southwick, C. H. (ed.). 1963. *Primate Social Behaviour.* Princeton, N. J.: Van Nostrand.

60. ____. 1967. An Experimental Study of Intragroup Agonistic Behaviour in Rhesus Monkeys *(Macaca mulatta). Behaviour,* 28, pp. 182-209.

61. Sprague De Camp, L. 1963. *The Bronze God of Rhodes.* New York: Bantam Books.

62. Stonier, T. 1964. *Nuclear Disaster.* Harmondsworth: Penguin.

63. Stott, D. H. 1962. Cultural and Natural Checks on Population Growth. *Culture and the Evolution of Man,* ed. M. F. Ashley Montagu, pp. 355-76. New York: Oxford University Press.

64. Thomas, W. L. (ed.). 1956. *Man's Role in Changing the Face of the Earth.* Chicago: University of Chicago Press.

65. Thompson, W. S., and Lewis, D. T. 1965. *Population Problems,* 5th ed. New York: McGraw-Hill.

66. Townsend, P. 1966. Poverty in Britain. *Poverty,* 1, pp. 5-9.

67. Wellman, P. I. 1966. *Spawn of Evil* (violence in pioneer America). London: Transworld.

68. White, L. 1964. *Medieval Technology and Social Change.* Oxford University Press.

69. Woolley, Sir Leonard. 1963. *The Beginnings of Civilization,* vol. 1, Part 2 of UNESCO *History of Mankind.* London: Allen & Unwin.

70. Wright, Q. 1965. *A Study of War,* 2nd ed. Chicago: University of Chicago Press.

71. Wynne-Edwards, V. C. 1962. *Animal Dispersion in relation to Social Behaviour.* Edinburgh and London: Oliver & Boyd.

Newspaper Articles

Daily mail

72. Burch, S. 1964. Crime in U. S. A. 27 July, p. 2.

73. Cook, A. 1965. Children in Vietnam. 20 Jan., p. 2.

74. Cost of living in Britain. 1964. 25 June, p. 11.

75. Couple who lost count of children. 1965. 30 Nov., p. 7.

76. Kidel, B. 1965. Slump in house-building, U. S. A. 31 Aug., p. 2.

77. McLeave, H. 1965. Battered children in Britain. 22 Aug., p. 10.

78. Nash. R. 1964. Large classes in British schools. 28 April, p. 10.

Evening standard

79. School demands in Surrey. 1967. 17 Aug., p. 12.

17

Population, crowding and human behaviour

Paul Ehrlich and Jonathan Freedman

How does population density, or crowding as it is usually referred to, affect human beings? Few questions of such importance are so little understood. Interest in the broader problem of overpopulation has fortunately blossomed over the past few years. By now all reasonable people appreciate the threat that the world's increasing population presents. But the consequences of overpopulation must be distinguished from the effects of population density *per se*.

This distinction is clearest and most important in our great urban centres. Certainly the cities have monumental problems. They are centres of crime, drug abuse, poverty, welfare cases, unemployment, riots. Some authors have suggested, indeed have unhesitatingly assumed, that many of these ills are inevitable consequences of the high population density prevailing in the cities. They claim that crowding *causes* mental, physical and social breakdown. If this were true, we would obviously be in serious trouble even if we could reduce our total population because people have always concentrated in the cities. If it were true, we would be forced to abandon the cities, or at least greatly reduce their size. But is it true? Does high population density produce bad effects by itself?

Evidence from animals

It is important that the effects of crowding itself, not crowding in conjunction with poverty, malnutrition, noise and filth, be clearly understood. Crowded slums

---

SOURCE: *New Scientist and Science Journal,* Volume 50, No. 745 (1971). Reprinted by permission of Drs. Paul R. Ehrlich and Jonathan Freedman and the editors of *New Scientist and Science Journal.*

should be eliminated even if crowding by itself is of positive benefit to human beings. But as the world becomes more and more packed with people it is critical that we be able to predict how human performance and interpersonal relationships will change even if crowding is not accompanied by other deterioration of the environment. For instance, the soundest ecological strategy may well be to encourage tall, high density dwelling units in cities instead of suburban sprawl. Farm land will be at a premium as the world food problem worsens, and suburbs are all too often built on farmland. In addition, resources (including energy) can be conserved by housing people more efficiently and closer to their jobs. Obviously we would hesitate to take that course if crowding *per se* were in some sense "bad"; if, for instance, it led to antisocial behaviour or to mental or physical deterioration.

There is a number of studies that demonstrate disruptions produced by overcrowding in rats, mice and other animals. John Calhoun and his associates have observed rat colonies in enclosed areas that were provided with sufficient food and water and allowed to grow. Rats are very good at reproducing and quite soon these colonies were teeming with animals. When the number of rats became quite large, social and physical pathologies began to appear. Males became either overly aggressive or unnaturally passive; they became homosexual; they invaded the nests of pregnant females; and some became cannibals. Females no longer built adequate nests, nor cared for their young sufficiently, and as a consequence infant mortality soared. And so on. Whereas with fewer animals, the colony functioned well, all animals had separate nests and raised their young successfully, with the larger population the social structure broke down and eventually the colony's continued existence was in doubt. Similar observations have been made of a wide variety of animals ranging from mice, rats and voles to deer and even monkeys. There is little question that as population increases, at some point it begins to have extremely negative effects on the animals involved.

Adaptable man

Two types of conclusions have been drawn from these studies by those interested in the human population explosion. One group finds solace in the results. They look to natural controls on the size of the human population. When we get "too crowded," population growth will cease: people will lose interest in sex or die of stress, or women will resorb foetuses, or Jonathan Swift's "modest proposal" will be instituted and parents will eat their young. It is difficult for us to view such a "solution" with equanimity, but it will never be the "solution," in any case. It is clear that many other limiting factors (food, raw materials, capacity of environmental systems to handle wastes) will come into play long before the human population reaches a size at which density itself will pose a limit. People living in Manhattan, Tokyo and other extremely crowded areas today do not show such behavioural pathologies to a significant degree. But if only 25 per cent of the land surface earth were populated to the density of Tokyo, the world population would be some 600 billion people. This is perhaps 500-1000 times more than the planet can support in reasonable comfort on a permanent basis.

Another group uses the rat data as the basis of a scare tactic – "if we don't stop population growth, then . . . ," and the list of behavioural horrors is produced. The argument given above more or less deals with this line of reasoning. Other horrors will get us first.

A more fundamental objection to both of these points of view involves the problem of extrapolation from results of rat experiments as a basis for predicting human behaviour. It is always chancy and dangerous to generalise from the reactions of nonhumans, particularly when relatively complex, social behaviours are involved. Humans are marvellously adaptable. They adapt to noise levels and to levels of frustration that cause complete behavioural breakdown in other animals. This fantastic adaptability is, of course, one reason why man has survived and has increased in numbers so spectacularly; it is also one reason why men now find themselves living in conditions that are, in certain ways, exceedingly unpleasant. If he were not so adaptable, he might have stopped the increase in noise, filth and general frustration before it reached its current levels.

Density and crime

To discover how density affects humans, we must study humans. Unfortunately, there is very little research of this type, and much of what there is has produced ambiguous results. The difficulty of pinning down the effects of density by studying existing conditions is illustrated by statistics on the relationship between crime and density. There is no question that in the United States crime is, in the words of the National Commission on the Causes and Prevention of Violence, "primarily a phenomenon of large cities." Whereas there are 1,070 crimes per 100,000 people in rural areas, there are 2,376 in the suburbs, 3,430 in cities of 50 to 100,000 population, and 5,307 in cities over a quarter of a million population. The figures for violent crimes are more dramatic. Six cities with populations over a million contain 10 per cent of the country's population, but contribute 30 per cent of the major violent crimes. The rate of major crimes in the big cities is more than five times greater than in smaller cities, eight times greater than in the suburbs, and 11 times greater than in rural areas. Obviously, the larger the city, the higher the crime rate. It would, however, be a mistake to interpret these statistics as indicating that higher population density causes higher crime. To begin with, the cities differ considerably in their population densities, and those with the greatest density do not necessarily have the highest crime rate. For example, the densities of our three largest cities range from New York's 26,000 people per square mile to Los Angeles's 5,500, with Chicago's falling in between at 16,000. Yet, New York, with the greatest density, has a much lower crime rate against persons than either of the others; and Los Angeles, with the lowest density, has by far the highest rate of crime against property. Thus, within a particular type of community, higher density does not always go along with higher crime rate.

More important is that many other factors tend to be associated with high density. The most obvious is income level – poverty and dense living usually go together. They go together not because high density causes poverty, but because poor people can afford only crowded, sub-standard housing. Also, poverty and crime tend to go together. Most crimes against property or people (except homicide – often a family affair) are committed in poorer neighbourhoods and by poorer people. The reasons for this need not be spelled out, except to say that a rich man rarely engages in mugging; and a man with a new car rarely steals another one. Given these two relationships – that density is associated with poverty, and poverty with crime – the fact that density is to some extent also associated with crime is not surprising. The question is whether it is the density or the poverty or perhaps some other factor entirely that causes the crime.

A recent study by Pressman and Carol attempted to answer this question by comparing metropolitan areas that vary in density and are equivalent in terms of poverty level and other characteristics. This was done by complex statistical procedures rather than actually finding areas that are exactly comparable, but the result is the same. Using this technique the authors found that high density itself, with income level and other factors controlled, is not related to crime rate. That is, metropolitan areas of higher density have no more crime than equivalent areas of lower density. It is not the density that has the bad effect.

The need for experiment

Another form of aggression that may be associated with crowding is war. Again the statistics are provocative, but rigorous analysis is difficult. For instance, in 1969 El Salvador, with a population density of 782 persons per square mile of arable land and Honduras, with only 155, went to war. The Organisation of American States suggested that population pressure in El Salvador was a major cause. It seems unlikely to us, however, that crowding was a crucial factor. Shortage of resources, especially land and jobs, appears to us to have been critical. Stanford political scientist, Robert C. North, has been systematically analysing the role of population pressures in generating wars. Pilot statistical studies of European powers have shown some relationship between rates of population growth and involvement in wars. Again, however, the exact nature of the cause and effect relationships remains obscure, but resource considerations are probably much more important than density itself.

We conclude from these statistics on crime and war that aggression seems much less likely to be the result of density alone than of many other factors. Perhaps density has other negative effects. It has been loosely suggested that high density produces mental illness, physical deterioration, depression and other kinds of mental, physical or social breakdown. Analyses of statistics relevant to these possibilities produce much the same result as for crimes. There is a strong tendency for high population density to be associated with higher rates of mental illness, suicide, infant mortality and so on. But, as before, when other factors such as income and educational level are equated, the effect of density disappears. Areas of high density have no more mental or physical illness than equivalent areas of lower density.

Several years ago it became apparent to us that questions of the effects of crowding on the behaviour of people would be unlikely to be resolved without some experimental work on human subjects. In 1968, when we were both on the faculty at Stanford, we received a grant from the Ford Foundation which permitted us to initiate research in this area. Work was carried out by us in collaboration with Simon Klevansky and Michael Katz at Stanford in 1968-1969 and has been continued by Freedman, and his co-workers, Alan Levy, Judy Price, Robin Welte and Stanley Heshka, after Freedman moved to Columbia.

We conducted a series of studies on the effects of density on various behaviours and reactions. All of the studies followed the same basic model. Groups of people spent four hours in rooms that were either very crowded or not at all crowded. The "crowded" rooms were designed so that every person had a seat, but there was no space for anyone else to fit in the room. In other words, there were as many people as there possibly could be without them actually sitting on or physically interfering with one another. For example, in one study the room was 35 square feet and held nine people, thus allowing less than four square feet per person. In contrast, the less-crowded rooms allowed 15-20 square feet per person. Keep in mind that we were not interested in the effects of density when it became so great that people were actually physically uncomfortable, or when odours or temperature became unpleasant. We wanted to know if crowding itself, apart from these other conditions, produces negative effects.

Skills in a crowd

This experimental method obviously is limited in many important respects. The most critical is that the time span is relatively brief compared to many real life situations, although quite long compared to most laboratory experiments. The crowding is very intense, more than ordinarily occurs in natural settings (except the New York subways) for this length of time. But four hours is still only four hours. And since the subjects know that the time is limited, they know that they will eventually get out of the crowded environment. How the effects of this intense, short-term crowding compare to less intense, long-term crowding is unknown, but ordinarily we would expect the direction of the effects to be similar even if their magnitude is different.

Our first series of studies focused on the effect of density on performance of a variety of tasks. We discovered that there was no effect. The individuals dutifully and competently crossed out sevens on a sheet of random numbers, memorised words, counted erratic clicks coming over a loudspeaker, solved anagram puzzles, formed words from scrambled letters and made up original and ingenious uses for a variety of common objects such as a brick. They did all of these tasks equally well regardless of the size of the room. The degree of crowding had no noticeable effect on any of the tasks, nor did any effect show up over time.

In contrast, our second series of studies revealed that more complex forms of behaviour and emotional reactions are influenced by population density. We now have evidence that the degree of crowding has some effect on competitiveness, vindictiveness and liking for others. But the effects are not simple. The fascinating aspect of this work is that men and women appear to respond in opposite ways to the level of crowding we have used.

Males compete

Our first study consisted of putting high school students in either small or large rooms, letting them get to know one another, discuss various topics and play a mechanical game requiring a high level of coordination between partners. The groups were either all boys or all girls. During the last hour of the study the groups engaged in a game that allowed each person to choose either a cooperative or competitive play. The game is called the prisoner's dilemma, because it is based on the classic problem of two men (Jack and Bob, say) accused of a crime who, questioned separately, are given the opportunity of either confessing and incriminating his partner, or else not confessing and trusting his partner not to do so.

In our study, we did not threaten the students with sentences – instead we offered them money. If they all chose blue, they would each get five cents (not much money for affluent suburbanites, but there were many trials and it could add up). If, however, three chose blue and one chose red, the one choosing the red would hit the jackpot and get 30 cents while the others would lose 20 cents apiece. But if more than one chose red, they also lost. Thus, the cooperative play is to choose blue, hope everyone else chooses blue and take a sure five cents a trial. But by competing and choosing red, each individual might gain a lot more at the cost of a loss to the others and the risk of losing himself. A dilemma, though not as serious as that facing Jack and Bob.

Under these circumstances, a clear pattern emerged – the boys played more competitively in the small room while the girls played somewhat more competitively in the larger room. That is, crowding increased competitiveness among boys and slightly decreased it for girls.

A second experiment used a different setting, different subject population, and different measures. Men and women over 18 were recruited by classified ads in newspapers. The subjects ranged in age from 17-80, and represented a wide variety of ethnic groups and educational and income levels. Once again they were placed in either a large or small room for approximately four hours. During that time, they first engaged in informal discussion and then listened to a series of taped courtroom cases for which they served as the jury. The group discussed some cases openly and did not discuss others, but for all cases each individual indicated his own decision separately and privately. In addition, the subjects responded to a questionnaire on which they were asked how much they liked the other members of the group, how much they enjoyed the session and other similar questions designed to measure their subjective reactions to the experience.

Females cooperate

The pattern of results is similar to that of the previous experiment, but differs somewhat in emphasis. Just as before, the men respond more negatively to the small room, while the women show the opposite tendency. The men give somewhat more severe sentences in the smaller room than they do in the larger room; while the women are lenient in the smaller room. Unlike the previous result, however, this difference between rooms is much stronger for the women than for the men. Crowding has an even stronger effect on the individual's subjective reactions. The men in the small room find the experience less pleasant, like the other members less, consider them less friendly and think they would make a less good jury than the men in the large room; whereas every difference is reversed for women who rate the experience more pleasant, the other members more likeable, friendlier and a better jury in the small than in the large room.

Thus the results of the two studies are quite consistent. Apparently under these circumstances, men respond negatively to crowded conditions – they become more competitive, somewhat more severe and they like each other less; whereas women respond positively, become more cooperative, more lenient and like each other more. Interestingly enough, when mixed groups took part in this last study, no effects of crowding were observed for either the groups as a whole or the men and women separately.

This dramatic difference between the sexes is intriguing and difficult to explain. Some might be tempted to interpret it as evidence for innate feelings of territoriality among males that are not present in females. Despite the simplicity of this explanation, it seems highly implausible. It is true that defending their territory from encroachment is seen primarily among males of other species, but the people in our rooms are hardly protecting territory in the usual sense, nor is there any evidence that women are generally any less protective of their homes than are men. Although it is obviously silly to deny certain innate differences between human males and females, this does not seem to be one of them.

A more likely explanation is that in our society men and women learn slightly different reactions to social situations and close physical contact in particular. There is evidence, for example, that two men who are talking stand farther apart than do two women, suggesting that men are less accepting of physical contact with other men than women are of contact with other women. Men are also probably somewhat more prone to be suspicious of other men than women are of other women. However, the exact form that these hypothesised differences take is sheer speculation. The main point is that our findings are probably due to learned rather than to innate differences, and are affected by the specific situation (as evidenced by the disappearance of the effects with mixed groups).

How should we interpret this and the previous research on density? The first answer is "with great caution." The studies of the cities are still very rough. Any work with massive amounts of data collected under uncontrolled conditions must be considered only suggestive. Our experimental work suffers from the opposite problems – it was well controlled, but produced relatively little data, on very few people, and under special conditions. With that important disclaimer, we must note that this is all we have to go on at the moment and some tentative conclusions can be drawn.

Getting along in crowds

There is little evidence that population density *per se* produces dramatic effects (negative or positive) among human beings. Those who predict loss of efficiency or total breakdown of productive activity as population density grows will find no support in the available data. Density had no effect on performance. At first thought this might be surprising, but a similar lack of effect has been found for other factors such as exceedingly loud noises. Man is remarkably good at ignoring distracting stimulation so even if crowding were unpleasant (which is not at all certain), it might not affect performance.

The evidence from the cities and from our studies also showed no dramatic effect on anti-social behaviour. There was no relationship between a city's population density and crime or other such behaviour. Our last two studies did indicate that all-male groups were somewhat more competitive and severe under crowded conditions, but the effects were not large, were balanced by opposite effects for all-female groups and disappeared entirely in the more natural mixed-sex groups. This is not to deny the effects, but to put them in perspective. Nothing we or others have found indicates that density is a major (or for that matter even substantial) factor in causing mental or social breakdown.

We should therefore not be surprised that the cities, despite their monumental problems, continue to function, and that the people on the underground do not suddenly turn into a brawling mob. The problems of the cities have increased enormously over the past 10 years, a period in which their population density has remained static or even declined in most instances. The problems are not caused by density *per se,* and will not be eliminated merely by reducing density.

This is of the utmost importance. Critics of the cities have correctly cited overcrowding as a major problem but in their zeal some critics have confused the logistic and economic problems caused by the concentration of population with supposed negative effects of crowding *per se.* It is certain that Manhattan's 75,000 people per square mile present difficulties in transportation, providing enough jobs and houses and schools, keeping the parks green, disposing of waste, eliminating pollution and on and on. But there is no reason to believe that this great concentration of population has negative effects on people. The difference between these two statements is crucial. If we view the problems as primarily logistic and economic, we can fight them and get something done. If we decide that crime is inevitably higher in the cities because crowding causes crime, the only answer would be to disband the cities – and this would be a bad mistake even if it were possible. We happen to disagree in our feelings about cities (Ehrlich hates them, Freedman likes them), but we agree that cities serve some functions extremely well. Overpopulation is a problem that must be solved, but high concentrations of people may well turn out to be desirable as long as we deal with the technical problems.

The second conclusion from this research is that whatever effects density does have are complicated. They depend largely on who is being crowded and the situation in which the crowding occurs. We did find that there are times when crowding has negative effects on at least some people; there are other times when it has positive effects. We cannot specify details, but the general point is clear. The few instances we can cite are provocative. All-male juries or cabinets or international conferences should probably be avoided, or at least be given spacious quarters. Better still, women should be included, not only to give them equal representation, but because apparently any negative effects of crowding disappear when the sexes are mixed. There is thus strong argument to eliminate the secretive meetings of men in back rooms deciding our fates – and bring them out into the open where their decisions are less likely to be aggressive.

More generally, the question of whether or not high concentrations of people are desirable depends on the particular situations and the types of behaviour involved. It seems likely that no simple answers will emerge – that for some people and for some purposes, high density is a bad idea, while for other people and for other purposes, it is fine.

PART FIVE

Further views from psychologists and psychiatrists

Psychologists and psychiatrists, by virtue of their clinical perspective and training, are likely to view human aggression and violence in terms of response to events of life history and as artifacts of individual development, rather than as species-specific, culture-specific, genetic, and/or evolutionary phenomena.

In the course of reviewing several recent semi-popular books, Leonard Berkowitz, a professor of psychology, points out a number of oversimplifications and errors of reasoning in these applications of popular biology to human behavior. His warnings are specifically directed against extrapolations from one species to another (from geese, lemurs, and baboons to man, for instance), and against the "word-magic" of analogizing with terms such as "instinctive," "appeasement gestures," "ritualization," and "catharsis," by which unrelated (or questionably related) activities or events may be associated merely by applying the same term. He also questions the concept of "sublimation," the hypothetically therapeutic release of pent-up aggressive energy in sports or other modes of acting-out. As he points out, recent savage eruptions between participants as well as spectators at hockey, basketball, and football games seem to indicate the arousal rather than the dissipation of aggression.

Gilula and Daniels, who are psychiatrists, offer interesting insights into the meaning and function of violence in contemporary Western culture. The current mystique of the gun as a symbol of male potency and self-dramatization is brought under scrutiny in the course of their analysis of the role of the mass media in rationalizing violence in this society.

Finally, Lauretta Bender, a child psychologist, discusses her failure to discern "inborn or instinctive aggression" in normal children.

18

Simple views of aggression

Leonard Berkowitz

The Territorial Imperative by R. Ardrey; 390 pages; currently Dell paperback, $2.45. (Atheneum, 1966).

On Aggression by K. Lorenz; 320 pages; $5.75; Harcourt, Brace & World, 1966.

Man & Aggression, edited by M. F. A. Montagu; 178 pages; $5.00 cloth, $1.95 paper; Oxford University Press, 1968.

The Naked Ape by D. Morris; 252 pages; $5.95; McGraw-Hill Book Co., 1968.

Human Aggression by A. Storr; 127 pages; $5.00; Atheneum, 1968.

The theme of this essay will be drawn from a dust jacket. On the back of the book *Human Aggression* by the British psychiatrist Anthony Storr, we find the following comment by Konrad Lorenz, widely renowned as the "father of ethology": "An ancient proverb says that simplicity is the sign of truth – and of fallacy. . . . However, if the simple explanation is in full agreement with a wealth of data, and quite particularly, if it dovetails with data collected in altogether different fields of knowledge, simplicity certainly is indicative of truth." Four of the books reviewed here offer essentially simplistic messages. With the writers represented in the fifth work, I shall argue that conceptual simplicity advocated by these volumes is definitely *not* "indicative of the truth." All of the books deal with man's capacity for violence, a problem deserving – no, demanding – careful and sophisticated consideration. The four volumes I shall concentrate on, those by Lorenz, Ardrey, Storr, and Morris – and especially the first three – provide only easy formulas readily grasped by a wide audience rather than the necessary close analysis. Being easily understood, their explanation of human aggression helps relieve the anxiety born

---

SOURCE: *American Scientist,* Volume 57, No. 3 (1969). Reprinted by permission of the author and the publisher.

of the public's concern with war, social unrest, race riots, and student protests, but is an inadequate, and perhaps even dangerous, basis for social policy.

All four voice essentially the same message: Much of human behavior generally, and human aggression in particular, must be traced in large part to man's animal nature. Aggression often arises for innately determined reasons, they say. The authors differ somewhat, however, in how they believe this nature leads to aggression. For Lorenz, Ardrey, and Storr (whom I shall refer to as the Lorenzians), a spontaneously engendered drive impels us to aggression, even to the destruction of other persons. Morris, on the other hand, views many of our aggressive acts as genetically governed responses to certain environmental conditions and to signals sent to us by other people. Nonetheless, over and above their similarities and differences, all four volumes present a highly simplified conception of the causes of and possible remedies for human aggression, and I think it would be well for us to look at a number of these misleading oversimplifications.

The role of learning in human aggression

Facing the writers at their own level, one misconception I shall not deal with here is their relative neglect of the role of learning in human aggression. Our behavior is influenced by our experiences *and* our inherited biological characteristics. I have argued elsewhere that innate determinants do enter into man's attacks on others, primarily in connection with impulsive reactions to noxious events and frustrations. These constitutionally governed impulsive responses can be modified by learning, however. The Lorenzians do not appear to recognize this kind of modification in these volumes. They draw a very sharp distinction between learned and innately determined responses, thus ignoring what is now known of the complex interplay between nature and nurture. Lorenz has admitted this on occasion, and the journalist, Joseph Alsop, has recently reported him as saying, "We ethologists were mistaken in the past when we made a sharp distinction between 'innate' and 'learned.'" Of course, there is also an experience-is-all imperialism at the opposite extreme. In sharp contrast to many ethologists and zoologists, social scientists typically have long ignored and even denied the role of built-in, biological determinants. Ashley Montagu's critical discussion of Lorenz in his introduction to *Man and Aggression* is illustrative. "The notable thing about human behavior," he says, "is that it is learned. Everything a human being does as such he has had to learn from other human beings."

Some book reviewers for the popular press, aware of these opposing stances, have approached the present volumes in terms of this kind of polarization. *If* human aggressiveness is learned, Lorenz *et al.* are obviously incorrect, but on the other hand, innate determinants to aggression presumably must operate as described by Ardrey, Lorenz, Morris, and Storr. Ardrey, Lorenz, and Storr pose the issue in these simple terms. Critics dispute their views, they maintain, primarily because of a misguided "American optimism"; American social scientists, psychologists, and psychiatrists, having a liberal belief in the perfectability of man, want to attribute social ills – including violence – to environmental flaws which might be remedied rather than to intractable human nature. The critics certainly would recognize the existence of man's innate aggressive drive if they could only shed their honorable but mistaken vision of Utopia.

There are other alternatives, however. Some of human aggressiveness might derive from man's biological properties, characteristics which he shares to some degree with other animals. He might even be innately "programmed" to respond violently to particular kinds of stimulation, much as other animals do. But his animal characteristics do not have to function the way Lorenz and his associates say they do. The Lorenzian analysis of aggression can be criticized on a logical and empirical basis independently of any general assumptions about the nature of man.

The volume *Man and Aggression,* edited by Montagu, serves as a counterpoise to the Lorenzian books. A number of journalist-reviewers have assumed that Lorenz's views are shared by virtually all students of animal behavior. The Montagu volume clearly shows that there is not the unanimity of support that the laymen believe exists. Many eminent zoologists, as well as comparative psychologists, have taken Lorenz's analysis of aggression seriously to task. *Man and Aggression* is a compilation of generally damning criticisms of the Lorenz and Ardrey books by such authorities as S. A. Barnett, J. H. Crook, T. C. Schneirla, and Sir Solly Zuckerman, as well as Lorenz's old opponent, J. P. Scott. For those people who have read only the Lorenzian analyses, Lorenz may speak for all ethologists; Lorenz is equated with all of ethology in the Storr book, *Human Aggression.* Yet he is not all of the science of animal behavior, and there are many good reasons in the animal as well as human research literature to question the over-all thrust of Dr. Lorenz's argument on grounds besides the "overbold and loose" nature of the Lorenzian contentions generally recognized by many readers.

We need not here review the many objections to the Lorenz and Ardrey volumes that are summarized by the critics included in *Man and Aggression.* However, some of the oversimplifications and errors of reasoning and fact that are characteristic of these two books are also prevalent in the Storr and Morris works, and I think it is important to point out several of these common weaknesses in the extension of popular biology to human aggression.

The use of analogies

As nearly every critic of these Lorenzian books has pointed out, the writers are excessively free-wheeling in their use of analogies. They frequently attempt to explain various human actions by drawing gross analogies between these behaviors and supposedly similar response patterns exhibited by other animal species. Attaching the same label to these human and animal behaviors, the writers then maintain that they have explained the actions. For Lorenz, man is remarkably similar to the Greylag Goose. The resemblances (that occur to Lorenz but not necessarily to other observers) are supposedly far from superficial ones, and he believes that they can only be explained by the operation of the same mechanisms in man and goose. "Highly complex norms of behavior such as falling in love, strife for ranking order, jealousy, grieving, etc., are not only similar but down to the most absurd details the same . . ." and therefore, all of these actions must be governed by instincts.

The analogy emphasized by Ardrey, of course, is based on animal territoriality. Man's genetic endowment supposedly drives him to gain and defend property, much as other animals do, presumably because this territorial behavior provides identity, stimulation, and security. Basing part of his argument on a study of the lemurs of Madagascar, Ardrey contends that there are two types of societies, noyaux (societies said to be held together by the inward antagonism of the members) and nations (societies in which joint defense of territory has given rise to in-group leadership and cooperation). The examples of noyaux listed by Ardrey include, in addition to the Madagascar lemurs, herring gull colonies, certain groups of gibbons, and Italy and France.

Morris' analogy, needless to say, is between humans and apes. His theme is that "*Homo sapiens* has remained a naked ape . . . in acquiring lofty new motives, he has lost none of the earthy old ones." We cannot understand the nature of our aggressive urges, he says, along with Ardrey, Lorenz, and Storr, unless we consider "the background of our animal origins." Unlike the Lorenzians, however, he doubts the existence of an innate, spontaneous aggressive drive, and emphasizes, to the exclusion of such a drive, the genetically determined signals he believes both apes and people send to their fellows. All four authors make much of the control of aggression by supposedly innate appeasement gestures, although Morris seems to have greater confidence in their efficacy than do the others. He even tells us how we should respond to an angry traffic policeman on the basis of this analogy between human and animal behaviors: The policeman's aggression can (theoretically) be turned off automatically by showing abject submission in our words, body postures, and facial expressions. Moreover, it is essential to "get quickly out of the car and move away from it towards the policeman." This prevents the policeman from invading our territory (our car) and weakens feelings of territorial rivalry. The looks people give each other are very important signals, Morris maintains in accord with a rapidly growing body of experimental-social psychological research, but, in contrast to these investigators, he oversimplifies greatly. Morris contends that prolonged looking at another is an aggressive act. In reality, persistent eye-contact can also be a very intimate, even sexual, encounter, or may arise from a search for information or social support.

This type of crude analogizing is *at best* an incomplete analysis of the behavior the writers seek to explain. Important data are neglected and vital differences are denied. J. H. Crook's excellent paper in *Man and Aggression* (which should be read by every person who has written a favorable review of the Lorenz and Ardrey books) notes the many important considerations omitted by the Lorenzians in general and Ardrey's treatment of territoriality in particular. Where Ardrey, following Lorenz, maintains that territorial behavior is a highly fixed, species-specific action pattern produced by energy accumulating in certain centers in the nervous system, the truth cannot be packaged as easily as this. Many different conditions enter into animal territoriality. The outcome is a complex interaction of ecological and social conditions with internal states so that territorial behavior is far from inevitable as a species characteristic. Territorial maintenance, furthermore, involves different components, such as attack and escape. These components are probably governed by somewhat different, although often interrelated, mechanisms, and appear to be susceptible to different environmental and internal conditions. Given these complexities and the multiplicity of factors involved in the territoriality displayed by birds, we cannot make simple statements about the functions and causes of territoriality even in these species, and it is highly unlikely that human concern with property is controlled by the same processes. Crook's conclusion is certainly reasonable: "The likelihood that the motivation control of territorial behavior is at a different level from that of fishes and birds suggests that human resemblances to the lower animals might be largely through analogy rather than homology." Sixteen years ago, Daniel Lehrman remarked, in an outstanding critique of Lorenzian theory, "it is not very judicious, and actually is rash . . . to assume that the mechanisms underlying two similar response characteristics are in any way identical, homologous, or even similar," merely because the actions of different species or entities seem to resemble each other (in the eyes of the writer, we might add).

The notion of ritualization

The same comment can be made about the analogizing involved in Lorenz's and Storr's use of the notion of ritualization. Theorizing that there are evolutionary changes in behavior as well as structure, and that particular action patterns, such as appeasement gestures, have evolved from other behaviors, Lorenz argues that responses originally serving one function can undergo alteration in the course of evolution so that they come to have a different function as well. The drive or energy motivating the original action presumably still powers this altered behavior. According to Lorenz, the appeasement or greetings ceremonies performed by humans and animals alike have become ritualized in this manner through evolutionary developments but still make use of transformed aggressive motivation. Lorenz thinks that the smile of greeting, as an example, might have "evolved by ritualization of redirected threatening." Storr, adopting Lorenz's reasoning, also speaks of "ritualizing the aggressive drive in such a way that it serves the function of uniting" people. For both of these writers, diverted aggressive energy powers the social bonds which tie individuals together in affection and even love. Now, we must ask, is there really good reason to contend, as Lorenz does so authoritatively, that the human smile, the appeasement gesture of the macaques (baring the teeth), and the triumph ceremony of the geese must have evolved in the same way from some original aggressive display? The supposed similarity between the human, monkey, and goose behavior does not mean, as Lehrman pointed out, that the processes underlying these actions are "identical, homologous, or even similar." Elaborating further, in his essay in *Man and Aggression,* Barnett says there is no justification for the "confident, dogmatic assertions" Lorenz and his followers have made about the hypothetical process, "ritualization." Harlow's observations regarding monkey development are also troublesome for the Lorenzian analysis of the genesis of social bonds. Affectional patterns generally emerge *before* aggressive ones in these animals, making it unlikely that the earlier, affectional-social acts are "driven" by aggressive motivation.

The dangers of unwarranted analogizing can also be illustrated by referring to another example of "ritualization" mentioned by Storr. It appears that the Kurelu, a primitive people in the heart of New Guinea, engage in frequent intertribal warfare. But instead of killing one another, the warriors shoot arrows at each other from a distance just beyond arrow range and rarely hit each other. Although this type of warfare seems to resemble the threat ceremonies exhibited by a number of animal species, we certainly cannot argue that the Kurelu behavior and animal threats have evolved in exactly the same manner or are based on similar biological mechanisms. Furthermore, both action patterns may ultimately lead to a cessation of attacks – but probably for very different reasons. It is also improper to insist, as the Lorenzians do, that competitive sports are the same type of ritual as the Kurelu warfare and animal threats merely because some writers have applied the same label to all three sets of phenomena; the surface resemblances do not guarantee that all have the same evolutionary causes and that all operate in the same or even in a similar way.

When we come right down to it, there seems to be a kind of "word magic" in this analogizing. The writers appear to believe that they have provided an adequate explanation of the phenomenon at issue by attaching a label to it: a person's smile is an *appeasement gesture*; athletic events are *rituals* comparable to certain animal displays, etc. Storr shows just this kind of thinking in the "proof" he offers for the notion of a general aggressive drive. Aggression is not all bad, Storr insists (in agreement with Lorenz); aggression is necessary to the optimal development of man. It is "the basis of intellectual achievement, of the attainment of independence, and even of that proper pride which enables a man to hold his head high amongst his fellows." The evidence he cites for this statement is word usage: ". . . the words we use to describe intellectual effort are aggressive words. We *attack* problems, or *get our teeth* into them. We *master* a subject when we have *struggled with* and *overcome* its difficulties. We *sharpen* our wits. . . ." (Italics in the original.) Waving his words over the particular behavior (in this case, striving for independence and achievement), he has thus supposedly accounted for these actions – and has also swept aside the many studies of achievement motivation by McClelland and his associates suggesting that there is very little similarity between the instigation to aggression and achievement motivation.

Popular discussions of the role of evolution in behavior can also be criticized on this basis. Even if it can be shown that a given behavior pattern has "evolved," such a demonstration does not explain the performance of that action by a particular individual in a specific setting. The application of the word "evolution" does not really help us to understand what mechanisms govern the behavior in this individual or what stimulus conditions affect these mechanisms.

Instinctive human actions

The Lorenzians (and Morris as well) also display this same word magic in the ease with which they refer to human actions as instinctive. Without taking the trouble to specify the criteria they employ in making their designations, they go scattering the label "instinct" around with great relish. As an illustration, in his book *On Aggression,* Lorenz talks about people having an "instinctive need to be a member of a closely knit group fighting for common ideals," and insists that "there cannot be the slightest doubt that militant enthusiasm is instinctive and evolved out of a communal defense response." Doubts must exist, however. The Lorenzians offer neither a precise definition of what they mean by "instinct" nor any substantial evidence that the behavior in question, whether human aggression or militant enthusiasm, is innate even in their vague usage of this term. Several of the writers in *Man and Aggression* (e.g., Barnett and Schneirla), as well as other scientists such as Lehrman, criticize Lorenz severely for his excessively casual employment of the instinct concept. Lorenz elsewhere has acknowledged this imprecision in his popular utterances (see, for example, the previously mentioned article by Alsop), saying that he has used the word only in a shorthand sense.

Nevertheless, the over-simplification regarding "instincts" so prevalent in the Lorenz-Ardrey-Storr writings is difficult to excuse as only shorthand. To say this is not to deny the role of innate processes in human behavior; such determinants apparently exist. Psychologists, together with other students of behavior, have shown, as an example, that human babies have a built-in preference for certain visual stimuli, and do not start with blank neural pages, so to speak, in learning to see and organize complex visual stimulation. The difficulty is that ideas such as Lorenz's "instinctive need to be a member of a closely knit group fighting for common ideals" are, in actuality, extremely drastic departures from the more precise instinct concept found in technical ethological discussions. When they write for an audience of their peers, ethologists generally describe instincts, or better still, instinctive movements, as behavioral sequences culminating in "fixed action patterns." These patterns, which are at the core of the instinct concept, are thought of as rigid and stereotyped species-specific *consummatory* responses generally serving to end a chain of ongoing behavior. Can this definition be applied to "militant enthusiasm"? What is the rigid and stereotyped action that unerringly unfolds to consummate the hypothetical enthusiasm pattern?

Sports as outlets for aggression

We now come to the most important part of the Lorenzian instinct conception, and the feature that has the gravest social implications: the supposed spontaneity of the behavior. The stereotyped instinctive action is said to be impelled by a specific energy that has accumulated in that part of the central nervous system responsible for the coordination of the behavior. The energy presumably builds up spontaneously and is discharged when the response is performed. If the instinctive activity is not carried out for a considerable period of time, the accumulated energy may cause the response to "pop off" *in vacuo*. Aggression, according to Lorenz, Ardrey, and Storr – but not Morris – follows this formula. "It is the spontaneity of the [aggressive] instinct," Lorenz tells us, "that makes it so dangerous." The behavior "can 'explode' without demonstrable external stimulation" merely because the internal accumulating energy has not been discharged by aggressive actions or has not been diverted into other response channels as, for example, in the case of such "ritualized" activities as sports. If violence is to be lessened, suitable outlets must be provided. Lorenz believes that "present-day civilized man suffers from insufficient discharge of his aggressive drive," and together with Ardrey and Storr, calls for more athletic competitions – bigger and better Olympic games. (Denying the Lorenzian formulation, Morris maintains that we do not have an inborn urge to destroy our opponents – only to dominate them – and argues that the only solution is "massive de-population" rather than "boisterous international football.")

This conception can be discussed at various levels. Neurologically, for one thing, Lorenz bases his assertions on observations regarding cardiac and respiratory activities and simple motor coordinations. With such critics as Lehrman and Moltz we must question whether or not these findings can be extended to more complex neural organizations, to say nothing of human aggression. (The Lorenzian interpretation of these observations can also be disputed, as Moltz has shown in the 1965 *Psychological Review*.)

There are empirical difficulties as well as this problem of the long inductive leap. Basing their arguments on a number of studies, Hinde and Ziegler (the latter in an important 1964 *Psychological Bulletin* paper) have proposed that many apparent demonstrations of internally driven spontaneity can be traced to external stimuli and the operation of associative factors. The responses evidently are evoked by environmental stimuli rather than being driven out by spontaneously accumulating internal excitation. Moltz has also summarized evidence disputing the Lorenzian notion that response performance is necessary if there is to be a reduction in the elicitability of the instinctive action pattern. As Hinde has suggested in several papers, stimulus satiation rather than a response-produced discharge of instinctive action-specific energy may cause a lessening in response elicitability.

Complex aspects of animal and human aggression

Going from the simple motor coordinations of the lower animals to the more complex aspects of animal and human aggression, the available data are even less kind to the Lorenzian formulation. Of course Lorenz maintains that his ideas are supported by a substantial body of observations. They are upheld, he says, by the failures of "an American method of education" to produce less aggressive children, even though the youngsters have been supposedly "spared all disappointments and indulged in every way." However, as I have pointed out elsewhere in discussing this argument, excessively indulged children probably expect to be gratified most of the time, so that the inevitable occasional frustrations they encounter are actually relatively strong thwartings for them. There is little doubt that these frustrations can produce aggressive reactions, and Lorenz's criticism of the frustration-aggression hypothesis is a very weak one. Belief in this hypothesis, by the way, does not necessarily mean advocating a completely frustration-free environment for children. Child specialists increasingly recognize that youngsters must learn to cope with and adapt to life's inescapable thwartings, and thus must experience at least some frustrations in the course of growing up. Nor do most contemporary psychologists believe that frustration is the only source of aggression. Violence can have its roots in pain as well as in obstacles to goal attainment, and can also be learned as other actions are learned.

Aggression, in other words, has a number of different causes, although the Lorenzians seem to recognize (or at least discuss) only one source. Here is yet another erroneous oversimplification: their notion of a unitary drive that is supposedly capable of powering a wide variety of behaviors from ritualized smiling to strivings for independence or dominance. This general drive conception is very similar to the motivational thinking in classical psychoanalysis, but is running into more and more difficulty under the careful scrutiny of biologists and psychologists. Indeed, contrary to Storr's previously cited argument, there is no single instigation to aggression even in the lower animals. Moyer recently has suggested (in the 1968 *Communications in Behavioral Biology*), on the basis of many findings, that there are several kinds of aggression, each of which has a particular neural and endocrine basis.

The flow of aggressive energy

Also like the traditional psychoanalysts, the Lorenzians speak loosely of aggressive energy flowing from one channel of behavior to another. This hypothetical process, mentioned earlier in conjunction with "ritualization," must be differentiated from the more precisely defined response-generalization concept developed by experimental psychologists. Reinforcements provided to one kind of reaction may strengthen other, similar responses. Rewarding a child for making aggressive remarks can increase the likelihood of other kinds of aggressive reactions as well. The reinforcement influence generalizes from one kind of response to another because the actions have something in common. (The actor might regard both types of responses as *hurting* someone.) It is theoretically unparsimonious and even inadvisable to interpret this effect as an energy transfer from one response channel to another. The Lorenz-Storr discussion of ritualization, and the related psychoanalytic concept of sublimation as well, employs just this kind of energy-diversion idea. We cannot here go into the conceptual pitfalls of this analytical model. (The interested reader might wish to read Hinde's article on energy models of motivation in the 1960 *Symposia of the Society for Experimental Biology*.) But there is a fairly obvious flaw in the Lorenzian statement that pent-up aggressive energy can be discharged in competitive sports. Rather than lessening violence, athletic events have sometimes excited supporters of one or both of the competing teams into attacking other persons. This has happened in many countries: in England, as Crook points out and as Storr should have recognized, in this country at times when white and Negro high school basketball teams have competed against each other, and most dramatically, this past March in Czechoslovakia when the Czechs defeated the Russians in hockey. In these cases, the team supporters were so aroused, even when their team won, that they were extremely responsive to aggressive stimuli in the environment.

Experimental tests of the hostility catharsis hypothesis also argue against the energy-diversion idea inherent in both Lorenzian and psychoanalytic theorizing. This well-worn notion maintains, of course, that the display of aggressive behavior in fantasy, play, or real life, will reduce the aggressive urge. Although there is no explicit reference to a catharsis process in Storr's book, his belief that aggressive energy can be sublimated certainly is consistent with the catharsis doctrine. Lorenz comes much closer to a frank acceptance of this idea in his contention that "civilized man suffers from insufficient discharge of his aggressive drive," and in a bit of advice he offers to people on expeditions to the remote corners of the world. Members of socially isolated groups, he says in *On Aggression,* must inevitably experience a build-up of aggressive drive; outsiders aren't available to be attacked and thus provide an outlet for the accumulating aggressive energy. If a person in such an isolated group wishes to prevent the intra-group conflict that otherwise must develop (Lorenz insists), he should smash a vase with as loud and resounding a crash as possible. We do not have to attack other people in order to experience a cathartic reduction in our aggressive urge; it's enough merely to destroy inanimate objects.

Summary

Summarizing (and simplifying) a great many studies, research results suggest that angry people often do (a) feel better, and (b) perhaps even experience a temporarily reduced inclination to attack their tormentors, upon learning that these persons have been hurt. This phenomenon seems to be quite specific, however; the provoked individual is gratified when he finds that the intended target of his aggression has been injured, and does not appear to get the same satisfaction from attacks on innocent bystanders. Besides this, the apparent reduction in the instigation to aggression following an attack is probably often due to guilt- or anxiety-induced restraints evoked by the attack and/or the arousal of other, nonaggressive motives, and is not really the result of an energy discharge. Standard experimental-psychological analysis can do a far better job than the energy-discharge model in explaining the available data. Recent experiments indicate, for example, that the lessening of physiological tension produced by injuring the anger instigator comes about when the aggressor has learned that aggression is frequently rewarded. This tension reduction, or gratification, is evidently akin to a reinforcement effect, and is not indicative of any long-lasting decline in the likelihood of aggression; people who find aggression rewarding are more, not less, likely to attack someone again in the future. The reinforcement process can also account for the appetitive behavior Lorenz and Storr seem to regard as prime evidence for the existence of a spontaneous aggressive drive. Provoked animals will go out of their way to obtain suitable targets to attack, while youngsters who are frequently aggressive toward their peers generally prefer violent TV programs to more peaceful ones. But this search for an appropriate target or for aggressive scenes probably arises from the reinforcing nature of these stimuli rather than from some spontaneous drive, and again, does not mean that there has been an energy discharge when these stimuli are encountered. Quite the contrary. There is some reason to believe that the presence of such aggression-reinforcing stimuli as other people fighting can evoke aggressive responses from those who are ready to act aggressively – much as the sight of food (which is a reinforcement for eating) can elicit eating responses from those who are set to make such responses.

In the end, the Lorenzian analyses must be questioned because of their policy implications as well as because of their scientific inadequacies. Their reliance on casual anecdotes instead of carefully controlled, systematic data, their use of ill-defined terms and gross analogies, and their disregard of hundreds of relevant studies in the interest of an oversimplified theory warrant the disapproval generally accorded them by technical journals. But more than this, the Lorenz-Ardrey-Storr books can also have unfortunate social as well as scientific consequences by impeding recognition of the important roles played by environmental stimuli and learning in aggressive behavior, and by blocking awareness of an important social principle: Aggression is all too likely to lead to still more aggression.

19

Violence and man's struggle to adapt[1]

M. F. Gilula and D. N. Daniels

> The need is not really for more brains, the need is now for a gentler, a more tolerant people than those who won for us against the ice, the tiger, and the bear. (Eisley, 1946)

> Violence waits in the dusty sunlight of a tenement yard and in the shadows of a distraught mind. Violence draws nearer in the shouts of a protest march and in ghetto rumblings. Violence erupts from Mace-sprinkled billy clubs and a homemade Molotov cocktail. Violence of war explodes the peace it promises to bring. Hourly reports of violence bring numbness, shock, confusion, sorrow. We live in a violent world. (Daniels *et al.*, 1970)

Violence surrounds us, and we must try to understand it in the hopes of finding alternatives that will meet today's demand for change. Do we benefit from violence? Or is violence losing whatever adaptive value it may once have had? We present two theses. (1) Violence can best be understood in the context of adaptation. Violence is part of a struggle to resolve stressful and threatening events – a struggle to adapt. (2) Adaptive alternatives to violence are needed in this technological era because the survival value of violent aggression is diminishing rapidly.

SOURCE: *Science*, Volume 164 (1969): 396-405. This article represents a preliminary summary statement by the Committee on Violence of the Department of Psychiatry, Stanford University School of Medicine. The material from which the article is drawn is revised and greatly expanded in a book edited by Daniels, D. N., Gilula, M. F., and Ochberg, F. M., *Violence and the Struggle for Existence,* Boston, Little, Brown & Co., 1970. Reprinted by permission of the author and the publisher.

[1]We thank Dr. D. A. Hamburg and Dr. A. Siegel for their review and critique of this paper and M. Shapiro, C. DiMaria, and R. Franklin for their contributions in preparing this manuscript.

The shock of Robert F. Kennedy's death prompted the formation of a committee on violence in the Department of Psychiatry, Stanford University School of Medicine. We committee members reviewed the literature on violence and then interpreted this literature from the point of view of psychiatrists and psychologists. We discussed our readings in seminars and sought answers to our questions about violence. This article presents a synthesis of our group's findings and observations and reflects our view of adaptation theory as a unifying principle in human behavior.

We define pertinent terms and describe the adaptation process before we examine violence as it relates to individual coping behavior and collective survival. We then describe three theories of aggression and relate them to adaptation. Next, we discuss relevant examples of violence as attempted coping behavior and factors that foster violence and illustrate the urgent need for other ways of expressing aggression. Finally, we consider the changing nature of adaptation and suggest ways of coping with violence.

Definition of terms

Two groups of terms require definition: (1) aggression and violence; and (2) adaptation, adjustment, and coping. We found that these terms have quite different meanings for different disciplines.

We here define aggression (*Webster's*, 1966; Gould and Kolb, 1964; Hinsie and Campbell, 1960) as the entire spectrum of assertive, intrusive, and attacking behaviors. Aggression thus includes both overt and covert attacks, such defamatory acts as sarcasm, self-directed attacks, and dominance behavior. We extend aggression to include such assertive behaviors as forceful and determined attempts to master a task or accomplish an act. We choose a broad definition of aggression rather than a restrictive one because relations between the underlying physiological mechanisms and the social correlates of dominant, assertive, and violent behavior are still poorly understood. Hence, our definition encompasses but is broader than the definition of aggression in animals that is used in experimental biology (Boelkins and Heiser, 1970; Carthy and Ebling, 1964), which says that an animal acts aggressively when he inflicts, attempts to inflict, or threatens to inflict damage upon another animal. Violence (*Webster's*, 1966) is destructive aggression and involves inflicting physical damage on persons or property (since property is so often symbolically equated with the self). Violent inflicting of damage is often intense, uncontrolled, excessive, furious, sudden, or seemingly purposeless. Furthermore, violence may be collective or individual, intentional or unintentional, apparently just or unjust.

By adaptation we mean the behavioral and biological fit between the species and the environment resulting from the process of natural selection (Dobzhansky, 1962; Simpson, 1958). In man, adaptation increasingly involves modifying the environment as well. Here we want to stress that behavior, especially group-living behavior in higher social species like man, is a crucial element in natural selection (Hamburg, 1963). Adaptive behaviors are those that enhance species survival and, in most instances, individual survival. In contrast, we define adjustment as behavior of a group or individual that temporarily enhances the way we fit with the immediate situation. By definition, adjustment is often a passive rather than active process and does not result in an enduring alteration of behavior structure or patterns (*Webster's,* 1966; Kluckhohn, 1949). In fact, adjustment may have biologically maladaptive consequences in the long run. In addition, rapid environmental change or extraordinary environmental circumstances may render formerly adaptive behaviors largely maladaptive (Hamburg, 1963), that is, behaviors appropriate to past environmental conditions can work against survival in "new" or unusual environments.

We define coping as the continuing and usually successful struggle to accomplish tasks and goals with adaptive consequences. Put another way: "Behavior may be considered to serve coping functions when it increases the likelihood (from a specified vantage point with respect to a specified time unit) that a task will be accomplished according to standards that are tolerable both to the individual and to the group in which he lives." (Silber *et al.,* 1961) Whereas each specific sequence of task-oriented behaviors may or may not have adaptive value, coping taken as a whole is an adaptive rather than adjustive human process.

Definition of human adaptation

Every culture prescribes the range of coping behaviors available to its people, but within this range individual adaptive behavior is forged and tested in times of stress. Stressful or new situations paradoxically offer us both the danger of failure and the opportunity for learning. Stress can be dangerous when it overwhelms the individual or group. Either the situation itself or unpleasant feelings about the situation (including massive anxiety) may block our usual resources and prevent problem solving, and aggressive reactions that are both indiscriminate and protective may occur. We may show primitive forms of behavior: passive adjustment, withdrawal, falsely blaming others, indiscriminate rage, violence, or confusion.

Alternately, stressful events provide a constructive challenge and expanded opportunity for learning. In a stressful situation that is not overwhelming, we seek information helpful in dealing with the situation and try to apply this information (Hamburg and Adams, 1967). From information seeking and subsequent exploratory behavior come not only greater use of information and eventual mastery of new situations but also a sense of heightened self-awareness, enhanced coping skills, and personal growth.

A number of commonly occurring stressful life situations that may challenge and develop our coping skills have been recognized (Hamburg and Adams, 1967). These are associated with the transitions in life and include adolescence, separation from parents, and marriage. Other challenging transitions involve cultural stresses, such as war and the threat of war; rapid technological change; and physical events, such as drought, earthquakes, and famine. These transition points in life are important because they provide opportunity for learning and developing more sophisticated ways of coping with problems.

We have marvelous adaptive abilities for coping with varying, even extreme, situations. These abilities result from cultural evolution interacting with our biological evolution. Culturally we survive through complex communal living. Through our living groups we obtain satisfaction, develop identity, and find meaning to life. Basic social values are of special cultural importance, for they determine the limits of acceptable behavior, especially during times of stress. Biologically we are uniquely endowed for complex communal living. Such biological characteristics as aggression, the upright posture, prehension, speech, prolonged infancy and maturation, and profound development of the brain – all favor and allow for rich, dynamic, and complex living. Development of the cerebral hemispheres has played an especially important role in adaptation, for the cerebrum constitutes the biological basis of higher intelligence, self-awareness, complex language, and flexibility (Dobzhansky, 1962).

Thus through the interaction of biological evolution and cultural evolution, we have the equipment for adapting to and molding diverse environments. But this ability to adapt by manipulating the environment is now our cause for greatest concern, for in changing the environment, man changes the conditions necessary for his survival. We now are seeing an unprecedented acceleration of various man-made changes which call for accompanying changes in man, changes which we are having difficulty in making. While biological change is extremely slow, cultural change theoretically occurs at least every generation, although some aspects of culture (such as technology) change faster than others (for example, beliefs and customs). The term "generation gap" not only describes how we today view the battle of the generations but also alludes to the speed of cultural change and how people have trouble keeping pace. Living in the electronic age, we watch televised accounts of pre-agricultural-age violence and feel our industrial-age mentality straining to cope with the environment.

Since survival results from the long-range adaptiveness of our behavior, knowledge of adaptive mechanisms is important for understanding the role of violence in human behavior and survival. In the section that follows we shall relate three theories of aggression to adaptation.

Adaptation and theories of aggression

Aggression has helped man survive. Aggression in man – including behaviors that are assertive, intrusive, and dominant as well as violent – is fundamental and adaptive. Violence is not a result of aggression but simply a form of aggression. Nor is all violence necessarily motivated by destructive aggression. For instance, in the sadistic behavior of sexual assaults, violence is evoked in part by sexual motives. In other instances, violence can occur accidentally or without conscious intent, as in many auto accidents. Currently there are three main views of aggression – all involving adaptation – but each suggests a different solution to the problem of violent behavior. Broadly labeled, these theories are (1) the biological-instinctual theory, (2) the frustration theory, and (3) the social-learning theory.

(1) **The biological-instinctual theory**[2] holds that aggressive behavior, including violence, is an intrinsic component of man resulting from natural selection: Man is naturally aggressive. It is hard to imagine the survival of man without aggressiveness, namely because aggression is an element of all purposeful behavior and, in many cases, provides the drive for a particular action. This theory says that aggression includes a wide variety of behaviors, many of which are constructive and essential to an active existence. Stimulus-seeking behavior (for example, curiosity or the need to have something happen) is certainly at least as important a facet of human behavior as avoidance behavior and need-satisfaction. Seeking the novel and unexpected provides much of life's color and excitement. Aggression can supply much of the force and power for man's creative potential.

Psychiatric and psychoanalytic case studies are one source of evidence supporting this theory (cf. Fenichel, 1945; Lorenz, 1966; Storr, 1968; Solomon, 1970). Examples range from individuals with destructive antisocial behavior who express violent aggression directly and often impulsively, to cases of depression and suicide in which violent aggression is turned against the self, and to seriously inhibited persons for whom the expression of aggression, even in the form of assertion, is blocked almost entirely. Psychiatrists and other mental-health professionals describe many disordered behaviors as stemming from ramifications and distortions of the aggressive drive (Fenichel, 1945).

Animal studies (Boelkins and Heiser, 1970; Lorenz, 1966; Scott, 1958) (including primate field studies), studies of brain-damaged humans, and male-female comparisons provide behavioral, anatomical, and hormonal data illustrating the human predisposition to aggression. Among nonhuman mammals, intraspecies violence occurs less frequently than with humans (Carthy and Ebling, 1964). When violent aggressive behaviors do occur among members of the same species, they serve the valuable functions of spacing the population over the available land and maintaining a dominance order among the group members. Uncontrolled aggression in animals generally occurs only under conditions of overcrowding. Aggression in humans, even in the form of violence, has had similar adaptive value historically.

The biological-instinctual theory suggests that since aggression is inevitable, effective controls upon its expression are necessary, and reduction of violence depends upon providing constructive channels for expressing aggression.

(2) **The frustration theory**[3] states that aggressive behavior comes from interfering with ongoing purposeful activity. A person feels frustrated when a violation of his hopes or expectations occurs, and he then tries to solve the problem by behaving aggressively. Frustrations can take various forms: threats to life, thwarting of basic needs, and personal insults. This theory often equates aggression with destructive or damaging violent behavior. Major factors influencing aggressive responses to frustration are the nature of the frustration, previous experience, available alternatives for

---

[2] See Fenichel, 1945; Lorenz, 1966; Storr, 1968.
[3] See Berkowitz, 1962; Dollard *et al.,* 1939.

reaction (aggression is by no means the only response to frustration), the person's maturity, and the preceding events or feelings. Even boredom may provoke an aggressive response. As a response to frustration, aggression is often viewed as a learned rather than an innate behavior. According to this theory, frustration-evoked aggression aims at removing obstacles to our goals; hence the frustration theory also ties in with adaptation. The aggressive response to frustration often is a form of coping behavior that may have not only adjustive but also long-range consequences.

The frustration theory suggests that control or reduction of violence requires reducing existing frustrations as well as encouraging constructive redirection of aggressive responses to frustration. This reduction includes removing or improving frustrating environmental factors that stand between personal needs and environmental demands. Such factors include violation of human rights, economic deprivation, and various social stresses.

(3) **The social-learning theory**[4] states that aggressive behavior results from child-rearing practices and other forms of socialization. Documentation comes from sociological and anthropological studies and from observing social learning in children. Aggressive behavior can be acquired merely by watching and learning – often by imitation – and does not require frustration. Aggressive behaviors rewarded by a particular culture or subculture usually reflect the basic values and adaptive behaviors of the group. In American culture, where achievement, self-reliance, and individual self-interest are valued highly, we also find a relatively high emphasis on military glory, a relatively high incidence of personal crime, and a society characterized by a relatively high degree of bellicosity. Similar patterns occur in other cultures. From this theory we infer that as long as a nation values and accepts violence as an effective coping strategy, violent behavior will continue.

The social-learning theory of aggression suggests that control and reduction of violence require changes in cultural traditions, child-rearing practices, and parental examples. Parents who violently punish children for violent acts are teaching their children how and in what circumstances violence can be performed with impunity. Other changes in cultural traditions would emphasize prevention rather than punishment of violent acts and, equally important, would emphasize human rights and group effort rather than excessive and isolated self-reliance. The first step toward making the changes that will reduce violence is to examine our values. We must decide which values foster violence and then begin the difficult job of altering basic values.

In reality, the three theories of aggression are interrelated. Proclivities for social learning and for frustration often have a biological determinant. For example, the biology of sex influences the learning of courting behavior. Regarding violence, from these theories of aggression we see that the many expressions of violence include man's inherent aggression, aggressive responses to thwarted goals, and behavior patterns imitatively learned within the cultural setting. All three theories of

[4]See Bandura and Walters, 1963; Ilfeld, 1970; Wolfgang and Ferracuti, 1967.

aggression and violence fit into the adaptation-coping explanation. Violence is an attempt to cope with stressful situations and to resolve intolerable conflicts. Violence may have short-run adjustive value, even when the long-run adaptive consequences may in fact be adverse. It is the sometimes conflicting natures of adjustment and adaptation that are confusing and insufficiently appreciated. In some instances violence emerges when other more constructive coping strategies have failed. In other instances violence is used to enhance survival. Our species apparently has overabsorbed violence into our cultures as a survival technique. Children and adolescents have learned well the accepted violent behaviors of their elders.

All three theories help us understand violent behavior and hence suggest potential ways of reducing violence. In the following sections we consider current examples of violence from the perspective of those factors in our society that foster violence and from the standpoint of how these examples reflect the changing nature of adaptation.

Phenomenon of presidential assassination

Assassination is not an isolated historical quirk, eluding comprehension or analysis. The event is usually overdetermined by multiple but equally important factors: personal qualities of the assassin, a fatalistic posture assumed by the victim, and such factors in the social environment as political stereotypes, murder sanctions, and the symbolic nature of high offices.

Although assassination can strike down anyone, we have restricted our examination to assassination of presidents in America (Taylor and Weisz, 1970) by studying the personal qualities of "successful" assassins and of others who almost succeeded. Of the eight assassination attempts on American presidents, four have been successful. The following facts emerge. (1) All the assassination attempts were made with guns, all but one with pistols. (2) All the assassins were shorter and weighed less than average men of the period. (3) All the assassins were young adult Caucasian males. (4) All the assassination attempts but one were made by individuals who were seriously disturbed or even paranoid schizophrenics (Freedman, 1965; Hastings, 1965). The exception was the final attempt of two Puerto Rican nationalists to kill President Harry S Truman. The successful assassins, for the most part, were mentally unbalanced and had persecutory and grandiose delusions.

Assassination provides a method for instantly satisfying a need for personal importance. The delusional assassin very probably had a fantasy that once the act was committed, an outcry of favorable opinion and acclaim would vindicate what he had done. In most of the instances of attempted or successful assassination, escape plans were inadequate or nonexistent.

The life pattern of most of the assassins included extreme resentment toward others – a resentment aggravated by a long history of isolation and loneliness. Often the isolation stemmed from poor and inconsistent relations with parents and others early in life, which resulted in most of the assassins having resentment and mistrust of parental figures. Their resentment toward parental figures might have included the President (political symbol of parenthood) as the head of the federal government. In response to imagined unfair treatment from others and a distortion of his own inadequacies, the assassin turned his anger on the chief of state.

Typically the assassin had struggled for importance, success, and manliness, but had failed. At the time of the attempted presidential assassination, the assassin was on a downward life course. Haunted by resentment and failure and plagued with disordered thinking and distortions of reality, the assassin took action. Shooting the President was thus an attempt to resolve conflicts with which he apparently could not otherwise cope. Providing an alternate outlet for his violent dissatisfaction would be one way of preventing the potential assassin from killing. Perhaps the ombudsman (public complaint receiver) system would allow the would-be assassin to voice his grievances against his intended victim, thereby lessening his pent-up frustrations and reducing the likelihood that he would kill.

Our discussion of another important determinant of assassination – the victim's fatalistic attitude – is not restricted to presidential assassinations. The fatalistic thinking and actions of several assassination victims are reflected in their strong disinclination toward taking precautionary measures despite recognizing the existence of violent impulses in others toward presidents and presidential candidates. Robert Kennedy stated a view that he shared with Abraham Lincoln, Martin Luther King, Jr., and John F. Kennedy: "There's no sense in worrying about those things. If they want you, they can get you."[5] This attitude often leads to dangerous negligence that is an exaggerated form of denying that one is actually afraid of physical harm. Lincoln has been described as "downright reckless" (Cottrel, 1966) about personal safety. Robert Kennedy was quoted as saying, "I'll tell you one thing: If I'm President, you won't find me riding around in any of those awful [bullet-proof] cars."[6] The fatalistic attitude illustrated by statements like this is encouraged by our tradition of expecting physical courage in our leaders. Men who repeatedly and publicly proclaim their vulnerability may be unwittingly encouraging assassination by offering an invitation to the delusional, grandiose, and isolated person who dreams of accomplishing at least one important and publicly recognized act in his life. "Mixing with the people" is firmly embedded in the American political tradition, but it is also an accomplice to assassination. One way to cope with this problem would be legislation to restrict the contact and exposure of a President with crowds when his presence has been announced in advance.

Mass media and violence

Television could be one of our most powerful tools for dealing with today's violence. It could provide education and encourage, if not induce, desired culture modification. Unfortunately, it does little of either today, perhaps because the harmful

[5,6] "It's Russian roulette every day, said Bobby," San Francisco *Examiner,* 6 June 1968.

effects of televised violence have been glossed over. However, all the mass media do little to discourage and much to encourage violence in America. The Ugly American as a national stereotype is rapidly being displaced in the eyes of the world by the Violent American, his brother of late. This stereotype is fostered by the media but is sustained by the violent acts of some of our citizens. Armed with shotgun, ignorance, frustrations, or hunger, this Violent American can be seen today throughout our society. We are not all violent Americans, but mass media are giving us the violence we seem to want.

What effect do the mass media have (Siegel, 1970; Larsen, 1968)? All of us are probably affected by the media to some degree, but most research has focused on children, since an immature and developing mind is usually less capable of discrimination when responding to a given stimulus. One comprehensive review (Maccoby, 1964) described short-term effects that include the child's emotional reactions to what he views, reads, and hears. Long-term effects, what the child actually learns as a result of his exposure, may include vocabulary, factual information, belief systems, and such altered personality characteristics as increased aggressiveness. No one selects all the media materials available, nor does anyone absorb or retain the selected materials consistently or completely. Prior information, differing needs, and quality of life adjustment also help to filter the child's processing of the offered materials. Mass media effects also depend somewhat on the applicability of the learned material to the child's own life situation.

Similarly, as shown by another researcher (Berkowitz, 1968), frustration, the anger evoked by it, the overall situation, the apparent severity and justification of the violence viewed in a film – all relate to whether or not children use these aggressive responses.

A large study in Great Britain (Himmelweit *et al.,* 1958) showed that certain portrayals of violence are more disturbing to children than others. Unusual motives, settings, and weapons are more disturbing than stereotyped violence. For example, knives or daggers are more upsetting than guns or fist fights. Similarly, seeing violence or disasters in newsreels bothered children more than dramatized violence.

Another study (Schramm *et al.,* 1961) found that the average American child from 3 through 16 years old spends more of his waking hours watching television than attending school. First-graders spend 40 percent and sixth-graders spend 80 percent of their viewing time watching "adult" programs, with Westerns and situation comedies being most popular. By the eighth grade, children favor crime programs.

Can we justifiably say that the media teach violence? Television teaches more than vocabulary and factual information to the impressionable young viewer, who learns by identification and social imitation. Learning theorists have shown that children readily mimic the aggressive behavior of adults and that the degree of imitation is comparable whether the behavior is live or televised. In another study (Bandura *et al.,* 1961, 1963) nursery school children watched a film of adults aggressively hitting an inflatable plastic figure, a Bobo doll. Later these and other children were first mildly frustrated and then led individually into a room in which they found the Bobo doll and other materials not shown in the film. Those who had seen the film imitated precisely the film's physical and verbal aggression and made more aggressive use of other toys, such as guns, that had not been in the film. Film-watchers showed twice as much aggressiveness as those who had not seen the film.

These children were all from a "normal" nursery school population, and all showed some effect. This finding seriously questions the claim that such violence is learned only by deviant individuals. The findings apply equally to real, fictional, and fantasy violence. The impact on children observing aggressive behavior has been further corroborated in experiments in which live models, cartoons, and play materials were used. The idea that watching television satisfactorily releases pent-up aggressions (the catharsis theory) loses credibility in the face of these data from social-learning experiments. Watching dramatized violence may actually lead to subsequent aggressive behavior.

A tendency toward repeating certain behaviors viewed in the media clearly exists. The mass media teach the alphabet of violence, but whether or not the actual performance of violent behaviors occurs depends on personality, subcultural values, and other factors. The research to date indicates that the learning of violence must be distinguished from the performance of it. One fear we have is that restraints and taboos against violent behavior may diminish as the result of observing prohibited behavior being condoned and rewarded on the screen. Violence depicts a way of life; it is disguised by a cloak of history or locale and becomes acceptable. We are never taught "in this School for Violence that violence in itself is something reprehensible." (Wertham, 1966)

Even with the portrayed violence, the screen environment may be more desirable than the viewer's actual environment. In the culturally deprived American household the underfed, underoccupied, undereducated person may be an apt pupil of the school for violence. Such pupils more readily accept as real a violent world made of movies, newsprint, comic books, and video. The blurred line between fiction and reality grows fainter when there is nothing for dinner. Ghetto violence is one way of at least temporarily adjusting to intolerable personal frustrations and an unbearable environment.

Given the effectiveness of the mass media in achieving culture modification, we should determine whether the content of the media produces desirable or undesirable modification. How frequently is violent content offered in our media? According to a 1951 New Zealand study (Mirams, 1951), 70 American films had roughly twice as much violence per film as did 30 films from other countries. A 1954 study of network television programs (Purdue Opinion Panel, 1954) found an actual doubling from one year to the next in the number of acts or threats of violence, with much of the increase occurring during children's viewing hours. These studies were all conducted before the documentary and news depiction of violence became common, and thus these studies dealt essentially with fictional violence. More recent studies reflect the same trends, however. A New York *Times* headline from

July 1968, reads "85 Killings Shown in 85½ TV Hours on the 3 Networks."[7]

Thus the media's repetitive, staccato beat of violence and the evidence of its impact upon the most impressionable members of our society show that violence is valued, wanted, enjoyed. In teaching that violence is a good quick way to get things done, television and other media teach that violence is adaptive behavior.

Part of the tragedy is that the mass media could effectively promote adaptive behaviors like nonviolent protest and other alternatives to violence. The communications personnel and we consumers alike share the responsibility for seeing that our mass media develop their own constructive educational potential. At the very least, violence in the media must be reduced. The statement is hackneyed, the conclusion is not.

Mental illness, violence, and homicide

What is the relationship between mental illness and violence (Gulevich and Bourne, 1970)? Generally the stereotype of the mentally ill person as a potentially dangerous criminal is not valid. The act of homicide often raises the question of psychosis, but only a relatively few psychotic individuals are potential murderers. The stereotype is kept alive, however, by the sensationalist news coverage of the few homicides committed by psychotics.

Mental illness does not usually predispose one to commit violent acts toward others. The patient with severe mental illness (psychosis) is frequently so preoccupied with himself and so disorganized that he is more likely to commit suicide than homicide. A main exception is the fairly well-organized paranoid patient with persecutory delusions concerning one or more particular individuals, intense hostility and mistrust for others, and a pervasive tendency to blame his troubles on the world. However, this type of mentally disordered person constitutes a small minority and does not greatly increase the low incidence of violent acts committed by those identified as mentally ill. In fact, several comparative studies indicate that patients discharged from mental hospitals have an arrest rate considerably lower than that of the general population. In a Connecticut state mental hospital (Cohen and Freeman, 1945) the felony arrest rate was 4.2 per 1000 patients, whereas among the general population it was 27 per 1000. Compared to an arrest rate of 491 per 100,000 among the general population, New York state mental hospitals (Brill and Malzberg, 1962) reported a figure of 122 per 100,000 for male patients discharged during 1947. Ten thousand patients were studied. One state-wide survey of Maryland psychiatric hospitals (Rappaport and Lassen, 1964) showed that the mentally ill are involved in criminal behavior about as often as the general population.

Since mental illness of itself is not predictive of violence or homicide, we must look for other predisposing conditions. Predicting specifically who will murder is

[7] Associated Press report of 25 July 1968; *Christian Science Monitor* article; New York *Times*, 29 July 1968.

difficult because over 90 percent of the murders committed are not premeditated and 80 percent involve an acquaintance or family member (Bakal, 1968). One often demonstrated factor related to homicide is the excessive use of alcohol. Overindulgence in alcohol has been cited as one feature of the "pre-assaultive state" (deLeon, 1961). Persons who are preassaultive usually show some combination of the following five factors: (1) difficulty enjoying leisure time often associated with the heavy use of alcohol; (2) frequent clashes with close friends, spouse, and others; (3) history of many fistfights and evidence of past violence (such as scars) reflecting difficulty with impulse control; (4) fondness for guns and knives; and (5) being relatively young, usually under 45 years old. Comparing homicide rates for males and females universally indicates that a potential murderer is more often male than female. This difference reflects more frequent use of guns and knives ("male" weapons) for murdering as well as sex differences in expressing aggression.

Case histories of homicide reveal repeatedly that a person uses murder as a means of conflict resolution in an unbearable situation for which he can find no other solution. Predisposing factors for homicide include alcoholism, subcultural norms accepting violence as a means of settling conflict, a setting in which the individual experiences intolerable frustration or attack, helplessness resulting from the unavailability of or the inability to perceive alternative actions, intense emotions, and distortion of reality (perhaps even to the point where reality disappears because of personality disintegration). In the instance of blind rage, a person sometimes murders without realizing what he is doing.

The act of homicide may be viewed as attempted coping behavior. Homicide eliminates the immediate problem at a time when there seems to be no future or when the future seems unimportant, and the long-range consequences of the act are not considered. Put another way, homicide has adjustive rather than adaptive value.

Firearms control and violence

Violence by firearms has recently caused great concern (Gillen and Ochberg, 1970; Daniels *et al.*, 1970). The question of whether there is a gun problem is complicated by regional variations in both the actual incidence and the reporting of crime and multiple psycho-social variables, such as individual "choice" of homicide, population density, age, race, socioeconomic status, religion, and law-enforcement effectiveness.

Even so, the following statistics (Bakal, 1968) estimating the involvement of guns in various forms of violence in America indicate that a problem does exist.[8] In 1967 firearms caused approximately 21,500 deaths – approximately 7,700 murders, 11,000 suicides, and 2,800 accidental deaths. In addition, there were also about 55,000 cases of aggravated assault by gun and 71,000 cases of armed robbery

[8]Criminal Division, U.S. Dept. of Justice, *Firearms Facts* (16 June 1968); based in large part on the FBI's *Uniform Crime Reports,* 1967. Washington, D.C.: U.S. Gov't. Printing Office, 1968.

by gun. Between 1960 and 1967, firearms were used in 96 percent (that is, 394) of 411 murders of police officers. More than 100,000 nonfatal injuries were caused by firearms during 1966. A study in Chicago (Zimring, 1968) in which assaults with guns were compared to those with knives shows many more equally serious assaults with knives than with guns; but more of the gun assaults were fatal. Another study (Berkowitz, 1968) convincingly shows that the mere presence of a gun serves as a stimulus to aggression, that is, "The finger pulls the trigger, but the trigger may also be pulling the finger." The number of guns owned by citizens is unknown, but estimates run from 50 to 200 million (Bakal, 1968). In 1967 approximately 4,585,000 firearms were sold in the United States, of which 1,208,000 were imports. Lately, data from a 1963 World Health Organization survey of 16 developed countries (Bakal, 1968) give America an overwhelming lead in death rates for both homicide and suicide by firearms.

These data speak for themselves. What they do not show are the steady increases in all categories for gun-related mortality cited during the past few years. Firearms sales increased by 132 percent between 1963 and 1967.

Responsibility for legal restrictions on guns has generally been left to the states. Consequently, regulations on the sale of guns vary greatly. The lack of uniform laws and the ability (until recently) to buy guns in one state and transport them to another state have made it difficult to compare accurately the gun laws of different states. Even the so-called strict gun laws may not possess sufficient strength to reduce gun killings significantly.

Until 1968 there were only two federal laws of note (Congressional Quarterly, 1968). The National Firearms Act of 1934 imposes a tax on the transfer of certain fully automatic weapons and sawed-off shotguns. The Federal Firearms Act of 1938 requires a license for interstate sale of firearms and prohibits interstate shipment of guns to convicted felons, fugitives, and certain other persons. Two bills passed in 1968 go somewhat further but do not include firearm registration (Gillin and Ochberg, 1970). The Omnibus Crime Control and Safe Streets Act restricts interstate and foreign commerce in hand guns. The Gun Control Act also adds mail-order sale of rifles and shotguns to this restriction and prohibits over-the-counter sales to out-of-state residents, juveniles, convicted felons, drug users, mental defectives, and patients committed to mental hospitals.

Although the data do not provide an ironclad indictment against weak, inconsistent legislation, we believe that they make a convincing argument. What is more, more than two-thirds of the American people continue to favor stronger gun-control legislation (Daniels *et al.*, 1970). Even the frightening regularity of assassination has not resulted in strong legislation (that is, legislation requiring registration of guns and owners). How then can we account for the successful opposition to strong gun legislation?

Diverse groups comprise the one-third or less of Americans who do not favor stricter gun control laws. The most visible opposition group is the large (about 1 million members), well-organized National Rifle Association (NRA). With an immense operating budget (approximately $5.7 million in 1967), the NRA is an especially effective "gun lobby" (Harris, 1968). Another group, the Black Panthers, sees arms as necessary for survival. Eldridge Cleaver, Defense Minister of the Black Panthers, wrote, "We are going to keep our guns to protect ourselves from the pigs [police]." (Cleaver, 1968) Protection is also the issue in Dearborn, Michigan, where housewives are arming against the potential rioter and looter who might "invade" Dearborn from Detroit. Tragic escalation continues around the interplay of urban and suburban action and reaction.

Arguments opposing gun legislation can be divided into five overlapping categories.

(1) Gun control would cause the loss of rights and possessions. This argument takes various forms: Restrictive legislation is an effort to disarm American sportsmen and law-abiding citizens; legislation would result in the loss of the so-called basic American freedom, "the right of the people to keep and bear arms"; and maintaining an armed citizenry ensures the protection of American liberties, especially against tyrannies from the political right or left. A common fear is that gun laws could lead from registration to discrimination and finally to confiscation of all firearms.

Our traditional frontier and rural ways of life are disappearing, and with this change has come a decrease in our traditional freedom and individualism. For many opposing gun legislation, the actual and potential loss of a way of life and its prized symbol – the gun – make gun legislation a concern basic to the adaptiveness of our society. These opponents assume that restrictions on the "right to bear arms" endanger our way of life.

(2) Guns represent protection from dangers. The gun is seen as providing personal protection from and a means of coping with life-threatening dangers and destructive evil forces, be they criminals, drug addicts, rapists, communists, other subversives, mental patients, rioters, police, or racists. The NRA promotes this coping strategy in its official publication, *The American Rifleman* (116, nos. 2-5, 1968). A monthly NRA column, "The Armed Citizen," states that "law-enforcement officers cannot at all times be where they are needed to protect life or property in danger of serious violation. In many such instances, the citizen has no choice but to defend himself with a gun." The power of this argument depends upon a person's feelings of helplessness and mistrust in the face of danger.

Many people in urban areas or changing neighborhoods fear the rising crime rate and the breakdown of law and order. However, there is no documentation that an armed citizenry provides greater individual or group protection than an unarmed citizenry. On the contrary, the potential danger of such individual armed protection in our congested urban society includes harm to innocent bystanders, accidental shootings, and the increased likelihood of impulsive violence, which already accounts for over 90 percent of homicides in America.

(3) Crime is reduced by punishment and not by gun control. Several forms of

this argument state that gun-control legislation simply is not an effective way of reducing crime and violence: (1) Guns don't kill people, people kill people; (2) when guns are outlawed, only outlaws will have guns (because they steal them anyway); (3) crime is not associated with guns but with such social factors as population density, population composition, economic status, and strength of police; and (4) effective enforcement of present laws has not been tried.

Using stronger and even cruel punishment to cope with gun-using criminals has to date not been proven as an effective deterrent, and its use, we believe, is morally indefensible. The "crime and punishment" thesis ignores data showing that more than three out of four homicides and two out of three criminal assaults occur among family and friends, that is, most murders are committed by "law-abiding citizens." In addition, criminals can and do purchase weapons from legal sources.

(4) A gun represents strength and manliness. Gun literature usually implies this argument. Acts of heroism and bravery are associated with gun usage. Members of the NRA receive distinguished fighting medals. Pictures and advertisements reflect manliness and imply that gun usage means "standing up for your rights."

Guns may serve as a source of power, pride, and independence (the "equalizer" – for feelings of inferiority or inadequacy) and as the symbol of manliness and potency. Guns can and do represent these qualities in our culture, even to a pathological degree for some of us.

(5) Guns provide recreation and support the economy. Arguments here portray citizens as being restricted from and deprived of healthy outdoor life, the hobby of gun collecting, family recreation, and the fellowship associated with hunting and target shooting. For example, an article in *The American Rifleman* entitled "Happiness is a Warm Gun" (Herlihy, 1968) depicts a close father-son relationship based on shooting. Additionally, gun sales and fees are held to be important economic factors supporting hunting states and conservation programs.

These arguments indicate that the issue of gun legislation is pragmatic, ideological, psychological, and economic, and is not based upon sound empirical data. The fervor of the arguments accurately reflects the deep emotional attachments at stake. Indeed, the specific content of proposed gun laws often seems irrelevant. Tragically, the arguments confuse ideology with issues of violence that must be solved. If strictly pragmatic issues of protection were involved, better police protection and increased communication with the feared group or groups should diminish the fear.

Finally, we have found that the "statistics game" is often played by both sides of this particular controversy. By presenting selected statistics and invalid inferences, both sides have obscured the more important goals of reducing gun killings and violence.

Yet, on balance, data document the need for strong and more uniform firearms legislation. We know of no single issue concerning violence that reflects more clearly the changing nature of adaptation. Challenges of the complex urban society in which we live cannot be met with old frontier means of survival – every man protecting himself with his own gun. Yet, gun legislation is no panacea. While reflecting America's desire for action, focusing or relying on legislation alone tends to obscure basic issues of violence and how we persist in using both individual and collective violence as a means of resolving conflict.

Collective and sanctioned violence

An additional dilemma is that killing is neither legally nor socially defined as an unequivocally criminal act. The existence of capital punishment and war gives qualified sanction to violence as a means of resolving conflict. Both the general public and their leaders always seem to be able to justify any violence perpetrated on their fellow man. Thus in practice the legitimacy of violence is arbitrary and depends more on the will of powerful men than on moral, ethical, or humane considerations. In a sense, all sanctioned violence is collective, since it has group social approval. Certainly the existence of sanctioned violence abrades the concept of law and order.

We desperately need research on the psychological processes that permit an individual or group to view some violence as good (and presumably adaptive) and other forms of violence as bad (and presumably maladaptive). Although the history of violence in man is polymorphous, there likely are psychological mechanisms common to all cultures and times. For instance, the psychology of sanctioned violence everywhere depends on attributing evil motives to the "outsiders." Then because "they" are violent (evil), "we" *have* to be violent, or (twisted even further) because "they" are violent, it is *good* for "us" to be violent.

Thus people who have seen sanctioned violence being committed in the name of law, order, justice, moral obligation, and duty come to use violence themselves as a "just" means of solving their own problems. The people are acting as their government's representatives have acted – if the cause is just, the grievance real, then unlimited power and force can be used.

Nowhere do we better find this thinking reflected than in the actions of rioters (Bittker, 1970). Study of the 1967 Detroit uprising (Lowinger *et al.,* 1968; Darrow and Lowinger, 1968) showed that the rioters (young, better educated men who had experienced frustration of their rising expectations) viewed violence against the "system" as justified. Not surprisingly, their views of what justifies violence differed greatly from those of the law enforcers and of the middle-aged black citizens. To the rioters violence was a means of accomplishing goals seemingly not attainable by nonviolent means. Their belief in the power of violence is understandable. Civil disorders are serving in part as a catalyst for change and an instrument of achievement. Some uprising participants reported that violence provided a sense of manliness and strength. But do these supposed gains outweigh the damage of escalations of counterviolence and potential suppression? At least the hypothesis that violence purifies, enhances manliness, and strengthens identity is subject to empirical study.

The results of social-psychiatric field investigations like those in Detroit and at Brandeis University's Lemberg Center for the Study of Violence are useful steps toward understanding the psychological processes and conditions evoking collective violence. For instance, a Lemberg report (Spiegel, 1968) cited four socio-psychological antecedents to ghetto uprisings: (1) a severe conflict of values between dominant and minority groups; (2) a "hostile belief system" held by the aggrieved group, based considerably on reality; (3) a failure of communication between the aggrieved and dominant groups; and (4) a failure in social control resulting from either overcontrol or undercontrol. In short, these studies show that psychiatrists and psychologists can and must help to resolve the crisis of violence through field studies, facilitating communication between opposing groups, and making recommendations for social change.

But what of war? Behavioral scientists have grasped at all sorts of explanations for this species' warring behavior. Perhaps even this attempt to explain war is a cause of war; our ability to justify any form of violence is part of man's magnificent cerebral endowment. Many causes of war have been suggested: contiguity, habituation, social learning, predation, psychological defenses (for example, rationalization, blaming, denial, counterphobic tendencies among others), the host of fears associated with the human condition, territoriality and power, intolerable frustration, biologically rooted aggressive instincts, and sadism (Frank, 1967; Ziferstein, 1967; Freeman, 1964; Richardson, 1960). One wonders whether the mere distance and speed with which we kill are factors rendering meaningless the signals of submission that other animals use to halt violent encounters (Freeman, 1964). Often we literally no longer have to touch the results of our violence. The impersonal factor shows up in another way. Since war is an activity between organized nation states rather than angry individuals, decisions producing war often are made in a calculated manner by those who do not participate directly in any personal acts of violence.

The evidence of history is that war proves everything and nothing. An adequate analysis of the Vietnam war and of the myriad of other wars dotting history is far too great a task for this discussion, despite the relevance of war to the current crisis of violence (Richardson, 1960).

Although preventive measures are difficult to administer in the face of the contradicting sanctioned and unsanctioned violence, there are remedies to violence, and we have discussed some of them. More effort could be expended trying to understand the all-important relation between the excessive use of alcohol and homicide. Disseminating currently available information on how to identify a potential murderer will help. Despite Americans' conflicting feelings about guns, there is a gun-death problem today, and more effective and uniform gun legislation can keep guns out of the hands of those who are likely to act impulsively. The mass media can play an increasingly responsible and educational role, while reducing the amount of violence for violence's sake. Many positive potentials of the media have not yet been tapped. Citizen complaint agencies can be established, of which one possibility might be homicide prevention centers along the lines of the suicide prevention centers. Frustrated minority groups will become less frustrated when they are not blocked from responsible participation and self-determination. Peaceful resolution of conflict

(Ilfeld and Metzner, 1970) such as nonviolent protest and negotiation, reducing the amount of sanctioned violence, encouraging a shared sense of humanity, and moving toward rehabilitation rather than retribution in dealing with crime – all these are promising directions. Violence must be studied scientifically so that human behavior can be sustained by knowledge.

Changing nature of human adaptation: some speculations

Violence is unique to no particular region, nation, or time (Richardson, 1960). Centuries ago man survived primarily as a nomadic hunter relying on violent aggression for both food and protection. Even when becoming agricultural and sedentary, man struggled against nature, and survival still required violent aggression, especially for maintaining territory when food was scarce.

Then in a moment of evolution man's energies suddenly produced the age of technology. Instead of adapting mainly by way of biological evolution, we are now increasingly subject to the effects and demands of cultural evolution. Instead of having to adapt to our environment, we now can adapt our environment to our needs. Despite this potential emancipation from biological evolution, we retain the adaptive mechanisms derived from a long history of mammalian and primate evolution, including our primitive forms of aggression, our violence, bellicosity, and inclination to fight in a time of emergency. Where these mechanisms once responded more to physical stress, they now must respond more to social, cultural, and psychological stresses, and the response does not always produce adaptive results. Where violent aggressive behavior once served to maintain the human species in times of danger, it now threatens our continued existence.

In this new era, culture changes so rapidly that even time has assumed another dimension – the dimension of acceleration. Looking to the past becomes less relevant for discerning the future.

In the current rapidly expanding technological era, many once useful modes of adaptation are transformed into threats to survival. Territorial exclusivity is becoming obsolete in an economy of abundance. Vast weapons, communication, and transportation networks shrink the world to living-room size and expand our own backyard to encompass a "global village." Yet war and exclusivity continue. Our exploitation of natural resources becomes maladaptive. Unlimited reproduction, once adaptive for advancing the survival of the species, now produces the overcrowded conditions similar to those that lead to destructive and violent behavior in laboratory experiments with other species.

The rate at which we change our environment now apparently exceeds our capacity for adapting to the changes we make. Technological advances alter our physical and social environments, which in turn demand different adaptive strategies and a reshaping of culture. The accelerated civilization of technology is crowded, complex, ambiguous, uncertain. To cope with it, we must become capable of restructuring knowledge of our current situation and then applying new information adaptively.

Several factors give us reason to hope that we can succeed.

(1) Our social organization and intellectual abilities give us vast potential for coping. Knowledge and technology can be harnessed to serve goals determined by man. Automation makes possible the economics of abundance, but only our cultural values can make abundance a reality for all people. Medicine permits us to control life, but we have not yet seen fit to use this power to determine the limits of population. The technologies of communication and travel shrink the world, but man has not yet expanded the horizon of exclusion. We can learn to unite in goals that transcend exclusivity and direct cultural evolution in accordance with adaptive values and wisdom. The past need not be master of our future.

(2) Violence can be understood and controlled. The crisis is one of violence, not of aggression, and it is violence that we must replace. Aggression in the service of adaptation can build and create rather than destroy. The several theories of aggression and current issues of violence suggest many complementary ways of controlling and redirecting aggression. We have suggested some in this article. Furthermore, our brief review of theory and issues points to many possibilities for multi-dimensional research – an approach that we believe is needed rather than "one note" studies or presentations.

(3) Greater attention can be focused on both social change and adaptation processes. Cultural lag in the technological era produces not stability but a repetitious game of "catch up" characterized by one major social crisis after another and by behaviors that are too often only adjustive in that they bring relief of immediate problems while doing little to provide long-range solutions. Expanding our knowledge of the processes of social change and understanding resistance to change are of highest priority. Unforeseen change produces intolerable stress, anxiety, and increased resistance to rational change. These reactions inhibit solution-seeking behavior; evoke feelings of mistrust, loss, and helplessness; and lead to attacks on the apparent agents of change. We must develop the ability to foresee crises and actively meet them. We must dwell more on our strengths, assets, and potential as the really challenging frontier.

Conclusion

The current examples of violence and the factors encouraging it reflect our vacillation between the anachronistic culture of violence and the perplexing culture of constant change. We feel alienated and experience social disruption. Current demands for change are potentially dangerous because change activates a tendency to return to older, formerly effective, coping behaviors. Social disruption caused by change tends to increase violence as a means of coping at a time when violence is becoming a great danger to our survival.

America's current crises of violence make it difficult for us to cope with our changing world. Today's challenge, the crisis of violence, is really the crisis of man.

This crisis is especially difficult because violence, a once useful but now increasingly maladaptive coping strategy, seems to be firmly rooted in human behavior patterns. We conquer the elements and yet end up facing our own image. Adaptation to a changing world rests on how effectively we can understand, channel, and redirect our aggressive energies. Then man can close his era of violence.

Summary

We are uniquely endowed both biologically and culturally to adapt to our environment. Although we are potentially capable of consciously determining the nature of our environment, our outmoded adaptive behavior – our violent aggression – keeps us from doing so.

Aggression is viewed as multidetermined. It is inherent, caused by frustration, or learned by imitation. Violent aggression is a form of attempted coping behavior that we in America, as others elsewhere, use despite its potentially maladaptive and destructive results. Current examples of violence and the factors fostering it include assassination, the mass media, mental illness and homicide, firearms and resistances to restrictive gun legislation, and collective and sanctioned violence. These examples are considered from the perspectives of the changing nature of adaptation and the opportunities they offer for research. Among recommendations for resolving or reducing violence, the need for thoughtful research by behavioral scientists is stressed. But the major obstacle to removing violence from our society is our slowness to recognize that our anachronistic, violent style of coping with problems will destroy us in this technological era.

References

Bakal, C. 1968. *No Right to Bear Arms.* New York: Paperback Library.

Bandura, A., Ross, D., and Ross, S. 1961. *J. Abnorm. Soc. Psychol.* 63:575.

____. 1963. *J. Abnorm. Soc. Psychol.* 66:3.

Bandura, A., and Walters, R. H. 1963. *Social Learning and Personality Development.* New York: Holt, Rinehart & Winston.

Berkowitz, L. 1962. *Aggression: A Social-Psychological Analysis.* New York: McGraw-Hill.

____. 1968. *Psychology Today* 2 (no. 4):18.

Bittker, T. E. 1970. The choice of collective violence in intergroup conflict. *Violence and the Struggle for Existence,* ed. D. N. Daniels *et al.* Boston: Little, Brown.

Boelkins, R. C., and Heiser, J. 1970. Biological aspects of aggression. *Violence and the Struggle for Existence,* ed. D. N. Daniels *et al.* Boston: Little, Brown.

Brill, H., and Malzberg, B. 1962. *Mental Hospital Service (APA) Suppl. No. 153.* August.

Carthy, J. D., and Ebling, F. J. (eds.). 1964. *The Natural History of Aggression.* New York: Academic Press.

Cleaver, E. 1968. *Ramparts* 7:17.

Cohen, L. H., and Freeman, H. 1945. *Conn. State Med. J.* 9:697.

Congressional Quarterly. 12 April 1968. King's murder, riots spark demands for gun controls, pp. 805-815.

Cottrel, J. 1966. *Anatomy of an Assassination.* London: Muller.

Daniels, D. N., Gilula, M. F., and Ochberg, F. M. (eds.). 1970. *Violence and the Struggle for Existence.* Boston: Little, Brown.

Daniels, D. N., Trickett, E. J., Tinklenberg, J. R., and Jackman, J. M. 1970. The gun law controversy: Issues, arguments, and speculations concerning gun legislation. *Violence and the Struggle for Existence,* ed. D. N. Daniels *et al.* Boston: Little, Brown.

Darrow, C., and Lowinger, P. 1968. The Detroit uprising: A psychosocial study. *Science and Psychoanalysis, Dissent* (vol. 13), ed. J. H. Masserman. New York: Grune and Stratton.

deLeon, C. A. 1961. Threatened homicide—A medical emergency. *J. Nat. Med. Assoc.* 53:467.

Dobzhansky, T. 1962. *Mankind Evolving.* New Haven: Yale Univ. Press.

Dollard, J., Doob, L. W., Miller, N. E., Mowrer, O. H., and Sears, R. R. 1939. *Frustration and Aggression.* New Haven: Yale Univ. Press.

Eiseley, L. 1946. *The Immense Journey.* New York: Random House.

Fenichel, O. 1945. *The Psychoanalytic Theory of Neurosis.* New York: Norton.

Frank, J. D. 1967. *Sanity and Survival: Psychological Aspects of War and Peace.* New York: Random House.

Freedman, L. Z. 1965. *Postgrad. Med.* 37:650.

Freeman, D. 1964. Human aggression in anthropological perspective. *The Natural History of Aggression,* ed. J. D. Carthy and F. J. Ebling. New York: Academic Press.

Gillin, J. C., and Ochberg, F. M. 1970. Firearms control and violence. *Violence and the Struggle for Existence,* ed. D. N. Daniels *et al.* Boston: Little, Brown.

Gould, J., and Kolb, W. L. 1964. *A Dictionary of the Social Sciences.* New York: Free Press.

Gulevich, G. D., and Bourne, P. 1970. Mental illness and violence. *Violence and the Struggle for Existence,* ed. D. N. Daniels *et al.* Boston: Little, Brown.

Hamburg, D. A. 1963. Emotions in the perspective of human evolution. *Expression of the Emotions in Man,* ed. P. D. Knapp. New York: International Universities Press.

Hamburg, D. A., and Adams, J. E. 1967. *Arch. Gen. Psychiat.* 17:277.

Harris, R. 1968. *The New Yorker* 44:56.

Hastings, D. W. 1965. *J. Lancet* 85:93, 157, 189, 294.

Herlihy, W. W. 1968. *Amer. Rifleman* 116(no. 5):21.

Himmelweit, H. T., Oppenheim, A. N., and Vince, P. 1958. *Television and the Child.* New York: Oxford Univ. Press.

Hinsie, L. E., and Campbell, R. J. 1960. *Psychiatric Dictionary* (3rd ed.). New York: Oxford Univ. Press.

Ilfeld, F. 1970. Environmental theories of aggression. *Violence and the Struggle for Existence,* ed. D. N. Daniels *et al.* Boston: Little, Brown.

Ilfeld, F., and Metzner, R. 1970. Alternatives to violence: Strategies for coping with social conflict. *Violence and the Struggle for Existence,* ed. D. N. Daniels *et al.* Boston: Little, Brown.

Kluckhohn, C. 1949. The limitations of adaptation and adjustment as concepts for understanding cultural behavior. *Adaptation,* ed. J. Romano. Ithaca, N.Y.: Cornell Univ. Press.

Larsen, O. N. (ed.). 1968. *Violence and the Mass Media.* New York: Harper and Row.

Lorenz, K. 1966. *On Aggression.* New York: Harcourt, Brace and World.

Lowinger, P., Luby, E. D., Mendelsohn, R., and Darrow, C. 1968. *Case study of the Detroit uprising: The troops and the leaders.* Detroit: Department of Psychiatry, Wayne State Univ. School of Medicine, and the Lafayette Clinic.

Maccoby, E. A. 1964. Effects of the mass media. *Review of Child Development Research,* ed. L. W. Hoffman and M. L. Hoffman. New York: Russell Sage Foundation.

Mirams, G. 1951. *Quart. Film Radio Television* 6:1.

Purdue Opinion Panel. 1954. *Four Years of New York Television.* Urbana, Ill.: National Assoc. of Educational Broadcasters.

Rappaport, J. R., and Lassen, G. 1964. *Amer. J. Psychiat.* 121:776.

Richardson, L. F. 1960. *Statistics of Deadly Quarrels.* Pittsburgh: Boxwood Press.

Schramm, W., Lyle, J., and Parker, E. B. 1961. *Television in the Lives of Our Children.* Stanford, Calif.: Stanford Univ. Press.

Scott, J. P. 1958. *Aggression.* Chicago: Univ. of Chicago Press.

Siegel, A. E. 1970. Mass media and violence. *Violence and the Struggle for Existence,* ed. D. N. Daniels *et al.* Boston: Little, Brown.

Silber, E., Hamburg, D. A., Coelho, G. V., Murphey, E. B., Rosenberg, M., and Pearlin, L. I. 1961. *Arch. Gen. Psychiat.* 5:354.

Simpson, G. G. 1958. The study of evolution: Methods and present states of theory. *Behavior and Evolution,* ed. A. Roe and G. G. Simpson. New Haven: Yale Univ. Press.

Solomon, G. F. 1970. Case studies in violence. *Violence and the Struggle for Existence,* ed. D. N. Daniels *et al.* Boston: Little, Brown.

Spiegel, J. 1968. *Psychiat. Opinion* 5(no. 3):6.

Storr, A. 1968. *Human Aggression.* New York: Atheneum.

Taylor, R., and Weisz, A. 1970. The phenomenon of assassination. *Violence and the Struggle for Existence,* ed. D. N. Daniels *et al.* Boston: Little, Brown.

Webster's Third New International Dictionary. 1966. Springfield, Mass.: Merriam.

Wertham, F. 1966. *A Sign for Cain.* New York: Macmillan.

Wolfgang, M. E., and Ferracuti, F. 1967. *The Sub-Culture of Violence.* New York: Barnes and Noble.

Ziferstein, I. 1967. *Amer. J. Orthopsychiat.* 37:457.

Zimring, F. 1968. *Is Gun Control Likely to Reduce Violent Killings?* Chicago: Center for Studies in Criminal Justice, Univ. of Chicago Law School.

20

Hostile aggression in children

Lauretta Bender

Child psychiatrists and psychologists studying child behaviour, both normal and abnormal, have had to deal with Freud's teachings that aggression in children is hostile, a primordial reaction to ever-present frustration, an instinctive drive equated with the death instincts leading to death wishes as a normal developmental feature (Freud, 1922).

Although these theories have not been accepted by all psychoanalysts (Bender, 1963), the child analysts following Anna Freud and Melanie Klein have made these concepts basic to their studies of child development and to their educational and psychotherapeutic practices.

They believe in an inborn or instinctive aggression in which aggressiveness, hostility, guilt and anxiety form the expected or normal behaviour of children and that it is necessary to subject them early and persistently to education based on inhibitions, disciplines, restraints and restriction and to psychotherapy giving insight into their aggressive tendencies.

Anna Freud (Freud and Burlingham, 1943), while studying the English children evacuated from London in the Hampstead Nurseries, wrote: "It is one of the recognized aims of education to deal with the aggressiveness in child nature in the first four or five years." She stated: "The dangers of the war lie in the fact that the destruction raging in the outer world may meet the very real aggressiveness which rages on the inside of the child."

SOURCE: *Aggressive Behaviour,* Proceedings of the International Symposium on the Biology of Aggressive Behaviour, S. Garattini and E. B. Sigg, eds., Amsterdam: Excerpta Medica, 1969. Reprinted by permission of Excerpta Medica.

She claimed that the child must be safeguarded from the primitive forces of the war "not because horror and atrocities were so strange to them but because of the need to estrange the young child from the primitive and atrocious wishes of their infantile nature." However, the psychoanalytic literature does not record child atrocities as a result of stimulation from war experiences or as a result of primary aggressive drives.

In my own experience with disturbed children in New York City and State, where I have worked since 1934, I have never been able to confirm these theories. Wherever aggression, hostile or destructive, has been shown in the behaviour of children, it has been the result of some form of real developmental pathology in the context of an unsympathetic or actively disturbing social and environmental situation which has disorganized the normal constructive patterned drives and behaviour of the developing child.

I have postulated the normal drives in child development in the following way:

1. An inherent drive for normality determined by biological maturation, patterned with a direction towards a goal, and which can never be completely blocked or diverted by any pathology within the child or in his outer world.
2. An inborn capacity to relate and identify with other humans such as the mother, and thus experience love, social relations, communication and language.
3. An inborn capacity for fantasy, symbol formation and projection in all his experiences, and to communicate these experiences, thus reconstructing and mastering the outer world with creativity.

Therefore, destructiveness and hostile aggression in a child is a symptom complex caused by developmental pathology which disorganizes the normal constructive patterned drives, so that inadequate gratification leads to frustration.

My experience with aggressiveness in children is best demonstrated by presenting the case material on children I have known, who have actually been involved in the death of another human being. If the psychoanalytic theories were correct, instances of children causing a death should not be uncommon. But in 25 years of psychiatric practice in New York City and New York State, I have been able to collect only 33 cases of children under the age of 15 years, who have apparently been responsible for a death. These 33 cases were collected from the New York City Bellevue Psychiatric Hospital, the children's courts of New York City, the New York State mental hospital system, and correctional institutions. Included were only children that I was able to study psychiatrically personally and where all hospital, court and follow-up records were available to me. All cases were followed up at least 5 years after the homicidal incident.

By 1945 eight children had been observed who were held responsible for a death (Bender and Curran, 1940; Keeler, 1954). The conclusions were overwhelming, the death was always accidental and unexpected by the child. Neither had the child any concept of the irreversibility of death. The death occurred because the victim happened to be in the path of the activity initiated by the child and was unintentionally fatal. The child then responded with a severe depressive grief or mourning reaction. His life pattern changed critically from that point. He tried by every means in fantasy and by acting-out to deny the act and its consequences, the death of the victim and its irreversibility. He might even attempt to repeat the whole experience in order to prove that it could not have happened. These children needed long periods of careful psychiatric care to ameliorate their emotional disturbance and protect them from repeating the experience.

These children had all experienced early social deprivation but also had endogenous pathology such as schizophrenia, encephalitis, epilepsy, and primary learning disabilities. Subsequent follow-up into adulthood showed that their latent pathology was more severe than recognized at the time of observation following the incident. Three were chronically hospitalized as psychotic schizophrenics. Two epileptics were impossible to rehabilitate. Two others repeatedly failed in community adjustments. Only one child, a girl, subsequently made an adequate social adjustment.

In 1959 (Bender, 1959a) a more extensive study was reported on 25 additional boys and girls to the age of 15 years, who had caused a death. The conclusions this time were that a constellation of factors was always present when a boy or girl had caused a death. There needed to be a disturbed, poorly controlled, impulsive child, a victim who acted as an irritant, an available lethal weapon, and always a lack of protective supervision by some third person who could have stopped the fatal consequences.

Of the total 33 death-causing children studied psychiatrically, some combination of the following factors were found: (1) Organic brain disease with an impulsive disorder, an abnormal electroencephalogram, and/or epilepsy; (2) schizophrenia with preoccupations with death and killing in the pseudoneurotic phase of younger children, or with antisocial paranoid preoccupation in the pseudopsychopathic phase of the adolescent children; (3) compulsive fire-setting; (4) defeating school retardation (reading disability); (5) extremely unfavorable home conditions and life experiences.

The mode of death in younger children was by fire (6 children); drowning (5 children); pushing off of heights (2 children); choking (1 child). Deaths by fire and drowning were all purely incidental. The child's subsequent severe depression and grief-ridden reaction required psychiatric care. Nevertheless, of these 14 children, 6 were schizophrenic, 3 were grossly defective with developmental brain damage. The five involved in a drowning were all fire-setters and came from home and social situations that were grossly damaging. They had all been known to threaten to kill before the drowning. None were free from family, social and personal disorders. Multiple deaths (two and three) were caused by drowning and fire.

The 19 older boys, ages 11 yrs. through 15 yrs., caused deaths by stabbing with sharp weapons (7 boys); by repeated blows with a heavy object (6 boys); and by shooting (6 boys). Four younger boys, ages 6, 8, and 9, are included in these categories. This group showed the most pathology with clinically recognizable schizophrenia, epilepsy and/or significant brain damage diagnosed in all cases.

Our more recent studies have shown that definite pathology could always be recognized in these homicidally aggressive children or young adolescents since we have acquired more clinical experience with diagnostic procedures. Furthermore, the pathology was confirmed and appeared more obvious when follow-up reports were obtained. This was true of adolescent schizophrenics with pseudoneurotic and pseudopsychopathic defenses, who often appear to be symptom-free and not psychotic at the time (Bender, 1959b). There is a strong tendency in our culture, and even among professionals, not to recognize psychoses or endogenous pathology in young people, to deny or not ask for previous histories, and to seek only for sociological or psychogenic factors. Subsequent course, however, has confirmed the presence of pathology in all these youngsters.

An adequate and, preferably, repeated use of electroencephalograms has revealed impulse disorders and latent epilepsy even before it was clinically demonstrable in a surprising number of adequately studied homicidal adolescents.

The psychodynamics of a prepuberty child who has caused a death is that he experiments in fantasy and by acting out to determine if irreparable death is possible. An adolescent makes an effort to deny both guilt and feelings of guilt for his part in the act that caused the death and to claim amnesia or other repressive defense. Both are usually misunderstood and dangerous. Eight of the boys who had caused a death, afterwards were still threatening to kill whenever they were frustrated. Several expressed fear of their own ability to kill.

Fifteen of the 33 boys and girls, because of their early disturbed behaviour, had psychiatric evaluation before the incident that led to the death. In many of these, recommendations had been made which had not been followed. Five boys had been reported as very dangerous. Of course, it cannot be denied that many children are reported as dangerous who have not proven to be so.

Dr. Renatus Hartog, who examined Lee Harvey Oswald as a delinquent boy, is reported (Sibley, 1967) to have said after the assassination of President Kennedy that he had found the boy "potentially dangerous." He also estimated that 15% of the youngsters in the Youth House, a retention home for delinquents of New York City, who were referred to him for psychiatric evaluation, were "potential killers." Dr. Hartog does not report, however, that any of them actually did kill.

We are faced with the problem of determining why there is not more violence committed by the "potentially dangerous" recognizable by psychiatrists (Rappaport, 1967). This re-enforces the concept that a constellation of factors is required: endogenous pathology; unfavorable social environment; an irritating victim (or even an innocent bystander); a lethal agent; and a lack of protection.

In such a psychiatric evaluation of known child and adolescent killers there is no place for the psychoanalytic concepts of universal inborn aggressive or death instincts or death wishes, as formulated by Freud and many of his followers.

The current involvement in the United States, with violence in the world, in the Vietnam war and in the civil rights conflict, as shown by the assassination of Dr.

Martin Luther King and the reaction that followed, leads many professionals to believe (New York *Times,* 1967), as Anna Freud stated, that the children of our country are developing a dangerous tolerance for and acceptance of violence, aggression and destruction as a means toward achieving desired ends. Such tendencies are said to threaten an upward trend of juvenile delinquency. However, there is so far no evidence of increased violence in the young. Riots, etc., are not involving children. On the other hand, the current movement in the youth has been towards a hippie philosophy (Bingham, 1967), which is one of passivity, withdrawal from the turbulence of both the Vietnam war and civil rights conflicts, in that the war and the draft are rejected and interracial relationships are accepted.

I offer these data as evidence that murderous hostile aggression is not a normal pattern of behaviour for children. It occurs infrequently as a result of disorganizing pathology both endogenous and environmental in a constellation of factors, so that the death occurs without the intent of the child but as an unexpected occurrence.

References

Bender, L. 1959a. Children and adolescents who have killed. *Amer. J. Psychiat.,* 116, 510.

_____. 1959b. The concept of pseudopsychopathic schizophrenia in adolescence. *Amer. J. Orthopsychiat.,* 29, 471.

_____. 1963. Genesis of hostility in children. *Psychoanal. Rev.,* 50th Anniversary Issue, 95.

Bender, L. and Curran, F. J. 1940. Children and adolescents who kill. *J. crim. Psychopathol.,* 1. 297.

Bingham, J. 1967. The intelligent square's guide to Hippieland. *N.Y. Times Magazine,* September 24.

Freud, A. and Burlingham, D. T. 1943. *War and Children.* New York: Medical War Books.

Freud, S. 1922. *Beyond the Pleasure Principle.* London: International Psychoanalytic Press.

Keeler, W. R. 1954. Children's reaction to death in the family. *A Dynamic Psychopathology of Childhood,* ed. L. Bender, p. 172. Springfield, Ill.: Charles C. Thomas.

New York *Times.* 1967. An open letter to President Johnson from 206 clinical psychologists. News of the Week, December 24.

Rappaport, J. R. 1967. *The Clinical Evaluation of the Dangerousness of the Mentally Ill.* Springfield, Ill.: Charles C. Thomas.

Sibley, J. 1967. Youth problems restudied in the light of the Oswald case. New York *Times,* January 5, 75.

PART SIX

Viewpoints of cultural anthropologists

It is only fitting that cultural anthropologists have the last word, for they alone have fully explored the range of behavioral variability that can be effected by enculturation in man. Geneticists, zoologists, and ethologists, who are often unaware of their own cultural bias, and move unconsciously within that tight network of habits, values, and imperatives that constitutes the subject matter of anthropology, will almost certainly overstress the role of genetic directives. Conversely, cultural anthropologists (especially those of the older "superorganic" persuasion) will predictably designate learning as the major (if not sole) determining factor in human behavior. While the *tabula rasa* concept of a generation ago has been somewhat shaken and modified, still these three scholars make good cases for the appearance of aggressive traits under specific endemic stress conditions: sociocultural modes of adaptation elected by some peoples and rejected by others.

Louise Sweet, Edmund Leach, and Morton Fried have all carried out ethnographic research in non-Western cultures; all three also evidence deep interest in and concern with the social and political problems that beset their own contemporary societies. Their testaments that war and human violence are neither innate nor inevitable are well stated, and should be carefully and optimistically considered.

21

Culture and aggressive action[1]

Louise E. Sweet

Introduction

My purpose in this paper will be to consider aggressive activities, whether those of individuals or those of societies (groups) from the point of view that aggression by human beings at any level of manifestation owes more to cultural influence than to any particular factor that is innately biological in character. That is, while members of the human species may be observed to respond or act aggressively, it is of primary necessity to examine the cultural matrix in which they do so if we are to understand how this comes about. There is ample evidence and argument in anthropology as well as other behavioral sciences that such activities may be adaptive for survival in many instances and particular situations. I hope to underline this. But I hope also to indicate that such behavior may be highly patterned and enculturated into the individual

SOURCE: Reprinted by permission of the author.

[1] Much of the interpretation offered in this paper derives from a stimulating summer session class in "World Ethnography of Violence" conducted for the Department of Anthropology, University of Manitoba, summer of 1969. My idiosyncratic view of "Arab" aggressive action in the Levant owes much to being in Lebanon in 1964-1965 and 1969-1970, while teaching at the American University of Beirut; to lengthy discussions with colleagues and friends, such as the people of "Ain ad Dayr"; to the study of the Arab press of Beirut with the help of my assistant, Michel Dib Kandis; and to a number of publications which until recently have been awkward if not impossible to obtain in the United States (Dodd and Barakat, 1968; Hadawi, 1967; Rodinson, 1968; Sharabi, 1969, 1970; Jiryis, 1969). The literature of the dispute on aggression and "human nature" is large and growing, and I have referred to some of it here. One of the most important in giving direction to this paper is Ralph Holloway's "Human Aggression: The Need for a Species-Specific Framework" (1968).

member of a society, often expected of certain roles and social types (cf. Hobsbawm, 1969), and used to form explicit "norms" or styles that are taught, regardless of the "inherent potential" of the individual for agonistic display or of his or her previous experience and training. And, by way of sharp contrast, we find equally in other situations or societies that there is explicit enculturation for non-agonistic activity even under many stressful conditions.

Such a discussion is unlikely to arouse surprise or much controversy among most cultural anthropologists for whom feud, raiding, and warfare are staple problems for socio-cultural study (cf. Fried *et al.*, 1968; Norbeck, 1963; Peters, 1967; Murphy, 1957; Newcomb, 1950, 1960; Sweet, 1965; Vayda, 1961, 1969; Wolf, 1969). For most the "culturological" perspective holds: "Warfare is a struggle between social organisms, not individuals. Its explanation is therefore social or cultural, not psychological." (White, 1949:132) But the concept of the *inherently* savage and aggressive human species has recently re-emerged from the fields of ethology, primatology, "pop social science," and other quarters. One question to raise is whether this revival is in part rationalization by some for this stressful era of a sequence of devastating wars and genocides. Nevertheless, the reaction of many cultural and social anthropologists has been virtually one of shock that so obsolescent a concept could revive (Holloway, 1968; Leach, 1968). And the distinguished ethologist John H. Crook cautions:

> The fact that a given viewpoint is academically unsound may not lessen the impact nor prevent it finding expression in the social attitudes and political views of the less disciplined. In particular, views purveyed by Ardrey would suggest that the possible establishment of territorially defended racial enclaves in the United States and in other countries would be a biologically natural event. The casual adoption of such views reduces the likelihood of a more positive search for racial tolerance through mutual understanding and the effective implementation of human rights. The Ardrey argument could quite plausibly be exploited in a right wing ideology sustaining a racist or nationalist *status quo*. (Crook, 1970b:xxiii)

Therefore this essay is perhaps better aimed at a nonexistent journal, *Current Ethology*. Since there is no such amphitheater, however, it may be useful to address it to anthropologists. The line of argument is somewhat different from most previous discussions of human aggression, in that it does try to contain both "individual motivations" and "causes of war" within a single paradigm for analysis. All but this paragraph of the paper was, in fact, written before Andrew P. Vayda's "The Study of the Causes of War, with Special Reference to Head-Hunting Raids in Borneo" (1969) was available to the writer. Since we have long shared the ecological approach, it is not surprising that we hold roughly parallel perspectives of "aggressive" activities of human persons and societies as adaptive in their particular contexts.

After the definitions, general assumptions, and criteria relevant to the argument have been presented, brief analyses of four well known contexts of "response to stress" (a broader concept than "response to frustration") will be given to support it: the Bushmen of Thomas' *The Harmless People* and those of Richard Lee's further research (Thomas, 1960, 1965; Lee, 1968, 1969); the "fierce" Yąnomamö as presented by Napoleon Chagnon (Chagnon, 1968a, b, c; Chagnon *et al.,* 1970); the dwellers in "La Esmeralda," the Puerto Rican slum, as recorded in Oscar Lewis' *La Vida* (1968); and some reflections upon the variety of Arab responses to the establishment of Israel in 1947, the subsequent wars of 1956 and 1967, and especially the actions and violence of 1969-1970.

The cultural mechanism of human survival and conditions of stress

For some two million years culture has evolved as the increasingly sophisticated and powerful means of human survival in societies of larger and larger scales of organization, mobility, and diversity of environmental adaptability. The evolutionary trend has moved from simple, open, egalitarian societies of hunters and gatherers to regional affiliations of industrially based states. Society has evolved from familistically organized households to clusters and networks of corporate industrial systems overriding national boundaries. The ideological aspect of cultural evolution has moved from that of a supernatural cosmos to the materialism of a naturalistic, finite earth and outer space. Many particular societies have become extinct by conquest or other catastrophe; many have retreated to wasteland refuges; many have been absorbed into other societies. The evolution of culture has taken place on a grand scale. Most individuals of the human species have been born into and lived their lives through the socializing life cycles provided by their particular cultural systems, and died without issue or unique cultural impact, other than as "carriers" of their bits of culture.

In the course of evolution from simple cultural mechanisms of survival vulnerable to natural disasters, to our present mechanisms – many of seemingly invulnerable power to destroy the earth and atmosphere as well as to promote vast productivity – the human species has increased from the estimate of a few hundred thousand Early Men (Australopithecines) two million years ago to its approaching three billion members, with gloomy forecasts of an overcrowded planet within less than a century. Some ecologists warn us that the cultural mechanism of human survival has gotten out of hand and the ultimate strategic resources of space, water, and air are declining rapidly. Some ethologists and psychologists warn us, on the other hand, that the inherent bellicosity of man is such that we are more likely to destroy our species by an inherently aggressive response to stress, frustration, or the threats of others of our species. Murderous man in the end can only massacre mankind altogether (cf. Freeman, 1964). But if we turn to less sweeping perspectives and assertions on the nature of man, biological and cultural, the view may be more interesting and perhaps more encouraging (cf. Crook, 1968, 1970b; Tinbergen, 1968).

Demographically viable units (groups, societies) of the human species are maintained in their habitats by the sustaining capacity of their cultures. Culture is continuously transmitted socially within groups and subgroups, laterally in space and structure between individuals and groups, and vertically through time. Culture provides technical skills which enable members of the society to harness the necessary input of nutritive energy from the environment, to coordinate human activity to produce and exchange necessary goods, to mate and multiply, and to act in unison during times of stress. As each new individual is born into the unit, its biological maturation proceeds and, simultaneously, the enculturation process envelops it. The match between the two processes is crucial for the individual. The continuity and fit of the enculturation process to the maturation process of individual growth into effective social membership (cumulating through infancy, childhood, adolescence, adulthood, to old age) varies within and among societies. One of the variations appears to be the response to stress. Whether at the level of the individual member growing up in a society, or at the level of the whole social unit with its culture, stress appears to be inevitable for all members of the human species, and perhaps even more intensively so than it is for non-human species who do not experience the enculturation factor (except, perhaps in laboratories!).

This is the heart of the aggression-man-culture problem: is it valid to equate, or better, to relate aggressive action in individual behavior to aggression of one society against others? Does intensely enculturated competitive aggression of members within some, if not all, institutions of a society correlate significantly with that society's aggressive predations against others? Hilary Callan's extended discussion focuses upon the same issues from the social anthropologist's point of view and emphasizes the continuity of "structuring" of behavior both among humans and in other organisms at individual and societal levels.

> The problem of relating human aggression to human warfare boils down to a confusion about the "level" of individual or social organization at which the concept of "aggression" properly applies. I have no solution to offer, but I believe that one is to be looked for along the following lines: I have tried to suggest that "aggression" in animals is as much a structural concept as it is a functional one. . . . There is no reason to deny that much of this is true of human aggressiveness. But since human societies are conspicuously built around verbal and symbolic action in the broadest senses of these terms, it is to be expected that processes which have their roots in the biology of *Homo sapiens* will recur repeatedly at a number of "meta-levels" in human social life. (Callan, 1970:93)

The individual encounters stress continually through life in greater or lesser intensities. But it appears to be the nature of the human animal to be gregarious, to seek society, to relate to other members, to learn to communicate with others, to fantasize and imagine, and to explore and manipulate the environment assertively from birth. It is not agreed, however, that curiosity and active exploration, or hunting practices, are "aggression" (cf. Hinde, 1967; Washburn and Hamburg, 1968). Moreover, there is not yet convincing evidence for an instinct or drive for "aggressiveness" in the sense of hostile attack or agonistic display that is free not only from prior conditions that might elicit it, but also from tacit or explicit socialization to use such action "purposefully." Human beings may be active, irritable animals, but they seem to be born more socially oriented than angry. Anger comes later, and how to be angry and when to be angry is a product of experience and the enculturation process in connection with maturation. If, as is so well known, an infant or child does not experience affectionate communicative handling by adults, and especially by the mother or her surrogate, from birth, both maturation and enculturation of the child will not "take" in normal patterns and will be faulty. The capacity to cope with stress and to use the cultural means available for coping may not be effectively learned, and responses will then take the form of ill-directed, "impulsive" hostility, anger, etc. This is only one of the many possible variations of the individual experience of "cultural deprivation" as a form of stress (cf. Crook, 1968; Hamburg, 1970).

At the level of the particular society with its culture, all aspects of the culture are modes of adapting to the environment of the habitat and other societies. Intra-adaptation or integration among sub-units of the society, however simple or complex in organization, is also a contingency of survival. The success of the whole cultural system as an adaptive one lies in its survival through time, and, in turn, its success in supporting, maintaining, and continuing its population.[2] The society as well as the individual is notably dependent upon its culture. This is reflected in the common expression "socio-cultural system." The tests come in times of stress, of changes in the environment, which, if there are no modes of adjustment or adaptation, threaten the continuity of the socio-cultural system as an integrated unit.[3] There are at least three important areas of adaptation here: continuity of successful retention and enculturation of new members; successful response of the whole to changes in the physical habitat; and successful response in the event of threat from outside societies.

To expand very briefly upon these three areas of adaptation – in the case of the first, successful retention and enculturation of the members of the society implies the continuing presence of all of the demographic requisites of a self-perpetuating society: essentially, fertile males and females and oncoming generations. Among human societies, of course, size and composition vary widely, but fundamentally in line with the technologically productive capacity of the culture in conjunction with the resources of the habitat. Of course there may also be considerable variation within the territory of a single socio-cultural system insofar as its habitat is diverse in abundance and/or its technology specialized or differentiated to handle this diversity: the geographical distribution of population density is one important fact in this regard. The internal development of centers of population density higher than the particular socio-cultural system is or has been geared to handle has been a

[2] The temporal criterion in human socio-cultural systems is, ironically, grandly insignificant in relation to other organisms lower in the phylogenetic scale.

[3] While traits or institutions in particular socio-cultural systems under detailed analysis may be identified as "non-adaptive" or "maladaptive," this is tangential to the main line argument pursued here.

recurrent phenomenon in the histories of human societies. Population pressure, crowding, social circumscription (Carneiro, 1970; Chagnon, 1968a) are ways of expressing such conditions. Other equally important demographic facts are sex and age ratios, especially in connection with the division of labor and task organization.

Population control mechanisms abound in cultures as adaptations to these facts of survival, from infanticide practices to, perhaps, the mass human sacrifices of the Aztec ceremonials (cf. Stott, 1962). Enculturation to accept, desire, and practice these customs and others that seem equally anti-social to other societies may be the simple facts of socio-cultural survival in some systems. Ideological systems, a source of both individual and societal "motivation," are especially geared to handle the creation of heretics, martyrs, and heroes as well as spectators to the gladiators' circuses. This area of adaptation is just beginning to be explored in cultural ecology. The most recent recognition that an evolutionary process of social reorganization may be the adaptive mode under such conditions has been offered by Carneiro in reassessing the problem of the origin of the state (Carneiro, 1970). Outside of such cultural adaptations are, of course, the Malthusian imperatives of famine and plague.

Second, the adaptations of a cultural system to the nature of its habitat and changes in this realm as mediated by technology, have been systematically well-explored. Diurnal, annual, and longer-term cycles of such resource items as rainfall, rabbits, piñon nuts; the geographical distribution of harvests; the fluctuations of markets – all of these are among the best-known conditions eliciting cultural adaptations. The relevance of ceremonial feasts to nutrition and energy crises within small populations may be included here (Rappaport, 1968/1970). But the effect of strategic resources located outside the territories of polities at all levels of integration and the modes of access developed have been less often considered in the contexts of the present problem in anthropology, except in regard to trade or raiding and warfare in pre-industrial and pre-market societies.

Third, in the face of threat of attack or rumor of attack, by outside societies, the mode of response may again vary greatly. This has been detailed in particular studies, archaeological and ethnohistorical, and compared along a continuum in a number of cases (cf. Fried, 1952; Service, 1955).

For any socio-cultural entity we must also consider the parts and roles within the system among which more or less severe competition results in modes of conflict still largely controlled by institutionalization. These range from expulsion to vengeance, feud, raiding, and warfare (Peters, 1967), or from chest-beating contests to feuding, raiding, and occasional massacres of other villages (Chagnon, 1968b, c; see also Sweet, 1965; Norbeck, 1963).

All of these loci of stress and adaptation (or failure of adaptation) may or may not be consistent with each other within any given system responding to a variety of stresses. But it appears to be a basic if tautological dogma of functionalism and structuralism that there must be a certain amount of consistency for persistence to be successfully maintained, and the "ideal" of a stable state of adaptation achieved.

A paradigm of conditions for stress

In discussing the four socio-cultural contexts that follow, some systematic framework will make the task briefer and clarify the contrasts that will appear. Six general categories of stress conditions (the enculturation process is included) are proposed. I will attempt to address my discussion to the paradigm of comparison these supply across the four cultures or subcultures. The discussion is in no way complete; it is offered as an initial essay in cross-cultural comparison of the general problem – the relation of culture and "aggression" to the human problem of survival.

1. The enculturation process for individuals as they enter the society. Here distinction should be made among coordinative, controlling, and coercive enculturation processes. There seems to be a plethora of terminology that is heavily negative in its assumptions about the enculturation process: "normal" versus "abnormal," positive and negative sanctions, taboos of society, and the like, including the concept of "social control" – a pejorative product of anthropology's colonialist heritage, indeed! It is as if the norms teaching and enculturating elders of human societies acted upon the assumption, held implicitly by anthropology, that human behavior is to be restrained, channeled, and controlled – because "in the wild" it *is* wild, erratic, totally impulsive. Does this mean that it is, in short, inherently aggressive? On the contrary, as I have indicated above, man in the wild is by nature not necessarily so at all.[4] Cultural systems and transmitting elders work at the coordination of youth into the whole, and the modes range from indulgent guidance to puritanical rigor and authoritarianism. In complex societies, especially those that are stratified and elite-controlled, with great differences between rich and poor or powerful and powerless, the enculturation process, like institutions of social control, may indeed be coercive and brutal in certain spheres. Enculturation for docility or for other social comportment may be handled in many ways; each case must be examined (cf. Young, 1970; Loudon, 1970). In any event, the enculturation process, examined in its cultural context and in relation to the other conditions for stress indicated below, may tell us whether the individual in this or that system is developed into docility, cooperativeness, or aggressiveness, or is incited by frustrations built into the system to agonistic displays which are then rewarded or punished; especially, whether significant boundaries or areas are learned wherein aggressive behavior is "right" or "wrong." Then it may be appropriate to ask whether enculturation for aggression is *pervasive* in the society or whether it is localized in particular institutions such as military training, or in particular subcommunities as defensive adaptation with survival value for members of the sub-unit.

2. Crowding in non-human species is a frequent source of destructive and lethal aggressive response (cf. Russell and Russell, 1968). In human societies, it is questionable whether adequate systematic comparative consideration has been given,

---

[4]Nor, indeed, are many other animals and especially other primates, except under such stress conditions as I have illustrated here. See the group of valuable papers in Crook, 1970b.

and cultural adaptations to crowding unmistakably discerned. Much has been made of ghetto crowding; some work or speculation has appeared on social distance and spacing (cf. Hall, 1970; Murphy, 1964), but an overall concept might be useful. *Crowding,* in human contexts, is a multifarious term inclusive of the explosion of population densities beyond the carrying capacities of given techno-ecological systems; of seasonal crowdings that elicit adaptive handlings of friction through such devices as systems of etiquette, avoidance rules, song duels, and competitive but ceremonialized games. Concentration camps, refugee camps, *bidonvilles* such as La Esmeralda in *La Vida,* refugee enclaves (mountaineers and islanders, for example), and other marginal groups may all need separate consideration in terms of crowding.

Finally, we find increasing emergence of a belief in world-level crowding of the whole species of man, couched in terms of the "population crisis" (cf. Durand, 1967; Ehrlich, 1968). In any event, crowding may be an important stress variable, relative to and interacting with many other variables in different socio-cultural contexts. It may be crucial in a ghetto context (Watts on a hot summer night in 1965), but much more neutral in a Far Eastern *bidonville* where an elaborate traditional hierarchical social system, rich in the etiquette forms of coordinating and regulating people in an involution of social roles and relations, proves adaptive to any intensification of crowding conditions.

3. **Demographic imbalance** may result from the action of other variables. It may be caused by loss of men in warfare and of women by infanticide, raid, or distribution through polygamous monopolies by certain categories of men, or by increase in proportion of the elderly. On the one hand, competition for unexpectedly scant resources of men and/or women may set a sufficient stress situation demanding response by adjustment or adapting devices. On the other hand, an adaptive custom relevant to other stress problems may maintain or regularly create a demographic imbalance, which in turn is part of the adaptation of the cultural system as a whole to any or all of the three general areas crucial to socio-cultural survival. A most conspicuous example is the preference for males in such loci as the Levant where multiple and ethnically distinct societies are engaged in continuous competitive fighting, feuding, or warfare adaptation for survival; this preference may also be accompanied by a marked frequency of female infanticide by neglect. A shortage of females may thus be deemed adaptively related to this preference. The opportunism of cultural adaptation often seems inconsistent and paradoxical, as in the case of differential birth rates among Makiritare women taken as wives by Yąnomamö men, compared to those of their own women who practice female infanticide (Chagnon *et al.,* 1970). But perhaps in this instance it is not only compensatory, but otherwise useful.

4. **Resource shortage or failure** may engender a stress condition for all or part of the society, depending upon the regulations of access to resources, especially food. The shortage may occur regularly, intermittently, or only occasionally, or so rarely as not to lie within the "recognition" of the cultural tradition. Floods, droughts, fires, earthquakes, and decimations by disease – all these are generally features of the habitat and have been given considerable attention in recent cultural ecological

studies. We may include here special extreme features of the habitat, such as the intense Arctic cold, for which there *may* or, intersected by other factors, *may not* be adequate adaptation in the cultural system. The history of Eskimo communities, gradually incorporated into the Euro-American industrial expansion into the north, is a history of the loss of Arctic-adapted modes for nearly autonomous survival of small communities of hunters. The withdrawal of access to the superceding industrial technology and to the commercially provided resources which now sustain them will result, as in 1941-1942 near Fort Chimo, North Quebec, in a quick starvation process, but one without the cultural adaptations of pre-contact Eskimo culture which selected adult females for ultimate survival, by cannibalism if necessary (cf. Graburn, 1969:74,120).

However, little attention has been given in anthropology to strategic resource shortage in relation to industrially based technological systems. It is difficult for anthropologists to conceptualize at this scale of organization, although it has been attempted (cf. Watson and Watson, 1969; Worsley, 1967). As the typical giant corporate industrial institution becomes an international, even a supranational, means of production or distribution of necessary goods, I can suggest only briefly the importance of asking again whether warfare, which Carneiro (1970) has suggested is a typical dominating mechanism of polities organized as chiefdoms or states, is not also the final response of power-holding interests committed to maintaining power in a political type – the commercial or capitalist nation-state – that is becoming maladaptive for survival of the species. (The political scientist David Easton has suggested its possible ephemeral nature [1953:106-115].)

5. Attack or threat by other societies, directly or indirectly, by raid or rumor of raid, invasion, or infiltration by specialized exploiting institutions, is again one of the conspicuous and well-known sources of stress in previously more or less stabilized systems. Some comparative work has been done, as indicated above, and the variations of response bring up the question: Under what conditions may aggressive organized resistance in specialized military units emerge where mechanisms of such resistance did not previously exist?

6. Supernatural and mythological threats at both the individual and societal levels have motivated aggressive reaction in the past and still contribute to individual and social agonistic acts in complex contemporary societies. Witchcraft, bone-pointing, dying of bewitchment, the Ku Klux Klan's burning crosses and lynchings, are particular examples. Such threats seem to be secondary cultural responses to stressful conditions such as illness and death, economic crises, etc., which the individual's or society's cultural tradition does not or cannot define realistically.

In this brief elaboration on six modes of stress conditions it has been necessary to blur the distinction between *individual* aggressive action and that of the whole society (or a sub-unit of the society), in spite of the caveats of cultural anthropologists who call, and rightfully so, for recognizing war as a socio-cultural phenomenon. The process by which individuals are trained to destroy others violently by long distance weaponry or in person-to-person confrontation is now only too well known to men in recent wars and to those of the American public reached by the media that have published some of the evidence. Hence the *enculturation* factor takes on increasing significance. This blurring is as it should be. Except for specific cases of injuries to individuals whose biological and enculturation maturation has not sufficiently integrated them into the society as to be maintained, it highlights the necessity to re-examine systematically the origins and kinds of stress and the cultural modes of coping in all societies. The paradigm for analysis appears in Table I:

Table I *Paradigm for Analyzing Responses to Stress in Four "Cultures"*

Mode of Stress Conditions	*Culture I*	*Culture II*	*Culture III*	*Culture IV*
1. E: Enculturation process				
2. C: Crowding				
3. D: Demographic imbalance				
4. R: Resource shortage or failure				
5. A: Attack or threat by other societies				
6. S: Supernatural and mythological threats - Individual Societal				

Stress and aggressive activity in four cultural milieux

Even with the incomplete data available on each of the four cultural situations to be presented, detailed attention to each stress mode would finally result in a lengthy volume of recapitulated detail and analysis. Since my purpose is to establish a cross-cultural method of approaching the cultural factor in aggressive activity, I shall select with arbitrary ruthlessness what I feel to be salient features of each. It should be understood that the general evolutionary framework, wherein specific adaptation processes appear in systems at different levels of complexity, is implicit in this comparison.

Culture I: The Bushmen

Richard Lee (1968, 1969) has shown us that the *de facto* nutritional intake of the Bushmen he studied is fully adequate, and that, even in a drought year, their territory provides ample wild foods to sustain their band. Nevertheless, theirs is a harsh environment and the Bushmen practice generalized reciprocity and rigorous sharing of food, tools, musical instruments, etc. Even though Elizabeth Thomas' *The Harmless People* may be somewhat discounted as impressionistic and anecdotal, when we view it together with Lee's work we can appreciate that Bushmen and their culture provide an example of a system that rejects aggression and active conflict, emphasizes "harmony," and very rarely realizes "anger" in overt action. While the evidence from Lee is that Bushmen have adequate food resources in their ranges, incidents in Thomas' account suggest that Bushmen are sensitive to the presence of too many Bushmen with whom to share the amount of food immediately available. Their response is not an agonistic display, but, rather, verbal or facial expression or even refusal to eat at all. As Thomas recounts, a frequent response of the Bushmen is to consider carefully the sharing potential of a given resource factor. But even more frequent is the fear of other societies (an attack factor), whether Bantu, Europeans, or even "stranger" Bushmen. While Bushmen need and want material goods from others, these are secured only by trade or services. In general, the danger of forced labor draft by the more powerful societies is so great[5] that the Bushmen can only secure themselves by flight or docility. Therefore it is not surprising to find, in the brief anecdotes about infants, children, and youths, that issues emerge over food and eating. Children are nurtured and apparently never punished except possibly by withdrawing attention or ignoring them at key moments of separation of adult work from child's play. Later in life one must take the blame, or blame others, for something going wrong. Lastly, there are hints that something like "crowding" is felt and responded to even in their small groups, camping together in face-to-face relations. Groups fission and recombine easily: extended friction is thus avoided, and the range of social ties is extended widely. There is clear and formal space allocation to men and to women at the hearth, and the huts or nests of each couple are clearly respected. One of the rudest acts is to stare at another.

Almost a defenseless people, close to being defeated by want in the distribution of resources, driven from their habitat in the event of a major environmental disaster, and experiencing threat strongly from more powerful societies, they evidence enculturation of aggressive behavioral patterns neither within the society nor toward strangers. No clear demographic imbalance adaptation is shown in these few sources, although it is suggested that there are often more women than men in the camps. Indeed, it is not in the Bushman's nature to fight, resist, or protest. It is apparent that, in Southwest Africa, it would not be safe to do so.

[5] Lee emphasizes, and perhaps overemphasizes, the isolation of "his" Bushmen from external economic dependencies, but he is certainly correct in the structural sense that there is no "market" type of link penetrant to Bushman economy. Trade modes remain primitive, and "service" is essentially by capture.

Culture II: The Yąnomamö

The Yąnomamö people, as presented by Chagnon (1968a, b, c; Chagnon *et al.*, 1970), stand in sharp contrast to the Bushmen. Horticulturalists of the Orinoco Basin tropical forest, they live in villages of maximum and minimum size optimal for available gardening land, hunting groves, and the distance to these basic resources. Chagnon's study suggests that these resources are *not* unlimited and that the search and watchfulness for good gardening land is continuous. He also indicates that the Yąnomamö are "expanding" and pressing outward toward further forest and that there has long been pressure against them from more densely populated and highly organized societies. Moreover, the territory they occupy overlaps that of the Makiritare, a gentler people from whom they acquire wives.

The "fierceness" of the Yąnomamö is spectacular, but perhaps overdrawn. Women engage in female infanticide which contributes to a clear shortage of Yąnomamö women, and is related by Chagnon to the attacks between villages to capture women. There is wife-beating, threatening, fighting, and bickering inside the village. Villages fission after such quarrels. Chest-pounding duels, club-fighting, shooting (with arrows) take place within and between villages. The men engage in "aggressive" trade, uneasy alliances, revenge feuds, raids, and occasional massacres of other villages.

The men must be "fierce," and are taught to be, or how to appear to be. The men of one village must be "fierce" *vis-à-vis* other villages.

The Yąnomamö behave in styles we would call *violent* and *aggressive,* since others are struck, injured, and sometimes killed. But the modes are patterned, orderly, taught, required, and occur in response to simulated as well as real stress. Chagnon even indicates that he, too, was *taught* to be "fierce" by the Yąnomamö men.

Within and between villages there is an escalation series in modes of violence. Duels between young men can, in most contexts, be cut off at any point, usually by intervention of an older man who has long since proved his "fierceness," by withdrawal of a duelist, or by a rising and spreading mood of consensus (when men of two villages are engaged) that trade and alliance are preferable to hostile relations.

Lastly Chagnon does indicate (1968c) that at the outer boundaries of Yąnomamö territory the escalating series is not complete and that the greatest elaboration, as well as the largest villages, is found in the central areas. This pattern has been noted and suggests to Chagnon (1968a) a stress of population pressure, "social circumscription."

Such ritualized fighting, together with an uneven distribution of population and extensive female infanticide, certainly suggests a response of Yąnomamö culture to population and resource stresses in the "original" parts of their territory. In contrast to the Bushmen, they possess a technology adequate to attempt territorial expansion in one direction and to resist pressure from another.

Whatever the ultimate explanations may be, Chagnon makes it abundantly clear that Yąnomamö men are taught to be "fierce" and that they are clearly not so innately. Some do not even learn to be so successfully; others cease the displays once they are established elders. But the whole society, a congeries of villages, vacillating between alliance and enmity, requires and uses an ongoing strategy and ideology of intranecine fighting to keep up expanding or resistance action against surrounding peoples.

Culture III (subculture): Violence and aggression in a Puerto Rican slum (from Oscar Lewis' La Vida*)*

Lewis' well-known *La Vida* presents one "family" whose members live in the waterfront slum of "La Esmeralda" in San Juan, Puerto Rico, and in New York City. While there has been extensive criticism of the "culture of poverty" thesis (cf. Valentine, 1968) and of the bias built into Lewis' method of data collecting and presentation, *La Vida* can be used profitably as a relatively direct raw data source for examining the relationship between "stress" and aggression in a third cultural milieu.

La Esmeralda is a contemporary urban slum in a "modernizing" U.S. colony in the Caribbean. Contradicting the reality of Lewis' own concept of a "culture of poverty," there are many hints in *La Vida* that, poor as its denizens may be, La Esmeralda is not without community structure and orderliness. *La Vida* does indeed record a picture of aggression, violence, and other symptoms of stress in a situation of poverty in a complex society. Lewis' data focuses upon one group of kin. Women of the family have had to engage in prostitution on occasion to obtain money to support themselves and their dependents; Lewis points out that about one-third of the women of La Esmeralda do so. Few men in or connected with his family of study have either regular or well-paying jobs; all of them are unskilled laborers.

The location of "violence" (i.e., aggressive activity) in the network of social interrelations is clearly patterned, if not in fact institutionalized. It even has an adaptive aspect that emerges quite clearly in some contexts. Nevertheless, the underlying conditions of crowding, want of housing, clothing, and food, and a persistent money-income insecurity (in view of what it is well-known that money *could* buy) are always present. Thus verbal abuse and threat seem to be woven into all oral communication. Women fight women over men, even with razors. Men and women who have been living in a consensual marriage come to fighting with one another and break up. Mothers beat their children in several contexts, of which "discipline" is only one; often some other source of disturbance triggers a woman's attack upon her children.

Men do not usually fight other men, although there is some such action "to prove *machismo*"; hence they conform by a ritual response to challenge. Nor do brothers and sisters fight, nor mothers and sons. But fathers or step-fathers are sometimes known to have violated their daughters sexually; insofar as there is general social sanction against such "incest," such a rupture of taboo *may* be within the periphery of "aggression."

Lewis does not mention *riots* in either La Esmeralda or New York City. It is possible that, at the time he recorded his data, Puerto Ricans had not learned to riot communally. There are also instances of emotional disturbance, requiring hospitalization, among some of the women in the "family."

One recurrent mode of fighting is especially indicative of the patterning of violence – the use of the heavy and resentful quarrel to effect a change. There are households in which a woman is the main economic supporter, and in which the man – who has been working – has lost his job or his resources from a job. Such households will break up after one or more violent scenes. The unproductive male is thrown out, and some of the children may be dispersed to other kin if economic distress is very sharp.

Thus, even in this possibly biased recording of a social scene of poverty and seeming atomization of social life to a war of all-against-all, the violence is apparently neither random, spontaneous, nor even a completely idiosyncratic response to stress. It is still socio-cultural and located at points of intense culturally defined competition for survival. There also remain roles and status relationships where it does not occur. It seems hardly necessary to conclude that the children of La Esmeralda will also be so enculturated, unless conditions of stress change.

Culture IV: "Arab" societies and the "war" against Israel

The anthropological literature has demonstrated fairly conclusively that the label *warfare* is best applied to organized territorial aggression by polities – usually at the state level of organization and carried out by such specialized and highly trained military groups as armies, navies, marines, etc. Raids and ambush attacks (e.g., the Yąnomamö) followed by withdrawals characterize the hostilities between polities of less complex organization, with the possible exception of chiefdoms. An ecological barrier may be an important explanatory factor in most cases: most societies below the chiefdom level of organization are adapted to technologically limited environmental niches. The level of organization is, in fact, indicative of dimensional simplicity or complexity in techno-ecological aspects. But even in complex, pre-industrial agrarian states or empires the techno-ecological specializations are clearly marked and so simply integrated that excision of the ruling elite and its agencies leaves peasants, tribal pastoralists, town and urban craftsmen, and ethnic or religious enclaves in such political isolation that indigenous reintegration can, for extended periods of time, be effectively inhibited by external pressures.

This is the current situation in the Levant. With the partial exception of Egypt, long under severe economic and population pressures, and the explicit exception of Israel, there is no polity in the classical Near East (the Fertile Crescent) that possesses the fully operational institutions of a modern industrial nation-state (Sweet, 1963, 1968).[6]

---

[6]This drastic generalization overrides real contrasts between the decentralization of political power in such mountain areas as Lebanon and Palestine and the greater centralization in Iraq, Syria, and Jordan. The ready alliance of urban elites to governing powers, Ottoman or Mandate, is well known.

The responses of indigenous pre- and sub-Ottoman enclaves to the Mandate Period (1920-1945) of French and British semi-colonial control are not well known, but repeated resistance and rebellion in city and countryside took place, notably in the 1930s. Even the Mandate imposition of parliamentary forms and monarchial trappings scantly concealed the perpetuation of divisive fragmentation: the rural "tribalism," the mercantile familialism of towns, and socially or territorially enclaved confessionalism[7] – in short, the Ottoman *millets* and subsidized border tribes of nomadic pastoralists – which the Turks had left behind.

In the course of the consolidation of the state of Israel from 1947 to the present, indigenous people (Arabs, Levantine Greeks, Armenians, etc.) have been incorporated or pressed out of Israeli territory. Most of these have been peasants whose only sanctuaries were the camps supported at minimum subsistence by United Nations agencies (Aswad, 1970). Hostile backlash responses to expansionist moves by Israel have peaked several times, in 1956, 1967, and 1970, with the continuous friction expressed in raid and counter-raid over Israel's expanding boundaries. But it must be emphasized that, regardless of the intensive propaganda from all vested interests in the area and emanating from both Levantine and Western capitals, the indigenous and chiefly Arab peoples from Iraq west to the Tunisian border had *no* effective autonomous national political structures until the Egyptian "revolution" of 1952, and the Syrian and Iraqi revolutions of 1958 – possibly not even until 1970. None but Egypt was capable of containing internal discontent rising under increasing economic disruption except by force, and much less of engaging in expansionist or dominating war.

If one wishes to understand the nature of Arab aggressive activity in response to the colonization in the Levant of a European-styled, dynamic, and industrial nation-state – small and intensively organized, externally subsidized economically, and demographically and confessionally dominated by one religious community – one must look to Arab peasant villages and towns. Here one finds merchant and craftsmen families, the religious *millets* of the Ottoman Empire, the ethnic quarters, the Western-subsidized and favored "elites," the "aristocrats" of the Hedjaz enthroned with their "tribal" bodyguards by the British Mandates – all fragments from a pre-industrial empire which have been kept in fragmentation.

If one looks down into the most intimate domestic circles among these fragments, even the child (boy or girl) is enculturated to "despise" and "ignore" those outside his fragment, but to conduct himself with courtesy and hospitality toward them, in reticence, and with a readiness for patron-client alliance with that fragment or external power which is most powerful and friendly.

In 1969-1970, however, a specific organizational and integrating capacity not previously encountered emerged explosively out of the Palestinian refugee sector of the Gaza Strip. The Palestinian refugee camps dispersed within the territorial entities of Jordan, Syria, and Lebanon were brought under internal control by Palestinian

[7]Religious groups such as the Druzes, Maronites, Alawites, and Shi'ite Muslims.

refugees themselves, members of the P.L.O. (Palestine Liberation Organization). United Nations (UNRA) officials and Lebanese and other "authorities" were suddenly excluded from their previous powers and functions in the camps, and the resistance organization took over to create what has been described as a state within states. If, however, a Palestinian resistance and nationalist movement has been successfully mounted, the organizational principle is still by no means clear – apart from a segmentary and factional character of the ten or more allied "parties," each of which has offices in nearly every camp, whether Muslim, Christian, or mixed. Nor is the economic basis self-sufficient.

The late summer of 1970 saw an unsurprising internecine battle between the Western-trained and armed bodyguard-army of the royal regime controlling the remnants of Jordanian territory and the Palestinians' armed units from the camps near the city of Amman. In the course of the fighting Palestinian women, children, and other non-combatants were killed in a fashion regarded as "massacre." Subsequent events were interpreted as a military move to crush the emergent Palestinian organization by genocidal force, in which the Jordanian "army" was said to be instigated by external powers, namely Israel and the United States.

The whole scene of rapid reorganization (1967-1969) into a political movement culminating in this violence can best be understood as a response to the severe stress conditions of overcrowding displaced peoples numbering finally nearly two million – most of these in a territory virtually without food and other resources, except by import. Coupled with a new integrative mechanism emerging in the previously less well organized camps, the threat challenged the incumbent regime in Jordan.[8] These battles of the many kinds of Arabs and other segments of the Levantine people are not primarily with Israel at all, for Israel is the most powerful and economically well-off state in the Levant. They are still primarily in conflict with each other, all propaganda notwithstanding. The feuding is lethal because the feuders are well armed, but the verbal displays and funeral ceremonies for fallen "martyrs" far outrun the real scale of war and destruction among themsleves or wrought in small-scale guerilla forays into Israel, to which, in fact, they may have been incited by external agencies. The greatest *de facto* destruction has been of Arab houses, villages, and people by Israeli retaliations and expansion moves.

Thus, the traditional and ritualized Arab displays of "fierceness," of loud threat and counter-threat, of running conflict with much shooting in the air, of destruction of property rather than life, and of chivalry toward women and children except *in extremis,* suggest that Arab conflict rituals in the Levant have not yet entirely given way to chaotic violence under stress. Nor have they escalated fully into the systematic military strategies employed by the armies of industrial states such as, in this

[8]The reality of the resistance movement is gaining some force from the internecine fighting. As Aswad's analysis makes clear, the most important organizational elements are the refugee peasants of the camps, the emergence of an educated "elite" from the camps, and the sympathy of peasants from South Lebanon, Syria, and Jordan. There is also a very general resemblance to the situation of the Yąnomamö – the highest density of displaced Palestinians is in Jordan and the Gaza Strip where the violence concentrates.

area, Israel. Aggressive activity is still largely incited and contained within pre-industrial cultural patterns of competing local segments, even though the weaponry is up-to-date. But the emergence from the crowded Palestinian refugee camps in Jordan of an organized resistance movement involving a rebellious peasantry suggests at once the stresses of "social circumscription" and the adoption of new modes of organization and aggressive action previously unknown to these people. Much publicity has been given to the commando training of recruits from the camps, including boys and girls. Little has been given to that of the mercenary bodyguard of the Jordanian regime – which is far more sophisticated and deadly.

Concluding remarks

All four cases of aggressive actions show that under endemic stress conditions, socio-cultural means of handling such conditions in the interests of survival of the society (whatever its scale of organization) prevail in determining the behavior of individuals or groups. Fierceness is always "fierce" and fighting is often less lethal than noisy. Up to the commercial industrial level of organization, at least, the importance of people and their need for each other constrains and stylizes violence with institutions and customs for dealing with stress derived from scant resources, demographic imbalances, crowding, attack threats from other societies, or "supernatural" dangers. However, genocidal aggression and radical environmental destruction remain to be explained; perhaps it is giantism in cultural systems that is maladaptive, for it is the giant systems that destroy in these ways, directly or indirectly through their clients. And it is the "giant" political systems of the ancient and recent past that have repeatedly failed to survive, although many particular ethnic groups have persisted after the demises of such polities.

As a final more general proposal, it appears that the cultural process, as manifested in maturing individuals of societies, in the sub-systems of complex societies, or in autonomous societies, has the unique adaptive capacity to incorporate even aggressive action into the system, to structuralize, institutionalize, and retain it if it promotes survival of the unit.

Although, since Malthus, the slaughter of war has been regarded as a "population control," it is to be hoped that more life-preserving means of stress resolution will be invented, for these also have characterized the evolution of culture. Although man is the only species who engages in extensive and intensive intraspecies aggression from the individual response to the political, he is also the only species who has repeatedly enlarged his sphere of social coexistence and invented a diversity of conflict resolution rituals in the face of internal and external threats of extinction.

References

Aswad, Barbara C. 1970. The involvement of peasants in social movements and its relation to the Palestinian revolution. *The Palestinian Resistance to Israeli Occupation*, ed. Naseer Aruri. Wilmette, Ill.: The Medina University Press International.

Callan, Hilary. 1970. *Ethology and Society: Towards an Anthropological View.* Oxford: Clarendon Press.

Carneiro, Robert L. 1970. A theory of the origin of the state. *Science* 169: 733-738.

Carthy, J. D. and F. J. Ebling (eds.). 1964.. *The Natural History of Aggression,* Proceedings of a Symposium held at the British Museum (Natural History), London, from 21-22 October 1963 (Institute of Biology Symposium #13). New York: Academic Press.

Chagnon, Napoleon A. 1968a. The culture-ecology of shifting (pioneering) cultivation among the Yąnomamö Indians. *Proceedings, VII International Congress of Anthropological and Ethnological Sciences,* Vol. 3. Tokyo and Kyoto, pp. 249-255.

_____. 1968b. Yąnomamö social organization and warfare. *War: The Anthropology of Armed Conflict and Aggression,* ed. M. Fried, M. Harris, R. Murphy. New York: Natural History Press, pp. 109-159.

_____. 1968c. *Yąnomamö: The Fierce People.* New York: Holt, Rinehart and Winston.

Chagnon, Napoleon, James Neel, Lowell Weitkamp, Henry Gershowitz and Manuel Ayres. 1970. The influence of cultural factors on the demography and pattern of gene flow from the Makiritare to the Yąnomamö Indians. *American Journal of Physical Anthropology* 32: 339-350.

Crook, John H. 1968. The nature and function of territorial aggression. *Man and Aggression.* New York: Oxford University Press, pp. 141-178.

_____. 1970a. Introduction – social behavior and ethology. *Social Behavior in Birds and Mammals,* ed. John H. Crook. London and New York: Academic Press, pp. xxi-xl.

_____. 1970b. *Social Behavior in Birds and Mammals.* London and New York: Academic Press.

_____. 1970c. Sources of cooperation in animals and man. *Social Science Information* (International Social Science Council) 9:24-48.

Dodd, Peter and Halim Barakat. 1968. *River Without Bridges: A Study of the Exodus of the 1967 Palestinian Arab Refugees.* Beirut: Institute for Palestine Studies.

Durand, John D. (ed.). 1967. World population. *The Annals of the American Academy of Political and Social Science* 369. Philadelphia.

Easton, David. 1953. *The Political System: An Inquiry into the State of Political Science.* New York: Alfred A. Knopf.

Ehrlich, Paul H. 1968. *The Population Bomb.* New York: Ballantine Books, Inc.

Freeman, Derek. 1964. Human aggression in anthropological perspective. *The Natural History of Aggression,* ed. J. D. Carthy and F. J. Ebling. New York: Academic Press, pp. 109-127.

Fried, Morton. 1952. Land tenure, geography and ecology in the contact of cultures. *American Journal of Economics and Sociology* 11:391-412.

Fried, Morton, M. Harris and R. Murphy (eds.). 1968. *War: The Anthropology of Armed Conflict and Aggression.* New York: Natural History Press.

Graburn, Nelson. 1969. *Eskimos Without Igloos: Social and Economic Development in Sugluk.* Boston: Little, Brown and Company.

Hadawi, Sami. 1967. *Bitter Harvest: Palestine Between 1914-1967.* New York: The New World Press.

Hall, Edwin. 1970. *The Hidden Dimension.* Garden City: Doubleday (Anchor).

Hamburg, David A. 1970. Recent evidence on the evolution of aggressive behavior. *Engineering and Science* 33:15-24.

Hinde, Robert A. 1967. The nature of aggression. *New Society* 9:302-304.

Hobsbawm, E. J. 1969. *Bandits.* London: Weidenfeld and Nicholson.

Holloway, Ralph L., Jr. 1968. Human aggression: the need for a species-specific framework. *War: The Anthropology of Armed Conflict and Aggression,* ed. M. Fried, M. Harris, R. Murphy. New York: Natural History Press, pp. 29-48.

Jiryis, Sabri. 1969. *The Arabs in Israel 1948-1966.* Beirut: Institute for Palestine Studies.

Leach, Edmund. 1968. Ignoble savages. *New York Review of Books.* October 10, pp. 24-28.

Lee, Richard B. 1968. What hunters do for a living, or, how to make out on scarce resources. *Man the Hunter,* ed. Richard B. Lee and Irven DeVore. Chicago: Aldine Publishing Co., pp. 30-48.

____. 1969. !Kung Bushman subsistance: an input-output analysis. *Ecological Essays*, Proceedings of the Conference on Cultural Ecology, National Museum of Canada, 1966, ed. David Damas. Ottawa: National Museum of Canada, pp. 73-94.

Lewis, Oscar. 1968. *La Vida: A Puerto Rican Family in the Culture of Poverty – San Juan and New York*. New York: Random House (Vintage Books). Originally published in 1965.

Loudon, J. B. 1970. Teasing and socialization on Tristan de Cunha. *Socialization: The Approach from Social Anthropology* (ASA Monograph No. 8), ed. P. Mayer. London: Tavistock Publications, pp. 293-332.

Murphy, Robert F. 1957. Intergroup hostility and social cohesion. *American Anthropologist* 59:1018-1035.

____. 1964. Social distance and the veil. *American Anthropologist* 66:1257-1274.

Newcomb, W. W., Jr. 1950. A re-examination of the causes of plains warfare. *American Anthropologist* 52:317-330.

____. 1960. Toward an understanding of war. *Essays in the Science of Culture in Honor of Leslie A. White*, ed. Gertrude E. Dole and Robert L. Carneiro. New York: Thomas Y. Crowell, Co., pp. 317-336.

Norbeck, Edward. 1963. African rituals of conflict. *American Anthropologist* 65:1254-1279.

Peters, Emrys R. 1967. Some structural aspects of the feud among the camel-herding Bedouin of Cyrenaica. *Africa* 37:261-282.

Rappaport, Roy. 1968. *Pigs for the Ancestors*. New Haven: Yale University Press. Paper edition, 1970.

Rodinson, Maxime. 1968. *Israel and the Arabs*, trans. M. Perl. Harmondsworth, England: Penguin Books.

Russell, Claire and W. M. S. Russell. 1968. *Violence, Monkeys and Man*. London: Macmillan and Co., Ltd.

Service, Elman R. 1955. Indian-European relations in colonial Latin America. *American Anthropologist* 57:411-425.

Sharabi, Hisham. 1969. *Palestine and Israel: The Lethal Dilemma*. New York: Pegasus Press.

____. 1970. *Palestine Guerrillas: Their Credibility and Effectiveness* (Monograph Series No. 25). Beirut: Institute for Palestine Studies.

Stott, D. H. 1962. Cultural and natural checks on population growth. *Culture and the Evolution of Man*, ed. M. F. Ashley Montagu. New York: Oxford University Press, pp. 355-376.

Sweet, Louise E. 1963. National integration and ethnic and cultural diversity in the Lebanon. (Ms. paper read at the Conference on Lebanese Democracy, May 21-31, 1963, University of Chicago.)

____. 1965. Camel raiding of North Arabian Bedouin: A mechanism of ecological adaptation. *American Anthropologist* 67:1132-1150.

____. 1968. Four nations of the Levant and the Druzes. (Ms. paper presented at the symposium Local Cultures and National Identity in the Modern Middle East, 1968, Annual Meeting, American Anthropological Association, at Seattle, Washington.)

Thomas, Elizabeth M. 1965. *The Harmless People*. New York: Random House (Vintage Books). Originally published in 1958.

Tinbergen, Nikolaas. 1968. On war and peace in animals and man. *Science* 160:1411-1418.

Valentine, Charles. 1968. *Culture and Poverty*. Chicago: University of Chicago Press.

Vayda, Andrew P. 1961. Expansion and warfare among Swidden agriculturists. *American Anthropologist* 63:346-358.

____. 1969. The study of the causes of war, with special reference to head-hunting raids in Borneo. *Ethnohistory* 16:211-224.

Washburn, Sherwood L. and David A. Hamburg. 1968. Aggressive behavior in Old World monkeys and apes. *Primates: Studies in Adaptation and Variability*, ed. Phyllis C. Jay. New York: Holt, Rinehart and Winston, pp. 458-478.

Watson, Richard A. and Patty Jo Watson. 1969. *Man and Nature: An Anthropological Essay in Human Ecology*. New York: Harcourt, Brace and World, Inc.

White, Leslie A. 1949. *The Science of Culture.* New York: Farrar, Straus, Giroux.

Wolf, Eric R. 1969. *Peasant Wars of the Twentieth Century.* New York: Harper and Row.

Worsley, Peter. 1967. *The Third World,* 2nd ed. London: Weidenfeld and Nicholson.

Young, Virginia H. 1970. Family and childhood in a southern Negro community. *American Anthropologist* 72:269-288.

Ignoble savages

Edmund Leach

Human Aggression by Anthony Storr. Atheneum, New York. 127 pp. $5.00.

Sanity and Survival: Psychological Aspects of War and Peace by Jerome K. Frank. Random House, New York. 330 pp. $5.95.

Non-Violence and Aggression: A Study of Gandhi's Moral Equivalent of War by H. J. N. Horsburgh. Oxford University Press, London. 207 pp. 35s.

Violence in the Streets edited by Shalom Endleman. Quadrangle Books, Chicago. 471 pp. $10.00

War: The Anthropology of Armed Conflict and Aggression edited by Morton Fried, Marvin Harris, and Robert Murphy. American Museum of Natural History Press, New York. 262 pp. $6.95.

These books are all concerned with violence as a form of human behaviour, but they cover a very wide spectrum ranging from personal subliminal tendencies at one extreme to nuclear warfare at the other. It is quite impossible for a reviewer to treat the various arguments with equal justice, but I will start with a brief summary of what they are: Item 1 is short, lucid and persuasive. Storr brings an amateur's understanding of ethology to his professional psychoanalytical conviction that aggression is a necessary component of human nature. Salvation can only come through sublimation, and the space race to the moon, far from being a waste of money, is a much-to-be-preferred alternative to letting off the Bomb. Item 2 is likewise psychoanalytic but is more diffuse. Frank writes as if international politics were no more complicated than a game of tic-tac-toe. If generals and politicians make mistakes this must be because of psychological defects in their personality, so closer psychological understanding of the motives of leaders will solve all

SOURCE: *New York Review of Books,* 10 October 1968. Reprinted with permission from *The New York Review of Books.*

our problems. What terrifies me about this particular author is the way he keeps making confident simplistic predictions about situations of the utmost complexity. "If the world has not destroyed itself first, it is certain to move eventually to an economy of affluence in which there will be plenty of goods for everyone." For Frank the problem of overpopulation is simplicity itself: "perhaps all aid should be accompanied by massive programs of birth-control and of education for potential leaders, given either in American schools or by American teachers sent abroad." With a special high school in the Vatican perhaps? However, Frank is less certain than Storr that man is irredeemably aggressive and hopes that, by suitable education, our descendants may be persuaded to settle their disputes by techniques of non-violence borrowed from Gandhi. This is also the theme in Item 3. Horsburgh is a moral philosopher. His book is an account of both the theory and the practice of *satyagraha* together with a discussion of whether, in the age of nuclear deterrence, Gandhian methods might have application outside India. The manner is academic. Horsburgh's India never quite connects up with the real-life confusions of Madras, Calcutta and Bombay. I have failed to discover the word "caste" anywhere in the book. Item 4 is a symposium of 38 short articles about the sociology of violence internal to the nation state. It is mostly about contemporary America. It deals with facts rather than abstractions and is sometimes very good indeed. Item 5 is a report on the proceedings of a conference of anthropologists. It is about warfare rather than civil disturbance or individual aggression. (Incidentally, it is a marked weakness of all these books that the relationship between these three dimensions never becomes clear.) Here again there is a legion of authors. The outstanding contribution is Chagnon's account of social organization and warfare among the Yąnomamö, a tribal people living on the borders of Venezuela and Brazil. Also very valuable are the highly professional comments on ethology (con and pro) by Ralph Holloway and C. R. Carpenter which will serve as a useful corrective to views expressed in some of the other books. Especially important is Holloway's remark:

> that not only are the biological attributes of man unique, particularly his brain, but also ontogenesis in terms of interaction with a cultural milieu, and the nature of his social relations are also unique – that is, specific to man. This does not mean that other animal studies cannot be used for purposes of comparison, or that they cannot provide heuristic frameworks with which man may be examined. I do mean that man's behavior, in the holistic sense, cannot be reduced to the same frameworks available for describing non-human animals, including primates. (p. 37)

The rest of the volume is very patchy and the authors display a disappointing tendency to edge away from the crucial issue: In what sense is "primitive warfare," which in Chagnon's case refers to hostilities between intermarrying communities with a total population of about 50 individuals, comparable at all with "modern war" in which populations may run to several hundred millions on either side?

But now let's go back to the beginning. Warfare is like sin – it is quite safe to be against it. But why? Why should we suppose that peace is normal and war an aberration when the whole weight of European history has been just the other way round? For centuries the schoolboy heroes of the Western World have been modelled on Alexander the Great rather than Jesus Christ; our noblest virtues are those of the dying soldier, not the suffering priest; Utopia is always a version of Plato's Republic, a Spartan nightmare inhabited by fascist thugs. With this kind of educational background the amazing thing is that we are willing to spend so much time chatting peacefully to our neighbours instead of bashing them over the head.

But fashions change; moreover, fashions in morality are as ambiguous as decency in dress. Do we repudiate our sins just to make them all the more exciting? What should we make of the fact that Bikini Atoll, the scene of the world's first thermonuclear explosion, has become the bathing wear equivalent of a cache-sexe? Is our terror of the Bomb just a symptom of sadistic fascination? Instant disintegration is not self-evidently more unpleasant than lingering death by cannon ball and septicaemia, so why the outcry against the barbarity of nuclear warfare? Our much heralded restraint in these matters has merely reduced our inhibition against more "conventional" modes of annihilation. If we were less indignant about push-button warfare we might be more effectively disgusted by the horrors of napalm. However, there it is. Whatever may be the underlying psychology, Western Man has recently been jolted out of his traditional heroic stance. It is Goya rather than Napoleon who now holds the stage. Warfare has ceased to be respectable, and self-righteous intellectuals are free to denounce the whole bloody business without committing any heresy at all. But there is no salvation for the wicked. With Calvinist fervour our mentors declare that we are eternally damned in any case.

The trouble with such sudden shifts of attitude is that advocates of the new morality become so indiscriminate. Forty years ago sexual frustration was suddenly seen to be the universal source of every human ill; today it is "aggression" that lurks in Pandora's Box, and Konrad Lorenz replaces Freud as the prophet who will lead us into the next world – if not into the Promised Land. But pity the poor prophet! There is a Talmudic story of how Moses, being granted a vision of how his wisdom was to be perpetuated by the Rabbis down the centuries, failed to recognise his own creation; the ethologists will soon find themselves in a similar predicament.

"Aggression" can mean different things to different people. In politics a "treaty of non-aggression" clearly refers to moral decision; it is optional, not "instinctive." But in the new pseudo-sciences aggression becomes a basic drive, the quintessential relationship between paired individuals. For psychoanalysts it is quite explicitly hydra-headed, embracing in the first instance both physical violence and sexual love and then extending, by sublimated derivation, into every imaginable variety of human interaction. Storr, for example, cites one analyst as saying that: "at origin, aggressiveness is almost synonymous with activity" and another for the view that: "aggression springs from an innate tendency to grow and master life which seems to be characteristic of all living matter. Only when this life-force is obstructed in its development do ingredients of anger, hate or rage become connected with it."

Ethologists say much the same thing in their own special language – the outcome of evolution is that each individual animal is endowed with an innate tendency to act aggressively against its neighbours, whatever their species, in order to preserve its living space. This drive is not self-destructive because the sequence of stimulus and response which would ordinarily lead to violence can be modified by superimposed mechanisms ("ritualisation") which allow for courtship and friendliness.

At the back of this contradictory use of words is the question whether human beings are in any way different from trigger-operated automata. Does consciousness give us powers of decision and hence moral responsibility? Those who incline to a mechanical interpretation assume that aggression is innate, those who emphasise the significance of cultural variation – e.g., anthropologists, sociologists, political theorists – assume that aggression is subject to moral values. Until recently the mechanists appeared to be on the defensive, but the new ethological jargon is full of technical terms, like "imprinting" and "territoriality," which slither across the traditional distinction between innate ("instinctive") and learned ("cultural") behaviour, and this has allowed the popularisers to attribute all the evils of our Western society to human nature itself:

> We are the cruellest and most ruthless species that has ever walked the earth – each one of us harbours within himself those same savage impulses which lead to murder, to torture and to war. (Storr, p. ix)

Thus spake the Serpent in Eden! The doctrine of original sin revamped under the title "savage impulse" is the classic device for evading responsibility. In the 1920's it justified a new morality of sexual licence, in the 1960's it justifies a Cassandra-like warning of the last trump.

Three of these books make deferential obeisance in the direction of the Lorenzian revelation without any manifest good cause, but if they are in error much of the blame must lie with Konrad Lorenz himself. He is much too fond of an expository trick by which he first attributes human motives to animals and then suggests that animal behaviour offers lessons for human beings! This is not science but sentiment, but it is an example which proves irresistibly tempting to his imitators. No doubt there are a few very general facts which are true of all intercommunicating organisms, including man, so that we can learn *something* about human beings even by observing the behaviour of sticklebacks: but we shall get nowhere at all by trying to solve problems of human morality by generalising from an observation on chimpanzees. Yet this is precisely what Lorenz's disciples imagine that they are entitled to do. In the process, they dress up in mock scientific clothing all the crass errors of social theorists down the ages. Storr, for example, in expounding the concept of "territoriality," comes up with "what is implied is that society itself has evolved as a defence against aggression: and that animals and men learn to cooperate and communicate because they would destroy each other if they did not." He states this proposition as if it were a profound and revolutionary discovery. Anyone less blinkered by the narrow pre-conceptions of psychoanalysis would recognise at once that it comes straight out of Hobbes' *Leviathan* (1651). If Hobbes and Storr were right all sociologists would be wrong, but my professional colleagues need not despair; the matter is not so simple.

In ethological jargon "territoriality" denotes a somewhat complex syndrome of apparently instinctive behaviour which is often associated with intra-specific fighting in defence of a mating or food supply territory. It is also linked with the fact that, in most species, murder is rare. Animals may fight members of their own kind, but they do not usually fight to the death. Many species are endowed with "instinctive" mechanisms which inhibit a combatant from pressing home his victory against a defeated opponent (of his own species) whenever the latter exhibits appropriate signals of submission. No human society, ancient or modern, primitive or civilised, has ever developed customs which correspond at all closely to this total stereotype of "territorial behaviour." Indeed, most human fighting is not concerned in any way with either the conquest or defence of territory. But warfare between sovereign states can be thought of as a variety of "intra-specific fighting" and, on a gigantically inflated scale, it sometimes exhibits *some* of the characteristics of "territoriality" though without the crucial feature of an inhibition against actual killing. Without more ado Frank tells us that territoriality "can be faintly discerned beneath the complex behavior of humans," and Storr (following the lamentable example of Robert Ardrey) jumps in with "there can be no doubt that man, also, is a territorial animal" with the implication that all our internecine behaviour is instinctive rather than culturally conditioned. So much for the non-science of psychiatrical ethology!

Of course, the problems are real enough, but we do not help to solve them by introducing brutal oversimplifications and false analogies. Hobbes is very relevant. *Leviathan* was a tract against Civil War and in favour of authoritarian central government. Hobbes maintained that every individual has a natural right to be selfish and hence aggressive against all his neighbours, but that in order to live comfortably in society all men must reach a covenant to forego, in equal measure, a part of that individual sovereignty. Likewise families and communities must forego their natural rights in order that all may come together as parts of a single whole, the sovereign Commonwealth. The central authority in this Commonwealth must be endowed with coercive power so as to enforce the covenant of tolerance which has been accepted by its component elements. *Leviathan* is a masterpiece, but it suffers from many grave logical defects the most important of which is the assumption that the analogy between the State and a living creature can be taken quite literally. Most of the stock fallacies of sociological reasoning derive from this mistake and Messrs. Storr and Frank trot them all out once again. Societies are not organisms; they cannot breathe or gesticulate or suffer from high blood pressure. Words like "love" and "hate" refer to the emotional states of individuals, not of communities. "A nation at war" is not the same kind of entity as "an individual engaged in a fight." Social psychology is not just a blow-up of individual psychology, nor is it true that all men have the same vices as ourselves. Even if it were true that every American male resorts to outright violence on the slightest provocation, as the Endleman symposium might seem to suggest, this would still prove nothing at all about Man as a species. It may be that some thousands of individuals will have met with violent deaths before tomorrow morning, but even in societies in which human ferocity is given the most exaggerated valuation – and such societies exist – such killing is statistically a rare phenomenon. Chagnon's Yąnomamö are a case in point. His descriptions of repeated slaughter make one wonder how any society can survive at all. Yet three adults out of four die from causes other than violence. Most people throughout the world get through their whole lives without any likelihood of either killing or being killed. If a "natural" (i.e., uncultured) man could exist he would certainly be much closer to Rousseau's placid simpleton than to Hobbes' selfish brute. It is only Western politicians, generals and psychoanalysts who have the delusion that the world is populated by potential murderers.

Just how far the ethological evidence really has any relevance for the human situation is a matter of doubt, but its implication, if any, would be the exact converse to what Ardrey, Storr and Co. seem to suppose. What is surprising for an ethologist is that man, as conditioned by culture, frequently kills members of his own species whereas other animals in a state of nature seldom do so. Submissive appeasement gestures, analogous to those which can be observed in other animals, occur in man also, but they differ from one social setting to another and do not function effectively as inhibitors of aggression. This suggests that men kill other men not because of "instinct" but because of their cultural training. If Hobbes and Storr are right, then education in tolerance would be a waste of time. Man is instinctively violent, and we must stagger along as best we may by using the deterrent threat of counter-violence. But if they are wrong – as the new science of ethology in fact suggests they are – then the Utopian dream of a non-violent world society deserves to be taken seriously.

All living creatures discriminate between creatures of our kind and creatures not of our kind. Among non-humans this distinction is either known instinctively or else imprinted within a few days of birth, but man has the unique capability of being able to vary his discrimination as he chooses. Characteristically, as he becomes socialised, he applies it to a whole series of overlapping but mutually inconsistent categories. "We" comes to mean all sorts of different things according to the context in which "I" happens to be at any particular moment. The significant categories ("We Groups") differ as between one social system and another, but with us they include: family, class, community, ethnic group, dialect group, nation, sect, "race," caste, club, profession. This choice of self-identification has social consequences which Carpenter summarises by saying that with humans "conflict is a structural property of human societies." "We" and "they" become polarised – not through any instinct but because the rules lay down that this is so. If I am taught that members of category "X" are "people like me" then they are notionally my friends and I am under a social obligation to treat them as such, but if the members of category "Y" are "not like me" this gives a sort of legitimacy to potential feelings of hostility.

Since the categories do not coincide, my potential enemy in one context is my friend in another, but it is normally the obligations of friendship which predominate, and it is this that makes social existence possible. This is true in great affairs as well as small so that the bias of probabilities is always *against* the expression of hostility through open violence. The peculiarity of warfare is that normal animal and human valuations are turned upside down. Social pressures, which ordinarily serve to minimise overt hostility, are suddenly inverted so that the individual soldier is coerced into murdering complete strangers with whom he has had no previous contact. It is a crime to kill a neighbour, an act of heroism to kill an enemy, but who is enemy or who is neighbour is purely a matter of social definition.

The point I want to emphasise is that such behaviours are all matters of custom; they are primarily determined by social conventions, *not* by "instinct," or "imprinting," or "territoriality." The psychological states of mind of the human actors are a response to social forces. They are an effect, not a cause. It follows that if we want to modify the incidence of warlike attitudes, it is society that must be changed, not the human beings. In particular, we need to do everything possible to confuse the issue, to make it difficult for those who exercise leadership to draw sharp unambiguous boundaries between "we" and "they." Some boundaries stand out: language frontiers, skin colour frontiers, national frontiers. It needs more than wishful thinking to get rid of them. Polarisation in terms of such criteria is unavoidable, but it is only when the boundaries coincide that they become dangerous. The real risk lies in situations where territorial exclusiveness is combined with endogamy and with a studied avoidance of economic and social communication across the ghetto frontier. And do not forget that whole nations, as well as city enclaves, may be dominated by ghetto values.

The equation *We* : *They* : : *Friendly* : *Hostile* is the universal nexus through which new relationships are forged and old ones broken up, and I agree that this kind of polarisation could not develop at all unless human beings had an underlying potentiality to feel aggressive; to that extent Storr is right. If man did not possess aggressive instincts social life would be impossible. Even the most rudimentary sense of social solidarity depends on the feeling that "we" are different from (and potentially hostile to) "the others." But Storr is wrong when he implies that the actual expression of human aggression is *determined* by "psychological" factors. Psychology comes into it, but only in a very roundabout way. The establishment of relationships in society is not a mechanical matter but a voluntary social act, which takes place within an existing structure of social conventions. New links are created by the exchange of gifts (women, valuables, words, documents, etc.) between partners who had previously felt themselves to be members of separate (and therefore potentially hostile) groups. An Australian aborigine "makes friends" with his neighbour by exchanging sisters, an Englishman by exchanging dinner invitations, sovereign nations by exchanging documents of treaty. The exchange unites the opponents. They become "allies," friends. As dozens of anthropologists have been told by hundreds of informants throughout the world "we marry our enemies." This paradoxical attitude to the relationship between friendship and hostility is not just an odd quirk of primitive communities operating at the technological level of Chagnon's Yąnomamö; it has been part of the coinage of international diplomatic manoeuvre down the ages. Henry V wins the battle of Agincourt and marries the king of France's daughter. It is relevant here because it emphasises how completely arbitrary and *socially* determined is an act of war. The initial act of war is political, a move in the complex game of diplomatic chess. The manipulation of public opinion and the maintenance of public morale in the face of military adversity is, of course, a very essential part of the same game, but warfare is never "caused by" the public will in any simple sense. That is why the Ardrey/Storr/Frank assumption that war-making by a nation-state is a kind of human equivalent to "territorial" behaviour among, say, prairie dogs is so totally misleading. In a nation at war most individuals are not engaged in aggressive activity at all, and although all human societies may be thought of as systems of conflict (in Simmel's sense), most forms of human rivalry explicitly preclude the use of violence and have nothing whatever to do with either territorial or national self-identification. The latter point is expressly recognised by Storr but he still manages to use the ethologists' "territoriality" as the modal type of group solidarity and inter-group opposition and treats the whole issue as a simple modification of infantile motivation. The relevance of rules of legitimacy for an understanding of group behaviour is never recognised at all. Yet that surely is the problem? Man is not just a wild animal whose ferocious instincts must be curbed by society or sublimated into other channels; he is a social animal who is taught by society to exhibit hostility in some situations and friendliness in others. The difference is fundamental.

The Endleman symposium is a useful corrective to the Storr-Frank oversimplifications. It puts stress not only on the multiplicity of contexts in which violence is manifested in American life but also on the immense relevance of cultural phenomena, such as films and TV, which act as educational media and train the individual American to regard extreme violence as a normal feature of everyday life. Endleman's contributors are mostly, on balance, on the side of the angels, but they recognise their limitations. We do not know in detail just how such child-training expresses itself in the adult personality. Even those who are disgusted by a fantasy world which seems to offer nothing but "wars, rumours of wars, murders, rapes, arson and traffic accidents" have to admit that the world of Little Red Riding Hood was not all that much better. There are self-styled "experts" who would justify an excess of violence in the mass media on much the same grounds that they would welcome an excess of pornography on the bookstalls: the sheer surfeit may be cathartic. But we need more facts, and meanwhile it is not unreasonable to suppose that in our own society, as in any other, we would behave differently if we were educated differently. Gentleness as well as gentility is a product of training. The aggression which Storr and Frank are writing about may be, in a psychoanalytic sense, a universal phenomenon, but its manifestation as aggressive violence is not an attribute of man but only of Western industrial man who has been culturally conditioned to act with brutality in a ruthlessly competitive society. Of course, some may say: "But what does it matter? *Our* problems are those of 20th century industrial culture. Who cares whether man-in-the-beginning was Rousseau's noble savage or Hobbes' snarling brute?" I think it does matter, because what we think about man's ultimate nature must necessarily affect our prognosis of the future. If man is, as Storr asserts, "a competitive, aggressive, territorial animal" *by his nature,* then we are condemned to the fate which Storr predicts and apparently welcomes, the joys of free enterprise competition, in a world of rival nation-states intent on mutual annihilation. Oddly enough, out of these depressing premises Storr himself extracts a conclusion with which I can heartily agree: birth control should take priority over bomb control on the grounds that "the population explosion is, of all possible factors, the most likely to cause an explosion of a different variety. The hydrogen bomb is undoubtedly the most effective way of reducing world population." If, however, we reject or are willing to qualify our belief that man is lethally aggressive *by nature,* then there are practical alternatives to murderous competition.

It is easy to dismiss all doctrines of world government, world federation and the like as impractical idealistic pie-in-the-sky and certainly the contributions on this theme that are offered in these books are markedly lacking in conviction. Gandhi's doctrine of non-violence (*ahimsa*) had a bastard parentage – the pure milk of Indian asceticism being heavily spiced with essence of Tolstoi and Thoreau – but the mixture makes little sense when revamped to fit the social peculiarities of contemporary Euro-America. What really happened in India between 1930 and 1947 bears no relation to the official mythology which Mr. Horsburgh now distills into a universal code of moral practice. The myth may continue to influence the wishful thinking of the saintly and the oppressed – the late Martin Luther King was one of these – but it has only marginal relevance for the problems of real-life politics.

I am more impressed by Anatol Rapoport's argument, to which Storr draws attention, that in ordinary competitive games, including competition between business firms, the players take it for granted that "one's opponent is a human being like oneself." In contrast, whenever national honour and patriotism are invoked, the "enemy" are reduced to the status of wild beasts. But since so much of the modern capitalist world is now dominated by vast *international* consortia it has already been demonstrated that, in some types of macro-rivalry, sharply drawn national frontiers are superfluous. If this is so even in the dizzy world of high finance where cut-throat competition is treated as a virtue of the highest order, there cannot be any intrinsic reason why a comparable confusion of boundaries should not be achieved in the much more polite world of international politics.

In practice it is precisely here that we encounter a classic paradox. As communications improve and the worldwide network of economic relationships becomes more and more convolute, the intensity of local nationalism and patriotic slogans becomes ever more strident. Biafra is born to commit suicide precisely at the moment when the oil companies can guarantee that Nigeria has the resources to move into the modern world. Yet even this terrible case can be a source of optimism, it is so plainly futile. Bit by bit it is becoming apparent, even to Israelis, that in contemporary conditions victory in warfare is economically just as disastrous as defeat. It isn't moral principles that guide the operation of power-politics but calculated self-interest, and in these calculations the decisive factors are ceasing to be military. The difference between Hungary in 1956 and Czechoslovakia in 1968 still hangs in the balance, but certainly the issue does not turn on any change in Russian temperament; it is simply that some influential Russians may be beginning to suspect that crime doesn't pay any more. And once that is really understood we need not fear the Bomb.

But where should we go from here? Arguments about the perfectibility of man are like ultimate theories of cosmology. Big bangs or steady states, neither side ever has the last word. We are no more likely to be obliterated by a Doomsday Machine than to achieve perpetual peace in a rediscovered Garden of Eden.

But do not let us forget that even if we are born as animals, we grow up as men. It is right that the psychologists and the ethologists should remind us of our "instinctive" beginnings, but we should not exaggerate the virulence of our original sin. What we need to understand is not what is true of all mankind but what is true of some men and not of others. Why are some societies warlike and others peaceful? And it is the sociologists rather than the psychologists who will eventually provide the answers. In all this pile of paper the fourteen most valuable pages are those in which Lewis Coser (Endleman, pp. 71-84) summarises the theory of "relative deprivation" which provides a peculiarly satisfying explanation of why *different* low status sectors of society (e.g., the poor, the young, the women) react to violence in quite *different* ways in *different* types of revolutionary situations. It is through the pursuit of discriminations of this sort rather than through grand generalisations about human nature that we may hope to keep our runaway world in an approximate state of grace.

23

On human aggression

Morton H. Fried

Some time ago, during what seemed a simpler age, I sat in an introductory course in philosophy and heard the instructor ask if it was the natural fate of an acorn to grow into an oak. The mere phrasing of the question alerted the class, sophomores though most of its members were, to snags of reason. Quickly the instructor established that there had to be many more acorns than oaks. So great was the imbalance that it seemed sounder to conclude that the natural fate of the acorn was to rot, be consumed or otherwise perish long before it became a sapling, much less a tree. On further reflection, the class agreed that there were difficulties in declaring the growing of an acorn into an oak to be an unnatural event, and I seem to recall that we went on to another topic with some relief. There is much here that parallels discussion of the question of whether man is an innately aggressive creature.

When Charlotte Otten invited me to write a few pages on the problem of aggression in human behavior from the viewpoint of a cultural anthropologist, I was unhappy. I happen to be among the proponents of a scientific rule that states that you can't kill a bad idea. Clearly, Dr. Otten was asking me to attempt to invalidate this rule. The balance was tipped by her assurance that an extraordinary number of people seem to believe the nonsense that they are naturally aggressive, despite daily accumulation of personal evidence to the contrary. Acceptance of such nonsense at that level is merely irritating. Unfortunately, it implies the acceptance of a much more significant string of correlates and consequences, such as that war is inevitable, exploitation unavoidable, violence necessarily routine. In the train of the belief in innate

SOURCE: Reprinted by permission of the author.

aggression invariably follow certain related ideas – that races are and must remain unequal in intellectual and other endowments, that sexual equality is a chimera. Until quite recently, each of these items existed in a theoretical zone of its own, although quite a few social thinkers recognized their interdependence and could show the logical ties that bound them into a larger reactionary package. Now a wide-selling popular spokesman for the concept of innate human aggression has openly linked the various speculations into a single continuous theory, so evident that the lay reviewer has no difficulty in summarizing it:

> Therefore, to list some of the toastier conclusions he [Robert Ardrey] reaches along the way, it should be recognized that American blacks are innately superior to whites on the playing field and inferior in the classroom (yes, Arthur Jensen lives); Lionel Tiger is right about male-bonding tendencies and their implications for women. . . . (Lehman-Haupt, 1970: 41)

Ardrey's handling of the racial problem is somewhat more hedged than Lehman-Haupt indicates, but in general the latter's appreciation of Ardrey's position is quite fair (cf. Ardrey, 1970:62-65).

If the concept of the naturalness of human aggression is popular, we must admit that it is being well purveyed. A number of authors, including a few well regarded natural scientists, have made impressive international reputations and substantial amounts of money by writing cleverly about aggression in humans, purporting to demonstrate it to be natural and innate (like the acorn's capacity for developing into an oak?). Some writers have based their demonstrations on analogies, utilizing selected anecdotes relating to non-human animal behavior. Others have relied upon fanciful reconstructions of ethological evolution. A favorite tactic is to describe a human ancestry that traversed a period of dependence upon carnivorous predation, and this they suppose to have laid a brand, quite like the biblical mark of Cain, upon all of us.

As a cultural anthropologist I am obliged to look at the matter differently. Before proceeding, however, let me set one thing clear. I am quite pleased to leave to properly specialized colleagues the primary investigation of the phenomena that fall within the domain of their competences, the specifics of human evolution and primate ethology to name two. But a corollary must be swiftly added. The activities of research and generalization carried out by such colleagues are very much a proper subject of study for the cultural anthropologist, falling within his competence precisely because those activities are part and parcel of the cultural scene. On the same grounds, the activities of the non-professional, self-proclaimed "authorities" on such topics as human aggression, are also legitimate objects of scrutiny for the cultural anthropologist.

Manifest to the social scientists who look over the utterances attached to the theory of natural human aggression is a certain mythic quality. More than this, there is a cosmetic use of scientism in the packaging of ideas so that the most widely accepted ideology of the contemporary world is used to enhance ideas that lack the minimum rigor demanded of a scientific concept. In actuality, the preponderance of statements made in favor of the theory of innate human aggression is better characterized as pseudo-scientific.

One area in which the difference between a scientific and a pseudo-scientific statement becomes apparent is that of definition. The act of definition is crucial to scientific method. The only hope of achieving inter-subjectivity, much less the possibility of replication of research results, is through the careful rendition of the definition of the subject. Yet we are accustomed to the crudest types of definition in the area of pseudo-science. Consider, for example, the absence of a rigorous concept of race, or even of intelligence, in the bulk of the writing that finds innate invidious distinctions among different populations within the human species (cf. Fried, 1968). A similar difficulty arises with regard to the problem with which we are confronted: the concept of aggression is all too frequently left without specification in the arguments.

Dictionary definitions provide useful points of departure, although we should not expect specialists to regulate their concepts according to generalizations propounded for essentially non-technical use. When we turn, for example, to the concept of aggression, we cannot fault Konrad Lorenz for regarding it as "the fighting instinct in beast or man which is directed *against* members of the same species." (Lorenz, 1966: ix; italics in original) It is worth remarking that the original title of Lorenz's best known book, *Das sogennante Böse,* was not translated; the English title derives from the German subtitle, "Naturgeschichte der Aggression." To pursue the matter a bit further, it may be noted that the word "aggression" does not exist in German, except as a direct loan from English. Looking up "aggression" in a standard German-English dictionary yields "Angriff," and sometimes "der erste Angriff," which means "the first attack." It is precisely this concept that supplies the essential core of aggression. It does not apply merely to fighting but to the notion of a first or sometimes an unprovoked attack. Whatever complications face the ethologist studying non-cultural behavior when the qualification of first or unprovoked attack is added, there can be no denying that it offers enormous complexity to the student of cultural behavior. It is, of course, the verbal and ideological components that escalate the difficulties. One is tempted to say that in cultural society almost every instance of attack is viewed by one side as provoked and by the other side as unprovoked. Consideration of the merits of the various arguments comprises a major activity in many human societies, but is totally absent in all other animal situations.

Let me emphasize this point, because so much has been made of words like "threat" and "ritual" in order to culturalize situations that are otherwise devoid of cultural aspects. Indeed, if Lorenz presents a correct picture, the basic function of activities described by such terms seems to be to limit or forestall violence rather than to bring violence into being, as frequently happens in cultural society. All of this, of course, without mentioning that the usual instance of "threat" or "ritualization" among non-cultural animals involves dyads, or the simplest larger combinations, whereas in cultural society, even the simplest known, such situations take on their greatest significance as they provide an armature on which numerous individuals arrange themselves. Even in this instance, however, we quickly note that the socially significant activity we know as war is absent in many simple cultural societies.

To avoid misinterpretation, a further clarification must be added. I do not wish to suggest that the only valid approach to aggression and violence is through emic methodologies. Were that the case, it is evident that there would be no hope of coming to grips with such phenomena in animal behavior. Actually, my point of criticism is far simpler. It seems to me that shifting conceptions of aggression mar the contributions of various naturalists and most amateurs who have addressed themselves to such phenomena. A major source of variability has clearly been the diversity in the process of drawing analogies.

Analogy and metaphor can be useful in attracting attention to a problem and can even suggest the beginnings of a solution. There are strict limits, however, beyond which the suggestiveness of analogy and metaphor fails and becomes counterproductive. In short, analogy and metaphor can raise possibilities and thus guide more serious work, but they cannot function as a source of proof or even of demonstration, which is precisely the use to which they are put by those who urge upon us a theory of innate human aggression. The use of analogy in such hands comes to grief for various reasons or combinations of reasons. Let us look at three of the broadest and most common.

To begin with, analogies are frequently selected on haphazard grounds, opportunistically. A resemblance is spotted, often fortuitously, and seized upon. The precise points of resemblance are often blurred, particularly when the descriptions are warped to emphasize and optimize the postulated similarities. It is relatively easy to recognize this kind of prose as the following example may illustrate:

> In our nearest relations, the chimpanzee and the gorilla, there is unfortunately no greeting movement corresponding in form and function to laughter, but it is seen in many macaques which, as an apparent gesture, bare their teeth and at intervals turn their heads to and fro, smacking their lips and laying back their ears. It is remarkable that many Orientals smile in the same way when greeting. . . .
>
> In any case, it is tempting to interpret the greeting smile as an appeasing ceremony which, analogously to the triumph ceremony of geese, has evolved by ritualization of redirected threatening. The friendly tooth baring of very polite Japanese lends support to this theory. (Lorenz, 1966:178)

It is difficult to write a parody of such "science."

We can take further advantage of the preceding citation by turning our attention to the second prominent failing of such arguments: the contempt for phylogenetic sequence within a professedly evolutionary framework. In the instance quoted, no observations have yet been recorded of anything sufficiently similar to the "smile" in our phylogenetically closest relations, but this gives no pause to the theorist. It is instructive to compare the laxness of this method with the similarly deficient method of certain ethnologists who also reached very large publics some decades ago. A useful instance is furnished by J. G. Fraser, author of *The Golden Bough,* who achieved his goal of explication of commonalities in primitive religion by virtually ignoring the functional *mise-en-scène* of the individual elements he was abstracting from widely different cultural matrices. Precisely such neglect of functional situations is the third major shortcoming of the work of those who offer us elaborate theories of innate human aggression.

Returning briefly to the failure of supporters of the thesis of innate human aggressiveness to deal properly with evolutionary sequences, we note again the associated tendency to postulate certain ethological stages, such as one in which human ancestors are described as predatory carnivores. I will leave to other colleagues the problem of placing such a thesis in the context of actual knowledge of Australopithecines, who were the creatures usually associated with such behavior. Let me note merely that such predation, falling outside the species, throws little or no light on intra-speciational behavior. Since a variety of possibilities exists, it is absolutely necessary that the analyst control as far as possible the information relating to functional context and precise phylogeny.

Even within the species possibilities are so numerous as to make facile comparison, much less analogical reasoning, highly dangerous. Let me suggest merely a few of the many alternatives that may be discovered: unprovoked attack by an individual upon another individual of comparable age and the same sex; unprovoked attack by an individual upon another who is significantly junior, but of the same sex; unprovoked attack by an individual upon another who is significantly senior, but of the same sex; unprovoked attack by an individual upon another who is of comparable age but opposite sex; etc., etc. Obviously, there are a great many additional variations here, not to mention those which follow when additional variables are considered, such as actions involving aggregates rather than individuals, as well as widely differing situational contexts. Thus, discriminations must also be made on the basis of the behavioral placement of the aggressive act: in a sexual context; in a feeding context; in a context requiring intergenerational relationships; in a highly delimited spatial context (i.e., one in which a specific place is at stake); etc. It should be evident that the addition of cultural variables immediately creates the possibility of virtually exponential increase in the number of situational contexts.

Because the work that has been done in advancing the theory of innate human aggression fails to display the required degree of rigor suggested in the previous examples, it can be assigned at the present stage of its development to the category of pseudo-science. We can note at the same time that such pseudo-scientific pronouncements are completely understandable as projections from other aspects of the ideology of the culture which spawned them, and thoroughly functional parts of that ideology as well. With regard to the former assertion, we need merely be aware that the cultures that generate these modern myths are encapsulated in social systems which embody conflict, aggression and warfare as legitimate means of national conduct, however they may seek to repress autonomous individual violence. The fact that modern nation states employ warfare as a form of interaction does not make warfare any more natural than the suppression of collective violence among Eskimos makes it unnatural. The evidence studied by cultural anthropologists indicates that potential for violence exists in most, if not all, human populations. More importantly, however, are the indications that the potential is triggered and channeled by sociocultural factors. Indeed, those factors may lead to a total repression of all violent behavior whether by individuals or aggregates.

Few ethnographic examples are more dramatic than that presented by the American Indian population we know as the Comanche. When first encountered by non-Indian observers, the Comanche lived in the northern plains and moved about on foot, gathering wild vegetable foods and taking small game. All information available indicates that upon coming in contact with other population groups, particularly any that showed a propensity for violent behavior, the Comanche would run as fast as they could until they had physically separated themselves from the others. After living in this way for unknown centuries, the Comanche obtained horses and guns from the Europeans who moved into the plains. A transformation set in among the Comanche. It is not known how long this transformation took, but it seems to have occurred within a single generation. In any event, the Comanche moved southward and eastward and became a scourge, not only of other Indian populations, but of the Europeans as well. Comanche warriors inflicted terror from the Mexican frontier to Louisiana.

The spokesman for a theory of innate human aggression might leap to the conclusion that the Comanche story supports his views. I believe that the Comanche offer us a message to the contrary. The Comanche are simply one of many illustrations that may be offered to show that humans do not act out behavioral programs imprinted in their genes. Within the biological limits set by the human constitution there is an open possibility with respect to violence. With the possible exception of those rare humans who possess XYY genotypes, involvement in episodes of interindividual violence seems to be absolutely dependent upon sociocultural context. When we deal with examples of inter-group violence, with warfare, the dependence upon sociocultural context seems to lack exceptions.

Let me begin to conclude these few comments by referring to some ancient events in the history of Chinese ideology. More than two thousand years ago, the Chou dynasty, already considerably attenuated, was replaced by the short-lived but vigorous Ch'in. To explain their success, the Ch'in elite referred to the moral decadence of their predecessors, but that was not enough. It seems that they reinforced their claim to the "mandate of heaven" by projecting almost a millennium into the past a version of the events through which they themselves had so triumphantly come. In brief, they created a myth to explain how the dynasty they had deposed, the Chou, had itself come to power by deposing a weak and corrupt Shang dynasty.

The manufacture of myth is a recurrent cultural phenomenon to which the theory of innate human aggression pertains. The varieties of myth that are spawned are remarkable, including such things as just-so stories of racial superiority or inferiority, and quasi-scientific theories of perpetual female inadequacy based upon hypothesized inability to form significant intrasexual "bonding." Sometimes such myths take pseudo-historical form, as in the Ch'in version of the fall of Shang. Sometimes the "historical" is combined with the "scientific" to produce a projection of contemporary fears and horrors into a remote evolutionary past. This is what seems to have happened in the fabrication of the myth of "Neanderthal Man." The original fossil is sometimes called "Darwin's witness," to testify to the date of its discovery, 1859. Part of its Victorian heritage, however, is its clearly defined historical role: Neanderthal Man represents the brute that had to be cleared from the path of Cro-Magnon man, just as blacks, American Indians and Asians had to be swept from the paths of Europeans. In the case of the Neanderthal fossils, this was done by brutalizing them and casting them out of the human species. Immediately on the heels of this now generally repudiated separation was one stipulation of the early (albeit totally hypothetical) cases of genocide. The "Cro-Magnon" (i.e., the modern European) population is described as having fallen upon the Neanderthals, eliminating them. Alas for this widely accepted hypothesis of former years, it is now known that the general physical makeup of "Neanderthals" fell well within the range of our species, so that the discriminating of Neanderthal types is equivalent to contemporary exercises in racial biology. On the other hand, recent archeological evidence that shows that Neanderthals not only buried their dead, but covered them with flowers in the process, is merely embarrassing.

Archeologists are in the process of stripping away some of the myths about human evolution that make genocide the oldest human crime. Just as the Neanderthals are being rehabilitated, so it is likely that *Homo erectus* and the Australopithecines will be seen in clearer light. There is no real need to make them carry our modern burdens. In the same vein, it will be seen that the theorists of innate human aggression pander to an outmoded conception of human nature.

Man does not operate on the basis of intrinsically programmed behavioral sequences. There are no biological imperatives that require humans to resort to aggression and violence. Neither are there any genetic restraints on the use and applications of violence. It may be that the forces which move *Homo sapiens* to a violent career are more difficult to confront and change than are such things as genetic disposition. The sociocultural contexts in which violence appears may be more difficult to overcome than would be change in specific gene loci, given our present technology. Be that as it may, the problems that we confront are social, political, economic and educational. They are not biological as the exponents of the theory of innate human aggression would have it. If attempts are made to change the situation, they should be directed at those things which can offer relief, difficult as their accomplishment may be.

References

Ardrey, Robert. 1970. *The Social Contract* New York: Atheneum.

Fried, Morton H. 1968. The need to end the pseudoscientific investigation of race. *Science and the Concept of Race,* ed. Margaret Mead *et al.* New York: Columbia University Press, pp. 122-131.

Lehman-Haupt, Christopher. 1970. Review of Robert Ardrey, *The Social Contract. New York Times,* October 5, p. 41.

Lorenz, Konrad. 1966. *On Aggression.* New York: Harcourt, Brace and World.

Solecki, Ralph. 1971. *The First Flower Children.* New York: Alfred A. Knopf.

A B C D E F G 7 6 5 4 3 2